Praise for
Wharton on Dynamic Competitive Strategy

"*Wharton on Dynamic Competitive Strategy*
is an excellently crafted tour de force
which integrates many diverse frameworks
and principles for understanding dynamic
competitive strategy formation. It is
exceptionally readable, providing a rich
array of key ideas beautifully augmented
by examples which give life to these
principles. Every thoughtful executive will
want to read this book and keep it handy
as a reference."

David B. Montgomery
Executive Director
Marketing Science Institute
S. S. Kresge Professor of Marketing Strategy
Stanford University

"No other book captures the spirit of
Hypercompetition more than this one.
This compendium is fabulous testimony to
the immense contribution that academic
theory can make to practitioners engaged
in highly dynamic hypercompetitive
rivalries. *Wharton on Dynamic Competitive
Strategy* provides invaluable insights into
how to win in Hypercompetition."

Richard A. D'Aveni
Author of *Hypercompetition*

WHARTON ON DYNAMIC COMPETITIVE STRATEGY

Editors

George S. Day

and

David J. Reibstein

with

Robert E. Gunther

WILEY

John Wiley & Sons, Inc.

Published by John Wiley & Sons, Inc., Hoboken, New Jersey.
Published simultaneously in Canada.

For general information on our other products and services please contact our Customer Care Department within the United States at (800) 762-2974, outside the United States at (317) 572-3993 or fax (317) 572-4002.

Wiley also publishes its books in a variety of electronic formats. Some content that appears in print may not be available in electronic books. For more information about Wiley products, visit our web site at www.wiley.com.

Library of Congress Cataloging-in-Publication Data:

Wharton on dynamic competitive strategy / edited by George S. Day and
    David J. Reibstein, with Robert Gunther.
        p.   cm.
    Includes index.
    ISBN 0-471-17207-3 (alk. paper); 0-471-68957-2 (pbk.)
    1. Competition.   2. Industrial management.   3. Strategic planning.
4. Trade regulation—United States.   5. Industrial management—
United States—Case studies.   I. Day, George S.   II. Reibstein,
David J.
HD41.W494   1997
658.4'012—dc21   96-53177

Printed in the United States of America

10 9 8 7 6 5 4 3 2 1

GIVEN THE BOOK'S INCEPTION AND
COLLABORATIVE NATURE, WE DEDICATE THIS
BOOK TO OUR WHARTON COLLEAGUES AND
THE WHARTON SCHOOL FOR PROVIDING
SUCH A STIMULATING ENVIRONMENT.

PREFACE

DRAWING TOGETHER THE DIVERSE STRANDS OF STRATEGY RESEARCH

This book is a pioneering initiative to develop an interdisciplinary view of strategy, drawing upon the best work of diverse streams of strategy research. Researchers have conducted extensive studies and developed theories focused on specific parts of the challenges of strategy formulation and implementation. This book draws together these varied perspectives on strategy, for perhaps the first time, and places them in the hands of managers and students.

These insights have never been more needed. As the competitive environment becomes increasingly dynamic, managers need fresh perspectives and a sharply tuned understanding of the true nature of competition. They need to understand the interplay between the company, competitors, and the larger environment. With competition moving more quickly, they need to develop their peripheral vision and sharpen their perception. This is the goal of this book.

The Wharton School, with one of the largest and most diverse groups of faculty studying strategy, is in a unique position to bring all these researchers to the same table. In fact, that is how this project began. Several years ago, we organized a series of roundtable discussions by strategy researchers from several Wharton departments. During these discussions, we shared our perspectives on strategy and began wrestling with the challenge of joining our diverse insights to gain a more complete view of competitive strategy. In the process, all of us—even those with decades of experience in their specific disciplines—gained new perspectives on the challenges of strategy. We decided to open this discussion and this learning to a broader audience through this book.

The authors contributing to this volume include members of Wharton's management, marketing, public policy, and operations and information management departments, collaborating with colleagues around the world. Some of the insights of this volume have appeared only in academic journals, but our goal here was to extract the most useful perspectives and approaches for managers and students. The book is designed to provide the broadest possible overview of the key approaches to addressing today's dynamic competitive challenges.

This work reflects the Wharton School not only in name but in spirit. It is a demonstration of Wharton's mission to advance knowledge, encourage dialogue across disciplines, and make an impact on the practice of management worldwide. It reflects our goal of devoting the resources of one of the world's largest and finest groups of business faculty to addressing the theoretical and practical challenges that face business leaders today.

Since these perspectives developed from different streams of research and theory, there is not always a perfect fit. Nor is the goal of this work to produce one formulaic answer to the complex challenge of developing strategy. Instead, the following chapters offer diverse perspectives on analyzing strategy and diverse tools for formulating strategy. Not every lens will be appropriate in every situation, but they are all useful in some situations. By viewing your competitive challenges through these multiple lenses, you will be able to engage in the most important activity in strategy: developing creative solutions to your strategic challenges.

ACKNOWLEDGMENTS

We first want to recognize the expertise, enthusiasm, and cooperative spirit of the authors of this volume. Without their commitment to this multidisciplinary exercise, we would not have succeeded. Throughout the journey that culminated in this book, each author cumulated many debts to the scholars and practitioners whose work was used to guide and structure thinking. There are too many people to acknowledge here individually, but we hope we have given them their due within the chapters.

This project was sponsored and funded by the Huntsman Center for Global Competition and Innovation. Research centers play a unique and central role in shaping and encouraging research at the Wharton School by identifying issues, stimulating activity through funding individual and collaborative projects, and communicating through workshops, conferences, papers, and books such as this one. Each center aims to capitalize on the close proximity of many able scholars with shared interests. The centers also provide an important window into the world of practice, from which we elicit reactions to our research and draw guidance on priorities to pursue. The special mission of the Huntsman Center is to be the focal point for Wharton research on competitive strategy, innovations, emerging technology, and managing in global markets. Our activities are a tribute to Jon Huntsman, an alumnus of the School, who had the foresight to establish the Huntsman Center in 1988. He is a visionary entrepreneur who has had remarkable success as the founder, chairman, and CEO of the nation's largest private chemical company.

Many people contributed to bringing this enterprise to closure. To Robert Gunther goes a special thanks for working with us on the overall development of the book, integrating the sometimes divergent efforts of each of the authors, and for his contribution to the content. Special thanks go to Michele Klekotka, our administrative assistant, and Heidi Brown who previously held that position, who cheerfully bore the burden of keeping us organized and facilitated the complex communication web.

It should not go unsaid our debt of appreciation to our wives, Marilyn Day and Karen Reibstein, whose support and tolerance make our work and lives the joy that they are.

Our daily work is enhanced by the spirited challenges and insights brought to us by our colleagues at The Wharton School and the broader academic community, as well as the interactions we have with students and executives. Indeed, this book originated in a course for executives on Competitive Marketing Strategy taught at The Wharton School. The insights, applications, and issues raised by the executives in the program helped stimulate much of the thinking brought to this book.

It was only in the context of the Wharton community, with such diversity of expertise and experience, that a project as broad as this book became possible to envision and develop. We hope this work reflects the true depth and excellence of the School and its faculty.

G.S.D.
D.J.R.

CONTENTS

Contents

CONTENTS

INTRODUCTION

THE DYNAMIC CHALLENGES
FOR THEORY AND PRACTICE

Competition is moving so fast, even
the Energizer Bunny can't keep up. Its fierce competition with rival
Duracell for the $2 billion U.S. alkaline battery market heated up in
1996 over the issue of battery testers. In 1990, Duracell had introduced
an in-package tester in some of its batteries, a move that analysts estimated may have helped Duracell gain three points in market share over
the following five years.[1] The two rivals upped the ante by announcing plans for more expensive on-battery testers at the end of 1995, a
move that erased the advantage of Duracell's package testers.[2] Eveready
arrived first to market, beginning to ship several sizes of batteries with
built-in testers in May 1996. Duracell began shipping its first on-line
testers just a month later on its AA batteries.[3] Neither company dared
to let its rival introduce the innovation first, yet the result was that the
on-line tester provided less of an advantage for either company because
both had it; both boosted advertising and neither was expected to raise
its prices. (The two companies were simultaneously fighting in court

over the patent for the on-line testers.) The firms now had the burden of producing this added feature without it providing a significant advantage over rivals. And this was just one round of competition. As Eveready's advertising states, competitive interactions "just keep going and going and going."

Strategy is increasingly dynamic. As in the case of Eveready, an initially promising strategy can be undermined by the moves of rivals. The strength of a given strategy is determined not by the initial move, but rather by how well it anticipates and addresses the moves and countermoves of competitors and shifts in customer demands over time. The strategy's success also depends on how effectively it addresses changes in the competitive environment from regulations, technology, and other sources. As the pace of change in the competitive environment has increased in many industries, so has the need for the explicit recognition of this dynamism in the formulation of competitive strategies.

Globalization and technological change are spawning new sources of competition; deregulation is changing the rules of competition in many industries; markets are becoming more complex and unpredictable; and information flows in a tightly wired world enable firms to sense and react to competitors at a faster rate. This accelerated competition means it is no longer possible to wait for a competitor to make a move before deciding how to react. The new watchwords are anticipation and preparation, for every eventuality. Every move of a competitor is met with a rapid countermove, thus any advantage is merely temporary.

The most intense or hypercompetitive rivalries are seen in the cola wars where every move Coca-Cola makes is met by Pepsi-Cola, and every initiative by Pepsi is quickly countered by Coke.[4] So, too, with long-distance providers: Every advertisement by MCI immediately stimulates a response by AT&T, and vice versa. The result is an advertising war in which collective annual spending has topped $1 billion. The list is endless. As soon as Kodak launches a new disposable camera, Fuji will have a similar model ready for the market. Even banks have launched credit card wars, where every offer of gifts or reduced finance charges is soon matched.

No firm can afford to let its rivals gain an obvious lead for long. This is because customers make their choices based on what they perceive each firm has to offer when compared to the other available choices. What constitutes a *powerful* computer or an *inexpensive* airfare depends on the power of the other computers that are available in the market and the fares of the other airlines on the route. In short, the deciding factor is not how good the product or service being offered is, but rather, how good a value it is relative to the competitor's offering. Thus, managers cannot afford to be complacent about a good product, since some competitor's new offering will always be altering the perception of their product's quality.

Strategy is complex. The impact of a strategy is determined not only by the initial action of the firm but by the interaction of the strategy with competitors, customers, and other players in the competitive environment. The ripples of a strategy are sent out across customers and competitors and are then reflected back to the firm. It is this complex interaction of multiple waves of strategy and reactions to them, layer upon layer, that defines competition. As market boundaries become more blurred, bringing new outsiders into once stable industries, competition has become more complex and multidimensional. The options and threats facing companies are broader and more diverse, demanding a wider field of vision.

RETHINKING STRATEGY

In the light of the increasing intensity and velocity of competition, there is a growing sense that the ability of managers to formulate and implement competitive strategies has not kept pace. Consultants and academics have stepped into the void to offer an ever-changing and often conflicting array of frameworks and methods. Each is held out as the key to unlocking the puzzle of competition, but each is capable of illuminating only part of the picture. And, in their attempt to oversimplify strategy, these approaches often overlook crucial elements of the strategy process.

This book addresses these challenges by offering a dynamic and integrative view of competitive strategies. This view recognizes the value of diverse perspectives on such a complex issue, as well as the need to draw these perspectives into a coherent whole. Strategists cannot afford to look at the world from one point of view. Doing so is as dangerous as trying to navigate the freeway with one eye closed. Managers need, instead, a comprehensive framework that uses a variety of lenses and tools to understand a firm's competitive situation, find new sources of advantage, and formulate strategies that competitors are unable to match readily.

Without a dynamic view of strategy, managers risk clinging to strategies of the past when they no longer work. Without a complex and sophisticated view of competition, managers risk oversimplifying or ignoring a potential threat or opportunity. To examine the many aspects that need to be considered in formulating strategy, consider the situation through the eyes of one competitor in a very dynamic and complex market.

Silicon Graphics: The Complex and Dynamic Challenges of Modern Strategy

By the middle of 1996, Silicon Graphics (SGI) faced the greatest strategic challenge of its young life.[5] The company, founded in 1982 by Jim Clark and six students from Stanford University, had risen to become a $2.2 billion company and the dominant force in 3-D computer graphics.[6]

Initially, large computer and software companies paid little attention to this small firm in a tiny segment of the computing industry. But in the more than a dozen years since its founding, three-dimensional graphics became increasingly important to entertainment (creating dinosaurs in *Jurassic Park,* for example), automotive design, and even financial services, where three-dimensional graphs helped brokers understand sudden spikes in the stock market. Silicon Graphics created the market and was the leader.

In a niche that accounted for just 5 percent of the workstation market in 1990, SGI became the third largest manufacturer of workstations overall—later slipping to fourth behind Sun, Hewlett-

Packard (HP), and IBM—and certainly the leader in three-dimensional workstations.

Graphic Violence: Advantages under Fire. In mid-1996, SGI continued to have considerable advantages. As the inventor of the 3-D market, it had a strong brand image and powerful visual design capabilities. But SGI and the market were now big enough to attract the attention of huge rivals, every bit as menacing as the velociraptors generated by SGI's computers. Intel's next-generation microprocessors and Microsoft's NT software brought three-dimensional computing into the mass market. Sun, Hewlett-Packard, and others were also challenging SGI for leadership in workstations. With the rise of these new competitors, could SGI hold on to its advantages? Also, who was it competing against and how?

SGI faced two significant threats that could undermine its advantages:

- *Small-fish-in-a-big-pond syndrome.* By the new definition of the market, SGI went from being the big fish in three-dimensional graphics to being a small player in a much larger universe. With just 9 percent of the total workstation market in 1996, it was dwarfed by Sun, HP, and IBM, as shown in Table I.1. This change in its competitors presents it with a much steeper competitive challenge, particularly as these same competitors aggressively develop new graphics capabilities.

Table I.1
Workstation Market Share (1996)

Sun Microsystems Computer Corp.	36%
Hewlett-Packard (HP)	21%
International Business Machines (IBM)	12%
Silicon Graphics, Inc. (SGI)	9%
Digital Equipment Corp. (DEC)	7%

Source: *Computer Graphics World,* March 1996, p. 52.

- *The commoditization of 3-D graphics.* Trends in chips, software, and workstations are increasingly making three-dimensional graphics a built-in feature of computers or software. As Intel CEO Andy Grove commented, "There's nothing Silicon Graphics has that you won't be able to do on a $99 application on a PC two years from now." Intel's Pentium Pro was beginning to offer performance levels in three-dimensional computing comparable to SGI's systems from several years before.[7] Intel also joined with Hewlett-Packard to develop its next generation of microprocessors, which were expected to be powerful enough to blur the lines between personal computers and workstations, threatening the entire market. These mass-produced, low-cost chips could flood the market with three-dimensional graphics, undermining SGI's advantage. In addition, Sun, HP, IBM, and Digital were all adding three-dimensional graphics capabilities to their new workstations. Meanwhile, Microsoft included strong graphics capabilities in Windows NT. With a $130 million acquisition of animation software company Softimage, Microsoft appeared to be positioned to make further attacks into SGI's turf. In fact, in its 1996 launch of Softimage 3-D for NT, Microsoft compared its performance to Silicon Graphics workstations (although not SGI's current generation of systems). The implication, as summed up by a reporter for *Computer Graphics World,* was that "you can get Silicon Graphics performance at half the price."[8]

SGI continued to do what it has always done—define the leading edge of three-dimensional computing through "perpetual innovation."[9] (Its reply to Grove was that SGI's customers didn't want to wait two years for SGI graphics.) As CEO Ed McCracken commented, "We try to churn the market faster than our competition, and we try to be there first with new paradigms."[10] But unless SGI changes its strategy, its competitors could turn this successful strategy into a prison. Silicon Graphics cofounder Jim Clark, who left to create Netscape in 1994, cautioned that the company's strategy could trap it in "high-end hell," a prisoner of its own gold-plated niche. Often it is the mass market that sets the standards for the industry.

SGI's niche strategy and vertical integration have led some observers to compare the company to Apple Computer.[11]

Silicon Graphics has moved into these high-volume markets through a series of alliances. It developed chips for Nintendo video games, an animation studio with Dreamworks SKG, and interactive television for Time Warner. It also strengthened its position in the high end of the market with the $780 million acquisition of Cray Research in 1996. Rather than manufacturing for the mass market, the company was designing systems for partners who could carry its designs to the masses. The partnerships were designed "to capture share in huge new markets," said Stan Meresman, CFO of Silicon Graphics. "The point of partnering is to get your leading customers to be pushing you for things you can't quite do yet."[12]

But with an increasingly large pack of aggressive hounds nipping at its heels, will SGI become the next Hewlett-Packard or another casualty in the rapidly shifting competitive field of Silicon Valley? Much depends on how it addresses its strategic challenges.

The Competitive Challenges. Among the competitive challenges that face Silicon Graphics as it considers its next moves:

- What are the structures of the market and SGI's position? Is it competing against chip makers, workstation manufacturers, or software companies? Are its advantages from its capabilities in programming innovation or its strong brand image? What is the relationship among competitors in its industry? How could public policy change the competitive arena?
- What actions must SGI take to protect its position in the market? Should it lower price to prevent being too far out of line with the new software competitors? How quickly should SGI introduce its new product enhancements?
- How will its competitors react to SGI's actions? How do they view the competitive game, and what biases affect their behavior? How will their behavior change over time?
- What are SGI's options in formulating a competitive strategy? How can it respond creatively to the moves of its competitors?

How can it preempt its competitors? Will its commitments to such investments as supercomputers be a source of strength or weakness? How does antitrust constrain its strategic moves?

- How can it analyze strategy across multiple rounds of competition? It may be easy to develop strategies that will be temporarily effective, but which of its potential strategies will work in the long haul—especially after considering its competitors' reactions and potential changes in the competitive environment?

SGI is not alone in addressing complex and dynamic challenges. These are the types of challenges that many companies face in dynamic competitive environments. These are the challenges this book addresses through an interdisciplinary approach using a wide array of tools and insights from many streams of strategy research and practice.

THE PRICE OF FAILING TO RECOGNIZE THE DYNAMIC NATURE OF STRATEGY

Managers and their companies pay a stiff price for failing to recognize the dynamic nature of strategy. This price is exacted through missed opportunities and strategic errors. Two of the most common and serious errors are related to the failure to anticipate competitors' moves and the failure to recognize potential interactions over time. These examples illustrate the importance of a dynamic view of competitive strategy.

The Failure to Anticipate a Changing Market Structure

In the 1970s, Okidata produced an excellent dot-matrix line printer and won a significant share of the printer market. While Okidata continued to offer customers "the best damned [dot-matrix] printers on the market," Hewlett-Packard transformed customers' perceptions of what a good printer was. First, HP introduced an imported ink-jet model that had some advantages over Okidata's line. Then, it offered the Laserjets, a family of highly reliable printers based on a technological breakthrough that made them faster and quieter, provided greater resolution, and even gave them substantial resale value. Okidata quickly lost its leadership position to Hewlett-Packard.

Soon the new HP printers proved their worth in the workplace, and Hewlett-Packard captured the respect and loyalty of many of Okidata's former customers. Okidata complacently watched its share of the printer market erode, stubbornly continuing to market a product in what was now only a narrow slice of the overall printer market. By failing to grow and evolve with the market, Okidata lost its once powerful position. It made the mistake of assuming that a strategy that worked well in the past would continue to work well in the future. In fact, strategies that worked well in the past are the most likely targets for attack by competitors who define the market differently.

The Failure to Consider Potential Interactions over Time

Okidata's failure to keep moving forward is one form of strategic error. Another is a failure to understand the potential interactions of competitors over time. A move that works effectively at the outset may then be undermined by subsequent moves of competitors and changes in customer perceptions. After initially gaining an advantage from the move, the company may ultimately find itself worse off because of its own "brilliant" strategy.

For example, one British bank felt it could gain a competitive advantage over competitors by opening on Saturdays in addition to the normal Monday through Friday hours. Initially, the move attracted an influx of new customers. The customers were delighted that a bank had finally started to provide extended hours, making it more convenient to do banking. The bank, however, failed to adequately consider an important question: Would competitors just sit by and watch their customers defect? It did not take long before most rival banks were forced to respond in kind. While the banking customers were better off, the net effect for the industry was for all the banks

9

to increase their cost of doing business without any appreciable increase in the level of banking. In short, the same level of banking was spread over six days instead of five.

In mature markets, in particular, competition is, at best, a zero-sum game, where one firm gains at the expense of the others. The more intense the rivalry, the more likely it will deteriorate into a negative-sum game in which the process of competition imposes costs on all the players.

An aggressive move to penetrate a market will backfire if the competitive response significantly raises the cost of doing business. For example, when a firm greatly increases its advertising expenditures, and competitors follow suit, there will be no net gain for anyone, just higher costs.

An even more destructive outcome is for the move to escalate into an all-out war. Such mutually destructive behavior is seen in the price wars that have eroded profits in airlines, computer software, automobile tires, disposable diapers, and many other markets. After one firm sets off the confrontation by cutting its price, a series of retaliatory price reductions are quickly launched by its rivals, because no one wants to lose customers, volume, or share. Seldom does volume increase enough to offset the impact on margins of the decline in average price level.

Besides the current battering to profits, the long-term danger is that once customers' expectations about the correct and reasonable price are driven to an unrealistically low level, the situation is difficult to reverse. Worse, as the rivals increasingly emphasize price, their customers become more and more price-sensitive. When the price war ends, the customers' behaviors may be drastically changed.

This change in customer behavior was an unanticipated result of the pricing strategy of a building products manufacturer. After losing market share to new and aggressive competitors that undercut its prices, the manufacturer changed its pricing policies. It allowed its sales force to cut special deals with customers who were considering defecting to a lower-priced rival. The company continued to charge a premium for its products, and it reversed its market share decline—in the short term. But over time, the customers paying a premium price learned that others were receiving the same products for less. They began negotiating harder on price, driving down the profits of the company and the industry. Price-shopping customers were less loyal and profits were even thinner. What initially looked like an effective strategy turned out to have negative consequences when customer and competitor actions were taken into consideration.[13]

The difficulty of addressing competitive reactions is heightened because competitive games are played in the fog. Managers have their own blind spots, and the true intentions and resolve of competitors are deeply and often deliberately obscured. Their responses are likely to be misunderstood and underestimated.

During the postmortem debriefing, it is usually easy for managers and students to clearly identify the failures of analysis or managerial fortitude that led to the mistakes. It is clear now that Okidata should not have clung so tenaciously to the eclipsed slice of the market for computer printers. It is clear the British bank should have thought twice about instituting Saturday hours. But how could it have been clear at the time managers were formulating these strategies? Unfortunately, managers rarely see the issues so clearly during the critical strategy formulation stage. How can they understand the dynamic nature of competition and its impact on their strategies? How can managers anticipate the moves by competitors that could undermine their strategies? How can they consider the complex forces that affect whether their strategies succeed or fail?

THE NEED FOR AN INTEGRATIVE VIEW ON STRATEGY

To meet the demands of this increasingly complex and dynamic environment, managers need new tools and perspectives. There are a variety of theories and approaches that can help managers better understand and anticipate competitive challenges. Okidata managers might have benefited from a more thorough understanding of their sources of advantages and how they are eroded. They might have been better prepared if they had examined potential scenarios for the future, including one in which there is a radical shift in printer technology. The bankers in the preceding example might have employed game theory or a simulation to try to anticipate the moves competitors were likely to make in reaction to the addition of Saturday hours. They might have considered whether this commitment to extended hours provided a defensible advantage over rivals.

Unfortunately, because most strategic perspectives arose out of independent disciplines, theorists approach strategy from a variety of directions. Like civilizations that developed in different parts of the world, each stream has its own separate culture and language. Sometimes there is more compatibility among the perspectives than is at first apparent.

This book, because it draws upon experts in different fields as well as those with an overview of several perspectives, aims to translate these diverse languages and explore the similarities and connections that underlie the differences. This integrative view draws together some of the different camps of strategy and brings fresh perspectives, such as public policy, to the table. Among the perspectives collected in this volume:

- *Resource-based and structure-conduct-performance perspectives.* These two frameworks have been among the most powerful and useful approaches to analyzing and formulating competitive strategy. The resource-based view, popularized by Gary Hamel and C.K. Prahalad, focuses on the firm's resources (assets) and capabilities and how these internal strengths provide advantage over rivals.[14] The structure-conduct-performance (positional view), most closely associated with the work of Michael Porter, examines the firm's relative position in its industry and the forces that either sustain or erode this position. (For example, one firm may stake out a position of low cost while another becomes a differentiator.) These views are two sides of one competitive picture, one perspective focusing on defining *what* advantages need to be created and the other focusing on *how* to create them.
- *Game theory and behavioral views.* This book also unites the sometimes conflicting perspectives of game theory and psychological behavioral theory. Game theory, an ancient science used by the

early Chinese military to examine moves and countermoves, has become increasingly popular in analyzing and planning competitive strategy. It allows managers to systematically analyze their incentives and payoffs as well as those of rivals. But behavioral theory reminds us that actual strategic interaction is anything but logical and systematic. It is conducted by human managers with their own foibles and blind spots, as well as organizations with their own weaknesses. The behavioral perspective examines what managers or companies are likely to do in a given situation and the simple heuristics used for formulating strategy. These two views, however, are complementary. Rigorous game theory takes as its starting point the mental models of competitors. If these are effectively figured into the equation, the model should reflect the incentives and moves of competitors, warts and all. The behavioral perspective reminds us of what those warts are so we can become more aware of our biases and those of our rivals in developing and implementing strategy.

- *Public policy and technology.* One of the voices on strategy that has been largely ignored by strategy theorists and practitioners is public policy. In some markets, public policy defines or redefines competition. Yet many companies view public policy as a small functional area in their organizations and do not explicitly include it in their analyses of strategy. This book examines the relationship between public policy and competitive strategy and considers the constraints imposed by antitrust regulations. The book also examines the impact of technology in reshaping competitive advantages. Technology can often turn a current advantage into a liability. Both public policy and technology are most often considered in strategy only as a part of the external environment. The chapters in this book emphasize that they must be an integral part of the strategy formulation process.
- *Scenarios, war games, and simulations.* The book includes an examination of several strategic approaches for testing the impact of competitive strategies. It draws together diverse techniques that have been used to rehearse and experiment with strategies, including the perspectives of scenario planning, war gaming,

conjoint analysis, and strategy simulations. In dynamic environments, these approaches are particularly important in helping managers to think through the multiple stages of competitive interactions before making the first move.

- *Signaling and actions.* The options for strategic moves are often broader and deeper than managers realize in formulating strategies. Although managers often focus on direct actions, there are many other aspects of competitive moves, which are highlighted in this book. The role of signals should be carefully considered in formulating strategy and interpreting the moves of competitors. The book also emphasizes the diverse options that managers have in formulating strategies, including developing plans for preemption and choosing among a wide range of different reactions to the moves of rivals.

These are just a few of many insights of different disciplines that are brought to bear upon strategic challenges in this book. These perspectives, while largely complementary, are not completely so. There are sometimes lively debates among the participants about the strengths and weaknesses of different views.

KEY MANAGEMENT CHALLENGES

This book is structured around four key challenges facing managers in developing competitive strategy:

1. Understanding advantages in a changing competitive environment.
2. Anticipating competitors' actions.
3. Formulating dynamic competitive strategies.
4. Choosing alternative competitive strategies.

These challenges are illustrated in Figure I.1. To develop effective strategy, managers need to understand the arena of competition and sources of advantage, anticipate moves of rivals, know their own

Figure I.1
Formulating Dynamic Competitive Strategies

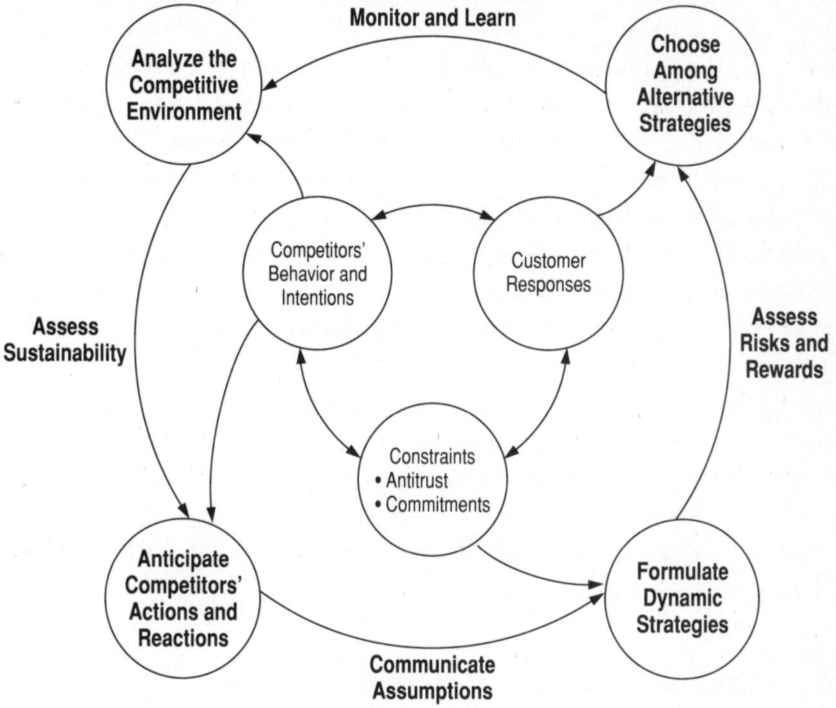

Monitor and Learn

Analyze the
Competitive
Environment

Choose
Among
Alternative
Strategies

Competitors'
Behavior and
Intentions

Customer
Responses

**Assess
Sustainability**

**Assess
Risks and
Rewards**

Constraints
• Antitrust
• Commitments

Anticipate
Competitors'
Actions and
Reactions

Formulate
Dynamic
Strategies

**Communicate
Assumptions**

competitive options, and analyze the potential impact of a given strategy. The parts of the book look at each of these issues in turn.

Understanding Advantages in a Changing Competitive Environment

The book begins by asking: With whom am I really competing? Many times companies waste precious resources responding to other companies in the same industry, but with whom they are not really competing. To be a true competitor, the firm has to be selling to the same set of customers or market segment and serving some of the same functions. If the firm is selling to a totally different segment, its actions may not affect one's sales, share, or profit. Imagine an airline serving an international airport responding to a price cut by a competitor serving a distant metro airport—thus unnecessarily engaging in a price war. That competitor needs to be watched closely so its intentions are understood and possible effects of the price cut on traffic patterns are identified. Chapter 1 shows numerous ways to identify who are the true or prospective competitors worthy of monitoring and preventing from gaining a competitive advantage.

Once this set of competitors is identified, the next question is: What advantages does the firm have over these competitors? A primary goal of strategy is to create and sustain these advantages. Chapter 2 examines the sources of advantage and ways that change over time. Finally, arenas and advantages are shaped or reshaped by changes in public policy and technology. The closing chapters in Part I explore these changes. They look at both the opportunities and threats created by public policy and technological change. They examine how policy windows open and close, and how being a leader in one generation of technology is very often the recipe for failure in the next.

Anticipating Competitors' Actions

The next challenge is to understand how competitors will respond to a given action and how they are likely to move in the future. To do this, managers need to understand the competitive games rivals are playing and the payoffs from different strategies. They also need to understand the competitors' motives and interpretations of rivals' actions. To do this, it is necessary to understand the biases and simple heuristics that color competitors' decisions. Finally, they have to have a sense of how these payoffs and perspectives will change over time as a result of competitive interactions.

Part II is a guided tour of the mind of the competitor through the perspectives of game theory and behavioral theory. Managers' mental models strongly influence how they interpret competitive intelligence and formulate alternative competitive strategies. These mental models are necessarily simplifications that managers use to make sense of complex and confusing competitive arenas. This section will provide a better understanding of what makes rivals tick and provides the tools to analyze their potential competitive actions and reactions. It also explores how companies learn, adapt, and coevolve over time. Finally, this part examines patterns of competitive relationships—such as leader-follower relationships—that shape actions and reactions.

Formulating Dynamic Competitive Strategies

Once one understands sources of advantage and potential moves of competitors, the next challenge is to explore the firm's strategic options. Part III explores a range of possible options as well as constraints on those options. It looks at the diverse options for reacting to a competitive move and the possibilities for preempting a move. It also explores how signals can be used as part of competitive strategy. This part also examines the use of commitment as a positive element of competitive strategy.

Part III then explores some of the limitations on competitive strategy. The first constraint is commitments; that is, irreversible moves and investments. Sometimes limiting options can be an effective competitive strategy. The second constraint on strategy is antitrust legislation. The closing chapter in this part explores the ways that antitrust limits strategic actions and how this issue should be raised early in the strategy formulation process.

Choosing among Alternative Strategies

The final challenge is to analyze the long-term impact of various potential strategies to select a strategy to implement. Strategies do not succeed or fail in one round. Usually, company A moves, company B responds, company A counters, and so on. As in the example of the bank that moved to Saturday hours, what looks like a great strategy in the first round might turn out to have terrible side-effects.

Once managers have conceptualized and generated potential strategies, they need some mechanism for evaluating the potential consequences of each of these strategies in the light of multiple rounds or multiple scenarios of competition. Part IV examines three tools for analyzing strategy over multiple rounds or scenarios of competition. The first is conjoint analysis, which explores multiple rounds of new product introductions, in the light of competitor and customer responses. The second approach is a strategic assets framework that examines the necessary resources and capabilities of the firm across different competitive scenarios. The third approach is strategy simulation, which allows managers to rehearse one strategy or experiment with a variety of possible strategies. These simulations provide insights into the "chemical" reactions among competitors that are often not apparent in the dry analysis of strategy on paper. To the extent that these experimental models can be made to reflect the actual dimensions of competition and the mind-sets of competitors, they can come close to embodying the complex dynamics of competition. Any such evaluation must incorporate one's own strategy, as well as that of the competitors, in a dynamic assessment—that is, how each competitor might react to the moves of the other.

Conclusion

This book proposes a process for developing dynamic competitive strategies: Assess the context of competitive moves and advantages, understand the potential moves and mind-sets of competitors, formulate strategies, and test these strategies before making irreversible moves in the market.

Although this is a straightforward process, it is by no means a simple formula. There are not three things one must do to lead in the market. And even if there were, there would very likely be a different three things tomorrow. Managers need to continually assess and reassess their options and competitive situation. They need to be vigilant and alert. Above all, they need to be able to learn, both from their own experiences and from the studies and experiences of others. This book is an excellent place to begin, or continue, what must be a lifelong process of learning about competitive strategy. In a fast-paced, complex environment, this ability to learn may perhaps be the most sustainable competitive advantage.

PART I

UNDERSTANDING ADVANTAGES IN A CHANGING COMPETITIVE ENVIRONMENT

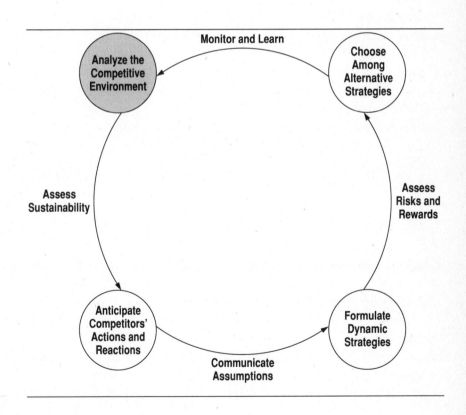

$\mathbf{A}$uto and phone companies are competing with banks in the credit card war, and big banks are creating their own long-distance telephone networks. Should Chemical Bank treat Microsoft, Intuit, and AT&T as competitors?

Dell Computers used an unconventional mail-order approach to computer sales to become a Fortune 500 company just eight years after its founding. Its success was then challenged by rivals who matched its strategy and continued to push forward technology. Electronics superstores appeared. Powerful players such as Compaq began direct marketing products. How could Dell continue to build and renew its advantages?

The Bhopal chemical accident of December 1984 meant that large chemical firms would be under increasing scrutiny by regulators around the world. Similarly, airline deregulation radically altered the competitive landscape in the U.S. airline industry. How can companies anticipate and help to shape and respond to such legislation?

Hong Kong Shanghai Bank Corp. (HKSB) held accounts from 75 percent of households in Hong Kong. But aggressive rivals such as Citibank began "cream skimming" the most profitable customers. HKSB's broad reach became a liability because it meant it also had to serve unprofitable customers. What can companies like HKSB do to respond to such competitive threats? This section examines these and other changes in the competitive environment and the nature of advantages within it.

ARENAS AND ADVANTAGES

One of the fundamental questions of competitive strategy is: Where do you have an edge over rivals? In dynamic environments, the sources and nature of these advantages often undergo rapid changes.

To assess your advantages over rivals, you must first determine the meaningful set of competitors for comparison. Should you look at companies in the same product market, those with similar capabilities, or potential substitutes? Sears may have had an advantage over other department stores in the 1980s, but not over specialized retailers such as The Gap. Should it now consider as competitors other department stores, category killers, catalog retailers, or even the television shopping networks and on-line interactive services? In an environment in which industry definitions are often in flux, the first challenge is to determine the arena of competition. Chapter 1 explores a variety of approaches for developing definitions of the competitive arena.

Once the relevant set of competitors is determined, the second question is: Does the company have a sustainable edge over the competition? Some would argue that there are no longer any sustainable advantages except a strong brand and an educated and committed workforce. A more complete and practical answer comes from a three-step process developed in Chapter 2. The first step asks whether we have demonstrated we have an advantage by delivering superior customer value. The next step is to understand the sources of these advantages. These are the superior assets and distinctive capabilities that set our organization apart from competitors. The final step asks how long these advantages can be sustained by putting impediments in the way of competitors' efforts to imitate or leapfrog, and investing to refurbish the advantages or find new ones. This process is part of a never-ending cycle of creation and erosion of advantages that must be mastered to achieve superior profitability.

UNDERSTANDING FORCES OF CHANGE: PUBLIC POLICY AND TECHNOLOGY

Two of the prime forces of change in shifting arenas and advantages are public policy and technology. Trends toward regulation or deregulation can fundamentally alter the nature of the competitive environment, yet many managers examine the impact of public policy only as an afterthought. Chapter 3 explores the interaction between policy and competitive strategy and shows how managers can integrate policy considerations into their process of strategy formulation.

Technology is another powerful force in shaping arenas and advantages. Chapter 4 shows how shifts in technology can erode the existing advantages of dominant firms. The chapter specifically examines how changes in technology and regulations in banking and other service industries are creating opportunities for new entrants to take away the most profitable customers from the large firms. Thus, the once sustainable advantages of large firms become "sustainable disadvantages" as these corporate giants are held back by old technology, past commitments, regulations, and other forces.

Part I offers tools and insights into understanding the nature of advantages and how they change in dynamic competitive environments. Any approach to competitive strategy needs to begin with an understanding of the definition of arenas, sources of advantages, and the forces of change.

CHAPTER 1

ASSESSING COMPETITIVE ARENAS: WHO ARE YOUR COMPETITORS?

GEORGE S. DAY

The Wharton School, Department of Marketing

One of the primary issues facing managers in formulating competitive strategy is defining the arena of competition. Where are you competing? Who are your competitors? How attractive is this competitive arena? This chapter examines definitions of the competitive arena, particularly from the perspective of either customers or competitors. It also explores the forces that make a given arena more or less attractive.

One of the significant competitive challenges for managers is to accurately define the existing boundaries and structure of the competitive arena—in order to understand, outmaneuver, and react to existing rivals—without making dangerous oversimplifications that can blind one to changes that will upset the prevailing rules.

Some arenas have well-defined, stable boundaries within which clearly identifiable competitors interact. Most of the classic cases used to study industry and competitive analysis fit this description. Procter & Gamble versus Kimberly Clark in disposable diapers, DuPont in titanium dioxide, or the place of Whirlpool in the appliance industry are readily described and predictable. The cola wars are being fought between Pepsi-Cola and Coca-Cola in the soft drink markets

---

Portions of this chapter are adapted from George S. Day, *Market-Driven Strategy* (New York: Free Press, 1990). Hubert Gatignon made a number of useful contributions.

of virtually every country on the globe. Each is contesting a myriad of end use and distribution segments within the cola market, and each has many other nonalcoholic beverage rivals striving for a share of the consumer's stomach. While the rivalry is fierce, it is taking place in a well-defined market, in accordance with well-established rules.

As competition becomes more dynamic, the arena boundaries become fuzzier, and rivals more difficult to identify or anticipate. Entire industries are converging and overlapping, as with chemical imaging and electronic imaging. Previously clear distinctions between office products, consumer electronics, telecommunications, and entertainment are eroding. Thus, the functionalities and customer benefits of the personal computer have so evolved that it is both a consumer product with an entertainment function, and a business and productivity device. Where does the retail financial services market begin or end now? Should Chemical Bank treat Microsoft, Intuit, and AT&T as competitors?

The continued disruption of once stable arenas that permits unexpected competitors to come out of nowhere is a result of technological change, globalization, deregulation, or demanding customers and channels. Auto and phone companies are competing with banks in the credit card war, and big banks are creating their own long-distance telephone networks. Firms with little respect for industry conventions are able to overcome the existing boundaries and establish new patterns of interaction, as Dell Computer has demonstrated by bypassing established channels for personal computers and going directly to customers.

No single approach can adequately describe and explain such complex, fast-changing, and multidimensional arenas. The primary purpose of this chapter is to provide readers with a variety of tools for making sense of these shifting arenas to reduce the confusion and ambiguity. This requires viewing the market from the perspective of both customers and competitors. Then, the chapter explores the competitive forces that determine whether these arenas are attractive or unattractive. This chapter thus defines the context of the rest of the book, for to have a meaningful discussion of strategy, one must first define which competitors should be considered.

SCOPE OF THE ARENA

How narrowly should the competitive arena be defined? A competitive arena may be as broad as an industry or as narrow as a product market. The broadest definitions of the automobile industry would encompass all makes of cars in the global market, as well as the light truck and minivan categories because they can be used for personal transport. A narrow arena definition might be limited to light trucks in California or luxury sedans in Germany. The arena definition is determined by choices along four dimensions:

- The array of product or service categories (single product versus broad category).
- The classes/segments of customers (single versus multiple segments).
- Geographic scope (single region or country versus global).
- Number of activities in the value chain (many versus few).

Seldom can one arena definition be used for all purposes. Tactical decisions call for a different definition of the arena from strategic decisions. Tactical decisions, such as short-run budgeting and performance evaluation, usually rely upon narrow definitions, corresponding to the short-run concerns of product and sales managers, who regard their market as "a chunk of demand to be filled with whatever resources they can command." Here the definition of customers is limited to those who are currently served, while competing products are those that look alike, perform the same functions, and are sold through the same channels.

In contrast, strategic decisions require broader market definitions to embrace:

- Presently unserved market opportunities;
- Changes in technology, price levels, and supply conditions that broaden the array of perceived substitutes; and
- Potential competitive entrants from adjacent markets.

Sticking with a narrow definition for too long can make a firm vulnerable. For example, American firms are still prone to restrict themselves almost entirely to their domestic market. After all, it is a large, known entity. This provincialism has given their foreign competitors breathing room to develop a global capability from a protected home base. Many markets such as ceramics and pharmaceuticals are inherently global, and market position depends on share of worldwide sales. It is no longer possible to participate in only one part of this market.

IDENTIFYING ARENAS

One of the key ways to identify a competitive arena is to examine patterns of substitution. Substitution can be viewed from a *demand-side* perspective to account for all the ways customers can satisfy their needs, or a *supply-side* perspective to include all the competitors with the capabilities to serve these customers. These two perspectives are closely intertwined. To a customer, coffeemakers satisfy different needs from food appliances, and thus are not usually substitutes (although they may both serve as gifts on some occasions). The customers' consideration set may include all types of coffeemakers, whether percolator or drip varieties because these are perceived to be functional substitutes, as shown in Figure 1.1.

Manufacturers of coffeemakers will take a broader view than their customers. They may see their competitors as all food preparation appliances, and all the present and prospective competitors with the capacity to design, produce, and distribute coffeemakers. Here the question is the extent of feasible sharing of manufacturing facilities, R&D capabilities, enabling technologies, sales forces, and brand names.

Substitution from the Demand Side: Customer-Defined Arenas

From the demand side, a market consists of shifting patterns of customer requirements and needs that can be served by an array of competitive offerings. This array goes beyond *substitutes-in-kind*—all those

Figure 1.1
Product–Industry Hierarchy

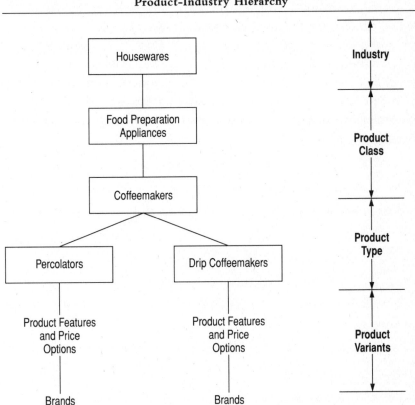

George Day: *Market-Driven Strategy,* New York: The Free Press, 1990, page 97.

products that look alike and represent the same application of a distinct technology to the provision of a distinct set of customer functions. It also encompasses *substitutes-in-use.* For coffeemakers, instant coffee is a substitute in use; it serves the same function, but in a very different way.

The customer perspective considers all the ways customer needs can be satisfied in a given usage or application situation. In some social entertainment situations, wine coolers may compete more with certain beers and wines than with other beverages. Seldom, however, is a substitute a straightforward replacement:

- The substitute may perform a wider range of functions. Thus a word processor is much more than a typewriter, by virtue of being able to store and manipulate text.
- Substitution may result if the buyer decides to perform the function, rather than buy it. The alternative to a gourmet dinner purchased in the deli section of the supermarket is one made from scratch. In the property and casualty insurance market, buyers are increasingly turning to self-insurance or setting up captive insurance subsidiaries.
- Another type of substitute is the used, recycled, or reconditioned product. Rebuilt automobile and aircraft engine parts are a major threat to the sale of new spare parts. One of the advantages of the steel minimills is the ability to use low-cost scrap steel.

Properly defined markets are bounded by sharp discontinuities in customer needs or benefits sought, and the degree of substitutability of the product or service alternatives for satisfying these needs. According to this rule, a material such as nylon competes in several different end-use markets such as tire cord, carpeting, and hosiery, since the customer needs in each application are very different. Thus, there is a distinct market for synthetic carpet fibers, but not a single nylon market. Substitutability implies that the purpose or application, rather than product features, as such, becomes the organizing theme for considering alternatives.

Analytical Methods to Determine Customer Substitution. Which products do customers consider as substitutes? Substitutability can be gauged by studying the actions of customers (behavioral) or by asking them to define their decision sets (perceptual).[1] The best known *behavioral* methods are based on cross-elasticities or brand-switching data. On the face of it, a cross-elasticity measure directly addresses the question of whether two products are substitutes and hence in the same competitive set. This measure is based on the proportional change in the sales of one product due to a shift in price of another product. For example, if a 10 percent reduction in the price of insulated copper cable caused a 5 percent reduction in the sales of insulated aluminum cable, the two types of cable would be considered substitutes. In practice, such studies are extremely difficult to undertake, because many factors usually contribute to changes in product sales other than changes in the price of substitutes.

Brand-switching measures of substitutability are widely used within such categories as food and health-care products that have high repeat purchase rates. These measures are interpreted as conditional probabilities, since they describe the probability of purchasing Brand A, given that Brand B was purchased on the last occasion. Consumers are assumed to be more likely to switch between close substitutes than between distant ones.[2]

While behavioral measures provide the best indication as to what customers have done, they do not necessarily reveal what they might do under changed circumstances. *Judgmental* data, in the form of perceptions or preferences of product or brand alternatives, give better insights into future patterns of competition. Also, the methods for analyzing this data to identify product-market boundaries are better able to handle large numbers of potentially competitive alternatives.

Customer judgments of substitutability can be obtained simply by asking a sample of customers to indicate the degree of substitutability between all possible pairs of products or brands on a rating scale. The results of such analyses are seldom useful, however, for customers lack a specific context within which to make their judgments. For this reason, *substitution-in-use* techniques have been developed that give good insights into product-market boundaries. Customers are asked to judge the appropriateness or acceptability of a number of potentially competitive products for specific conditions of use. In a study of proprietary medicines, for example, respondents were asked whether each of 52 medicines was acceptable for a wide variety of usage situations ranging from "when you have a stuffy nose" to "when you have a fever."

This approach presumes that the set of products provides a reasonable sample of the benefits being sought by the customer, and that two usage situations are similar if similar benefits are desired in both situations. If so, a market can be defined as a set of products that are judged to be appropriate within usage situations in which similar patterns of benefits are sought.

29

With information on perceived substitutability or similarity of the alternatives in the choice set, it is possible to create a spatial map of the competitive arena that locates the brands or products in a two- or three-dimensional space. Alternatives that are perceived to be very similar are located close together, while those that are not considered to be competitive are far apart. The dimensions of the reduced space provide the reasons why the alternatives are similar or different.

The map of consumers' perceptions of women's clothing retailers in Washington, DC, shown in Figure 1.2, illustrates what can be learned from such maps.[3] Customers used the two determinant attributes of value and fashionability to distinguish among 23 store chains. Some of these stores—notably Kmart and Nordstrom—are

Figure 1.2
Map of Women's Clothing Retailers (1990)

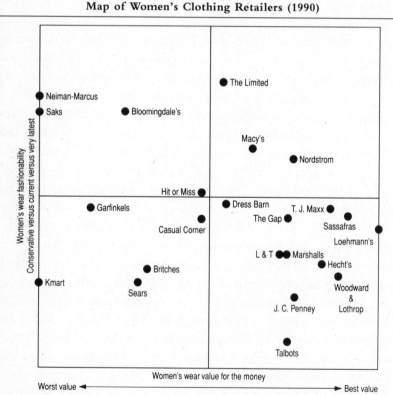

perceived as very different from one another and therefore are not competitors. Others such as Neiman-Marcus and Saks are directly competitive, but both are seemingly at a disadvantage to Bloomingdales, which is seen as equally fashionable but offering better value. Gaps in the map may be latent opportunities, but may also be infeasible or undesirable. Perhaps, very high fashion and value are not compatible, and stores in the position of worst value with conservative fashion are vulnerable and under great pressure to improve.

Substitution from the Supply Side: Competitor-Defined Arenas

Customer-defined arenas reveal patterns of substitutes that are perceived to offer similar or closely related functions. The contrasting supply-side approach starts with all the competitors who could possible serve the needs of a group of customers. This gives a different picture because it explicitly considers technological similarity, relative production costs, and distribution coverage.

This supply-side perspective addresses the following questions:

- Which competitors are serving related product classes with the same technology, manufacturing processes, material sources, sales force, and distribution channels?
- What is the geographic scope of the market? Is it regional, national, or global?
- Which competitors should be included—only those presently serving the market or potential entrants with a capacity to compete?

These questions are vital to an understanding of the relative cost standing of a business, and degree of transferability of experience into related arenas.

To draw the boundaries of the arena, the supply-side approach looks for significant discontinuities in the pattern of costs, capital requirements, and margins along the product and customer dimensions. These discontinuities create barriers that insulate prices and profits within a product market from the activities of competitors outside the market.

31

They also discourage easy entry by potential competitors. When boundaries are properly defined, the relative profitability of competitors within a market can meaningfully be compared.

When the arena is defined as broadly as an industry, it often presents a very different definition from the customer-oriented perspective. It may encompass product classes that are only loosely related on other criteria such as customer needs satisfied, similarity of functions provided, or production methods. Thus the helicopter industry includes both military and commercial helicopters, even though the respective customers don't see them as interchangeable. The cost position of many consumer packaged-goods firms is dictated by their experience in sales and distribution through grocery outlets, and advertising and sales promotion to mass markets, for these activities are a significant proportion of total cost.

Strategic Groups

The boundaries drawn by both customers and competitors, as well as the history and capabilities of the firm and competitors, lead to a clustering of firms into a few coherent strategic groups. Within these groups, firms look alike in their scope of activities and market coverage, follow similar strategies, and compete much more intensely with each other than with firms in other groups.[4] There is usually little mobility between groups, even when there are persistently large differences in their average profitability. Firms are prevented from shifting readily between groups because of differences in cultures, resources, market access, and technology, and the threat of rigorous retaliation from the incumbents in the other groups.[5]

Strategic groups are a useful intermediate level of analysis between the broad industry and the individual firm. They are valuable for separating the rivals that demand close and continuing attention from those at the periphery of concern. Moves by the firms in the same group will be quickly countered, while initiatives from within other groups don't call for a reaction. To understand these groups, consider the profound differences that would have to be surmounted to move between the following groups:

- Captive producers of electronic components such as semiconductors and merchant firms producing for the open market.
- Boutique wineries selling by mail order and high-volume, mass-market producers.
- Full-line national brand makers of major appliances and private-label producers.

One of the most useful applications of strategic groups was a forecast made by a McKinsey team of the strategic groups that would likely emerge after the deregulation of five industries.[6] They accurately foresaw there would be one group of national distribution, full-line companies such as Merrill Lynch in brokerage and Burlington Northern in railroads. The second group was the low-cost producers such as Charles Schwab in brokerage and Southwest Airlines entering the industry following the loosening of the rules and competing with stripped-down offerings that appealed to price-sensitive buyers. The last group contained the focused specialists serving a specific segment such as Ryder Systems in trucking and Goldman Sachs in brokerage.

While strategic groups are useful for identifying arenas, it would be both foolish and dangerous to assume the current strategy groups are a fixed and unquestioned feature of the arena. All arenas and the strategic groups they encompass are in flux, and it is important to have a well-reasoned point of view on how they are likely to change.

FIVE FORCES THAT SHAPE THE STRUCTURE AND INTENSITY OF COMPETITION

In addition to determining the boundaries of the competitive arena, managers also need to determine whether the arena is an attractive one. Do they want to enter or remain in this arena? The attractiveness of a certain industry or product market depends upon how the economic value created for customers is shared throughout the value chain. This is the chain of activities that obtains and transforms inputs and then sells, distributes, and services the output to the end customer. Each activity in this chain adds value to the product or service.

The cumulative value of the activities is whatever the customer is willing to pay for the stream of benefits that has been created. (Realized price is not necessarily an indicator of the amount of value created, especially if customers were able to exercise bargaining power and force the price down. They might have been willing to pay more to get the benefits but were able to exploit weaknesses among their suppliers.)

Who captures the value created for the customer? This depends on the relative influence of the players in the arena—the rivalry of competitors, threat of new entrants, customer power, supplier power, and threat of substitutes.[7] These five forces—along with several other factors in the environment—shape competition and determine the overall attractiveness of the arena, as illustrated in Figure 1.3.

Strong bargaining power of customers or threats from substitutes will limit the prices (and value captured) by firms in the market.

Figure 1.3
Forces Influencing Arena Attractiveness

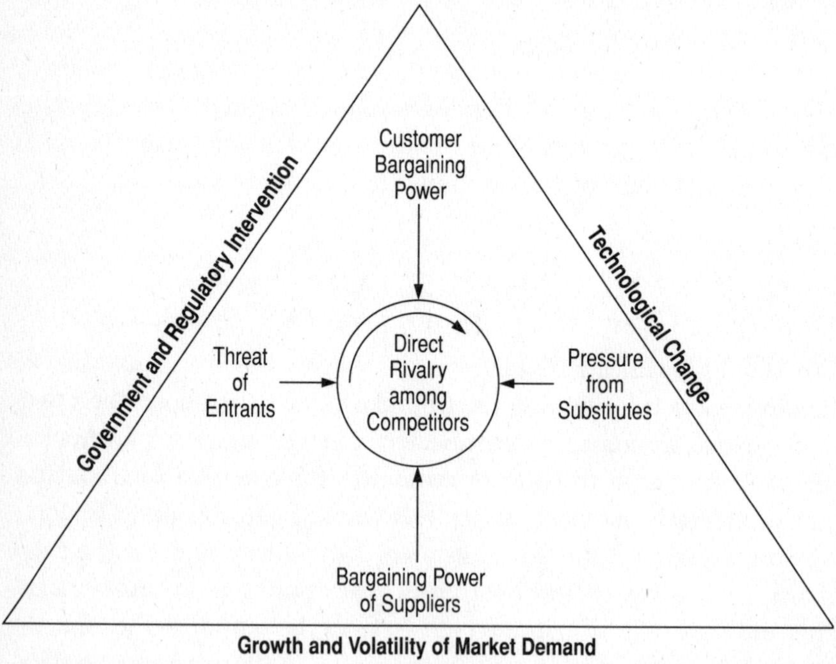

Powerful customers are usually more costly to serve. Strong bargaining power by suppliers will allow them to capture more value by raising costs of input materials and services. The intensity of competition among direct rivals can drive down prices and raise costs of meeting competition with new products, enhanced service coverage, advertising, and sales coverage. These forces of competition will be modified—either abated or accentuated—by three additional influences: government intervention, technological change, and market growth. The rest of this chapter will address each of the five forces and the additional influences.

Direct Rivalry among Competitors

In some arenas, the direct rivals coexist comfortably, and appear content with their respective market shares. Other arenas are constantly on a war footing, as the competitors look for a temporary edge with price cuts, promotional deals, ad blitzes, and aggressive new product spending. Others have to match these moves to protect their position, and waves of price-cutting escalate to the point where much of the value created is dissipated. The domestic airline industry, in its eagerness to fill seats to cover fixed costs, has a long history of behaving this way, despite experience that tells them that cut-price market expansion is short-lived and erodes profits while leaving shares unchanged. The following factors determine whether the direct rivals are in a state of war, peace, or perhaps observing an uneasy truce.

Structure of Competition. Rivalry is most heated when there are a few equally balanced competitors, or when numerous small players serve the same market and try to make moves they hope the others won't notice. A small number of stable competitors doesn't always lead to reduced rivalry. In the otherwise attractive market for industrial lasers, there are only two competitors, Spectra-Physics and Coherent Radiation, but neither has been profitable. Deep-seated antagonism between the managers of these implacable rivals often leads them to use their resources to attack and retaliate against each other, with price-cutting being a favorite weapon.

When competition is concentrated among a few companies and one competitor clearly dominates, by virtue of a share at least 50 percent larger than the second, rivalry is more subdued. The followers coexist under the leader's umbrella, and seldom challenge the price structure for fear of retaliation. This is especially likely when differences in cumulative experience mean the leader has much lower costs than anyone else.

Structure of Costs. When fixed costs are high, the emphasis is inevitably on capacity utilization. Whenever there is excess capacity, competition reverts to a volume-grubbing contest, with price as the main weapon. As often happens in the pulp and paper market, these price cuts are quickly matched by other competitors also striving to maintain their capacity utilization.

Extent of Differentiation. An absence of perceived differences among competing alternatives means the conversation with customers soon turns to prices, terms, and sales conditions, and rivalry intensifies. This rivalry is muted when there are large perceived differences, for customers then develop strong preferences and loyalties that make them more resistant to competing offerings. Long-run attractiveness is further enhanced when the differences are difficult to imitate. The necessary conditions for sustainable differences, or advantages, are considered in the next chapter.

Customer-Switching Costs. These costs tend to tie buyers to one supplier, who is then protected from raids by others. These costs are high when the product is durable or specialized, when the customer has invested a lot of time and energy in learning how to use the product, or has made special-purpose investments that are useless elsewhere. A commitment to a computer operating system makes it very difficult for a customer to switch between computer systems without expensive software development, retraining, and general disruption.

Diversity of Strategies and Objectives. When all competitors adopt similar strategies, have similar cost structures, place equal emphasis on short-run profitability versus market share, and are managed by people from the same backgrounds, they naturally understand one another's intentions and can accurately anticipate their reactions to strategic moves. When the players come from diverse backgrounds (where some are foreign-based, some are closely held, and others are state-owned), and vary in size and objectives (some are low-overhead local producers, while others are global players), and thus have different ideas about acceptable profits, they will follow conflicting strategies that eventually depress average profits.

Exit Barriers. These hurdles keep companies trapped as participants in a market even when profitability is miserable. Excess capacity remains as a drag on everyone's profits, but no one is willing to shut down unneeded plants. This happened in the early 1980s in the market for float glass, because the large U.S. firms that controlled the capacity were unwilling to either write off the fixed assets and suffer the impact on earnings, or to sell to foreign manufacturers who wanted to establish a position in the United States, because this would introduce a new threat to the profitable parts of their glass markets.

Threat of Potential Competitors

Easy-to-enter markets soon become overcrowded to the detriment of future profit prospects. One reason is the increased power handed to customers who can wring concessions from existing suppliers by threatening to buy from an offshore competitor or encourage a company from an adjacent market to enter. Once the new entrants have established a beachhead, they frequently go on to assault the entire market, and intensify the level of competition.

The seriousness of the threat of entry depends on the height of entry barriers that impose disadvantages on prospective entrants and depress their expectations of profitability. These barriers are created by:

- *Factor cost advantages.* Such advantages of incumbents are created by lower labor or capital costs, preferred access to raw materials, favorable locations, or proprietary technology.

- *Economies of scale.* These are a deterrent if they force the prospective entrant to spend heavily on facilities, advertising, sales force coverage, distribution, and so forth to achieve a cost advantage. The aircraft engine business has very high-scale thresholds in all functions; severely limiting the number of possible players.
- *Differentiation and switching costs.* Not only do these factors abate direct rivalry, they also deter new entrants.
- *Channel crowding.* Most distribution channels have limited capacity, and restrict the number of product lines they will handle. Computer retailers have space for about five manufacturers at a time. Each new line of computers imposes fixed costs, ranging from training to allocation of shelf space, spare parts management, and so forth. New entrants must either chase niche segments or pay substantially larger margins to offset the retailers' extra costs. Sometimes the incumbents have preempted the existing channels, with long-run or exclusive arrangements, leaving the prospective entrant with the cost of establishing a completely new channel.

Expected Reactions of Incumbents.   Barriers to entry will be raised or lowered depending on how aggressively the incumbents have defended their position in the past. If they have ignored previous entrants or been unwilling to take a short-run profit reduction to protect their position, then further entrants will be encouraged. When they have retaliated hard in the past, regularly signal their deep commitment to the market, and have deep pockets to back up their threats, then a prospective entrant would be foolish to make a frontal attack. A flank attack on a small, unprotected segment may be the only way to enter.

Turning Barriers into Gateways.[8]   The height of the perceived barriers depends on who is looking at them. A well-endowed entrant from an adjacent market may be able to nullify them if it has a strong brand name, a ready-made distribution and services network, or lower costs because they source offshore. Incumbents may be restrained from retaliating if the entrant has deep pockets or signals a willingness to spend heavily to gain a position. Airbus Industries entered the U.S. market by offering financing provided by European governments that even Boeing was unwilling to match. Late entrants sometimes gain an advantage from being late. They can employ the latest technologies, while copying the best practices of the incumbent, and improving in areas where customers appear to be dissatisfied.

Customer Power

There are a wide range of relationships between customers and sellers. At one extreme are tight, just-in-time manufacturing systems, where, for example, suppliers of auto parts become extensions of the auto assemblers. At the other end of the spectrum are mass-market drug makers selling to customers of branded cold remedies in super-combo drugstores. The ability of auto makers to force down prices by playing competing suppliers against one another is legendary—to the detriment of the suppliers' profitability. Cold remedy makers are not as vulnerable to bargaining pressure because their end customers are not price-sensitive; but they still face aggressive retailers who control access to the shelves and extract sizable promotional allowances, quantity discounts, and other charges for the privilege. The extent of customer power in these and other situations depends on the credibility of their bargaining leverage and their sensitivity to price, each discussed next.

Customer bargaining leverage is enhanced when there are:

- Few customers making large-volume purchases. Consequently, the supplying firm becomes dependent and faces considerable excess capacity if the relationship is severed. This is the plight of private-label suppliers to large retailers such as Sears.
- Few constraints on the customers making a switch from one supplier to another; either because there is little differentiation, the costs of switching are low, or there is a cost-competitive substitute. If so, loyalty is ephemeral, and the conversation soon turns to price.
- Credible threats of backward integration, which can and will be used to wring concessions on prices and terms under the threat that the "make" alternative may become more attractive than continuing to "buy." This threat continually overhangs the beverage can

market, where more than 25 percent of all cans are made by the beer and soft drink companies. Similarly, large long-distance customers such as banks and governments often contemplate bypassing the public telephone network to build their own systems. Some large liability insurance customers are protesting high premiums by self-insuring and spreading the risk among many operating units.

- Customers who know their suppliers' costs or have learned that the supplier badly needs the business to soak up excess capacity.

Price sensitivity is a measure of how important lower prices are to the customer, and hence the intensity of their demands for concessions. Sensitivity is heightened when:

- The product or service has little influence on the performance or quality of the end product. Conversely, when the consequences of failure are very severe, such as items that are integral to the operation of a system, the buyer pays little attention to price.
- The cost of the product is a significant proportion of the customer's total costs. Purchasing scrutiny focuses on the larger-cost items first; incidental items may escape a thorough analysis of the costs of alternatives.
- The customer is suffering poor profitability and looks to the supplier for help. When survival is at stake, the pressure for concessions can be intense.

When these factors describe buyers who perceive few differences among the competing suppliers, the pressure on price is further intensified.

Supplier Power

The ability of large suppliers to withstand bargaining efforts by their customers and increase their share of the value created depends on:

- Their size relative to the customers'. This is especially noticeable in the negotiating advantages of large textile fiber manufacturers relative to their small, dispersed customer base.

- The reliance of the customers on the supplier's product, either because they can't get equivalent quality elsewhere, or they are locked into the supplier to the extent that the cost of switching is much greater than any benefits a new supplier can promise.
- The credibility of their threats to integrate forward in their value chain and sell directly to the end customer. This threat will blunt aggressive attempts by customers to get better prices.

Threat of Substitutes

The availability of an acceptable and available substitute that performs the same functions or offers the same benefits puts a ceiling on the average prices that can be charged, and thus limits the amount of value that can be created. For example:

- Fiberglass insulation for homes competes with foam sheets and blown-in, sawdust-based insulation.
- High-fructose corn syrup can be immediately displaced as a sweetener for baked goods and soft drinks when beet or cane sugar becomes cheaper.
- The use of overnight express delivery for documents is being constrained by improvements in the performance and cost of facsimile transmission.

As discussed, these substitutes also can be used to determine the boundaries of the competitive arena. Depending on where these lines are drawn, some of these substitutes could be seen as direct competitors. For example, if the high-fructose corn syrup manufacturer defines its arena as including all sweeteners, it would include beet and cane sugar makers as its competitors. The key is to account for similarity in customer functions performed or benefits provided, and look beyond physical similarity.

ASSESSING ATTRACTIVENESS

Each force of competition works in conjunction with the other forces to determine the long-run profit prospects for the average firm in a competitive arena. Although they provide a useful framework for analyzing the attractiveness of arenas, their joint effect is very difficult to establish with any precision, for several reasons. First, the relative importance of the specific factors underlying each force is unknown, and probably varies across arenas. Some guidance as to which factors are likely to be important can be extracted from Profit Impact of Market Strategies (PIMS) data, on the performance of 2,200 businesses. These findings are summarized in Figure 1.4.

As shown by the PIMS results, attractive markets with above-average profitability are those where customers tend to make purchases from a large number of suppliers (implying low supplier power), and customer purchases tend to be diffused (low customer power) and small in average size. Another factor, high market growth rate, which is discussed next, is also positively associated with industry attractiveness.

These factors seldom all point in the same direction. It is more likely that some will be favorable, but their positive effects on profits will be negated by other factors that are unfavorable. Even when two factors do point in the same direction, their effects are not always additive. Sometimes they multiply, as when strong buyers amass even greater-than-expected bargaining power by playing off two warring suppliers.

IMPACT OF MACRO TRENDS

A further complication is the impact of trends in the macroenvironment that can accentuate or dampen the impact of the five forces. The influences of government intervention, technological change, and market growth operate indirectly so their impact is harder to predict. But they can't ever be overlooked, for they sometimes emerge to become the dominant influence on attractiveness.

Government and Regulatory Intervention

This influence, discussed in greater detail in the following chapter, is pervasive. It is especially strong when the intervention defines who competes. Regulatory requirements often restrict entry, usually because

Figure 1.4
The Impact of Market Factors on Profitability: Evidence from PIMS*

Within the PIMS database that describes the environment, strategies, and performance of more than 2,200 businesses are variables that correspond to most of the factors that influence market attractiveness. The data allow us to compare rates of return (ROI) for hypothetical businesses that operate within attractive markets (specifically, they are rated in the top 20 percent of each factor) with other businesses that are in markets at the bottom fifth on each factor. These two businesses are otherwise assumed to be the same on the other strategic factors known to influence profitability, such as quality, market share, and investment intensity. Thus the differences in their performance are solely due to the varying intensity of the competive forces.

Factor	Unattractive Market (Each factor in the bottom 20%)		Attractive Market (Each factor in the top 20%)	
	Level	Impact On ROI	Level	Impact On ROI
Market growth rate	−4%	−1.2	+11%	+1.1
% purchases from top three suppliers	17%	−0.8	70%	+0.8
Purchase importance (% of customers total purchases)	5%	−3.0	<1%	+1.8
Purchase amount (average size of purchase)	$10K+	−4.0	<$1K	+5.2
TOTAL IMPACT (variation from average pretax ROI of the 2,200 businesses of 22.4%)		−9.0%		+8.9%

To put these results into perspective, the prototype business operating in an unattractive market would have an ROI of 13.4% (that is, 9.0% less than the average ROI of 22.4%). The business fortunate enough to serve an attractive market would have an ROI of 31.3% (when all other factors are held constant).

*R. D. Buzzell and B. T. Gale, *The PIMS Principles: Linking Strategy to Performance,* New York: *The Free Press,* 1987.

there is a scarce resource such as a radio or television broadcast frequency to be allocated. Performance or safety standards are more subtle barriers, especially when they favor the incumbents in the market. Testing of drugs to satisfy FDA safety requirements can take five to seven years. Pollution standards may determine whether there is even a market. If acid emissions standards for power plants burning coal are loose, then there is little or no demand for scrubbers of the stack gases. As standards tighten, the market suddenly becomes much larger.

Regulatory rulings have had a powerful influence on industries such as telecommunications. AT&T was prevented by law from meeting MCI's prices on long-distance service for seven years after deregulation to give the entrant time to get established.

Technological Change

No competitive force is immune from the restless effort of technology. Substitutes are creations of technology, and become increasingly threatening as price-performance improvements are made. While this displacement effect is obvious, other consequences are more subtle: Information technology may help to open a gateway for new entrants by eliminating the need for large-scale distribution, and rivalry may increase if new manufacturing technology makes short production runs feasible and accelerates product design cycles. The balance of power with customers or suppliers may also shift, depending on where the technology is developed. Otis Elevator reduced the bargaining power of service customers by tying them into a computer monitoring system that anticipated breakdowns. Chapter 4 offers a more detailed examination of the impact of technology.

Growth and Volatility of Market Demand

Vigorous growth generally enhances market attractiveness, because demand may exceed supply and diminish the pressure on prices. Meanwhile, the rivals in the market are preoccupied with building capacity to meet demand and are less likely to react to losses in their share.

Unfortunately, high–growth markets lose their luster if a surplus of competitors is attracted, and each brings unrealistic market-share expectations. This is a volatile situation that eventually leads to a wrenching shakeout.[9] The odds of a surplus of competitors go up when the market and its growth rate have high visibility, and firms in related markets are anxious that they not miss an inviting opportunity; there are few apparent limits to growth to dampen the enthusiasm of prospective entrants; barriers to entry are low; products employ an existing technology rather than a risky or protected technology; and some potential incumbents have low visibility and surprise everyone when they emerge.

When growth slows, there is a noticeable shift to competition for market share, where gains by one firm are resisted by other firms trying to avoid reductions in their capacity utilization. Meanwhile, customers are becoming more knowledgeable about the product, and less willing to pay a price premium. At the same time, slowing growth reduces the threat of new incumbents who are likely to be deterred by the overcrowded conditions.

CONCLUSION: THE BENEFITS AND LIMITATIONS OF THE COMPETITIVE FORCES FRAMEWORK

Competitive arenas are complex, moving targets for strategists. Their structures are continually shifting in response to changing buyer requirements, product and process innovations, currency and factor cost fluctuations, or anything that upsets the competitive balance. The competitive forces framework offers a robust and systematic approach to analyzing these threats and opportunities, and thus explaining why some arenas have better profit prospects than others. Its greatest virtue is that it demands thinking about the future of the arena, as a consequence of shifts, disruptions, and trends in the underlying factors.

Attractiveness of arenas is not set in stone. The payoff from understanding the competitive forces is when managers begin to think how they can change strategy to alter the attractiveness of their market to their advantage. These are "change the game" strategies that dampen the competitive forces, perhaps by dramatically increasing differentiation, raising switching costs, or using capital investments to raise the minimum scale of operations to deter potential entrants. Markets do not unfold inexorably, with the firms on the sidelines as interested observers. Their strategic responses also determine the future of the market. Even when prospects in the overall market are poor, there are usually protected segments that offer superior profitability.

Although the competitive forces framework is quite robust, and capable of being applied to diverse settings, there are some weak spots and limitations that require caution. First, it is vulnerable to all the problems of arena definition discussed earlier—and often there is little guidance on where to place the boundary. This is especially troublesome when boundaries are fuzzy, or arenas are converging because of changes in technology and functionality. While substitution effects matter when there is a convergence, it is seldom clear when a substitute should be taken seriously. How big a threat does videoconferencing pose to the airline or hospitality industries? So, managers need to determine when to see a substitute as a competitor.

A second problem with the standard formulation of the five forces framework is the lack of consideration of complements, such as the effect of personal computer sales on computer disk drives, or the availability of programming for high-definition television. Similarly, hardware can't function without software, but software writers won't produce programs until a critical mass of hardware exists. In recognition of this co-dependency, groups of technology companies are forming economic webs that use a common architecture to deliver independent elements of an overall value proposition. One of the most pervasive webs is that of Microsoft and Intel, which meshes hardware and components, software development, channels, and training. Netscape is mobilizing a web of other companies that are developing the complementary technologies to enable commerce on the Internet. What makes a web of complements work is a technological standard that reduces risk by allowing firms to make investment commitments in the face of technological uncertainty, and a lead firm that is willing to maximize the size of the web by giving away value to other firms. Rivalry then takes place between webs.

A third problem is the implicit assumption of the five forces framework that each player adopts a single, well-defined, and unchanging role. This doesn't begin to capture the complexity of emerging industries in which the distinctions between customers, suppliers, and competitors are increasingly blurred, and the rules of engagement keep changing.[10] Rivals may actively collaborate, as Sony and Philips are doing in developing common optical media standards and supplying components for one another. These multiarena contacts may reduce the intensity of rivalry in any single arena.

Fourth, the competitive forces framework presents the interaction of customers and suppliers as a zero-sum game—evoking images of the exercise of uncompromising bargaining power. Increasingly, buyer-seller relationships are being recast as collaborations or partnerships with a positive-sum outcomes. An adversarial mind-set is contrary to the spirit of trust, information sharing, and joint decision making that is demanded in durable relationships.

Finally, the competitive forces framework is mostly focused on differences in average industry profitability. Yet profit differences *within* an industry are, on average, several times larger than profit differences *between* industries.[11] Why, in the same arena, do some firms earn strong profits and other barely survive? The purpose of the next chapter is to shed some light on this second component of profitability through an understanding of relative competitive advantages between firms.

CHAPTER 2

MAINTAINING THE COMPETITIVE EDGE: CREATING AND SUSTAINING ADVANTAGES IN DYNAMIC COMPETITIVE ENVIRONMENTS

GEORGE S. DAY

The Wharton School, Department of Marketing

Within a given arena of competition, companies seek to build and sustain competitive advantages over rivals. Advantages are based on the assets and capabilities of the firm that yield superior competitive positions. In dynamic environments, companies must increasingly focus on strategies for renewing advantages. This chapter examines how advantages are created and identified. It also explores how advantages are eroded and how companies can prevent or slow this erosion.

Strategy is about seeking a competitive edge over rivals while slowing the erosion of present advantages. Few advantages can be sustained indefinitely, for time eventually renders them obsolete. In slower moving environments, firms can sustain advantages for relatively long periods before they are replaced. In dynamic environments, this process of the creation and erosion of advantages accelerates. As advantages become increasingly temporary, managers are shifting their emphasis from seeking an unassailable static advantage to building organizations that continually seek new sources of advantage. Understanding the key sources of advantage and how they are sustained or eroded has thus become more crucial than ever in formulating competitive strategies.

This chapter offers guidance—derived from available theory and "best practices" of successful firms—on how to assess the nature and magnitude of present advantages and the reasons why they have been sustained. The persistence of advantages in the future and what moves are needed to enhance or defend them depends on the intentions, capabilities, actions, and reactions of competitors. Thus, this chapter serves as a prelude to the rest of the book, which is concerned with these questions.

THE DOUBLE EDGE OF SHIFTING ADVANTAGES

An environment of rapid shifts in advantage is a double-edged sword. The shifts create opportunities for companies to establish new advantages in a market, but as the competitive environment continues to change, these new advantages are themselves vulnerable to attack. This is what economists have referred to as the "Law of Nemesis," by which every situation bears the seeds of its own reversal.[1] High-profit opportunities ultimately attract competitors who strive to match, leapfrog, or neutralize the advantages of the leader.

The Case of Dell Computer

Dell Computer lived with this Law of Nemesis through several shifts in the market for personal computers. It used the changing sources of advantage in personal computing to become a Fortune 500 company just eight years after its founding. By 1993, it had become the world's fifth largest PC maker. But Dell later found itself buffeted by the same forces that had propelled it forward.

Dell's advantage was developed from the recognition that sophisticated personal computer buyers were getting little from traditional storefront retailers. Michael Dell realized that these users would be comfortable giving up the face-to-face service and support of traditional dealers for the lower prices of mail order. Initially, Dell reached this high-end market segment directly through ads in trade magazines, with low prices as the incentive.

Dell's strategy was readily imitable, and price was not a sustainable edge. Soon Dell faced a crowded field of mail-order rivals competing on price. Dell's next move was to augment its core product with guarantees, unlimited toll-free technical support, and one-year free on-site service. To keep ahead of clone makers that simply assembled standard components, Dell raised the stakes by manufacturing PCs to order. This kept Dell's inventories and financing costs low, while investments in flexible robots enabled the company to become a low-cost manufacturer.

The most durable source of Dell's advantage has been its mastery of direct-relationship marketing. The company developed the capability to monitor and analyze each of the 7,000 to 8,000 calls received every working day, to extract fine-grained insights into problems, needs, and emerging segments. Neither dealers nor other manufacturers were able to develop this level of direct feedback from the market. This advantage was then married to investments in R&D in hopes that Dell could become a technology leader. These dual strengths allowed Dell to listen closely to how the market responded to its innovations and act quickly on what it learned.

This was not enough to keep Dell ahead of the competition. The two big draws of direct sales—price and convenience—were almost matched by low-price electronics superstores, and competitors like Compaq and IBM, which entered direct marketing with promises of faster delivery, longer warranties, and new installation services.

In response to these competitive challenges, Dell expanded its limited presence in retail distribution and launched a new line of notebook computers. Both moves proved ill-advised and contributed to a $40 million loss in 1993, even though sales had increased by 40 percent:

- Lack of capacity meant the firm had to outsource production of the notebook computers (and low-cost desktop computers) to third-party manufacturers. While this saved initial costs, quality control suffered and service costs rose significantly. Moreover, the first designs were not up to industry standards.
- Operations slipped out of control under the combined stresses of rapid growth and inability to track activities with either

third-party manufacturers or retailers. Dell often could not tell how many units had been sold at a store, nor could it check its warehouse inventory. These were serious shortcomings as margins were increasingly squeezed by intensifying competition.

To reverse the deteriorating situation, the response of CEO Michael Dell was appropriate: "We're constantly reinventing ourselves," he said. By 1993, he had hired a new team of seasoned computer industry executives. This team decided to refocus on Dell's core strategy of selling directly to customers. The company made heavy investments to overhaul its information systems and improve logistics to ensure prices remained competitive. An especially painful decision was made to shelve the entire line of notebook computers for nine months and watch a fast-growing market from the sidelines. This enabled Dell to reenter with a competitive product using leading-edge technology. The reward for the renewal effort was a profit rebound to $150 million by the end of 1994, and sales growth to $5 billion annually by 1996.

Dell's case shows how quickly advantages can erode—and be re-created. Can Dell continue to protect its current advantages from further erosion by rivals? How can it "reinvent itself" to build new advantages for the future? Because a competitive advantage depends upon the company's actions as well as those of its rivals, it takes more than effective action to sustain them. Sustaining advantages requires effective *interaction* between the firm and its competitors—building its resources and position while preventing competitors from eroding them.

THE COMPETITIVE ADVANTAGE CYCLE

How do companies create and sustain advantages over their rivals? Researchers and managers have developed several views of the factors that account for differences in profitability among firms in the same industry. Two prominent perspectives on competitive advantages are that they result from either the firm's position in the industry or its resources and capabilities. According to the structural forces approach, advantages result from securing a defensible cost or differentiation *position* in the most attractive segments of the total market.[2] In contrast, the resource-based view relates superior performance to the distinctive, hard-to-duplicate *resources* of the firm.[3] These resources—comprising integrated combinations of assets and capabilities—are cultivated slowly over time, can't be readily traded, and limit the firm's ability to adapt to change. These assets and capabilities determine how efficiently and effectively a company performs its functional activities.

Neither of these answers gives the full picture, but together they describe both the state of advantage and how it was gained. The position and performance of the firm in the industry describes the state of advantage, but this positional superiority is a consequence of relative superiority in the resources a business deploys. In turn, these resources are the result of past investments made to enhance the competitive position.

The creation and maintenance of advantages is thus a continuous cycle, as illustrated in Figure 2.1. At any time, businesses are endowed with a mixed bag of resources. Some of the assets and capabilities are no better than those of the competition, others are inferior, while a few are superior to the competition. These superior assets and capabilities are the source of positional advantages.

A position of competitive superiority and the resulting market share and profit rewards are continually subject to erosion by competitive moves and changes in the market. In this dynamic cycle, strategy has two purposes. The first priority is to put impediments in the way of competitors to protect current advantages. Because these barriers to imitation are being continually eroded, the business has to keep investing in new assets and capabilities. This process of renewal can be achieved by:

- Developing new assets. Intel has done this by investing in its "Intel Inside" branding,
- Upgrading existing capabilities through continuous improvement or radical reconfiguration of current processes,
- Acquiring the alternative resources that are threatening the company's current position. Thus, AT&T is investing in cellular

Figure 2.1
Competitive Advantage Cycle

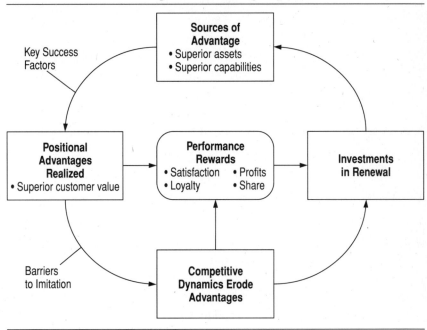

telephony now that its long-distance network is no longer as unique or critical as it once was.

- Investing to extend the resources into new competitive arenas, as Nucor has done by progressively moving from low value-added steel products such as bar stock into more differentiated and complex products such as thin-slab cast-steel sheets.

Thus the creation of advantages and their sustenance is a long-run, iterative process with ongoing demands for investment dollars and management energy and foresight. To sustain and renew advantages in dynamic environments, managers need to understand how advantages are created and how they are eroded. The sources of advantages and the forces that erode them are examined next.

THE SOURCES AND CONSEQUENCES OF ADVANTAGES

As noted, advantages are defined by position or by the assets and capabilities that underlie these positions. Positions of advantage deal with the *what* of competitive advantage, while superior resources—assets and capabilities—address the *how* of competitive advantage. Taken together, these two sources of advantage represent the ability of a business to do more (or do better) than competition. These advantages contribute to a successful competitive strategy, as measured by higher market share and profits as compared to the rest of the industry.

Positions of Advantage

From the vantage point of customers or competitors in a market, positional superiority defines advantage. Positions within the market have been described by several different frameworks. One of the earliest frameworks was that companies either staked out positions of low cost or differentiation in relation to customers and rivals. A later framework presents alternative *value disciplines* through which companies define their competitive positions.

Low-Cost versus Differentiation. The simplest view is that positional advantage can be achieved either by *differentiation* through providing superior customer value or by achieving the *lowest delivered cost*. According to this view, these two generic strategies involve fundamentally different routes to competitive advantage, and firms must make a choice between them because they are usually incompatible.[4] To ensure superior profitability with a superior value strategy, the price premium the customer is willing to pay must exceed any costs of providing the extra value. Similarly a low-cost strategy must offer acceptable value to customers to maintain prices close to the average of competitors. When a low-cost position is achieved by sacrificing too much quality, for example, the price discount demanded by customers will more than offset the cost advantage, and the profit gains are lost.

Like all simplifications, the notion of two generic routes to positional advantage comes at a price: Important strategic insights and possibilities are missed. The first deficiency of the low-cost versus differentiation framework is that companies sometimes pursue both strategies simultaneously. Firms like Kellogg prosper by simultaneously lowering costs and gaining price premiums with superior customer value. One reason is that superior product quality can indirectly lower costs.[5] Higher quality leads to higher market shares, and this, in turn, reduces total costs due to experience effects and scale economies. This trade-off between cost and differentiation also is undermined by the evidence that "quality is free." Quality improvements may raise product quality while lowering total costs because of lower reject rates, lower costs of adjustments and field repairs, and higher customer satisfaction. It is possible for firms to be the low-cost leader while differentiating themselves.

The second problem of these generic strategies is that they are not talking about the same things. A differentiation strategy is framed in external customer terms, and competitive advantage is achieved by offering superior quality. The lowest delivered-cost strategy is framed in relation to rivals, emphasizing the companies' costs relative to competition. This strategy does not offer a clear inducement to the customer.

These two concepts—cost and quality—are brought together in the concept of customer value, which is the sum of perceived benefits received minus perceived costs incurred in acquiring and using the product or service. The superiority of a lowest-delivered cost strategy is only evident to the customers when the benefits are the same as the competition and the only difference is that the price is lower. This has an especially unfortunate consequence in capital-intensive industries, with undifferentiated products, of focusing attention on price competition because there isn't much else to talk about. Yet we know that customers in most markets consider many attributes beyond price before they make a choice. This focus on customer value led to the creation of a second framework for viewing positional advantage as a set of value disciplines.

Value Disciplines. The framework of value disciplines uses a consistent externally oriented schematic for framing the generic strategies. Ultimately, all strategies win or lose by their ability to consistently offer superior value to a distinct customer segment. Recent studies of market leaders have revealed three such strategies or "value disciplines."[6] Each strategy differs in the core value proposition; the capabilities, assets, and business systems to be mastered; and the organizational structure and culture that is needed. The basic premise is that it is not possible to be all things to all people, because the requirements of different customer segments within a market usually diverge. One segment may emphasize high performance; another wants low prices and dependability; and a third values quality of relationships, trust, personalized service, and advice when choosing a supplier. Each value discipline excels at meeting the needs of one segment, while offering acceptable performance on the attributes that are less important:

- *Operational excellence* means the provision of consistent quality at the best price, through a standardized business system that minimizes the cost and difficulty the customer will face in acquiring the product. The leaders of this strategy invest heavily in integrated low-cost transaction processing systems and understand how to optimize their business processes across organizational boundaries. Exemplars are Wal-Mart, AT&T Universal Card, and Southwest Airlines.
- *Customer responsiveness* strategies put the emphasis on the careful tailoring and adaptation of products and services to increasingly precise requirements. There is a strong orientation to addressing the distinct needs of individual customers or microsegments to nurture long-term relationships with customers. This requires an organization empowered to make decisions close to the customer, and systems that facilitate multiple modes of producing and delivering products and services. Companies such as Lutron Electronics, Merrill-Lynch, and Nordstrom's excel here.
- *Performance superiority* is attained by continuous, fast-paced innovation that yields a steady flow of leading-edge products that consistently push the state of the art of technology or enhance a customer's use or application. Companies with this focus are open to new ideas, sensitive to latent customer needs, and effective at

mobilizing teams to pursue these opportunities. Leaders here are companies such as 3M, Hewlett-Packard, Sony, and Gillette that are usually first to market.

These value disciplines are vulnerable to the problems of oversimplification that beset all efforts to define generic strategies. The three types of advantage are not always at odds with each other, and for structural reasons a firm may excel at two at a time. Sometimes there seems to be no choice of value discipline, as everyone is forced by the segment structure or the economics of capacity utilization to pursue the same strategy. When the dominant resource is capacity, firms gravitate toward the efficiency benefits of an operational excellence strategy. When brand equity and relationships are the critical resources, the natural strategy is customer responsiveness. But if the industry is knowledge-based, and the most important assets are patents and cumulative learning and skills, then performance leadership is mandatory for superior performance. As markets mature and the differences among competitors shrink, it may be desirable to pursue another value discipline to offer customers a new reason to choose the company.

The real question is how long will a follower take to match the leader in the eyes of the customer? The incentive to do so is great, and consequently the resulting positional advantages may be modest and short-lived. This speed of matching an advantage is often determined by how quickly rivals can create the assets and capabilities needed to achieve a given position.

Assets and Capabilities: How Advantages Are Created

Underlying a positional advantage is a distinctive set of assets and capabilities. Thus, a company that pursues a customer responsiveness strategy must have flexible systems, motivated staff with a "have-it-your-way" mind-set, and related capabilities to deliver this strategy.

Superior assets are the tangible resource endowments the business has accumulated. Since they often have physical presence, can be given a monetary value, and can be readily counted, they get the most attention in competitor analyses because it is possible to make direct comparisons of competitors on such assets as:

Scale and scope of facilities and capacity utilization.

Distribution coverage.

Number of service- and salespeople.

Expenditures on advertising and promotion support.

Financial capacity and cost of capital.

Cost of raw materials and purchased inputs such as energy as a result of ownership of raw materials sources.

Geographic coverage.

Brand equity, whose value is based on goodwill built up from the residue of past successful efforts to compete.

Distinctive capabilities are the glue that holds these assets together and enables them to be deployed advantageously. Each of these capabilities is a complex bundle of skills and knowledge, exercised through the organizational processes that enable a business to coordinate activities, utilize its assets, and continuously learn and improve. Capabilities are exercised in typical business processes such as order fulfillment, new product development, and service delivery.

Capabilities differ from assets in that they are so deeply embedded in the organizational routines and practices that they cannot be traded or imitated. Capabilities are obscured from view because much of their knowledge component is tacit and dispersed along four dimensions:[7]

1. Accumulated employee knowledge and skills.
2. Knowledge embedded in technical systems including software, linked databases, and formal procedures.
3. Management systems that exist to create and control knowledge.
4. The values and norms that dictate what information is to be collected, what types are most important, and how it is to be used.

Every business acquires many capabilities that enable it to carry out the activities necessary to move its products or services through the value chain. While most of these capabilities will simply be comparable to those of competitors, a few will have to be done well if the business is to outperform its competition.

Wal-Mart's ability to manage a cross-docking logistics system gives it a significant edge over Kmart.[8] This system is part of a broader customer pull system that starts with individual stores placing their orders based on store-movement data. These orders are gathered and filled by suppliers in full truckloads. These loads are delivered to Wal-Mart's warehouses, where they are sorted, repacked, and dispatched to stores. The transfer from one loading dock to another takes less than 48 hours, sharply cutting the usual inventory and handling costs.

Because distinctive capabilities are difficult to develop, they resist imitation: Kmart knows full well what Wal-Mart has accomplished with its logistics system and can readily buy the hardware and software, but has been unable to match the underlying capability. Wal-Mart's processes are not readily visible because they cut across different organizational units. And since much of the collective knowledge is tacit and dispersed among many individuals, a competitor cannot acquire the requisite knowledge simply by staffing with the best available people. As Marvin Bower, the legendary leader of McKinsey & Co., observed while ruminating on the risks of having agencies and consultants serve competing clients, possibly divulging privileged information:

> As a matter of realism, the interests of competing clients would not be harmed by an almost complete exchange of information among the people serving the two competing companies . . . . I am convinced that the history, makeup, ways of doing business, attitudes of people, operating philosophy, and procedures of even directly competing companies are ordinarily so different that information could be exchanged between them with no harm to either.

Another attribute of distinctive capabilities is that they are robust and can be used in different ways to speed the firm's adjustment to changes in the environment.[9] Honda, for example, has been able to apply its companywide mastery of engine and drive train technology development and manufacturing processes to create distinctive capabilities in a variety of related markets such as generators, outboard marine engines, and lawn mowers.

It is less clear whether Honda's distinctive capability in dealer management—used to develop a network of motorcycle dealers that was better managed and better financed than the part-time dealers of competitors—also aided entry into new markets. On the one hand, Honda's skill at managing dealers has been of value in the auto market where Honda dealers consistently receive high ratings for customer satisfaction. It is harder to say whether the logic of Honda's diversification into related markets was really guided by a desire to exploit this dealer management capability. More likely it was the ability to gain a multiplier effect, by combining both these distinctive capabilities, that shaped the moves into new markets.

Performance Outcomes

The most popular indicators of a successful competitive strategy are market share and profitability. They are closely related at any given point in time, although the reasons for the correlation have been hotly disputed. Other measures of performance, such as customer satisfaction and loyalty, are increasingly used because they directly reflect customer responses to positional advantages and thus can be leading indicators of changes in share and profitability.

Market Share.   The premise is that we can distinguish winners from losers by the proportion of transactions or volume they have gained, just as the outcome of a horse race is shown by the final standings. The analogy can be quite misleading, for competition is played out over many time periods, while the rules of the game keep changing. Thus it may be dangerous to extend the interpretation of market share from an indication of past performance to a predictor of future advantages.

This doesn't mean current market share won't be a good predictor of future market share in many markets. We will be more confident of maintaining a large share when the positional advantages are hard for competitors to match, and the market boundaries are stable. Dominance of a market in which competitive forces are evolving rapidly is no guarantee of future advantage. Since most positional advantages decay over time, we are likely to find the share of large firms slipping (or converging toward the mean), while small firms typically gain share.

Profitability.   Current profitability is the reward from past advantages after the current outlays needed to sustain or enhance future advantages have been made. Because profitability is influenced by actions taken in many previous time frames, it is unlikely to be a complete reflection of current advantages. When the environment is turbulent, it may be a misleading indication. The objectives of the business may also distort the signals that current profitability sends about the strength of the competitive position. Above-average reported profits may be extracted by harvesting the business and cutting investments in the sources of future advantage. Conversely, the business may decide to not take profits now but exchange them for increased market share with a penetration price.

Market Share and Profitability.   There is no denying these two variables are strongly related; on average, for each 10 percent difference in share, there is a corresponding 4.7 percent difference in return on investment for the businesses in the PIMS database.[10] However, this seemingly innocuous fact has been widely misinterpreted and misused, to the detriment of sound strategic thinking. At one time, market share was viewed as the cause of profitability, due to economies of scale and experience differences. On sober reflection and reanalysis, a number of other reasons for the relationship have emerged that imply different strategic messages.

There is a competing view that profits cause market share. In this scenario, businesses that are lucky or especially insightful stake out strong and defensible positions early in the product life cycle. With the initial profit rewards, plus their superior skills gained from early learning about the market, they make astute continuing investments that enable them to grow faster than their less fortunate rivals.

Most likely, both mechanisms are operating concurrently, although the relative importance may vary as the market matures. In the early stages, first-mover advantages are most influential. With maturation, the challenge is to adapt the strategy to new requirements for success while capitalizing on the initial advantages. Some first movers can't shift their strategy quickly enough to cope with the fragmentation of markets, technology changes, and other shocks that offer gateways for new entrants. Thus, it is most accurate to think of both share and profitability as manifestations of superior capabilities, assets, and strategic direction.

In summary, market share is best viewed as an outcome of strategic moves, and a measure of success, and not an intrinsically valuable asset to be bought or sold. What counts are the fundamentals, as reflected in the relative position of the business on the key sources and positions of advantage.

Customer Satisfaction and Loyalty. Numerous companies have adopted customer satisfaction as their primary metric of performance. According to the Juran Institute, 90 percent of top managers from a sample of Fortune 500 companies agreed with the statement, "Maximizing customer satisfaction will maximize profitability and market share," and have acted on this belief by instituting formal methods for monitoring and improving customer satisfaction scores in their companies.

Unfortunately, customer satisfaction is difficult to measure, and satisfaction scores are often not correlated with subsequent behavior. In most businesses, 60 percent to 80 percent of customer defectors said they were "satisfied" or "very satisfied" on the last survey prior to their defection. This awkward reality has led an increasing number of companies to use customer loyalty instead. They were persuaded by a stream of research that found that customers who had been loyal to a company for five years were between 85 percent (credit cards) and 350 percent (industrial distribution) more profitable than new customers. Not only did loyal customers buy more, they were less price-sensitive, cheaper to serve, and did not carry the high costs of finding and attracting new customers. As Reicheld and Sasser found, companies are able to improve profits anywhere from 25 percent to 85 percent by reducing customer defections by 5 percent.[11] Perhaps more companies would adopt the loyalty metric if their accounting systems could show the value of loyal customers. Some companies are using customer retention—or length of relationship—as a proxy for loyalty. Unfortunately, simply keeping a customer on the books does not necessarily ensure or enhance loyalty, in the sense of a high level of their commitment or a high percentage of purchases, which is what drives profitability.

PERSPECTIVES ON ASSESSING ADVANTAGES

Managers view advantages through a variety of lenses. Surprisingly, although many managers would agree that advantages are shaped by the interactions among competitors, they often look only at themselves in shaping strategy. An in-depth study of the way managers viewed their competitive advantages in 190 businesses found that a high proportion—over 40 percent of the businesses in the sample—employed self-centered representations.[12] These businesses were clearly not happy with their view of the world, for they generally described their strategy as unstable, characterized by a lack of agreement within the management team. At the other end of the spectrum were market-driven businesses, focused simultaneously on customers and competitors. These firms reported a high degree of stability in the direction of their strategy and a strong consensus within the management team.

An internal focus is one kind of mental model, used to simplify the complexities of competition and impose order on ambiguous, multidimensional market settings. Most managers have well-developed mental models of their competitive position that shape the information they seek and the lessons they extract. These representations of advantages—or disadvantages—vary along two dimensions.[13] One dimension depends on whether the managers emphasize their internal capabilities and performance or look outside to assess their position. The second dimension describes whether customers or competitors are the most salient feature of the market. The combination of these two dimensions yields four types of representations, as shown in Figure 2.2. Each is a

Figure 2.2
Managerial Representations of Competitive Advantage

		Emphasis on Competitor Comparisons	
		Minor	Major
Emphasis on Customer Perspectives	Minor	Self-Centered	Competitor-Centered
	Major	Customer-Oriented	Market-Driven

coping mechanism that is a reasonable adaptation to the pressure points in the environment and the choice of strategy.

Competitor-Centered Assessments of Advantage

These are based on direct management comparisons with a few target competitors. This mind-set is most often found in concentrated, capital-intensive industries that have been stalemated because slow growth and technological maturity have reduced competition to a zero-sum game. In this setting, the players are constantly looking for an edge, so the emphasis is on "beat the competition." These businesses watch their relative cost position very closely, quickly match the marketing initiatives of their competitors, and look for sustainable advantages in technology. With high fixed costs comes a fixation on capacity utilization, so there are periodic bursts of price-cutting to protect market share and volume. Managers keep a close watch on overall market share and contracts won or lost to detect shifts in their competitive position. At all times they are sensitive to the relative sizes of their resources, especially distribution and sales coverage and plant capacity. Customers are not ignored, for they are the prizes gained by prevailing over the competition.

Customer-Oriented Assessments

These rely on customers to make the comparisons of the business with its competitors, rather than using the collective judgments of the management team. This perspective relies on detailed analyses of customer benefits and relative satisfaction with end-use segments, and works backward from the customer to the firm to identify the actions needed to secure new advantages. This market-back orientation is most evident in fragmented industries where there are numerous competitors, each trying to stake out a distinct position in a highly segmented market such as magazines. It is also found in service-intensive industries such as investment banking where new services are easily imitated, all the players have the same cost of funds, and entry appears easy. Relatively little time is spent watching competitors and making side-by-side comparisons with their capabilities and performance; the emphasis is on the quality of customer relations. Evidence of continuing customer satisfaction and loyalty is more meaningful than market share.

Self-Centered Assessments

These look at year-to-year improvements in key operating ratios, such as inventory turns, scrap rates, and sales per employee, to assess their position. There is usually a strong sales volume orientation, so sales growth is a key indicator of competitive performance. However, the absence of a direct comparison with other competitors means this is an inward perspective. This is why general merchandise retailers have so often been undermined by specialty retailers; an acceptable sales volume increase in products such as towels may mask losses in share to bath boutiques. A business can only afford or survive this perspective if it has no direct competitors, by virtue of a commanding technology lead or a well-protected market position, or if all the other competitors behave the same way and coexist comfortably.

Why should it matter how managers view their competitive positions? Markets are complex, ambiguous, and fast-changing abstractions, which are given meaning in the minds of managers by processes of selective attention and simplification. Otherwise they couldn't cope with the welter of trends and events that must be organized, analyzed for patterns, and acted upon. A customer-oriented or competitor-centered perspective helps simplify this unruly part of the environment, by guiding the choice of information to be selected and how it is screened and interpreted.

Simplification comes at a cost, which is the risk that only a partial and biased picture of reality is created. A competitor-centered perspective leads to a preoccupation with cost and controllable activities that can be compared directly with the corresponding activities of close rivals. This mind-set deflects attention from opportunities to serve customers better and encourages imitative strategies. It may even blind the firm to new forms of competition. Customer-focused approaches have the advantage of examining the full range of competitive choices in light of the customers' needs and perceptions of superiority, but lack an obvious connection to activities and variables that are controlled by management. There is a tendency to be insensitive to shifting competitive forces until it is too late. The organization with a market-driven representation achieves a balance between customer and competitor perspectives, and avoids the pitfalls of over-reliance on either dimension of the market environment.

THE EROSION OF ADVANTAGES

It is very tempting to presume that historically durable advantages and their rewards will continue into the future. The dangers of such a presumption account for the surprises of both the managers and equity markets as they overestimated the prowess of once secure firms such as Sears, IBM, DEC, Apple, GM, and more recently, Merck, and overlooked or underestimated new forms of competition.

There are many reasons for the inappropriate extrapolation of past durable advantages into the future. The term "sustainable" advantage implies an unwarranted momentum, persistence, and resistance to imitation. This semantic error is compounded by *ex post facto* identifications of the reasons for sustainability using a circular logic that leads to speculations that successful firms have had some enduring advantage that made them successful.

Sustainability is a matter of degree. Most advantages are transitory because they can be readily duplicated. The most contestable are price advantages for they can be readily countered by competitors. Most product innovation is also quickly contested. It is estimated that competitors are able to secure detailed information on 70 percent of all new products within a year of introduction.[14] Even improvements in internal processes are hard to protect—60 percent to 90 percent of all learning eventually diffuses to competitors.

Why Advantages Erode

The greatest threats to the advantages of most firms are changes in the "rules of the game" to which managers have been accustomed, and the creation of new advantages by competitors.[15] For example, U.S. domestic airlines such USAir, Delta, American, and United were long protected by their control of hub-and-spoke networks and investments in computerized reservation systems. This enabled them to gain the loyalty of frequent flyers who were locked into their reward programs. Unfortunately, these advantages were gained at higher costs, which were exacerbated by expensive and inflexible labor contracts. All these full-service airlines are vulnerable to low cost, no frills, point-to-point airlines such as Southwest Airlines with employee ownership and flexible work arrangements. Instead of gathering people at hubs in big cities, these short-haul airlines offer nonstop flights on routes to medium and small cities. Not only do they avoid congested airports, they also simplify ticketing and boarding procedures, so they are less vulnerable to system delays. Their lower costs permit aggressive price-cutting of as much as 70 percent below their established rivals on previously protected short routes. The pressure from these no-frills start-up carriers has mounted as more than 30 were launched between 1992 and 1995.

Advantages also can erode under external pressure or the arrival of outside competitors who can transfer well-honed assets and capabilities from related markets. The dangers posed by such capabilities predators are exemplified by AT&T, which entered the credit card market in 1990 and within two years became the fourth-largest card issuer in the United States. Because AT&T was the world's largest transaction processor, handling 100 billion minutes of call traffic a year through a worldwide long-distance network, the barriers between volume-based telecommunication and financial services were relatively low.

Markets differ widely in how long an advantage can be sustained before competitors imitate, neutralize, or leapfrog.[16] Extreme examples of short-lived advantages are found in the Japanese consumer electronics market where new products—usually variants on a theme—are matched in months or less. By 1993, Sony had introduced 160 models of its Walkman to withstand the onslaught of clones. Its innovations were being copied within 6 to 12 months. The frenetic pace of innovative imitation ensures that closely matched competitors who understand each other well and carefully watch one another can anticipate and respond rapidly to any initiatives. The only basis of sustainable advantage appears to be an ability to continuously innovate. This raises daunting questions when customers no longer value the blizzard of features and minor variations and start to buy for other reasons such as price.

At the other extreme are slow-moving industries in which firms have highly durable advantages based on assets or capabilities that are unique and tightly secured within the organization. Exemplars are pharmaceutical firms with patent-protected drugs, which had the best return on equity (24.7 percent) of all U.S. industry groups between 1990 and 1994. Other revealing examples are the Microsoft MS-DOS operating system and the Lotus 1–2–3 spreadsheet. These firms have unassailable positions based on the first-mover advantages of being able to set standards and create high customer switching costs and have high visibility as leaders in the market. Some of the most durable advantages are derived from close personal relationships such as investment bankers achieve with their clients. Here the actual investment products—market advice, merger screening, balance sheet management—are sophisticated but readily available. In a pressured, high-stakes deal environment, however, the clients are willing to work only with those advisors they know and trust. Such confidence must be earned over a very long period of time.

This difference in the speed of the erosion of advantages is reflected in the following three categories of competitive cycles:[17]

Class 1 (Slow-Cycle). These firms have highly durable advantages based on resources or capabilities that are unique, tightly secured within the organization, and strongly shielded from competitive pressures. These advantages may be based on patents, locational pre-emption, strong brand names, or tight buyer/supplier relationships. The reward is stable pricing, few cost reduction demands, and high profit margins that endure. The biggest threats are from changes in the environment, such as health care regulation, or a new technology that delivers superior benefits.

Class 2 (Standard-Cycle). Firms in this class generally face extended competition from a few firms that pursue the same capital-intense or mass markets. Because these businesses rely heavily on volume and the mastery of standardized processes and have to coordinate activities across widespread organizations, they navigate a carefully circumscribed territory.

Class 3 (Fast-Cycle). These organizations are found in markets with short product life cycles, fast profit margin compression, and seemingly perpetual sequences of innovation and then obsolescence of rapidly introduced generations of products. These products are "idea-driven"; that is, primarily based on a concept, technology, or idea.

SLOWING THE EROSION OF ADVANTAGES

Given that market conditions and competitors will erode advantages, how can individual companies work to slow this erosion and benefit from their advantages for as long as possible? Companies create barriers to imitation to prevent competitors from matching their advantages.

There are five conditions that tend to make an asset or capability a sustainable source of advantage:[18]

1. It is *valuable,* in that it makes a significant contribution to superior customer value.

2. It is *durable* and not vulnerable to rapid depreciation or obsolescence because of the pace of technological change, shifts in customer requirements, or the depletion of nonrenewable assets.
3. There is *causal ambiguity;* it is unclear to the competition how the source of advantage works.
4. Even if the competitors understand the advantage, they still can't *duplicate* it, either because they cannot amass the same assets or capabilities or they cannot find different resources to serve the same purpose.
5. The early movers are able to deter efforts at duplication with a credible threat of *retaliation.*

The last three conditions—causal ambiguity, duplicability, and credible retaliation—create the barriers to imitation that permit advantages to persist. They help explain why Chubb Corp. has continued to realize returns on shareholder equity of 20 percent in the property and casualty market, while the rest of the competition have seen average returns slide below 5 percent. Chubb focused on insurance coverage for expensive houses, and competed by offering attentive and highly knowledgeable personalized service. For example, Chubb clients can have all their worldly goods valued by an agent at the same time they are buying the insurance, thus eliminating the usual inconvenience of finding an appraiser, getting an evaluation, and then calling the insurance company. They have a reputation for settling claims fairly and quickly.

Chubb's competitors continually pursue this affluent market, but have not been able to incorporate the detailed knowledge of this market into their organizations, emulate the complex systems, or hire and train the right kinds of people. Chubb's competitors may not be fully aware of all the processes that underlie Chubb's advantage, and this causal ambiguity makes it harder for them to create similar capabilities. Chubb's rivals also cannot duplicate those parts they understand. And, even if a competitor could pass these first hurdles, it would face a threat of retaliation if it directly confronted Chubb in this affluent market. Thus, Chubb continues to sustain this advantage in full view of its competitors.

Next we consider each of these three barriers to imitation—causal ambiguity, barriers to duplication, and retaliation.

The Barrier of Causal Ambiguity

For a firm to imitate the strategy of a rival, it must first understand the sources of the rival's advantages, and then determine what resources would be needed to replicate or improve on the results. This will be greatly impeded if there is *ambiguity* about the causal connections between the actions of this rival and results. The greater the uncertainty over how successful companies realize their results, the more potential entrants are inhibited.

Causal ambiguity is especially characteristic of distinctive capabilities such as Federal Express' next-day delivery capability, which requires close cooperation among a whole chain of order takers, pick-up drivers, dispatchers, delivery people, and their coordination into a system comprising planes, vans, computerized tracking facilities, and automated sorting equipment.[19] By contrast, Atlantic Richfield's low-cost position in the supply of gasoline to the California market is largely determined by its access to Alaskan crude oil. The cause, in this case, is clear.

The difference is that Federal Express' capability has three features that make it hard to comprehend. First, its capability embodies *tacit knowledge* based on learning by doing or using, accumulated through experience and refined by practice. A rival trying to acquire this knowledge would have to replicate much of the learning process. At the extreme, the knowledge base may be so tacit and implicit that it resists all efforts at codifying the routines, decision rules, and protocols that make the system work.

Causal ambiguity is deepened when the capability requires a complex *pattern of coordination* among diverse types of resources. This means that few individuals have a complete grasp of the entire system. Thus a rival cannot copy through direct observation and may still not grasp the functioning of the capability even after hiring away key employees. Adding to the complexity are the norms, values, and beliefs that define what is appropriate behavior within the system and comprise the organization culture. These cultures are very resistant to efforts at transplantation.

Finally, there will be ambiguity when the assets are specifically *committed* to the activities in the process and cannot be used elsewhere. These are sometimes called *transaction-specific* assets in the context of relationships with outside agencies. These create a high degree of interdependency that is both hard to disentangle or imitate.

Barriers to Duplication

Once a potential rival comprehends the sources of advantage—however imperfectly—imitation requires the acquisition or development of the resources necessary to mount a competitive challenge. Sustainability depends on being able to impede these moves.

Direct acquisition of the necessary resources will be impeded or facilitated, depending on:

- *The immobility or scarcity of the resources.*[20] The best way to block imitation is to create one-of-kind resources such as Atlantic's access to Alaskan oil, geographically centered hub-and-spoke systems, meaningful patents, and close customer relationships that literally cannot be transferred. Next best is to embody the advantage in the complex relationships among large teams of people. This means the whole team has to be transferred, along with the communication channels and supporting systems. Even so, the climate and culture are unlikely to be re-created.[21]
- *The accuracy of the information about the value of the resource.* The established firm will usually have better insights into the productivity of the individual assets—given the capabilities it already has in place to utilize these assets. The rivals are thus facing a very imperfect market with very poor information about how much to pay, so they may well pay too much.
- Even if the specific asset or capability can be acquired, there is a risk that the value may not be realized because of short-term or continued degradation of productivity after the transfer as a

result of the organizational changes necessary to absorb the new capacity.

Given the risks of acquisition and integration of resources, some rivals will try to emulate a successful competitor either by developing most of the necessary capabilities and assets or finding a venture partner to fill in the major gaps, such as access to technology or markets. The replication will be aided if the rivals can readily observe the innovation (through reverse engineering) and have similar capabilities and serve the same market.[22] Most financial services advantages derived from innovations such as interest rate swaps, stripped bonds, and derivatives are notoriously easy to copy because rivals have the systems, people, and information in place. When product, process, or managerial innovations can be protected with patents or secrecy, then emulation is much more difficult. Thus, Merrill Lynch was able to obtain a long lead over its competitors with its Cash Management Account, which integrated four investor services into one account. The competitors were able to readily develop the technology because the hardware was available from several suppliers, but they lacked the organization infrastructure for bringing the innovation to market.

A further barrier to internally developing assets and capabilities comes from *time compression diseconomies*.[23] Some resources can be developed only painstakingly over long periods of time. For example, a reputation for exceptional quality requires consistency and continuous improvement over a long period of time. A rival that tries to rapidly achieve the same result through a crash program is likely to find it has incurred much higher costs than if it had made the same expenditures over a longer period.

Perhaps the most subtle barriers to imitation are rooted in the past commitments of the rivals to assets, capabilities, and policies, which cause their strategies to persist, even when they want to change. One effect of these commitments is to lock in the current direction. (The uses of commitment are considered in more detail in Chapter 13.) Rivals to Wal–Mart are constrained by past investments in stores that are inappropriately sized and whose locations preclude imitation of

Wal-Mart's efficient hub-and-spoke distribution. Similarly, Sears became locked into a high-low pricing policy whereby numerous deep discount sales were held to create store traffic. It effectively trained its customers to wait for promotions and "cherry-pick" the sales items. Sears wanted to switch to everyday low pricing, but couldn't afford the loss of earnings during the transition period needed to train its customers in a different patronage pattern.[24] Another type of commitment is rooted in organizational inertia, emphasizing preservation of the strategic status quo. One can speculate that Detroit responded too slowly to Japanese competition in the auto industry because of a high resistance to change stemming from a historic emphasis on making cars bigger, because the strategy worked in the past and because the necessary changes were clearly going to be painful and resisted by key stakeholders such as unions.

Credible Threats of Retaliation

A third way to create barriers to imitation is through threats of retaliation. Early movers may be able to deter imitation by rivals who might be able to overcome the barriers to duplicability with a credible threat of retaliation. Procter & Gamble (P&G) has been able to discourage frontal attacks on its core detergent and toothpaste markets by publicly signaling its intentions to defend these markets. Erstwhile invaders believe these signals because they are backed up with a long history of punitive retaliation against aspirants and frequent public reminders that P&G's first priority is maintaining share even at the expense of short-term declines in profits. These signals may be amplified by making early announcements of new products, building capacity ahead of market growth, or making other commitments to scale and scope. The defender also can play on the fear of the potential imitator that if it tried to match the early mover's size, total capacity would exceed foreseeable demand and industry profitability would be seriously eroded.

Signals of possible retaliation will be futile if they are misunderstood by a target competitor, who is holding a different set of market assumptions or lacks the means to appraise the consequences of the threat. Signals from some firms are routinely dismissed as mere posturing because there is no evidence of a deep commitment to a long-run intention to win.[25] When the entire organization is focused on beating competitors, this intent pervades all levels and ensures a consistent message will be heard by challengers as well as by distributors and customers. We will return to the issue of signaling of competitive intention in Chapter 12.

CONCLUSION: THE UNCERTAIN PERSISTENCE OF ADVANTAGES

Competition is an inherently dynamic process, and managers must be aware that artful competitors are constantly looking at ways to overcome their disadvantages and find new advantages. Thus, the assessment of persistence of advantages depends on getting answers to the issues addressed in the following chapters: What are the competitors intentions and capabilities? How are they likely to behave and respond to our initiatives? What are we capable of doing? And how will the customer and channel members behave?

Advantages depend upon the ability to create barriers to imitation to extend existing advantages. They also depend upon understanding how investments in renewal create new advantages as the old ones are eroded. In this way, the competitive advantage cycle is sustained. As we saw with Dell, in an era in which more businesses are becoming fast-cycle, the most persistent of all advantage may be the ability to continually adapt and pursue new bases of advantage.

CHAPTER 3

INTEGRATING POLICY TRENDS INTO DYNAMIC ADVANTAGE

ELIZABETH E. BAILEY

The Wharton School, Department of Public Policy and Management

The public sector is sometimes treated as an external factor in formulating strategy, yet public policies often serve as nonmarket drivers of company success. This chapter explores the effect of reduced economic regulation and increased social and environmental regulation on different competitors. We examine policy windows that create opportunities for firms to shape policy or its implementation. We describe the nature of political competition and offer prescriptions for strategy depending on whether the policy initiatives affect competing firms equally or unequally. Finally, we present a set of schematics of the interaction between the public and private sectors to help firms analyze policy trends and integrate them into competitive strategy.

In airlines, telecommunications, utilities, and many other industries, public policy defines the competitive playing field. Even in industries in which regulation is less visible, public policy on issues such as the environment can have a substantial strategic impact. Yet many firms do not consider the implications of policy as part of the process of analyzing and formulating competitive strategy. In assessing their strategic positions, managers should ask: What are the opportunities created by policy changes? What are the negative consequences of proposed policies? Should the firm be active or passive with respect to a public policy initiative? Should it adopt an individual stance or join in collective action? How can it best influence the governmental or social activist agenda?

The answers to these questions require an understanding of the interaction between public policy and private sector strategies. This analysis should include the direct effect of policy on the firm as well as indirect effects from the market responses of competitors.

An understanding of the public sector should be an integral part of a firm's overall strategy. In their strategic thinking, managers must develop connecting tissue between concerns originating outside the firm and the market strategies adopted by the firm. They should be aware of long-term patterns of change in the public sector that could influence the future growth path of industry profitability. The strategic interaction between the private and public sectors needs to be understood as a dynamic driver of competitive advantage.

This chapter explores this interaction between public policy and competitive strategy. It examines ways managers can integrate policy considerations into their analysis of strategic options. The chapter first examines how public policy is often overlooked by managers. It then discusses key policy trends and the rationale driving many current policy decisions. The chapter then explores the fortuitous events that create *policy windows* where firms can make an impact. Finally, the chapter looks at four strategies for developing dynamic advantages in light of various types of policy initiatives. The choice of strategy depends upon whether the policies reduce regulations or increase them, and whether they affect all players equally or create winners and losers among competing firms.

PUBLIC POLICY AND PRIVATE STRATEGY: AN INTERACTIVE PROCESS

Public sector policies can create and help sustain competitive advantage for firms, or can undermine and even destroy advantages, as illustrated in Figure 3.1. Consider, for example, an industry in which price and entry are regulated. Its marketplace arena and the value of its resources are sustained and protected by regulation. A public sector deregulatory initiative provides a new definition of the competitive arena. Smaller firms that had been geographically limited can expand their areas of operations, and new firms can enter and attempt to attract business

Figure 3.1
Policy Trends and Dynamic Advantage

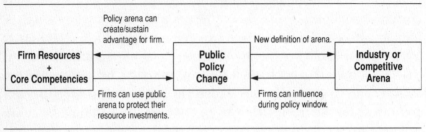

through lower prices. As shown in the right side of Figure 3.1, the new definition of the competitive arena causes changes in the boundaries of the competitive arena and in the mix of rivals. As shown in the left side of the figure, the key resources needed for competitive success change, and firms must develop new competencies in pricing and network design.

Firms can also influence the new policy initiative, as indicated by the inward arrows in the figure. Consider a proposed environmental law that will significantly increase the net costs to an industry. All firms in the industry may collectively seek to influence legislative and/or rule-making activities so as to meet the public need while minimizing the cost burden to the industry. Or consider the ability to influence policy toward piracy of a firm resource, such as computer software. Future profitability may, in large measure, be determined by the degree to which that industry can mobilize its government to force copyright compliance by other countries.

Strategists Ignore Policy

Traditional strategy literature does not explicitly focus on the interactions between strategy and policy shown in Figure 3.1. Yet this interaction affects advantages as defined by these theorists. Porter's model of competitive strategy identifies five market forces that need to be factored into a firm's strategic planning process.[1] These are: the threat of new entry, bargaining power of buyers, bargaining power of suppliers, the threat of substitute products and services, and rivalry among existing firms. His categorization does not focus on the important linkages between private strategy and public policy. Yet regulatory policy may determine whether entry can occur; antitrust policy may influence the degree of rivalry; new products may need to go through governmental approval processes; labor, antitrust, and trade laws may influence the bargaining power of buyers and suppliers; and trade policies may determine the degree of rivalry among international firms.

Similarly, the resource-based view of the firm, also treats public policy only indirectly. In this theory, there are four cornerstones of competitive advantage: superior resources, forces that limit competition, imperfect resource mobility, and *ex ante* limits to competition.[2] As argued here, superior resources (heterogeneity within an industry) often come from monopoly rents granted or rescinded by the public sector. Property rights are supported by law, permitting exclusive rights to many mineral or other scarce resources. Antitrust laws can rescind superior rents associated with monopoly. Similarly, *ex post* limits to competition, which sustain rents, are often granted by government policy. Much of the entry regulation practiced from the 1930s to the 1970s in the telecommunications and transportation industries gave sustainable advantage to those with current operating rights and handicapped companies attempting to enter as new competitors. Capital and labor mobility may also be constrained by governmental policy. Environmental laws (making a distinction between high and low sulfur coal, or failing to do so) may cause gains or losses in specialized factors of production that might affect one firm or locality more than another. Similarly, the existence of trademark, copyright, patent, and intellectual property laws all contribute *ex ante* to a firm's incentive to invest to achieve protected rents. Government disclosure regulations may lessen the degree of information asymmetries that underlie advantage and so provide *ex ante* encouragement to competition.[3]

PATTERNS OF POLICY CHANGE
Sometimes policy shifts may appear to managers to be random and perhaps even capricious, but there are some clear patterns of policy

changes. By understanding these patterns, managers can better anticipate future policy shifts.

Tracking Broad Policy Trends

Two major public sector trends during the past quarter century have
characterized government policy toward business. The first trend has
been the economic regulatory reform movement, including both
deregulation and privatization, which is part of a worldwide downsiz-
ing and reinvention of government. The second trend, somewhat contrary to the first, has been the significant increase in social and
environmental activism. This activism has resulted in major new legislation aimed at improving the quality of life for citizens, but often at
significant cost to industry.

Other public sector events can be subsumed under these two broad
headings. For example, the end of the Cold War has increased the market orientation of many former Communist economies. This trend fits
into the deregulation and privatization category, since the constraints
on firms are being relaxed. Another result of the end of the Cold War
has been a reduction in defense spending, which in turn has led to defense industry consolidation. Another public sector trend has been the
factoring of social and environmental issues into trade policy. Human
rights activism with respect to China, or *Maquiladora* issues with respect
to NAFTA, are best analyzed as part of the trend toward greater social
and environmental regulation.

In a study of the long-term trends in economic regulatory activity in
the United States, Richard Vietor found a move toward regulation and
then away from it.[4] In the 1930s, the major policy thrust was toward increased economic regulation of infrastructure sectors such as transportation, telecommunications, and energy. If you were a manager in
one of these industries, your destiny was in large part influenced by this
broad-based trend. But there was also a degree of constructive strategic thinking that could beneficially influence your future. All along the
time path, it was possible to influence both the legislation and its implementation. The earlier and the wiser the intervention, the better for
your long-term interests.

Continuous monitoring of the external environment would also have revealed the spread of the regulatory net over the next 30 years. As technological change continued to lower costs and to bring new modes of service into being, regulatory rules that had been designed for one transportation mode, such as railroads, were extended to more competitive modes, such as trucks and air and water carriers. The government entered the business of maintaining equity, not only for consumers, but also for supply among and within modes of transportation. The regulatory system became cumbersome. Regulations became ever more detailed, and even simple regulatory issues could take years to be decided. The heavy hand of economic regulation began to be felt, and the regulatory system began to break down.

In the mid–1970s, a wave of economic regulatory reform and deregulation began. Again, there was a degree of predictability about the trend, and some business leaders caught the vision sooner than did their rivals. The dilemma was that policymakers now recognized that regulatory intervention was imperfect just as marketplace competition was imperfect. Policymakers began to ask: Which is better in this situation—imperfect competition or imperfect regulation? Their solution was to seek minimal regulatory intervention for each circumstance. Economic regulatory policy began to be administered with a light touch rather than with a heavy hand.

Contestability Theory: Changing the Rules for Regulatory Policy

A new economic theory called *contestability theory* helped provide a practical template for reform.[5] The idea was to segment an industry into various markets and to seek to determine for each such market the extent of contests for the market that could take place under conditions of free entry and exit. Figure 3.2 provides a synopsis of this framework. In the 1930s template of regulation, the industry was treated as an integrated monopoly. Prices, entry, and service obligations were set by regulators. New entry was also overseen by regulators. In the 1980s template of deregulation, the industry was unbundled into its distinct activities—the unbundling could be vertical (separating electricity

81

Figure 3.2
Contestability Theory and Industry Unbundling

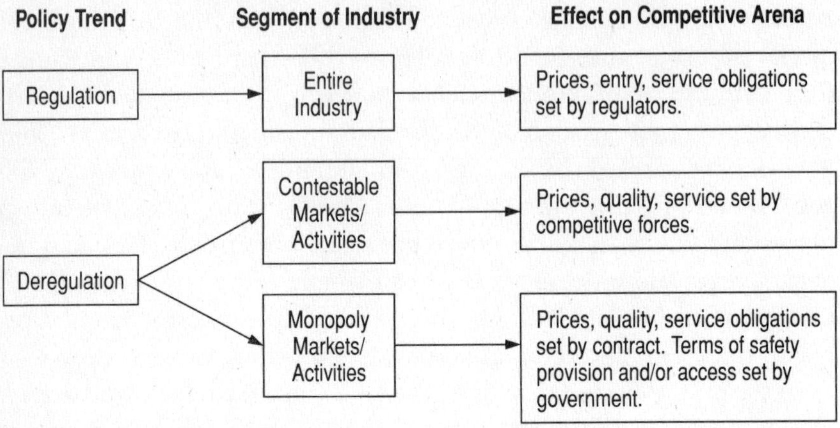

Policy Trend	Segment of Industry	Effect on Competitive Arena
Regulation	Entire Industry	Prices, entry, service obligations set by regulators.
Deregulation	Contestable Markets/ Activities	Prices, quality, service set by competitive forces.
	Monopoly Markets/ Activities	Prices, quality, service obligations set by contract. Terms of safety provision and/or access set by government.

generation from transmission and distribution) or horizontal (either geographically or by service categories). Each activity was then analyzed as to the degree of monopoly power remaining in the market/activity. For contestable markets/activities, there was an opening of competition in the market. Prices, quality, and service were set by competitive forces. For monopoly markets/activities, there was an opening of competition for the market by concession or lease or competition by substitutes. Prices, quality, and service obligations were set by contract. The right of access to the monopoly facility was mandated by government. In this process, regulators were clearly playing a role in defining the competitive arena and the nature of competition within it.

Figure 3.3 summarizes this unbundling for various infrastructure industries. Consider the railroad industry. Certain of its markets, such as the transportation of fresh fruits and vegetables, faced strong competition from trucks, even in regions where only one railroad provided service. Such markets were contestable and could be deregulated. Prices, quality, and service could be set by competitive forces. Other railroad markets, such as the supply of coal to an electric utility, were captive (not readily contested). For such markets, continued economic regulation was warranted, but even here, many new concepts that flowed

Figure 3.3
Economic Framework for Regulatory Reform

INDUSTRY	Contestable Markets: Deregulation	Captive Markets/Safety Concerns: Continued Regulation
Stock Brokerage	Commissions	Margin Requirements
Airlines	Domestic Rates and Routes	Airports Air Traffic Control Safety International Rates & Routes
Trucks	Rates and Routes	Safety
Rail	Competitive Markets	Captive Markets
Telephone	Terminal Equipment Long Distance	Local
Electric Power	Generation	Distribution

from the theory helped free up the players to try other mechanisms than command-and-control regulation. Freedom to negotiate long-term contracts (e.g., between the coal company and the railroad) was requested and granted, and the terms of these contracts were permitted to be kept private. In areas where it is safety concerns rather than captive markets that are at issue, traditional regulation continues.

Many managers are unaware of contestability theory, even though it may have a powerful effect in shaping their competitive environment. Most are at least somewhat aware of the broad regulatory trends, but many fail to factor them into the strategy formulation process. The more forward-looking firms in each industry, those that understood the shift toward deregulation and the new opportunities it offers, have been able to achieve dynamic advantage. Others have conducted business as usual in a public environment that has dramatically changed; they often find themselves competitively disadvantaged.

A Trend toward Social and Environmental Regulation

David Vogel describes the expansion of the political agenda over the past two decades to include the emergence of a strong public interest movement.[6] According to Vogel, environmental and consumer organizations have become important sources of countervailing power to business. These initiatives reflect an increase in public sophistication toward requiring increased social performance by large companies. Figure 3.4 shows the various regulatory trends by category. Social regulation is most often responsive to concerns about human rights (particularly in the workplace) and to protecting youth. Environmental regulation pertains mainly to the desire for cleaner air, water, and/or land. According to Robert Hahn and Thomas Hopkins, while the annual regulatory costs devoted to economic regulation have shrunk from $100 billion in the late 1970s to about $25 billion today (in 1990 dollars), social and environmental regulatory costs have risen threefold from about $75 billion in the late 1970s to more than $225 billion estimated by the start

Figure 3.4
Growth in Social and Environmental Regulation

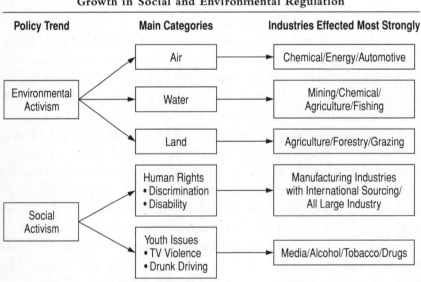

of the next century.[7] Many managers failed to see the strategic implications of this trend until it had already placed restrictions or added costs on their industries.

INTERACTIONS BETWEEN POLICYMAKERS, THE PUBLIC, AND INDUSTRY

In the policy arena, there are multiple players, each competing to have his or her perspective reflected in any new legislation or regulatory rule making. David Baron recommends that firms pursue an "integrated strategy," including both public sector and private sector considerations.[8] Managers should analyze public sector initiatives to see whether they will help or harm their business, and develop legislative, agency, and litigative strategies to influence these initiatives. The strategic planning should include a public policy awareness that is deeply understood at all points in the value chain and through the organization. Nonmarket strategy should not be the sole domain of government relations officers, but needs to involve advertising and marketing people, strategic planners, and area managers (for international operations), as well as top management and members of the board of directors. Firms should realize that social concerns may lead to changes in competitive advantage. They should promote an awareness of an ongoing loop of influence between the public and private sectors. New public sector initiatives may shape business opportunities in the marketplace, and new business initiatives often require governmental intervention or approval.

The organization also needs to be aware of the dynamic interrelationships between business, the public, policymakers (elected officials), and regulatory/executive branch agencies, as illustrated in Figure 3.5. Both industry and public interest groups submit input to influence policy. Consider the recent Contract with America. The public presence is shown in the right-hand arrow of Figure 3.5, as the public influences policy through newly elected members of the House of Representatives. On many of the Contract with America issues, business and industry associations also have self-interested (but not monolithic) views that tend to be reflected by the arrow coming from industry on

Figure 3.5
Policy Influence Chart

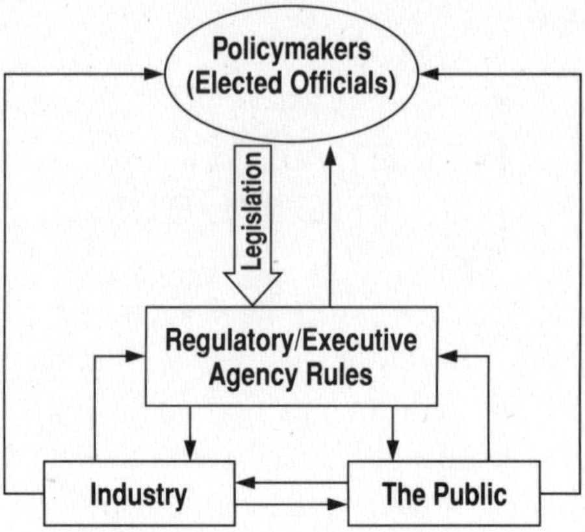

Adapted from Oster (1990)

the left. Policymakers issue new legislation which is interpreted and enforced by regulatory and executive agencies. Industry and the public also have links to the executive and regulatory bureaucracies.[9]

DYNAMIC EVOLUTION: POLICY WINDOWS AND MULTIPLE PLAYERS

In addition to examining interactions between players at a point in time, we can also examine the evolution of policy interactions over time. As shown in Figure 3.6, there are specific points in the strategy process when the private sector can influence policy development or implementation. The policy window reflects an empirical pattern that often appears for issues arising in the public sector. Such issues develop over time, beginning with issue identification. Various interest groups form and battle one another until a legislative consensus is reached. The legislation is then turned over to an executive or regulatory agency for implementation through a rule-making process. If one or more of the interest groups have been left out or are unsatisfied by either the legislative or rule-making decisions, those groups may well

Figure 3.6
The Policy Window

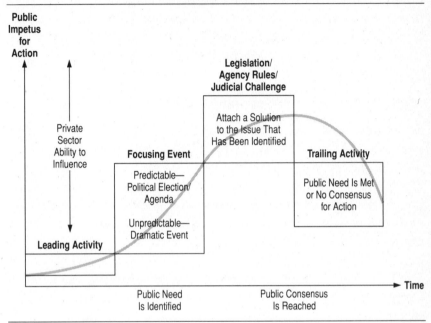

seek judicial relief. The eventual outcome, represented by the trailing activity box in the figure, is that no consensus is reached or that the public need is met, and the policy window for action passes for the time being.

The policy window portrays opportunities for action on given initiatives.[10] Such opportunities present themselves and stay open for only short periods. Some event will trigger a public impetus for action, which rises steeply for a short period of time. Typical events are the election of a new president (timing is predictable), or a disaster with extensive media coverage (unpredictable). The firms or public interest groups that will achieve dynamic advantage among the multiple players are those that are first to recognize that a policy window has opened. They will attach a solution to the issue that has been identified, overcome potential political difficulties by redrafting proposals, and thereby turn the politically propitious event to their advantage.

87

As indicated in Figure 3.6, the earlier that players become involved in the process, the more influence they have. This is why it is vital for managers to incorporate public policy issues into strategy formulation. Recognizing these issues after the policy windows close usually limits the company's ability to influence their development.

Multiple Strategic Players and the Policy Agenda

Sometimes, not all competitors are affected equally by a regulation; some win, while others lose. To be effective, each player needs to understand the relative concentration or dispersion of the benefits from supporting or opposing a policy alternative. The Wilson Matrix in Figure 3.7 describes four types of political competition.[11] The first is interest group politics. This occurs when one business or interest group expects to benefit at the expense of another. The public does not believe it will be affected much. Legislation, if passed, will have something to please each affected party. The 1996 Telecommunications Deregulation Act was of this variety. Consumers were not immediately gainers or losers, but two industry groups (long-distance carriers versus local operating companies) were diametrically opposed. The solution was that the long-distance market would open to local carrier competition shortly after the local telephone market had itself been opened to competition.

Entrepreneurial politics result when a policy alternative has widely distributed gains to society, but is opposed by one interest group, often one business or industry that will bear most of the cost. A political entrepreneur is needed to reflect the interests of those with dispersed benefits. Often this entrepreneur is a politician. Senator Ted Kennedy (D-MA) played this role in airline deregulation by championing consumer interests in lower air fares, even though most industry players were initially opposed. Commissioner David Kessler of the Food and Drug Administration is an example of a political entrepreneur from an executive branch agency who has recently highlighted the youth and tobacco issue.

Client politics occur when one firm or interest group gains disproportionately from a policy change (the benefits are concentrated).

Figure 3.7
Nature of Political Competition*

Distribution of Benefits from Policy Change

	Narrowly Concentrated	Widely Distributed
Narrowly Concentrated	**Interest Group Politics** • Some business or interest group expects to benefit at expense of another. • Public does not believe it will be much affected. • Legislation, if passed, will have something to please each affected party.	**Entrepreneurial Politics** • General benefits conferred at cost to be bourne by some business group. • Politician must mobilize latent public sentiment. • Opponents of plan are publically put on defensive. • Legislation associated with widely shared values.
Widely Concentrated	**Client Politics** • Some business or interest group expects to capture a disproportionate share of benefits. • It must organize a coalition and/or lobby to change perception of policy's effects and/or to justify its effects.	**Majoritarian Politics** • Issue must get onto political agenda. • There must be agreement that it is legitimate for government to take action. • Ideological objections must be overcome.

Distribution of Costs from Policy Change (left axis label)

*Adapted from Wilson (1980)

Norman Augustine, CEO of Martin Marietta Corporation, took the lead in modifying merger criteria in defense consolidations, smoothing the way for the Lockheed-Martin merger. Majoritarian politics, in contrast, typically involve major social issues—crime policy, social security—in which both benefits and costs are widely distributed.

The main lesson for any business that is seeking dynamic competitive advantage from a new policy initiative is that the information in Figures 3.6 and 3.7 need to be linked. Managers need to move quickly to take advantage of policy windows, but they also need to determine whether to move individually or to join with others based on the distribution of benefits and costs from the initiative. The speed and skill with which a firm implements its political strategy can enormously influence the outcome of the political competition and the positions of players.

FOUR STRATEGIES FOR SEEKING DYNAMIC ADVANTAGE

What actions should an individual firm take to support or block a public policy initiative? Figure 3.8 shows the broad policy trends and strategic responses by firms to gain as much advantage as possible in the dynamic environment created by changing public sector policies. This matrix examines each public sector trend, those that remove or lessen a constraint (decreased economic regulation) and others that add a constraint (increased social or environmental regulation). Managers must determine whether the initiative creates an incentive to

Figure 3.8
Strategy During the Policy Windows

	Prescriptive Incentive	
	Uneven Effect A firm's desire to set itself apart from its competitors.	**Even Effect** A firm's need to join with others to increase bargaining power.
Decreased Economic Regulation	Improve Relative Advantage	Improve Collective Advantage
Increased Social and Environmental Regulation	Mitigate Relative Disadvantage	Mitigate Collective Disadvantage

join with competitors or sets the firm apart from competitors. Consider, for example, a new command-and-control regulation that proposes a ban on a particular product. If all firms in an industry manufacture this product, their political activity might be collective, with all firms in the industry coordinating their efforts to oppose the ban. By such coordinated activity vis-à-vis the public sector, they can mitigate their collective disadvantage, as shown in the bottom right of Figure 3.8. Suppose, however, that the ban on a particular product affects one firm less than another, giving one firm a relative advantage. That firm may be able, after the ban, to use an alternative technology for which it has patents, but which was not cost-effective prior to the proposed ban. It may use this relative advantage to take individual action to support the ban, if it is better off on a net basis after taking the market consequences for its rival into account. Its rival sees only the confounding of the negative effect of the ban and its lack of substitute technologies. It would thus have an incentive to vigorously oppose the ban. Here, the two firms experience different outcomes from the proposed policy initiative, and hence their strategic political activity will differ. Each would try to mitigate its relative disadvantages, as shown in the lower left-hand box.

A similar analysis holds on the deregulatory side. There are a variety of public initiatives that can improve financial performance. There can be a loosening of a former governmental constraint, perhaps from deregulation or privatization, or from movement away from command-and-control regulation toward a more market-based system. One firm might be able to gain a relative advantage for itself by locking in a new market opportunity. Privatization might permit long-term exclusive rights in a newly emerging economy. Or, the use of marketable permits might permit cooperative advantages to all firms in an industry.

We next examine how companies respond to each of the four strategic situations depicted in Figure 3.8 and explore how policy changes create strategic threats and opportunities. To better understand the dynamic aspects of the prescriptive strategic initiatives depicted in Figure 3.8, we show how it is linked to Figures 3.5, 3.6, and 3.7.

Antitrust and Defense Consolidation: Improving Collective Advantage

There have been significant budgetary reductions for the defense industry in the last decade. Overall, the budget has been cut by a third in real terms from its peak in the mid-1980s. The part of the budget related to equipping U.S. military forces has been reduced by nearly two-thirds. As a result, there is excess capacity in the industry, and with it has come the pressure to consolidate. In several cases, such as the proposed Olin-Alliant Techsystems merger, the Department of Justice (DOJ) intervened to prevent the merger. While the Defense Department decided that the market for a particular form of tank ammunition would support only one supplier, the DOJ was unwilling to let one firm have a monopoly in this product.

The strategic response in defense industries has been to urge government to rethink its antitrust policies. The industry collectively encouraged the establishment of a Presidential Commission (along the top left-hand arrow of Figure 3.5). The policy window (Figure 3.6) was formed by social concerns about large layoffs in the defense industries as highlighted by the media. The Defense Department and elected officials from the most severely affected regions (such as southern California) were particularly interested in supporting an initiative that would better rationalize the industry. The commission recommended the formation of an antitrust unit in the Defense Department. Its purpose would be to articulate to the DOJ its view of why a particular merger in the defense industry would not do harm. One argument might be that the buyer (the Defense Department) was not an uninformed consumer, as DOJ assumed in its antitrust analysis, but rather was highly sophisticated in its contracting practices. In these circumstances, a market with only a small number of suppliers would not violate the intent of the Antitrust Act, which is to prevent the price-gouging of consumers that might occur when an industry tends toward a monopoly.

If the defense industry is indeed able to obtain regulatory relief from the antitrust laws, for reasons of monopsony supply and national defense, it would enjoy an improvement in collective advantage (upper right corner of Figure 3.8). A number of military suppliers would be freed to consolidate and improve their financial performance. As mentioned earlier, Norman Augustine, CEO of Martin-Marietta Corporation, was an early leader in seeing the benefits of supporting this particular end, and his client politics (Figure 3.7) helped create the new policy. He stood immediately to improve relative advantage by achieving a successful merger between Martin-Marietta and Lockheed, while simultaneously improving collective advantage for all defense companies.

Airline Deregulation: Improving Relative Advantage

The Airline Deregulation Act, passed in 1978, profoundly affected the market opportunities available to firms in the industry. For the first time in 40 years, airlines could determine their own operating strategies by entering and exiting any route they wished within the United States. They were free to set prices rather than having to adhere to a price formula set by the Civil Aeronautics Board. So the deregulatory action by government opened up new possibilities for market competition that previously had been blocked. Initially, support for deregulation came from only a few firms. New entrants, such as Southwest, had a structural cost advantage and supported the policy initiative (upper left block of Figure 3.8). But among the major airlines, only United Airlines supported deregulation. It was the largest carrier and did not anticipate much chance for further growth from continued regulation. Moreover, its size might well confer a structural advantage under deregulation (upper left block of Figure 3.8). The politics (Figure 3.7), were entrepreneurial because the benefits were widely distributed to the public, and the costs would come in changes imposed on the major companies in the industry. There was a policy window (Figure 3.6) for reducing the size and scope of government caused in part by recent oil price shocks.

Airlines spent the first decade after deregulation focusing on individual market strategies of their rivals. Robert Crandall of American Airlines took the first private initiative, moving its headquarters to Dallas-Fort Worth where it would build its hub-and-spoke system. It initiated many creative ideas in marketing and pricing, such as SuperSaver fares and Frequent Flyer programs. It thus enjoyed, *ex post,* a dynamic relative advantage from decreased economic regulation (Figure 3.8) that it had not anticipated in advance. However, this advantage was not as long-lived as American might have liked. Most large airlines began to make similar strategic decisions. Each airline found that its best strategic choice was to provide nationwide service, operating to all U.S. points through one or more hub airports, where it held a dominant share of traffic.[12] Larger trunk carriers bought out the smaller local service carriers, which had been surprised to find themselves relatively advantaged in the early deregulatory years by their control of regional traffic and their new ability to initiate longer-haul services at their hubs.

By the 1990s, many of the larger carriers decided that their market strategy involved becoming global. They wished to provide one-stop shopping for their airline customers to destinations throughout the world, rather than only to points within the United States. To implement the new international strategy, airlines had to work through the regulatory and executive agencies, along the middle left arrow in Figure 3.5. In terms of Figure 3.8, there was an opportunity to improve relative advantage to those firms, such as American, Delta, or United, which could arrange to purchase international routes from other carriers, such as Pan Am, TWA, Braniff, or Eastern. But, such transfers of route authority required foreign government approval. Government permissions also had to be sought to gain approval of new international routes or alliances. So an industry whose competitive strategy was greatly affected by a downward legislative movement from policymakers to industry in the late 1970s (Figure 3.5) found itself proactive in creating a reverse movement from its largest players to government trade negotiators in the early 1990s, as they sought to take advantage of this new policy window.

The Chemical Industry after Bhopal: Mitigating Collective Disadvantage

From Earth Day 1970 through the early 1990s, governments here and abroad piled on regulations, setting ever more sweeping and costly environmental goals. The mandates constrained many industries, including, at first, those that were generating big, obvious sources of pollution, such as air pollution associated with oil- and coal-powered electric utility plants, and water pollution caused by releases of chemical companies into the waterways. As time went on, there was an extension of concern to issues such as cleaning up toxic waste dumps, preventing major process accidents, protecting an expanding list of endangered species, reducing greenhouse gases, phasing out chemicals found to be toxic in laboratory animals. Many of these sweeping environmental statutes, such as the Clean Air Act, the Superfund Act, and the Resources Recovery and Conservation Act, bear the restriction that regulators cannot consider costs when setting standards. In terms of Figure 3.5, the initiatives commenced from the public rather than from industry, moving into the policy arena from the right-hand arrow.

These new mandates have begun to interfere more and more with the ability of business and citizens to make sensible decisions concerning their property, processes, and products. A new understanding of the cost associated with zero-risk mandates and pristine cleanups has arisen. New reform ideas are currently being floated, such as requiring an assessment of the true degree of risk and a cost-benefit analysis whenever a federal agency issues a major new rule. A second area of concern has been at state and local government levels, where there is a desire for a "no money, no mandate" law; that is, permitting at the federal level the enactment of expensive new requirements only when funds are provided to pay for them. A third area of reform concerns property rights, and the provision of compensation when environmental actions severely limit the use and lower the value of private property.

As with economic regulation and deregulation, those businesses that are staying closer in touch with the environmental regulation and reform movements, have learned how to influence their tide. They understand the consequences to them of the policy changes, and through political intervention as well as voluntary action, are gaining a competitive edge over their rivals. The Responsible Care Program in the chemical industry provides an interesting example. Spurred by the threat of high-liability awards in the aftermath of the policy window created by the Bhopal accident of December 1984 (Figure 3.6), the larger firms in the chemical industry acted swiftly in taking initiatives to prevent future accidents, thereby to economize on their liability exposures. Members of the Chemical Manufacturers Association voluntarily established a code of conduct for their members, which required the adoption of a complex array of risk management practices and procedures. This collective action (Figure 3.8) went beyond the regulatory compliance requirements of the time. The chemical industry leaders had caught the vision of the future, and realized that more stringent regulations were on the way. The Community Right-to-Know and Emergency Planning Act of 1986 included many of the voluntary process safety improvements (a link from industry to Executive Agency rules in Figure 3.5), and still others were later codified by regulatory agencies into new process safety management regulations. Collective disadvantage (Figure 3.8) was thereby significantly mitigated when compared to the expense that would have been incurred had the regulations been agency-imposed.

Human Rights in China: Mitigating Collective and Relative Disadvantage

The U.S.-China dispute over human rights presents an excellent example of mitigating both collective (1993) and relative (1996) disadvantage, the remaining left-hand box in Figure 3.8. In 1993, President Bill Clinton wished to give human rights concerns in China a higher profile. He announced an executive order linking improvements in human rights in China to U.S. renewal of China's most-favored nation trade status. The Chinese were given a year, from June 1993 to June 1994, to make measurable improvements in human rights areas, such as dismal treatment of political prisoners and sale of products made by prison labor. At the time, the order was widely praised by law makers, China experts, and human-rights groups as an excellent compromise that acknowledged the concerns of Congress on human rights but deferred any punishment of China for a year.

The 1993 announcement involved entrepreneurial politics (Figure 3.7). The signal was from government to business, and it created a year-long policy window (Figure 3.6). During the year in which the executive order was in place, there was intense lobbying by a number of large American companies including Motorola, General Electric, IBM, and Xerox. These companies coordinated their activities, since each had significant investments in China and regarded China as a major market (an industry link, left-hand arrow of Figure 3.5). By joining and directing strenuous efforts both to the White House and to Congress, the companies were able to mitigate collective disadvantage (Figure 3.8) and thereby retain and expand their share of expanding Chinese markets.

A new twist began to occur in the next two years, when piracy of intellectual property rights became an issue. A presidential policy window (Figure 3.6) in favor of the software interests was created, since Silicon Valley supported President Bill Clinton in the 1992 election. When the 1995 piracy agreements were insufficiently implemented by China, this window ensured that there was the political will to seek a strengthening of these agreements. The interests of industry giants such as Walt Disney and Microsoft were arrayed on one side as they attempted to mitigate their relative disadvantage (Figure 3.8). Other industry giants were arrayed on the other side, as China retaliated by withdrawing airplane orders from Boeing in protest to the pressures from the United States on intellectual piracy. The need for business to take a very broad look at the strategic implications of the policy initiatives taken by other industry groups became overwhelmingly apparent.

CONCLUSION

More and more management attention is devoted to strategic issues involving business and the public sector. Some 56 percent of CEOs spend more than 10 days a year in Washington, and 39 percent spend over 20 days there.[13] But often this time is spent in reacting to policy late in the game. By becoming aware of policy issues earlier and incorporating them into the strategy process, managers can improve their strategic planning. By understanding the broad policy trends, their current and future impact, and options for responding to them, companies have a better chance of enjoying and sustaining dynamic competitive advantage as a result of public sector initiatives.

One way to increase this awareness of public policy is to support boundary spanners, the individuals within a firm who are open to external trends, both societal changes and market innovations, by other firms.[14] Such individuals aid the transformation process of the firm in helping it overcome institutional conformity and permitting it a degree of protection from the changing policy environment. It is vital that business provide support to these individuals. They are key to catching the trends early so that their business can capture the economic rents associated with being in the forefront of major policy and technology change.

CHAPTER 4

TECHNOLOGY-DRIVEN ENVIRONMENTAL SHIFTS AND THE SUSTAINABLE COMPETITIVE DISADVANTAGE OF PREVIOUSLY DOMINANT COMPANIES

ERIC K. CLEMONS

The Wharton School, Department of Operations and Information Management

Technology-driven environmental shifts are one of the most powerful forces changing the nature of competitive advantage. This chapter explores how these shifts not only undermine current sources of advantages, but often undermine the whole basis for thinking about strategy and regulation in an industry. This can rapidly transform a competitive advantage into a competitive disadvantage. This chapter examines the impact of these changes in banking and other service industries, discusses the reasons large incumbents are often unable to replicate the strategies of nimble new entrants, and offers recommendations for mitigating these disadvantages. As described in the discussion, the challenges faced by incumbent firms go far beyond the simple anticipation of emerging technological trends. There are complex interrelationships among technology, public policy, and firm-level strategy. These interactions define the strategic impact of new technology, often in ways that are not initially apparent in understanding the technology itself.

The assistance of my colleagues at the Wharton School—David Croson, George Day, Matt Thatcher, and Bruce Weber—is gratefully acknowledged, as is the assistance of officers at banks, credit card issuers, telecommunications firms, and insurance companies in North America, Europe, and Asia.

99

A combination of environmental shifts have invalidated not only the strategies of incumbent firms, but also the assumptions upon which their strategies are based. Changes in technology and regulation have enabled new pricing structures and new distribution channels. These changes create significant opportunities for new entrants, who apply IT and database marketing to attract the most profitable segments away from the incumbent.

Paradoxically, successful incumbents are often unable to replicate these new strategies. Indeed, it is usually their previous success that limits their ability to respond. Prior commitments by incumbents to customers and suppliers and investments in distribution frequently constrain the strategies available to large firms and facilitate "cream skimming" by new entrants. Moreover, existing regulatory regimes, developed in response to previous abuses of industrial giants, now frequently cripple large service firms.

There are a limited number of truly useful steps that incumbent firms can take to protect themselves. These include updating doctrines (a shared set of assumptions about resources, capabilities, and objectives), creating flexible strategies, and negotiating more enlightened regulations.[1] This chapter examines the challenges faced by these dominant incumbents and briefly discusses strategies they can use to address these challenges.

COMPETITION IN BANKING: HONG KONG SHANGHAI BANK

With 75 percent of households in Hong Kong holding accounts at Hong Kong Shanghai Bank Corp. (HKSB), it is difficult to imagine a bank with broader marketplace presence, or with more apparent marketplace dominance. But beneath this dominance is a strategic vulnerability that it shares with many dominant firms. HKSB's customer base has been characterized in informal conversations as being composed of "love 'ems" and "kill yous." It is believed that 20 percent of its customers generate all HKSB's profits, and that 20 percent of its customers actually cost HKSB money.

A typical "kill you" is a low-balance retail customer that performs his or her transactions in the branch with a teller. Conversely, a "love 'em" may be characterized as a high-balance customer whose reliance upon nonbranch interactions that are not based on time-consuming teller transactions makes them profitable to serve. Its pricing structure, like that of most banks, tends to subsidize the "kill yous" through the "love 'ems." As long as this complete base of customers remains intact, it continues to make a profit.

But now Citibank, taking advantage of new technology and relaxed regulations on global competition, has begun to challenge HKSB's profitability in the market. Citibank has not attempted a frontal assault on all segments of HKSB's broad market share. It has, instead, gone straight for the "love 'ems" segment, developing distribution channels and pricing strategies for its products and services that are attractive primarily to the most profitable Hong Kong customer segments. The newly contested consumer banking market in Hong Kong has opened up an avenue for opportunistic cream skimming by Citibank, which is now HKSB's most dangerous and profitable rival.

What are the conditions that have allowed Citibank and other entrants to make this type of attack on dominant incumbents? In this chapter, we discuss three reasons why incumbents face this type of threat:

1. *It is easy to attack.* The structures that once protected the positions of dominant firms are crumbling. Shifts in technology, relaxation of regulations and other barriers to entry, and the ease of acquiring necessary assets through outsourcing have made it increasingly easy for new entrants such as Citibank to attack established competitors. These changes also make it increasingly difficult for established players to rely upon their existing resources to protect their position in the marketplace.

2. *It is attractive to attack.* HKSB's history of undifferentiated pricing—common to all major banks—helped create an opportunity where it was attractive for new entrants to attempt to capture the most attractive customer segments from HKSB. Significantly,

Citibank did not attack all segments of HKSB's market, nor did it "offer to help HKSB defer the costs" associated with serving its share of the "kill yous." Rather, Citibank targeted those customers for whom the costs of service and the service prices charged had the widest gap, and thus provided the greatest opportunity. It has become attractive for new entrants to attack even in markets where established players have historically enjoyed significant advantage due to scale, market share, and lower average costs. The attacker may be able to be the low-price service provider for its targeted customers, even if it does not enjoy lower average costs.

3. *It is difficult for established players to defend themselves.* Dominant players such as HKSB would appear to be well positioned to respond to threats posed by new entrants. But restrictions on their flexibility—including outdated technology infrastructures, long-term commitments to customers, inappropriate corporate culture, and hostile regulation—make it difficult for them to defend themselves. Regulators concerned with public welfare, or consumer activist organizations, may make it extremely difficult for large banks to close unprofitable branches, to withhold services from unprofitable market segments, or to impose service fees on unprofitable accounts. Fixed investments in existing distribution systems, such as branch banking networks, may be difficult to recover.

HKSB's Options

In the absence of an effective response, the profitability of HKSB's consumer bank will fall as rivals target attractive customer segments and leave the bank with customers that are costly to serve and produce limited revenues for the bank. What are its options?

- *Raise prices.* As profits decline, HKSB may raise prices for its remaining customers in an attempt to regain profitability; and more customers will defect to alternative service providers. This will lead to further decline in the bank's profits and further deterioration of costs, a second round of price increases, and additional defection of remaining attractive customers.

- *Move to differential pricing.* Instead, HKSB might attempt to introduce differential pricing strategies such as charging small accounts for access to branch tellers and applying fees to low-balance accounts to recover the costs of providing services. This move, however, could be blocked by social policy, public outcry, and unfavorable publicity if small, unprofitable accounts are driven from the banking system.

- *Introduce new technology.* The bank may pursue technological alternatives including new means of distribution and cost-reducing alternatives that do not exclude the "kill yous" entirely. HKSB's ability to respond may depend on its ability to distribute banking products with fewer tellers and branches and by encouraging use of ATMs, kiosks, and telephone service centers. As with imposition of service fees, actions taken to move customers to low-cost technological service delivery systems will need to be targeted especially at small-balance accounts. Unfortunately, these may be precisely the accounts that are most resistant to technological alternatives to teller-based interactions.

It is no surprise that the bank is pursuing a combination of change in pricing structure to encourage its most expensive customer segments to consider lower cost technology-based distribution systems and the active development of such systems. The bank's participation in the introduction and marketing of Mondex, a leading-edge smart card alternative to cash, is but one example of new service distribution possibilities that the bank is exploring.

FROM DOMINANCE TO DEATH SPIRAL

HKSB is not alone. Our research has shown that in a wide range of industries, new entrants are using IT applications to pick off the most profitable customers of large incumbents. Why can't incumbents simply mimic the behavior of these newcomers, especially given their often superior resources and position in the market? It is because the incumbents, for all their dominance (often *because* of their dominance), are far more limited in their ability to change quickly, both because of prior commitments to customers and infrastructures and because of regulations designed for a previous age.

Average Cost Pricing

One of the central strategic vulnerabilities of large incumbents is their historical pricing structures. Established players often have engaged in *average-cost pricing*. They set prices based on the average cost of serving a broad range of customers, even in the presence of wide differences in the costs and benefits of serving these customers. This entailed a cross-subsidy, as good credit risks paid an additional 150 basis points or more to subsidize the credit risk of other credit card holders, or as local telephone customers in Denver or Manhattan paid higher rates than necessary, subsidizing local telephone service to remote regions of Colorado or upstate New York. It was often justified, especially in telecommunications, by the social benefits of universal access to the telephone network, or of universal access to credit and to the banking system.

Moreover, this cross-subsidy was difficult to avoid in many industries, such as retail banking, since customer profitability analysis was poorly understood and expensive to perform. However, just as four new entrants are currently competing to provide local telephone service in Manhattan, which has been made attractive by Nynex's charging rates well above the true cost of service in Manhattan, new entrants can be expected to challenge established banks for at least some segments of the market. Moreover, just as these new telecommunications service providers are not attacking Nynex in New York's upstate rural farming counties, it is reasonable to expect that new entrants in banking will selectively target only the established banks' best customers.

Average-cost pricing can provide comfortable profitability for established players when their customers are representative of the entire market and when competitors are not cream skimming. New entrants, however, frequently seek to capture market share by attempting to attract their competitors' most profitable customers by offering them preferential pricing; these prices are better than the prices that these customers have been charged under average-cost pricing but are substantially higher than the true costs of providing service to this selected group.

For example, credit card issuers serve customers that differ significantly in their profitability. Historically, dominant players charged most or all of their customers the same annual fee and the same APR. Increasingly, new entrants are engaging in differential pricing and are targeting their offerings to attract certain profitable segments of the market; this leaves the established players with the less-profitable customers.

Credit card customers who have reliable sources of income, who use their cards actively, maintain large outstanding balances, and who use the revolving credit feature of their cards rather than paying balances in full each statement period are the most profitable customers. It is easy to identify some of these attractive customers. For example, tenured high-school teachers and university faculty members have secure incomes and a low risk of defaulting, but frequently earn less during the summer months; this often leads to making smaller monthly payments during the summer and thus to borrowing on their cards.

Using demographic and predictive data, card issuers such as Signet Bank have targeted these low-risk, high-income borrowers, and have used lower annual fees and lower APRs to attract them away from established bank card issuers.[2]

Death Spirals

As a result of average-cost pricing and cream skimming, the incumbent is left with less-profitable accounts. The logical response would be to raise prices for these remaining accounts to ensure profitability. But this is a very dangerous strategy (even assuming it is not blocked by regulatory concerns such as affordable universal access). If the incumbent responds by raising the charges for its remaining accounts, more of its best customers will be courted and will defect to its cream-skimming rivals. This, in turn, creates more pressure on profits, so the incumbent may raise prices again, causing more of its remaining good customers to defect. Thus the incumbent enters a death spiral, a self-reinforcing cycle of boosting prices and losing market share that ultimately leads to the firm's collapse. This is obviously not an effective response to these attacks.

Our recent research—conducted with banks, financial services firms, and telecommunications companies in North America, Europe, and the Far East—suggests that the problems faced by incumbents are quite severe, and may be difficult to resolve simply by attempting to duplicate the strategies of new entrants. Incumbents *must* respond in order to avoid catastrophic loss of market share and profitability, which can lead to bankruptcy. Yet there are often significant structural reasons why incumbents *cannot respond effectively;* this leads to a new phenomenon, the *sustainable competitive disadvantage* of previously successful organizations.

Newly Vulnerable Markets

Dominant incumbents were previously considered secure because of scale, captive customers, and other resources. The combination of technological, market, and regulatory changes, along with historic pricing structures have made these secure markets *newly vulnerable markets*.[3] These are markets in which, as shown in the HKSB example, the once-secure incumbent is now very vulnerable to attack. We consider the three reasons for this vulnerability in more detail next:

1. Ease of attack.
2. Attackers' advantage due to targeting.
3. Defenders' disadvantage due to flexibility restrictions.

Each of these factors is affected by information technology.

Markets Are Newly Easy to Attack

A range of changes makes it increasingly easy for new entrants to begin to compete with established banks, even in markets where these banks have historically enjoyed apparently dominant market positions. While not all of these changes may appear to be directly driven by information technology, most will readily been seen to be significantly influenced by this technology:

Technological change. A number of technological changes have reduced the value of scale and market share, and thus have reduced the cost advantages of very large institutions. In particular, the drop in cost of computing make it possible even for banks with smaller market share to afford hardware, while the growth of shared ATM networks and the increased availability of outsourced software make it possible for these smaller banks to acquire necessary software. At present, hardware vendors like Unisys and IBM, software vendors like EDS, and even established clearing banks like Barclays, are all competing as outsourcers of check-processing services in the United Kingdom. The availability of inexpensive computing, shared support, and outsourced software and services, all reduce the former advantages of large banks and reduce barriers to entry. This calls into questions previous strategies aimed at buying market share, for example, by buying another bank's credit card portfolio.

Alternative distribution channels. Technology also enables a wide range of alternative delivery systems. Just as ATMs provide alternatives to tellers and expensive "brick-and-mortar" branch networks for access to cash, newer technological developments may further erode the importance of branch networks. Branch networks require significant scale to justify secure buildings in convenient central locations, with a suitably impressive external façade. Electronic home banking, smart-card alternatives to cash and to ATMs, telecommunications-based banking kiosks, and other changes may significantly reduce the importance of scale; as important, they may be much less expensive than branch networks, both in absolute terms and in terms of costs per customer and costs per customer transaction. This further reduces barriers to entry and increases vulnerability of markets for banking services. Moreover, it diminishes the value of banks' investments in real estate and in traditional retail branch banking distribution networks. Similarly, changes in telecommunications technology make it possible to combine digital voice, digital data, and entertainment within a single connection, or local loop, into each home; this reduces the value of the local telephone companies' investments in copper local loop, while making it far easier for cable companies to attack with new, high-speed, integrated digital services.

Changes in customer preferences. Consumers are increasingly comfortable with information technology, and consequently increasingly willing to use alternatives to traditional banking. The recent acceptance of Intuit as a provider of home banking services in the United States, the general acceptance of direct debit as an alternative to checking for paying merchants and service providers in the United Kingdom, and the rapid increase in consumer acceptance of a variant of direct debit in France all suggest that the role of traditional banking services, and thus of branch networks and of traditional banks, may be changing. This acceptance of technological alternatives to traditional banks will facilitate moving customers away from their existing banking relationships and toward new entrants with new service distribution channels; this makes it easier to enter markets, since these new channels may also be much less expensive than branch networks, both in absolute terms and in terms of costs per customer and costs per customer transaction. This further reduces barriers to entry and increases vulnerability of markets for banking services. While adoption of alternative technology-based forms of distribution has not been fast historically, this move has been easiest with the most sophisticated segments of banking customers, which have also been among the banks' most profitable customers. Changes in customer preferences are occurring more slowly for travel services without traditional travel agents and for insurance through mail without traditional insurance agents; they are, however, already sufficient to have raised concerns among the largest travel service firms and insurance companies.

Regulatory change. Erosion of Glass-Steagall in the United States is making it easier for nonbanking financial institutions to attack banks and for banks to attack securities firms and insurance companies. The erosion of restrictions on interstate banking likewise encourages banks that are facing problems in their domestic markets to attack the most profitable segments of the market in other banks' regions. International restrictions on retail banks are being removed by reciprocity agreements such as the European 1992 Accords, which allow banks and other financial institutions that are licensed to operate in one country to operate on equal footing with domestic banks in all countries that are party to the agreement. In many instances, these regulatory changes would not lead to significant changes in the actual degree of competition, were it not for improvements in information technology. Deregulation of telecommunications in the United States in 1996 would not have been possible without technological improvements that permit interoperability, allowing companies to choose specific segments of telecommunications in which to compete. Similarly, given the scale-intensive nature of many banking and insurance operations, deregulation would not have led to changes in the degree of competition without technical outsourcing and other changes, as described.

Markets Are Attractive to Attack

Because it is now easier to attack many markets does not assure that competition will increase; new competitors will attack incumbents in their established markets if these markets are attractive to attack as well as easy to enter. Regulators and technological change have made it easier to attack many markets; the pricing policies of many established players, in a wide range of industries, contribute greatly to making their markets attractive to attack. Consumers vary greatly in the costs that their service providers incur by providing them service and in the revenues that they produce for them. This is equally true among customers for credit card services or for demand deposit banking products, for health insurance or life insurance, or for telecommunications services:

- Some banking customers maintain large balances, conduct few transactions, and seldom need assistance from tellers or account officers.

- Some health insurance clients have far better claims history than their fellow employees; others have worse family medical history and thus are far more expensive to serve.
- Some customers for telecommunications services live in cities, where the local loop running between their homes and the telephone company's central office switch can be quite short, and where numerous customers can be served with a single large-capacity cable or fiber; other customers live in remote and mountainous regions, and their local loop is long, expensive to install, and cannot be incorporated into that of neighbors.

And yet, historically dominant, established players have frequently followed very simple pricing strategies:

- Very few banks impose charges for teller usage, and virtually all banks in Britain and France practice uniform pricing for banking services such as checking; indeed all British and French consumers enjoy free checking privileges, even those who are consistently unprofitable for their banks to serve. Profitable accounts were subsidizing the banks' provision of banking services to unprofitable accounts, increasing the number of consumers who have access to banking services.
- All employees who select a particular health insurance plan are charged the same rates, despite their claims history and medical conditions (excluding certain preexisting medical conditions). This enabled insurance providers to offer service to all employees, both those with attractive claims histories and those that did not enjoy excellent health, and enabled all employees access to affordable insurance.
- In the interest of providing universal service for telephone customers, state regulators have encouraged significantly overcharging customers in urban areas to create profits that are used to subsidize telephone service for rural areas.

This has led to a significant gap between the *costs* of providing services to individual customers that were incurred by their bank or service providers and the *prices* that these customers were actually charged for these services. The greater this gap is for a market segment or an individual customer, the more attractive it will be for a new entrant to target this customer or segment. The greater the gap between cost and price, the greater the discount that the new entrant can offer (lower price), and the greater the remaining profit margin to the new service provider after the customer has been captured (gap between new price and cost for this customer). This gap may have been created for any of a variety of reasons:

- It may be the result of simplistic *historical pricing errors*. Until recently, it was extremely difficult for banks and credit card issuers to perform detailed customer profitability analyses.
- It may have been encouraged by the *historical near monopoly position of the service provider*. Before HMOs began to compete with Blue Cross to be the providers of employee health benefit plans, there was no need for Blue Cross to perform profitability analyses on individual households.
- It may be the result of *deliberate regulatory policy* aimed at encouraging universal access to banking, telephone services, or other entitlements. This enabled regulators to have the private sector provide the entitlements through implicit transfers that result from overcharging some consumers and undercharging others.

The policy of uniform pricing worked well for established players, for regulators, and for society, as long as all players in the market adhered to it. However, the attraction of the gap between costs and prices for some segments of the market and the ease of entry as described suggest these policies will have to be abandoned.

Moreover, information technology makes it possible for attackers to develop precise and accurate predictive models, based on publicly available economic and demographic data, to guide their targeted attacks on the most profitable market segments. Many established players have been slow to employ differential pricing and to use their historical transaction data from each customer; reluctantly, they have been forced to develop IT-based targeting measures to protect their customer base.

Indeed, as one major credit card issuer explained: "Once a competitor starts down the slippery slope of differential pricing, our only choices are to follow or to be forced out of the market!"

Restrictions on Established Players: The Uneven Playing Field

It would be natural to expect an established player, under attack by new entrants, to emulate the strategy of its attacker. That is:

- If an attacker relies upon new technology for alternative low-cost distribution or for distribution systems that are valued highly by the bank's most attractive customers, then the established defender should copy this distribution system, and begin to scale back its reliance upon traditional distribution. This would enable it to reduce its infrastructure and its fixed costs.
- If an attacker is focusing only on the best accounts, the defender should begin to shed its least attractive accounts; once again this would enable it to reduce its infrastructure and its fixed costs.
- If an attacker is charging differential rates, attacking the defender's best accounts while saddling the defender with loss-making business, then the defender should increase rates for unattractive customers while decreasing them for its best accounts in order to retain its most attractive business. Information embedded in transaction histories should always give the defender an advantage: The attacker is using demographic and economic data in predictive models to *guess* which accounts to target, while the defender is using actual history accumulated over several years and should *know* which accounts to defend.

External Commitments and Regulations

Unfortunately, each of these moves is more difficult than it might initially appear. As just noted, prior commitments and regulation are among the most important factors limiting the actions of large incumbents. There are also a variety of other factors that place the defender at a disadvantage:

- *It is difficult to abandon assets* that previously have been useful or valuable, or that previously have been seen as a measure of success. A senior vice president at a New York money center bank and his strategy consultant together closed over a hundred of the bank's branches, greatly improving the bank's profitability, and no doubt preserving the jobs of several senior officers. However, the decision to close branches was seen as very painful, and they report that "our senior colleagues are still gunning for us." Similarly, the investments of the Bell operating companies in billions of dollars worth of copper wiring may now be of very little value, since it is an ineffective way of providing digital data, digital telephone services, or high-quality image capability for the delivery of video entertainment, and represents an unacceptably high loss if this sunk asset needs to be written off. Likewise, insurance executives may find it extremely difficult to shed large and expensive agent-based distribution forces.
- *Regulators may limit options available to incumbents.* Regulators may have very little patience for an established player that wishes to shed its unattractive business. Universal service is often believed to be a social good; banking, telecommunications, and other services are often seen as entitlements, albeit entitlements that are provided by the private sector, and that dominant players may be forced to provide as part of the cost of their previous success. Similarly, in the insurance industry, regulators may wish to protect the highest risk segments of the market by maintaining their insurability, especially if their high risk is due to genetic factors outside their control, rather than due to avoidable behaviors such as smoking or alcohol consumption.

  Regulators and consumer activist organizations have made it very difficult to change the pricing structure of large players. Just as Nynex will be forced to continue offering rates in upstate New York that are below the true cost of providing service, large banks that have enjoyed significant market share may have to provide banking services to the poor and the elderly. Regulations like those prohibiting "red lining" make it difficult to close unprofitable branches. Consumer response, adverse publicity, and extremely unflattering press coverage make it difficult to impose fees for services that were previously provided without charge, especially if these fees are imposed on only some accounts. An account that represents a historical pricing error to the bank will on national television be portrayed as someone's grandparent, afraid of using an ATM, and unfairly denied access to a teller.

- *Contracts with customers also limit incumbents' options.* Service firms may be limited by contracts that they have created with their customers. In particular, pricing errors may be backed up by contracts that are binding on the service firm that issued them, but not binding on the customer; thus, the firm will have to honor them if the customer wishes, but the customer will be free to exit if he or she can get a better offer. Consequently, as attackers target the defender's best customers, existing contracts allow them to leave; these same contracts often do not allow the defender to drop or reprice existing accounts. Credit cards now allow for repricing when they are renewed, or automatically as interest rates change, allowing incumbents to respond when they are attacked. Thirty-year fixed-rate mortgages used to represent a significant risk to banks, but much of the risk appears to have been reduced by the move to variable rate mortgages. However, very few mortgage issuers appear to be using differential pricing, based on consumer attributes like risk or amount of the consumer's down payment; if new mortgage companies were to begin effective differential pricing, we might expect to see the best credit risks seeking to refinance their mortgages, while the remainder would of course choose to stay with their existing companies rather than pay the rates that would now be demanded in the marketplace. Similar examples can be found in life insurance and other service industries; indeed, members of the board of a major European financial services firm believe that one of the major advantages enjoyed by their new U.S. life insurance operations is its current lack of U.S. market share.

Internal Inflexibilities of Structure, Culture, and Vision

Not all restrictions on the options available to incumbents are externally imposed. The firms themselves create additional restrictions to their own ability to defend themselves:

- *Existing information infrastructure is often poorly suited to detailed customer profitability analyses,* making it extremely difficult to use historical transaction data to perform the studies needed to drive improved targeted customer pricing models.

   "I don't know whether $1.00 of marketing expenditure produces $1.00 of revenue or $2.00."

- *It is difficult to abandon customers,* or to abandon an even-handed policy of treating all customers equally.

   "You're suggesting that I charge one customer 8.9 percent APR and another customer 14.9 APR for the same type of credit card. I can't do that!"

- *It is difficult to reduce prices* at a time when profits are under pressure due to outside attack.

   "We brought you in to increase profits. Now you're suggesting that I give away 500 basis points for some of my accounts!"

- *The problem may not even be perceived correctly,* due to what George Day has termed "causal ambiguity." Firms are unlikely to respond correctly when they are unable to identify the strategic causes of their current problems.

THE NEED FOR A NEW REGULATORY VIEW

Regulation has not addressed the challenges of the new technology and the threat of cream skimming and death spirals. Much of regulatory policy in the United States has been directed at limiting the economic abuses of near-monopoly competitors.[4] This has been due to the historical experience with monopolists, and in turn due to the advantages they enjoyed due to economies of scale or to natural monopolies in bottleneck resources like the local loop that connected a subscriber's home to the telephone network. Consequently, regulatory policy is largely targeted at achieving economic efficiency by controlling the behavior of (apparently) dangerously dominant incumbents. Regulators are still fighting the ghosts of Standard Oil when the competitive environment has been fundamentally transformed. Now the regulations that were designed to protect consumers from the power of large incumbents are leaving these incumbents vulnerable to attack by smaller new entrants, even when these new entrants are less efficient and could not survive under a more even-handed regulatory regime.

Regulatory policy seeks to achieve the efficiency that would be achieved in a perfectly competitive market, despite the fact that the conditions of perfectly competitive markets (a large number of small firms, none able to set prices and all required to accept the prices set in the marketplace, no barriers to entry or exit, and no economies of scale) will not be achieved in any industry in need of regulation. A surrogate, *perfect contestability* is more easily modeled, and forms the basis of a regulatory policy that does the following:

- It establishes *ceiling prices,* based on prices that would be observed in perfectly contestable markets; the regulated player is not allowed to charge above these prices. By charging above these prices, manufacturers and suppliers are demonstrably overcharging, which is possible only in the absence of effective competition. The reasons for ceiling prices are (self evidently) to avoid exploitation of consumers in product markets that are not facing competitive threats.

116

- It establishes *floor prices,* below which the regulated player is not allowed to charge. This initially appears unnecessary as a regulatory tool. Undercharging, it is argued, over the long term is possible only if the regulated player is overcharging elsewhere. Thus, the reasons for floor prices are to prohibit the dominant player from cross-subsidizing threatened product markets via profits from other product markets that do not face competition, and thus to prohibit the incumbent from setting prices artificially low to discourage competitive entry, and making up losses by overcharging in other areas.

Note that this view of regulation is aimed at:

- Controlling the pricing behavior of the incumbent.
- Eliminating cross-subsidies *between product types* that are believed to discourage competition from more efficient new entrants.

Current regulatory change often requires a transition period in which the behavior of incumbents continues to be more closely regulated than that of new entrants. However, it is incumbents rather than new entrants that are at risk in newly vulnerable markets, as discussed previously. New entrants that operate less efficiently than incumbents can enter profitably simply because of the cross-subsidies *between accounts* that incumbents are required to maintain. This suggests a regulatory transition period in which the incumbents will be at a severe competitive disadvantage.

CONCLUSION: STRATEGIES AVAILABLE TO PREVIOUSLY DOMINANT FIRMS

We have shown that technology-driven shifts in the competitive environment have made it easier and more attractive for new entrants to attack, and harder for dominant incumbents to defend their once-secure markets. In particular, prior commitments, such as historical pricing, legally binding contracts, sunk investments in distribution systems, and past regulations have all limited the responses of incumbents. These changes have transformed the incumbents' former competitive advantages into competitive disadvantages.

Given these competitive disadvantages, how can established, dominant organizations respond effectively as their historical strengths are transformed into weaknesses? Clearly, the advantages of new entrants are structural, and cannot be attributed to complacency, to slow decision processes and slow reaction times, or to an outdated corporate culture of the incumbents. Indeed, the very factors that created and sustained the strength of dominant players may have become weaknesses that cannot easily be divested. New management teams and new strategies alone cannot begin to redress these structural problems. The following are suggestions that incumbents may pursue for developing an effective strategic response to cream skimming new entrants:

- *Cut costs.* Take actions to decrease costs, to improve the ability to withstanding the attack of a cream-skimming competitor. Recent megamergers in banking, like the merger of Chemical Banking and Chase Manhattan, are aimed at achieving increased efficiency through the consolidation of branch networks and the closing of duplicated facilities; thus, they may be seen as part of a cost control strategy that will buy both organizations additional time to respond. These are classic activities to survive market shakeout; alone, they will not be sufficient for dealing with competitors with structural advantages such as better costs due to alternative distribution and better revenues due to better selection of customers and better pricing of service offerings. In other industries, previously dominant incumbents have considered dramatically different cost-cutting strategies for surviving shakeout. The U.S. telecommunications companies with the widest distribution on the costs of providing local service have actually considered shedding their highest-cost regions, either selling them or actually giving them away, to escape the burden imposed by regulators' policies of uniform pricing.[5]
- *Develop alternative distribution systems,* including home banking, wireless distribution of local telephone service, or agentless distribution of insurance products. This entails a fundamental

reexamination of products and services that must be offered to different market segments, and of the means of distribution that will be most effective and least expensive for dealing with these customer segments. This may entail a very radical departure from strategies classically employed to survive industry shakeout. The chief executive of at least one major U.S. insurance company has concluded that new entrants with lower-cost alternative distribution systems will eventually force his company out of the market. He has decided to develop a direct distribution arm, to increase the chances that the attacker that eventually destroys his company will at least be owned by his company.

- *Take actions to increase pricing flexibility,* to facilitate emulating the strategy of cream skimming new entrants. This entails maintaining far better information on customers than is done in most service organizations, performing far better market research, and developing the databases and applications to support the development and targeting of new products and new services and to support new pricing strategies. This is becoming vitally important to banks, to securities firms, and even to stock exchanges as they prepare for increasing competition from electronic off-exchange dealing systems.[6]

- *Learn to lobby more effectively* for preservation of regulatory protection, restricting the ability of new entrants to attack the market. As was discussed in Chapter 3, much of regulatory policy has been informed by the structure of manufacturing telecommunications and heavy industry, and by their patterns of abuse in the late nineteenth and early twentieth centuries, modified to reflect current social and environmental concerns. As we discussed, however, there is little to suggest that the regulatory apparatus is well suited to protect the needs of the incumbent in a period of regulatory transition. This may imply that an activist regulatory policy should be a strategic concern of many firms. It suggests also that the absence of regulatory policy as a factor in most competitive industries models, and its absence from the list of board-level strategic decision areas, represent major gaps in our understanding and implementation of strategy. Moreover, Chapter 3 suggests analysis of regulatory windows, optimal times to exert necessary influence upon the regulatory process. Attempts at influencing regulatory policy are likely to be more effective if they can demonstrate, in terms that regulatory economists expect to see, that policies will have the unintended effect of encouraging reduced economic efficiency through the entry of inefficient cream skimmers. This is likely to be more effective than asserting the fundamental lack of fairness in an uneven playing field.

- *Learn to deal more effectively with the news media* and to present the case for differential pricing more effectively to the press. This may help assure that when incumbent banks impose fees and service charges on their unprofitable customers, or when local telecommunications providers cut rates in big cities and increase them in remote rural areas, it will be seen correctly as a defensive move aimed at protecting the firm and its shareholders from the attack of opportunistic new entrants who are freeloading in the market.

  Lobbying for continued regulatory protection may be a lost cause in many industries, including banking and local telecommunications services. However, if the social benefits of universal access were better and more effectively described, and the social costs of opportunistic new entrants were better understood, perhaps established players could achieve a phased regulatory shift, during which new entrants would be forced to absorb some of the costs of continuing universal service.

- *Learn to understand the profound threats and to manage the organizational resistance and risks associated with strategic change.*[7] A history of success reinforces a company's existing behaviors until they are enshrined as core competences and difficult to change. As companies—or, more precisely, their officers—learn what has worked in the past, it is difficult to change these behaviors, and difficult even to perceive the need to change. Early environmental signals of change will be weak, easily ignored, or outweighted by historical evidence, and these core competences will come to represent core rigidities; ultimately, they will become core incompetences. Seeing the threats will be difficult. Calling attention to these threats, and suggesting alternative courses of action that replace core competences and devalue existing skills, will be resisted; indeed, it will often be risky to suggest such change. Organizations will need to learn to sense their environments, recognize threats, and respond in ways that were not previously possible or necessary.

Above all, managers of dominant firms need to recognize the current challenges posed by technology-driven changes in the environment and anticipate future challenges that might arise. They need to be aware of the possibility that their current advantages may become liabilities. The sooner executives can recognize the impact of these changes, the more effectively they can begin to build the internal organizational structures and resources to meet them. And the earlier they can see these challenges, the sooner they can begin lobbying for changes in regulations that will reduce their strategic vulnerability.

PART II

ANTICIPATING COMPETITORS' ACTIONS

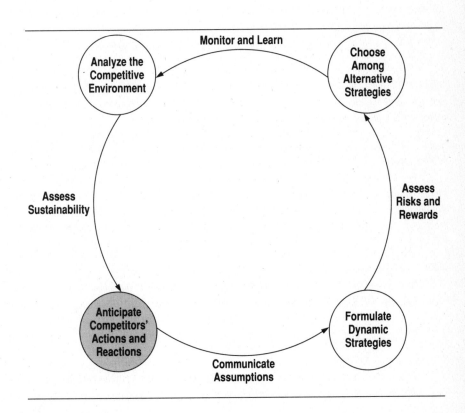

The first mover in a new market must decide how to respond to future potential entrants. If it lets other companies into the market, it will sacrifice part of its share. On the other hand, it has to invest to keep them out. How many entrants should it allow in and how much should it be willing to spend?

Southwest Airlines moved into the Baltimore-Washington market by initiating a fare war on several major routes. Two existing carriers—USAir and Continental—rose to the challenge and offered major discounts of their own. There followed 15 months of a bitterly fought price war. Why do companies engage in such no-win competitive battles? How can such price wars be avoided?

The senior vice president of a leading pharmaceutical firm faces a wide range of challenges, including managed care, price pressures, and competitors' mergers. How do managers cope with such complexity? How will competitors respond? And how do these mental models change over time?

The head of fixed income funds at a large investment company is developing strategies to gain a larger share of the bond funds market and increase fees. Among his options: he could decrease the load on the company's funds, raise management fees, maximize operating efficiencies, increase advertising, or acquire other boutique firms. But the challenge is that the success of his action depends on his rival's reactions. How can he better anticipate these reactions?

A U.S. company is planning to enter a foreign market. A key element in its decision process is to understand the nature of competitive relationships among the current local players. Is one of the firms the price leader? Do local players act competitively or in collusion? What is the pattern of relationships in the market and how will it affect the moves of the new entrant?

The success or failure of your strategy is not determined by your actions alone. The moves of rivals determine whether a price cut becomes a price war, whether a hot new advantage becomes a cost of doing business, whether a current position of strength becomes a position of weakness.

The following chapters examine these and other challenges from a variety of perspectives—including game theory, behavioral theory, and the view of coevolution. These chapters provide insights into the choices and mental models of rivals and help managers to anticipate the responses of competitors.

GETTING INSIDE THE HEADS OF COMPETITORS

But how do you know how your competitors will react to your strategies beforehand? How do you anticipate their next moves? You cannot peer inside the heads of the managers of a competitor, but there are a set of tools and approaches that can help you understand them. You first need to understand the nature of the competitive game. Who are the players? What are their relative costs and benefits (payoffs) for various moves? To understand these payoffs and possible moves, you have to understand the mind-sets of rivals—the rational and sometimes irrational forces that will shape their strategies. Finally, you need to understand how the nature of the game, the perceptions of rivals, and your own strategy are changed by successive interactions. As competitors learn and coevolve, they change their views of the game.

To understand the competitive game, we look to an approach that is gaining increasing currency among managers: game theory. Game theory looks at the definition of the competitive game and payoffs of different strategies. If all its other choices are suicidal, it may be pretty clear how a competitor will react to a given move. This allows you to see the best moves of your competitors, given your different options, and also to examine how these tradeoffs change over a series of moves. Chapter 5, which opens this part, provides an overview of game theory and its key uses and implications for managers in developing competitive strategy.

On the other hand, people are more complex than a simple model. As history amply demonstrates, they will not always be strictly "rational." They apparently will make suicidal moves. They will take unexpected risks or act in ways that may seem to be downright foolish—sometimes with surprisingly good results. The managers who are shaping your rivals' strategies are not automatons. Their decisions are shaped by their own biases, history, and views of the industry. Chapter 6 looks at the competitive game from the perspective of individual and group psychology. This behavioral approach examines what managers actually do and the many biases that influence their actions.

Even this view of the game is not fixed and unchanging. Competitors do not act and react the same way over time. Instead, they learn and change through the process of interacting. The mental models and the competitive situations of rivals change over time. Chapter 6 begins to examine this learning process and Chapter 7 offers a deeper perspective on it, which the authors call coevolution. They examine how this coevolutionary perspective can draw together the rational view of game theory and the psychological view of behavioral theory into a common framework. Coevolution is concerned with the interplay between companies and how their actions and perspectives on competition change and evolve as a result of their interactions.

Chapter 8 then discusses an empirical study that explores how competitors will react to your moves. If you take a certain action, how will they respond? Will they ignore it or fight aggressively? By analyzing competitive moves in the airline industry over a period of eight years, the authors provide practical insights into how the nature of the action, the nature of the rival, and the nature of the acting firm influence competitors' reactions.

Finally, the closing chapter of this section examines patterns of interaction that define competitive relationships in a given market. For example, some markets exhibit a clear pattern of leader-follower relationships. Others show a more independent movement while still others are collusive. Chapter 9 examines these three models of relationships and presents several tools that can be used to assess the nature of relationships in your industry. Understanding these patterns provides key insights into the expected moves of rivals.

Interaction with competitors is one of the key dynamics of competitive strategy. This interaction changes how you think about strategy. Through game theory, behavioral theory, and emerging insights of coevolution, you can gain a better understanding of the moves of competitors. This will help you to better understand their moves and reactions in developing and implementing your own competitive strategies.

CHAPTER 5

GAME THEORY AND COMPETITIVE STRATEGY

TECK HUA HO

University of California, Los Angeles,
Anderson Graduate School of Management

KEITH WEIGELT

The Wharton School, Department of Management

How can you understand the mind-sets of your rivals and anticipate their moves? Like players in a game, you and rivals affect one another by your actions. The outcome of this game and the best strategies depend on how the game is defined and played. What are the payoffs for a given strategy? How do these payoffs change over the course of multiple moves by the players? Given these payoffs, what is your best move and what are the likely moves of your competitors? This chapter examines the application of game theory to competitive strategy, providing an overview of key aspects of game theory and showing how they are related to fundamental and timeless strategic principles.

In his seminal strategic treatise, *The Art of War,* Sun Tzu writes: "Thus, it is said that one who knows the enemy and knows himself will not be endangered in a hundred engagements. One who does not know the enemy but knows himself will sometimes be victorious, sometimes meet with defeat. One who knows neither the enemy nor himself will invariably be defeated in every engagement."

Game theory provides a formal methodology for knowing oneself and one's competitors. It helps analyze and anticipate the strategic moves of rivals. It also shows how a firm's actions and those of its competitors are interrelated, linked by a strategic umbilical cord. This chapter introduces basic concepts of game theory and then uses them to examine key strategic principles. In exploring these principles, we show how game theory can be applied to issues such as interpreting signals, sequential market entry, setting production quantities, and reputation.

GAME THEORY'S 2,500-YEAR MARCH INTO THE BOARDROOM

The principles of game theory were applied by Chinese military planners 2,500 years ago. Modern economists expanded and formalized these principles. Game theorists recently celebrated their first half-century by winning the 1994 Nobel prize in economics. While this award illustrates game theory's maturing as an economic discipline, the usefulness of game theory in business strategy has only recently begun to be recognized.

Similar to more common tools such as BCG's Strengths-Weaknesses-Opportunities-Threats (SWOT) analysis or Porter's five forces model, game theory is a tool of strategic analysis. We show how managers can use game theory to:

1. Create a common language for modeling strategic situations.
2. Classify situations and transfer strategic insights across contexts (e.g., markets, products, organizations).
3. Channel resources only to assets that significantly improve the firm's competitive market position.
4. Generate specific prescriptions if enough relevant information is available. For example, game theory has been used in bidding an optimal price for bandwidth channels in the recent FCC auction; deciding whether to enter a new product market and choosing whether to issue an affinity credit card.

Even if parameters are not known exactly, game theory can help classify strategic situations, which is often a critical step in strategic planning. This classification may either offer new insights or simply confirm those already known. Game theorists have studied extensively many categories or classes of games, and have developed strategic insights about game parameters. A celebrated example is the Prisoner's Dilemma game, whose key insight is that individually rational action can hurt the group as a whole. This insight has been applied, but not restricted to, strategic situations such as price wars, intrafirm cooperation, and international trade.

Because game theory is a model with restrictive assumptions, some managers question its relevance to real competitive situations. All formal models require some simplification of reality to be used. Even for skeptics, however, game theory generates core strategic principles and insights that belong in the toolbox of all managers. Further, game theory provides a method of formal analysis of these principles.

This chapter provides an introductory review of game theory for the layperson.[1] After a brief discussion of key concepts of game theory, we examine several strategic principles through the lens of game theory. These principles can help analyze many recurrent issues in competitive analysis, including cooperative and noncooperative behavior, trade-offs between individual and group goals, short- and long-term payoffs, and altruistic and self-interested behaviors.

KEY CONCEPTS OF GAME THEORY

Any strategic analysis should create a common mental model of the underlying strategic situation. It is difficult to communicate ideas among managers if they do not share the same mental model. Because of the exactness of its language, game theory is useful in precisely describing strategic situations. The theory uses visual representations and a unique set of terms to describe situations; this enforces the creation of a common mental model among managers. Thus, game theory provides a consistent framework for structuring competitive decision problems. This structuring process, in turn, focuses managerial attention on relevant competitive factors and helps configure a firm's resource base for strategic advantage.

In this chapter, we provide a rudimentary "vocabulary lesson" so readers unfamiliar with game theory can follow our examples. (Those familiar with the theory should feel free to skip this section.) Game theorists *visually* represent strategic situations in one of two related ways. Figure 5.1 shows a situation where two firms (A and B) are introducing a product and must decide whether to advertise. This representation is called a *normal* or *matrix form* game. Consider it a summary of the strategic situation. It identifies all players (Firms A and B), their available strategies (advertise or not), and payoffs associated with all consequences (if Firm A advertises, and B doesn't, then A receives a payoff of 9, and B a payoff of 7).[2]

Figure 5.2 shows the same strategic situation in an *extensive form game*. Extensive form games illustrate all the information of normal form games (players, available strategies, consequences, and associated payoffs), but add a time dimension. Specifically, they show whether the game is a simultaneous or sequential move game (any normal form game is one of simultaneous moves).

The game in Figure 5.2a, is a simultaneous move game: Decision nodes are represented by squares, and random shocks by circles. The dotted line linking Firm B's decision nodes represent an *information set*— managers at Firm B do not know whether they are at the left (Firm A advertises) or right (Firm A does not advertise) decision node. So they must select their action without knowing Firm A's choice. Thus their moves are simultaneous. Even if both players do not move at the same time, they act "as if" they do because they do not know the choices of the others.

Figure 5.1
An Advertising Game

Firm B		Firm A	
		Advertise	Don't Advertise
	Advertise	11, 6	16, 1
	Don't Advertise	7, 9	21, 3

Figure 5.2
Extensive Form Game

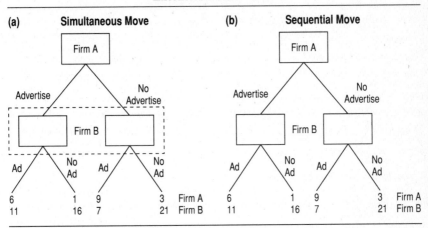

Figure 5.2b shows a sequential move game. Note that the only difference is the absence of a dotted line linking B's decision nodes in Figure 5.2b. This indicates that B's managers know A's decision before choosing their strategy. Thus, their moves are sequential.

A Strategic Umbilical Cord

As indicated in Figures 5.1 and 5.2, strategic situations are characterized by interactive payoffs—one player's actions affect the payoffs of others. For example, in Figure 5.1, if managers at Firm A choose to advertise, they realize either a payoff of 6 or 9, depending on whether B's managers advertise. This interdependency is prevalent across strategic situations. Game theory's capacity to analyze strategic situations lies in its explicit recognition of the mutual interdependence of players (because of interactive payoffs). So, in strategic situations, managers must consider themselves connected by a strategic umbilical cord: No independent optimal strategic choice exists; optimality is conditional on the actions of others. One player's actions can cause others to change their actions, and vice versa. Hence, managers need to understand the strategic perception of others; that is, what characteristics do others ascribe to the situation, and how do these characteristics affect their strategy choices?

For managers, a key implication of game theory's focus on interactive payoffs is that strategic planning is a process-based function. Because the strategic umbilical cord ties you to others, as you move, you move others, and vice versa. Strategic situations are never static; they continually evolve. If managers recognize the relevant strategic variables, then any disadvantage is an opportunity; any success, a potential failure. Within the sphere of strategic interdependence, you shape the future.

Equilibrium Strategies

A distinct feature of game theory is its prescriptive power: It identifies which strategies players should choose by designating equilibrium strategies. Equilibrium strategies are characterized by three traits: stability, optimality, and rationality. First, no player has an incentive to unilaterally shift from its equilibrium strategy. Second, it is a strategy of mutual best response: My action choice is optimal given others choose their optimal choices. Third, all players are rational and believe others are rational. The most commonly used equilibrium concept is the Nash equilibrium, an array of strategies (or action choices) such that each player believes he or she is doing the best he or she possibly can, given the actions of others.[3]

In Figure 5.1 the Nash equilibrium is that both firms advertise. One can interpret this as a prediction regarding the future strategies of each firm, assuming that each firm will try to maximize its payoff. If both firms advertise, then Firm B has no incentive to shift to another strategy. If B shifts to "Don't advertise," it would earn a payoff of 7 instead of 11. The same reasoning holds true for Firm A. If Firm A shifts to "Don't advertise," its payoff is 1 instead of 6. So by advertising, each firm is doing the best it can, given the other is doing the best it can.

Equilibrium strategies depend on the configurations of players' strategic states. We define a strategic state along four dimensions:

1. *The feasible strategy set.* The set of possible strategies for the player. Managers may shift equilibria by enlarging their feasible

strategy set. That is, they may play strategies that were previously assigned a zero probability. For example, before Frank Perdue differentiated his chicken via a brand name, managers in that industry had assigned a zero probability to a differentiation strategy. Or, when John D. Rockefeller entered the oil industry, it was regarded as a commodity business with low-profit margins. Using a strategy of vertical integration, Rockefeller shifted the equilibrium and was handsomely rewarded for it.

2. *Information flows.* The flow of information also affects the structure of the game. First, is information perfect or imperfect? This relates to our earlier discussion of sequential or simultaneous moves. If information is perfect, then managers recognize previous moves of others (i.e., a sequential move game); if information is imperfect, managers do not completely know the previous actions of others (i.e., a simultaneous move game). Obviously, this type of uncertainty can affect strategic choice. Is information complete or not? In a complete information setting, players know (with certainty) all strategic configuration dimensions (e.g., payoffs, feasible strategy sets, identities of players, and so on). Information is incomplete if some uncertainty exists among players about relevant strategic variables. When this occurs, players may have different mental models regarding the strategic situation. Any information gathering that helps reduce this uncertainty may help managers in choosing a strategy.

3. *Payoffs.* Payoffs are the level of rewards that players receive from a given outcome. For example, in Figure 5.1, if both firms advertise, Firm A receives a payoff of 6 and B a payoff of 11. A player's payoff depends on its underlying preference function, so different players can realize different reward levels from identical consequences. Because the reward level depends on the subjective preferences of the manager, managers can shift equilibria (i.e., change the strategy choice of others) by changing the reward level associated with an action. For example, preemptive entry into a market can change the payoff associated with the subsequent market entry of others.

Payoff structures can define strategic situations; for example, zero-sum game versus nonzero-sum games. In a zero-sum game, the total payoff space shared by players remains constant. So any gain by one player must result in a loss to another player. This is typical of many bargaining situations. In nonzero-sum games, the payoff space varies. When the payoff space is increasing (as in high-growth markets), all players can increase their payoffs.

4. *Players.* Both the number of players and their identities are important. As the number of players change, payoffs to individual players may also change. For example, in forming strategic alliances, identities are important because of the subjective nature of payoffs. A payoff not highly valued by one player may be highly valued by others.

A situation's strategic configuration can significantly affect the underlying nature of the interaction. Game theorists have developed a classification scheme of games that can be used to identify important types of strategic situations. We describe some classes of these in the following discussion of several strategic principles.

STRATEGIC PRINCIPLES

Although game theory has much more depth and complexity than presented in the preceding brief overview, perhaps its greatest power is in presenting very simple, but crucial, strategic principles. The importance of strategic principles, which we illustrate with game theoretic models, were recognized by Chinese philosophers 2,500 years ago and are contained in the seven military classics.[4] Principles expounded in the military classics were considered so valuable that the unauthorized possession of a classic was punishable by death. At the time these books were written, China consisted of a collection of individual states, each striving to survive in a very competitive environment. Alliances between states were perpetually changing, and there was a constant threat of war. The Chinese belief that there is no distinction between theory and application meant strategic principles were well tested.

So, while the techniques available to strategists have certainly improved, both in the sophistication of modeling (e.g., game theory, decision analysis) and analytic power (computers versus Chinese "counting sticks"), the importance of these principles remains constant. Given this consistency, we use insights of classic Chinese philosophy to help explain their more formal game theoretic interpretations.

Principle 1: Use Strategic Foresight

Unlike Westerners, the Chinese did not define knowledge as a mapping from theory to objective reality; their knowledge was the ability to trace out or unravel a strategic situation. Today we might characterize this as *strategic foresight;* game theory can be used to analyze future competitive actions. It is the ability to analyze a strategic situation, anticipate where it is going, and then make decisions today that will favorably affect future payoffs (since strategy is a process). Thus knowledge corresponds to controlling the dynamics of the strategic situation—we shape the future by manipulating strategic variables. The Chinese refer to this ability as "taking care of the great, while the great is small." Game theorists call this ability *backward induction.*

Example: Credible and Noncredible Signals. When managers of a firm state their intention to do something, should they be believed? Backward induction can help determine whether the signal is truly in line with the payoffs of the action. For example, when a firm acquires another firm, managers at the acquiring firm (Firm 1) may fear that managers at the acquired firm (Firm 2) will fight relentlessly if their autonomy is threatened. So managers at Firm 1 publicly promise to adopt a hands-off policy and give managers at Firm 2 autonomy. If managers at Firm 2 believe this promise, they acquiesce to a friendly takeover. However, the promise is not credible, as shown in Figure 5.3.

The acquisition scenario is the following: Managers at Firm 2 must decide whether to agree to a friendly takeover, or fight it. If they fight (R) they realize a payoff of 1 (because they keep their independence), and managers at Firm 1 realize a payoff of 1 (because they don't incur the costs of a hostile takeover). If they agree to a takeover (L), then

Figure 5.3
Acquisition Game

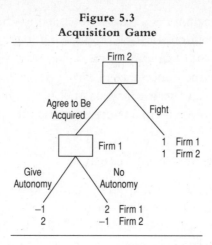

managers at Firm 1 must choose their strategy. They can keep their promise and give autonomy to Firm 2 (L). Then managers at Firm 1 realize a payoff of -1 because even though they paid for Firm 2, they cannot impose their preferences, control, and monitoring systems, and more on it. However, managers at Firm 2 realize a payoff of 2 since they both have their freedom and the use of Firm 1's resources. Or, managers at Firm 1 can renege on their promise (R), and not give managers at Firm 2 their autonomy. Now managers at Firm 1 realize a payoff of 2, since they induced Firm 1's managers to agree to a friendly takeover, and now they can impose their monitoring, control, and incentive systems on them. Conversely, managers at Firm 2 realize a payoff of -1, since they forgo their managerial freedom. If you were a manager at Firm 1, which payoff would you choose?

Game theorists suggest managers use backward induction to solve this game. That is, a manager should go to the game's end and trace out what each player should do along the "choice path." For example, if managers at Firm 1 reach their decision node, what will they do? They could either give autonomy and realize a payoff of -1, or not give it and realize a payoff of 2. Clearly, they prefer a payoff of 2 over -1, so they will not give autonomy.

But, from Figure 5.3 we clearly see that managers at Firm 2 would agree to a takeover (move left) only if they thought they would receive a payoff of 2 (managers at Firm 1 give them autonomy). If they did not believe the promise, they are clearly better off retaining their freedom (a payoff of 1 versus -1).

So if they use strategic foresight (i.e., backward induction), they should not believe the promise by Firm 1's managers (since it is not credible). Good strategic players should always anticipate the future actions of others—they must consider future moves in choosing today's strategy. Managers who are myopic do not anticipate the future, because they fail to realize the processlike nature of strategy. Such managers may make good short-run decisions, but may not be as successful in the long run, because they lack strategic foresight.

This dynamic can be seen in many actual examples of corporate acquisitions. For example, just 99 days after IBM spent $3.5 billion to acquire Lotus, Jim Manzi, the CEO of Lotus quit because of differences about managerial control. The *Wall Street Journal* noted that ". . . IBMers grumbled that Mr. Manzi campaigned in the press to win broader powers inside the company," and that IBM could be hurt by ". . . disarray and disruption in Mr. Manzi's wake—more executive departures, delays in development . . ."[5]

Lotus was not alone. AT&T spent $7.48 billion in 1990 to acquire NCR. Five years later, it took a $1.2 billion charge, laid off 10,000 employees, and lost $500 million in a nine-month period. Another *Wall Street Journal* article stated, "[AT&T] let many top NCR executives exit, then rankled an embittered and balky workforce and hostile management by imposing its own culture on the new property."[6]

Finally, in 1995, ITT paid $1.7 billion for Caesar's World Inc. In June 1995, CEO Henry Gluck, the man responsible for building Caesar's, quit. He said the ". . . breakup happened faster than he expected and left him with a more diminished role than he had anticipated."[7]

Could these outcomes have been predicted through the use of strategic foresight?

Example: Sequential Market Entry.   Another area in which backward induction can be useful is in anticipating how many firms will enter a market. Performance measures such as capacity utilization, market growth, and prices are influenced by entry by others. In some markets, firms enter sequentially. As more firms enter the market, per-firm profits generally decrease.[8]

Table 5.1 offers a stylized example of the impact of market entry. It shows the profits per firm (think of these as the present value of the future earning stream) for one firm and for all players if other firms enter. When there is only one firm in the market, it earns $20 million. If two firms enter the market, then competition drives per-firm profits to $16 million.

Entrants enter sequentially. Customers exhibit brand loyalty, so incumbents can use advertising to deter entry. To enter, an entrant must spend twice the total spent on advertising by an individual incumbent firm. Assume all incumbent firms provide the same level of advertising. For example, if two firms are in the market, and they each spend $5 million on advertising, an entrant must spend $10 million on advertising to successfully enter the market.

How many firms will enter the market and how much should Firm 1 spend to keep others out? The profits in Table 5.1 are gross before any spending on advertising. To act as a deterrent, advertising must

Table 5.1
Sequential Entry Game

Number of Firms	Profits per Firm ($ millions)
1	20
2	16
3	7.5
4	—

be directed against a specific entrant. Hence, if Firm 1 tries to keep out Firm 2 and fails, its advertising cost is considered sunk and nonsalvageable. If you are the manager of the incumbent firm (Firm 1), how many firms should you expect to enter the market, and what is the net per-firm profit?

Most individuals respond that two firms will enter the market, and their net profits will be $12.25 million. They reason that if two firms enter the market, each must spend $3.75 million (one-half of $7.5 million) to keep out the third entrant. Their net profits will thus be $12.25 million (16 − 3.75). If the first firm wants to keep out the second firm, the first firm must spend $8 million (one-half of $16 million). Its net profit would equal $12 million. So it is better for the first firm ($12.25 million versus $12 million) to let the second firm enter the market and share the cost of keeping out the third firm. Unfortunately, this reasoning is wrong, because it doesn't use backward induction.

The correct way to view the situation is if the first firm lets the second enter the market, then the per-firm profit is $12.25 million. But if the first firm wants to prevent the second firm from entering the market, it only has to spend $6.125 million, not $8 million. For if the second firm enters the market, it is looking at a payoff of $12.25 million, not $16 million (see Table 5.1). Managers at the second firm should realize if they enter the market, they will have to spend $3.75 million to keep out the third entrant ($16 − 3.75 = $12.25 million). So Firm 1 is better off spending the money on advertising to keep out the second firm ($20 − 6.125 = $13.88 million). Hence, using strategic foresight, only one firm should enter this market, not two.

Both the acquisition and advertising examples illustrate the importance of strategic foresight. Managers have to realize they must think about the future when making today's decisions: In both examples, strategic actions taken early in the game affect later behavior. Because of the interdependence between players, managers can control the strategic situation, and help determine its future path.

Given the importance of this principle, it is imperative that managers be taught to think about the long-term implications of decisions.[9] Simple game theoretic examples like these may encourage managers to think more about these long-term implications.

Principle 2: Know Yourself as Well as Others

As noted in the preceding examples, many strategic decisions depend on understanding the structure of the game and the payoffs from the view of the competitor. In other words, it is important "to be sure you are playing the right game." Managers who successfully use game theory create models that mirror reality—their models capture the essential elements of the actual strategic situation.

Many managers underestimate the difficulty of this task, and fail to carefully construct models. Most managers learn game theory through examples like those in the preceding figures, where payoffs are given and feasible strategy sets and players are specified. In real strategic situations, determining these payoffs, players, strategy sets, and other factors is half the battle. Information is not perfect and complete as it is in most examples.

Most individuals are trained to solve game theory models, but receive scant formal training in constructing them. This is unfortunate, for much of game theory's strategic value is derived from forcing managers to correctly model the strategic situation. Given the evidence of the poor decision-making abilities of individuals, discussed by Meyer in the following chapter, managers should engage in a disciplined process of constructing a game model of their strategic situation.[10] To construct these models, managers must specify the number and identity of players, feasible strategy sets, and underlying preference functions. And, most important, they must specify both their beliefs and those of others regarding these strategic dimensions. This is why Principle 2 is so important.

Many times it is said that game theory forces you to view the situation from the viewpoint of others. This is a half-truth, and like many half-truths its use will produce suboptimal results. What game theory suggests you do is to view the situation as others do. In *The Book of Five Rings,* the famous samurai warrior Musashi states: "Small men must know thoroughly what it is like to be big men, and big men must know what it is like to be small men."

If you are to think like others, you must adopt their mind-set. Musashi was discussing sword fighting, where small men use different strategies (e.g., quickness, maneuverability) relative to big men (e.g., strength, reach) because each relies on different resources. So if a big man anticipates the moves of a smaller opponent without adopting his mind-set, he will likely be wrong (with fatal consequences), because he will anticipate the moves of a big man.

Similarly, in today's business world, many entrepreneurs have different mental models from managers at Fortune 500 firms. Managers at large firms have different resource bundles, incentive plans, decision-making procedures, and so on. When the large firms treat their opponents like large firms, they are often surprised when these nimble entrepreneurs outmaneuver them. Even managers at firms that diversify into new markets often have initial difficulties because they haven't grasped an understanding of their rivals' mind-sets.

Because of the strategic umbilical cord of interactive payoffs connecting a firm to other players, a manager cannot know him- or herself well unless he or she knows others well. One's strengths and weaknesses are defined relative to those of others. Some managers have difficulty "knowing themselves" because they must recognize both their strengths and weaknesses (and those of their organizations). Managers often overlook weak points and focus on strengths. Those who ignore weaknesses find it difficult to be successful strategists. Since managers should pit strengths against others' weaknesses, weaknesses must be recognized to identify vulnerable areas.

Example: Production Quantity Game. Figure 5.4 is a game-theoretic example of why Principle 2 is important. It illustrates a simple quantity-type (i.e., Cournot) game. You and a rival share the market. While you know your cost function with certainty, you are unsure about your rival's costs. Figure 5.4a shows the situation where your cost function is higher, relative to that of your rival. Figure 5.4b shows the opposite situation.

Game theory suggests if your strategic situation is that represented in Figure 5.4a, you should produce low quantities of the good (and your rival, high quantities). If the strategic situation more closely resembles that in Figure 5.4b, you should produce high quantities of the good (and your rival, low quantities). So the predicted optimal strategy is

Figure 5.4
A Production Quality Game

(a) High-Cost

		You	
		Produces High Quantities	Produces Low Quantities
Your Rival	Produces High Quantities	4, 1	8, 4
	Produces Low Quantities	1, 5	3, 3

(b) Low-Cost

		You	
		Produces High Quantities	Produces Low Quantities
Your Rival	Produces High Quantities	2, 2	5, 1
	Produces Low Quantities	4, 8	3, 3

conditional on the characteristics of you and your rival, namely who has the higher cost function. The absolute level of the cost function is of less strategic importance than the function's relative level.[11]

This example again illustrates the strategic value of constructing payoff matrices (even for simplified situations). Once you know whether your cost function is relatively higher or lower, choosing the optimal strategy is straightforward. The difficulty is in deciding your cost level, relative to that of rivals. Many times, this requires a lot of thought about the strategic situation, including rational reasons (or evidence) about why you think your cost function is lower (or higher) than those of rivals.

Benchmarking studies are one way managers heed the advice of Principle 2. These studies provide a measure of a firm's performance relative to that of others. For example, Motorola initiated the six-sigma program as a result of benchmarking vis-à-vis Japanese companies. Benchmarking studies help motivate organizations to move to new goals and to "convince" agents of the feasibility of such goals. In this sense, through benchmarking studies, managers use the principle of knowing others and themselves to motivate organizational improvements. However, managers must also recognize the principle's value in formulating strategy. It is this use that creates the most strategic value.

Sometimes it is impossible to determine all the attributes of a competitive game. Uncertainty about others' characteristics is the norm for most business-related strategic situations. Although this uncertainty does complicate modeling, game theory can help managers think about its implications. When managers are uncertain about attributes of others, they can use *incomplete information game models.* These models assume managers hold different information sets about game parameters (e.g., payoffs, player attributes, and so on). Because managerial beliefs are dependent on information sets, and beliefs affect strategic choice, managers must consider the beliefs of others. As previously shown, if I think my costs are lower than my rival's, I will choose a different strategy than if I think they are higher. If one player has lower relative costs, but its managers believe it has higher costs, they will act accordingly.[12]

Principle 3: Differentiate between One-Time and Repeated Interactions

Many times, game theory prescribes different behaviors for identical strategic situations depending on whether the game is played once or repeatedly. Repeated interaction increases the strategy space and allows today's strategy to depend on past history. The Chinese recognized this and summarized it in the following principle: "When there is trust in verbal agreements, the trust is there before the words."

For instance, in repeated play, a penalty for past uncooperative behaviors can be built into the current strategy. Because of this strategy space expansion, prescriptions for optimal behavior can change. For example, in a single-shot Prisoner's Dilemma game, the optimal response is to "defect." If players were to play the same game repeatedly, then it could be optimal to exhibit cooperative behavior— if players care about future payoffs, since any defective behavior could be penalized in the future.[13]

Repeated interaction also can change the ways firms behave in incomplete information games. Next we show how managers can use corporate reputations to generate future rents.

Example: Reputation. Firm B is the dominant player in a growing market it developed. Your firm, Firm A, is one of several thinking about entering B's market. Imagine you are a manager at Firm A, and you must decide whether to enter B's market. You are unsure about some characteristics of managers at Firm B. These managers may be "weak types" who would rather share their market with you than start a price war. Or they may be "tough types" who do not want to share, and are willing to start a price war to keep you out. These two scenarios are shown in Figure 5.5. Looking at the figure, your decision is straightforward—if you know the incumbent's true type. If the incumbent is a weak type, you enter the market; if it is tough, you don't enter.[14]

This is an example of why Principles 2 and 3 are so important. The more you know about rivals, the better you can anticipate their next move and use this information in choosing your action. In this example, if the rival is weak, enter: if tough, stay out.

However, when uncertain about characteristics of others, managers form beliefs about them. Managers at Firm B should exploit the uncertainty. If they are smart (though weak), they recognize the incentive to mimic the behavior of tough types. If they do (i.e., start a price war), they may convince other entrants they are actually tough and not enter. And why is this convincing? Because when uncertain, we seek

Figure 5.5
Type of Incumbent

(a) Weak

		You (Entrant)	
		Enter Market	Do Not Enter
Incumbent	Share Market	2, 2	6, 1
	Start Price War	0, 0	5, 1

(b) Tough

		You (Entrant)	
		Enter Market	Do Not Enter
Incumbent	Share Market	−1, 2	3, 1
	Start Price War	1, 0	7, 1

information to resolve the uncertainty. We infer a player's type from available information; that is, we look for "signals" about types. (These signals are discussed in more detail in Chapter 12.) One signal is past behavior—we infer future behavior by examining past behavior. This behavioral history is what game theorists call *reputation*.

By acting tough against early entrants, managers at Firm B establish a reputation for being tough. This reputation then generates future rents because it causes later entrants not to enter. Although costly in the short run, the mimicry of tough types by weak ones is profitable in the long run (given reasonable assumptions about discount rates and time horizons).[15]

There are many examples of reputation-building behavior in markets, usually by firms that are admired for their management skills. Procter & Gamble has clearly cultivated the image of being a tough competitor, by forcefully responding to any entry into its markets. Intel is currently establishing a "tough type" reputation in the chip market. It seems determined to hold its leadership position at all costs. Between 1990–1995, Frito-Lay expanded its market share in salty snacks from 43 percent to 52 percent. The *Wall Street Journal* noted: "[Frito-Lay] continues to expand its realm. I'd tell anyone else trying to get into the business, don't try to expand, don't try to impinge on Frito's territory or you'll get crushed."[16]

Reputation models help explain many aspects of strategic planning. Besides entry deterrence, they can explain why producers use noninformative advertising to signal the quality of their products, the widespread use of consulting and accounting firms, and even corporate culture.[17] Repeated interactions thus change the competitive game because managers change their perceptions after each round. Also, payoffs for a single round of play may be very different from those of multiple-round games, so it is important to understand at the outset whether the game is one-time or repeated.

Principle 4: Managers Must Unify Minds to Promote Cooperation

We have focused on competitive strategic situations. In business, these are commonly represented by interfirm interactions. However, game theory is also useful in analyzing cooperative behaviors—either within firms or within alliances among different firms. In these situations, the emphasis is on promoting cooperative behavior.

All the Chinese classics discuss how important, yet difficult, the "planning" of cooperation is. As one classic notes, "As for the Tao of the military, nothing surpasses unity." Or, as Napoleon more recently remarked, "In war, morale is to materials as 3 is to 1." Unfortunately, many managers underestimate the significant difficulty of building cooperation within groups. Simple game theory models pinpoint the source of difficulty.

The Chinese model of unity is based on mutual trust. Individuals sacrifice personal goals for group goals when they "commit" to a group goal. Individually, though, the question is, "Yes, I'll sacrifice as much as you, but how do I know you are sacrificing the same as I?" Unless everyone trusts others to be as committed as they to group goals, support for group commitment is incomplete. Mutual trust is not.

Figure 5.6 shows why. Group members choose an "effort contribution" toward group goals represented by seven numbered levels. Your payoff depends on your contribution and those of others. Contribute significantly less than others, you free-ride off them; significantly more, they off you. Individuals want to coordinate their effort with that of others.

All players should select the maximum effort level of 7, since everyone realizes the highest possible payoff ($5.00). No player can possibly receive a higher payoff by choosing any other effort level. So if players want to coordinate their effort with that of others, then everyone should want to coordinate on 7.

The key caveat to this thinking is that you must trust others to provide their maximum effort, for if they don't and you do, your payoff is negative: They simply free-ride off your effort. So if you don't trust others to give maximum effort, you hesitate to give yours. And if group members think this way, they choose a suboptimal effort level. This line of thinking results in organizations where members give effort levels of say 3 or 4. This results in mediocre performing organizations or alliances; mediocrity sets in because of a lack of mutual trust.

Substantial empirical evidence shows the modal response to this game is 4.[18] One question research has addressed is: How does one measure group effort? Some studies use the median effort of players: If there are

Figure 5.6
The Median Effort Game

		Group						
		7	6	5	4	3	2	1
	7	$5.00	−$2.00	−$2.50	−$3.00	−$3.50	−$4.00	−$4.50
	6	$4.75	$4.50	−$2.00	−$2.50	−$3.00	−$3.50	−$4.00
	5	$4.50	$4.25	$4.00	−$2.00	−$2.50	−$3.00	−$3.50
You	4	$4.25	$4.00	$3.75	$3.50	−$2.00	−$2.50	−$3.00
	3	$4.00	$3.75	$3.50	$3.25	$3.00	−$2.00	−$2.50
	2	$3.75	$3.50	$3.25	$3.00	$2.75	$2.50	−$2.00
	1	$3.50	$3.25	$3.00	$2.75	$2.50	$2.25	$2.00

seven group members, group effort is equal to the group's median choice. Using this measure of group effort, the modal choice across studies is 4.

However, some believe corporations are better represented by minimum effort games. This is the view that the chain is only as strong as its weakest link, so group effort is equal to the lowest level selected by any member. Getting a product to the final consumer involves several functional areas: purchasing, manufacturing, design, engineering, manufacturing, distribution, service, and more. If only one person performs poorly, then the entire organization is blamed. So if you receive poor service, you tend to blame the organization, not the individual serviceperson.

When minimum effort games are played, the modal response is lower than 4. Trust is even more important in these games because if only one group member chooses low effort, the entire group is punished. And, while many managers recognize the importance of trust-building, most organizations have a difficult time building trust among agents.[19] And this trust-building can be even more difficult across organizations.

Our example illustrates that game theory's strategic value is not limited to competitive strategic situations. It is also useful in modeling strategic situations where cooperation and coordination are optimal strategies. In addition to formal modeling, game theory can be used as a powerful training device to show group members the consequences of not building mutual trust.

CONCLUSION

As shown in the preceding examples, game theory provides a variety of insights to competitive strategy. It helps managers understand and apply key strategic principles such as those discussed. Further, game theory can be used for more detailed modeling and analysis of these principles and the competitive situation.

Our overview of principles and applications of game theory for strategic analysis emphasized the situational dependency of any strategy. Understanding and anticipating the moves of rivals—the payoffs and players and their perceptions—determines the structure of the game, and, ultimately, its outcome. The rightness or wrongness of a strategy depends on the situation. There is no optimal strategy across all strategic situations. Because of this situational dependency, strategic planning is an evolving process. If you don't like your current situation, you have the power to change it.

By changing in a strategic situation, you change others. There is a strategic umbilical cord connecting you to others. As they move, you move, and vice versa. Game theory explicitly models this dependency via interactive payoffs. And it identifies strategies that help managers anticipate the moves of rivals and improve their payoffs.

The four strategic principles we discussed are important in shaping strategy, whether or not formal game theoretic models are used to analyze the strategic situation. The first principle is that managers must possess strategic foresight and be able to look ahead. Only by doing so can they configure their resource base in the most advantageous position for the future. Next, we stressed managers must know themselves and their competitors. This principle follows since a manager's payoff in any strategic situation depends on the company's strategic state relative to that of others. The third principle highlights the importance of recognizing the difference between one-time and repeated interaction in strategic situations. Finally, we stressed the importance of coordination in an organization. Only when managers unify their minds can their organization be an effective competitor.

These examples show that game theory, when used correctly, can be a very powerful modeling tool. Like any planning tool, game theory has its limitations, but these limitations are not as great as generally perceived. We believe game theory's use in the future will grow as managers become familiar with models, and computer programs help managers configure strategic situations. However, lest managers forget, analytic models are always replaced by newer more sophisticated ones. It is the underlying strategic principles that remain unchanged.

CHAPTER 6

BEHAVIORAL THEORY AND NAÏVE STRATEGIC REASONING

ROBERT J. MEYER
The Wharton School, Department of Marketing

DARRYL BANKS
The Wharton School, Department of Marketing

As Ho and Weigelt wrote in the preceding chapter, game theory, at its best, takes into account the mind-sets of competitors in defining the competitive game and payoffs. But what are the biases of rivals that cause them to act contrary to the predictions of rational game theory? What shortcuts do they use to make complex strategic decisions? And do these quirks affect strategic actions and outcomes? In this chapter, based on a behavioral perspective, we examine the heuristics managers use to make decisions and the sometimes irrational human biases that define and influence their perceptions and actions. Managers often don't behave as expected by the simple application of the principles of game theory. And, particularly in complex environments, they often produce good results. We explore empirical studies showing how managers approach games and how they learn in the process. We also examine the situation in which a sophisticated player (who is aware of both game theory and behavioral research) plays against a naïve opponent.

In the summer of 1993, Southwest Airlines heralded the arrival of its new service into Baltimore-Washington International Airport (BWI) by doing what it does best: initiating a fare war on several major routes. Although the two existing carriers—USAir and Continental—were not financially equipped to engage in a pricing battle with Southwest (each faced higher cost structures), they nevertheless met the challenge by offering major discounts of their own. What ensued over the next 15 months was one of the longest and most severely fought price wars in recent domestic airline history—a war that transformed BWI into the nation's fastest-growing airport, and alas, also helped USAir to turn in the worst yearly financial performance in its history.

Why did the carriers allow themselves to be drawn into such an unprofitable pricing pattern? To a game theorist, this price war—as well as the hundreds of others just like it that routinely erupt in the industry—has an easy and familiar explanation: The combatants were simply acting as rational firms inevitably do when faced with what game theorists call a finitely repeated Prisoner's Dilemma, a game that prescribes a dominant strategy to defect (match the low price) at each point in time. The explanation goes something like this: In a market where goods are largely undifferentiated, supply exceeds demand and firms are shortsighted, there is a temptation to gain a momentary (or endgame) advantage by undercutting on price. Once firms realize this potential, price-cutting, in theory, perpetuates *ad infinitum,* as firms repeatedly conclude that a low price is their best one-period response to whatever the competition might do. It is both the best defensive reaction to a price cut by a competitor, and the best offensive reaction to price increases.

While often cited, there is an important missing element to this explanation of fare wars. Since the detrimental effects of fare wars are common knowledge (the BWI carriers were industry veterans who had first-hand experience with the effects of such wars in the past), why are they initiated in the first place? Game theory indeed predicts price-cutting as a rational *short-term* strategic response in Prisoner's Dilemma, but it also predicts that if players recognize that the game is infinitely repeating—presumably a better characterization of actual industry thought—competing firms should *cooperate*. Perhaps reflecting this, fare wars invariably come to a conclusion at some point. The BWI market, for example, saw intense fare competition come to an end in late 1994. Since then, there has been a sustained period of relative cooperation. One might be tempted to conclude that the industry has thus finally discovered the wisdom of cooperation, but such an analysis would seem naïve. If the past is any guide to the future, fare wars will likely return to BWI at some point, as they intermittently have to almost all domestic airline routes over the years.

MUTUAL UNCERTAINTY

So what explains the chaotic pricing behavior of firms in the airline industry? One possibility is that we are simply looking at behavior that lies outside the domain of the rational theory of games. Although firms may appreciate the value of cooperation, the cooperative equilibrium is, perhaps, occasionally disrupted by periodic fits of irrationality—spawned, say, by rogue carriers who have suddenly forgotten the lessons of their economics courses.

But such a dismissal may be off the mark. It is important to note that a strategy of strict cooperation predicted by game theory arises *only* from the assumption that firms share a common belief about the game they are playing and its payoffs, and most critically, that each confidently believes the other will act rationally on this common knowledge. If we withdraw this assumption—as would seem a more realistic characterization of the real world—then the predictions the theory offers about how firms should rationally conduct themselves become less clear. In particular, the prescriptions game theory offers for "optimal play" now depend on the conjectures firms make about the knowledge and rationality of their opponents—beliefs that may not and need not follow from standard economic textbooks. In this sense, what may seem to the outside as an industry mired in chaos may, in fact, turn out to be a set of firms rationally responding to mutual uncertainty about each other's rationality.

This chapter takes up an obvious question that follows from this discussion: If a firm cannot be sure that its opponents will follow rational principles of game theory when making its strategic choices, how should the firm best formulate its own strategies? Our goal is to complement the earlier discussion of the theory of games by Ho and Weigelt (Chapter 5). As they note, to accurately model a game, managers need to understand the mind-sets of competitors. This chapter explores these mind-sets, drawing upon insights from the psychology of strategic reasoning—knowledge about the way competing managers might be expected to depart from the prescriptions of economics when viewing a given game structure. The conclusions we reach about how games tend to actually be played—and how a firm can best exploit this psychology—are essentially twofold:

1. When working through strategic business problems, managers are likely to be subject to a number of simplistic reasoning biases, resulting in strategies that are often quite dissimilar to those that would be prescribed by rational economic analysis. Intuitive strategies, for example, tend to be excessively myopic (exploring potential actions only over short time horizons), are biased toward case- or example-based understanding of consequences, and display an aversion to actions that are dissimilar from past experience.

2. The most effective strategies of play against naïve opponents often will *not* be those prescribed by textbook game-theoretic analyses of problems. Opponents will be unlikely to fully recognize the long-term value of cooperation, will be poor at reading cooperative signals, and may be exploitable (at least in the short run) in ways that rational analyses of game theory do not recognize.

Our central message is that knowing how competitors *will* reason—and the limits to one's ability to anticipate competitive actions—is thus an essential consideration that must be taken into account before naïvely applying game-theoretic principles when formulating strategic plans.

In the next four sections, we elaborate on these ideas. We begin by reviewing some of the basic tenets of how economic theory suggests rational firms should solve complex problems of business strategy, and then the heuristics that seem to describe how they are actually solved in practice. We then discuss the results of work that has explored performance in competitive games under uncertainty, and outline how a firm might adjust strategies for play against naïve opponents. We then attempt to reconcile the positive and normative views of game theory by taking up the problem of long-term strategic evolution—the idea that firms may be suboptimal in the short run, but that over time, normative game theory may provide an increasingly better account of how firms strategically interact.

THE THEORY AND PRACTICE OF COMPETITIVE GAMES

One of the longstanding difficulties in using classical game theory as either a descriptive or prescriptive tool for studying real-world problems of strategy is that its solutions presume a sophistication in strategic reasoning likely to be held by few real managers. To illustrate, consider the following simple game of full-information bargaining, known as the centipede game.[1] The game goes something like this:

> Player A is presented with a pot containing two payoffs, one large and one small. A has the option to stop the game immediately by accepting the larger of the two amounts (with player B receiving the smaller), or let it continue, with Player B then having the opportunity to stop or pass. Each time both players elect to pass, the pot is enlarged by some multiple k (for example, 10). This process is allowed to continue for a specified finite number of periods, and terminates when one player elects to accept the larger award.

It turns out that the game-theoretic solution to this game is simple, unambiguous, and perhaps surprising: Player A should accept the first offer, spurning the possibility that a greater award might be obtained by waiting. The rationale goes something like this: Player A would be presumed to first think ahead to the final period T, and observe that he or she must accept in the first half of the final period, or B will take the entire pot. Now, since A presumes that B is also thinking along the same lines, he or she must also conclude that B will never let the game get that far, since B would surely terminate the game given a chance $T-1$ rather than let A get the larger amount on T. Extending this string of, "since A knows that B knows that A knows . . ." logic back to the game's origin, it yields the inescapable conclusion that A should always take the first offer. The solution is unique and dominant; once both players recognize this logic, the first player never has an incentive to unilaterally deviate from stopping at the first opportunity.

As noted in the chapter by Ho and Weigelt, this type of reasoning, known as backward induction, is central to the prescribed solution of most finitely repeated games in classical game theory. But is this how individuals will actually reason through such a game when playing for stakes? Perhaps not surprisingly, the answer seems to be a decided no. The standard experimental finding is that the pot is allowed to expand for several trials, even among highly experienced players.[2] One take on the results is that even if it occurred to some individuals to engage in strictly rational backward induction, its prescribed solution is of little relevance since they have little faith that their opponent will act as traditional game theory would prescribe.

When we begin to construct games that resemble problems actually faced by firms in natural settings—for example, by introducing uncertainty in payoffs—computational complexities increase considerably. Consider, for example, a problem in product launch-timing explored by Lippman and Mamer, which we will examine in greater detail later in the chapter:[3]

> You are one of a number of firms trying to develop a product for entry in a new market. For each firm, product development is governed by an R&D department that periodically produces a new product idea. When a new idea is generated, its quality is probabilistic, drawn randomly from a uniform distribution of quality values—say, between 0 and 1,000. The longer you wait to introduce the product, the higher the quality, but also the greater likelihood a rival will move first to market. The first firm to elect to enter the market receives a reward tied to the highest product quality it has managed to produce to date, with all other firms

receiving nothing. If the cost of R&D is constant per period, there is no discounting, and all game parameters are common knowledge, how should you decide when to enter the market?

Although this example is set in a more meaningful context than the centipede bargaining game, it remains quite simplified as a model of the real-world problem of a product launch in technology markets. In natural settings, for example, firms will face uncertainty concerning how consumers will respond to new technologies; imitation is possible; and, of course, it will never be the case that a close second to the market is precluded from profits. Yet even for this highly simplified problem, the likely optimal solution turns out to be beyond the intuition of even the most sophisticated managerial experts (and many economists as well).

To see this, we will provide a brief glimpse at the problem's normative solution. First, theory prescribes that it is optimal for both players to decide to enter using what is called a *threshold-quality policy:* At the start of the innovation process, each player should decide that it will enter the market as soon as its R&D department develops an innovation with a quality at or above some threshold level. This rule is certainly simple enough, but computing the optimal value of this threshold is much less so.[4] First, both players would be assumed to derive the same general equation for the long-run expected profits, which would be yielded by any pair of thresholds, as well as a *best-response function,* or an equation describing the threshold that should be set for any given threshold used by an opponent. With a bit of math, one can show that these response functions will converge to a unique *equilibrium:* a common threshold from which neither player stands to gain by unilaterally deviating. In the case in which the quality uniformly varies from 0 to 1,000, the equilibrium is 333, or one-third of the distribution of innovation values. Put another way, the fully rational player in this game will enter the market as soon as the R&D division produces an innovation value of 333 or higher.

Would naïve managers actually engage in anything like this type of reasoning when faced with such a problem? Intuition suggests not. For starters, it is not even obvious that all players would see a constant threshold–quality policy as being the "best" way to play this game (for example, some might think to use more complex rules that adapt to how the opponent is playing). Even if they did, it would seem unlikely that they could intuitively calculate the rational equilibrium threshold, or even hazard a correct guess as to what it might be. (The rational equilibrium of 333 would not seem a natural focal point.)

It is in this discrepancy between what theory prescribes people *should* do and what they plausibly *will* do that the core dilemma of game theory lies: The rational solution to nontrivial games presumes computational reasoning skills unlikely to be held by real managers of firms. Yet problems that are far more complex than those treated by economists are routinely faced and resolved by firms, often to a high degree of intuitive satisfaction. If there are competitive disadvantages that arise from failing to endow managers with training in advanced mathematics and game theory, they have apparently gone unnoticed by most firms.

EFFICIENT SHORTCUTS THAT SHAPE MANAGERS' DECISIONS

If managers do not use the mathematics of dynamic decision theory to solve complex problems, how are such feats of intuition achieved? Over the past 50 years, a large literature in experimental psychology and economics has sought to examine the degree to which individuals are "intuitive decision theorists" when resolving uncertain and dynamic decision problems. The overwhelming view of this work is that individuals, indeed, rarely approach problems as a decision theorist might hope, but rather attempt to solve them using heuristics that are often quite remote from the solution methods of decision theory.[5] Yet, the *consequences* of this difference in solution methods are often mild: while individuals can fail at tasks that seem trivial to the decision theorist (for example, failing to recognize the equivalence of two restated versions of the same problem), they can perform surprisingly well at tasks that, to the theorist, appear quite complex (for example, knowing how frequently to replace goods in a dynamic market with uncertain changes in technology).

While there are no ironclad principles of decision making that characterize intuitive solutions to dynamic tasks, they nevertheless reflect a few unifying themes, which we outline in turn.

Learning by the Case Method: Pattern-Matching as a General Solution Heuristic

Managers often reach decisions by referring to examples of similar problems whose solutions are already known.[6] Business schools use this pattern in teaching students through the case method. We teach chess players to become experts not by training them to be better brute-force calculators, but rather by enhancing their ability to recognize standard openings and closings, and by studying classic games played by past grand masters. Likewise, the best pool players are unlikely to be those with the best grades in calculus and physics; they are more likely to be those with the best ability to recognize table positions, and the cue-movement protocol this implies.

But for all its merits, case-based reasoning also has its dangers, the most familiar being suggesting wrong solutions by overgeneralizing past examples. In other words, managers take away the wrong lesson from the case. For example, consider the plight of Mattel Toy Company, which, in the mid-1980s announced to the press that it had stumbled on the Holy Grail of the toy industry: a formula for producing market winners. Specifically, the firm attributed much of the success of its highly profitable Masters of the Universe toy line to a unique—and highly costly—research and promotion program, which included detailed consumer testing led by a staff of child psychologists, followed by integration of the toy line with a 30-minute television cartoon series.[7] Of course, one might have looked at this inference as an extreme case of overconfidence in case-based reasoning. While the support program was certainly associated with the success of the Masters line, the firm could just as easily have attributed its success to any number of other, less observable and controllable factors (such as timing, competition, and so on).

Perhaps not surprisingly, Mattel's "formula" later proved to be a one-time wonder. The same research and promotion process failed to produce a winner in its next major series launch, Marshall Bravestarr (1986), and gradually Mattel reverted to its pre-Masters skepticism about the value of large up-front investments in single new product ideas.

In recent years, a rather large literature has developed in psychology that has helped systematically document both the pervasiveness and limitations of case-based reasoning as a problem-solving heuristic. To illustrate, we recently undertook an investigation exploring how managers learn to set price over time when demand is uncertain.[8] We posed a mix of marketing managers and MBA students a variation of the following abstract problem, implemented on a computer:

> You have been hired as the manager of a new, patented drug that is about to be launched for sale in a new market. You are, however, initially uncertain about how sensitive customers will be to variations in price: they may be either all highly price-sensitive (implying a low price to maximize profits) or all price-insensitive (implying a high price to maximize profits). Your job is to set price in each of a number of decision periods so as to maximize total profits over time, observing actual demand as you go.

Participants were further told that demand was given by one of two probabilistic linear functions (which were graphically displayed), and that, at the start, the two demand functions were equally likely.

This problem has a rather straightforward normative solution. In the first two periods, the rational decision maker actively experiments with price by setting it at alternating extreme high and low levels, quickly discovering whether the market is of low sensitivity (in which case, sales will remain high even at a high price) or is of high sensitivity (in which case, sales will vanish at a high price). Once this discovery is made, pricing on subsequent trials becomes a simple matter of setting price at the level that would maximize profits for the known, demand function.

Did subjects do this? To the contrary, subjects displayed extreme conservatism in pricing, rarely experimenting with high and low price values as optimal theory would predict. Rather, they initially set price at a medium (or compromise) level, and then made small adjustments up or down in each period in response to observed changes in demand. The consequence was that, even after many trials, prices remained lower than they should have been in low-sensitivity markets and higher than they should have been in high-sensitivity markets.

Subjects appeared to use a case-based reasoning heuristic, where the outcome of prices set in the past were used to guide prices set in the future. The prices set by subjects appeared to follow the principle of "if it worked well in the past, charge it again," coupled with an aversion to setting prices whose demand consequences were unknown. After observing the profit outcome of a safe initial price, subjects adjusted price either upward or downward depending on the effect of the last price change. These small upward or downward adjustments then continued until the profit gains were no longer clearly noticeable—which generally left subjects short of the optimum prices that they could have charged.

Despite these illustrations of the weaknesses of case-based reasoning, we should stress that, by and large, these weaknesses are overcome by its efficiencies. Specifically, in a world in which relationships are complex and there is insufficient experience to deduce these relationships (the common case in strategic management), simple pattern-matching heuristics provide a useful mechanism for rendering judgments that would otherwise be unfeasible; if a price or product-launch strategy worked with satisfactory results before, it is a reasonable guess that it will not fail miserably if applied to similar situations in the future. Although case-based judgment has the downside of reducing the speed of discovery, it is also a reasonably safe solution method in settings where being "approximately right" is a sufficient outcome.

It's All Relative: Reference-Based Judgments

How do individuals use case examples in the course of learning and problem solving? The attractiveness of outcomes tends not to be assessed in any absolute, time-invariant sense (as is presumed by optimal decision theory), but rather almost always relative to the outcomes offered by known cases or focal points of reference. The effect is similar to popular optical illusions in which the same object looks smaller when placed next to a large object than when placed next to a small object. Individuals often judge the attractiveness of prices relative to "reference prices,"[9] and the attractiveness of strategies relative to defaults.[10]

A rather vivid example of the consequences of reference-based judgment arose in an experiment we designed to explore the degree to which individuals make rational decisions about how many units to buy (or stockpile) of a frequently consumed good that appears "on sale" during periods of inflation and deflation.[11] Our central finding was that respondents did a poor job of intuitively indexing price for the effects of inflation and deflation, leading to underbuying (insufficient stockpiling) during periods of inflation, and overbuying (excessive stockpiling) during periods of deflation. The prime reason is that respondents tended to assess price relative to prices they had paid in the past rather than what they would likely be paying in the future.

An important additional characteristic of reference-based judgment is that individuals tend to be *loss averse* when considering the consequences of new actions relative to those offered by focal cases.[12] Specifically, a negative change from a reference point is almost always seen as greater than a comparable positive change. While there is a large literature of examples of loss aversion, an immediately relevant example arises in our study of the uncertain pricing problem just described.[13] In that work, we found that subjects were more likely to adjust prices downward when they found that sales were below expectations than adjust prices upward when sales were above expectations.

Managerial Myopia: A Bias toward the Short-Term

One of the most difficult aspects of dynamic planning is reasoning the consequences of future courses of action. Most individuals are not endowed with the powers to do this well; even if individuals wanted to act in a completely optimal manner when making sequential decisions, short-term memory limitations alone preclude the possibility of exhaustive searches over future contingencies for all but the most trivial of problems. What is most troubling for normative theories of sequential decision making, however, is that empirical evidence of the way in which individuals assess future consequences of current decisions (e.g., the long-term value of alternative investment vehicles) suggests that errors in such assessments are far from random. Rather, individuals act in a nearsighted fashion, as if long-run consequences are undervalued relative to immediate consequences.

The Bias of Subaggregation.   One factor that contributes to the apparent tendency of individuals to act in a nearsighted fashion is that they tend to have poor instincts for computing long-term costs and benefits; when faced with assessing the long-term value of a considered action, intuitive estimates tend to be systematically lower than actuarial values. To illustrate, consider how a group of 125 Wharton MBAs (many finance majors) intuitively solved the following—seemingly straightforward—problem in assessing the cumulative cost of storing goods:

Imagine you are making budgeting plans for an upcoming 16-week academic semester. You know that you will consume exactly one bag of groceries per week, and you have two options for paying for these groceries: (a) Pay $10 a week for each of 16 weekly bags ($160 total), or (b) buy all 16 weekly bags in the first week at $6.50 a bag ($104 total), and pay a storage charge of 50 cents per week per bag. Assume that there are no transactions costs (e.g., all groceries are delivered) and the money cannot be used for other purposes or accrue interest. Which payment method would you prefer?

The answer to this question is a matter of straightforward, albeit tedious, arithmetic: One simply computes whether the $56 savings one realizes by purchasing in advance is larger than the cost of storing those groceries over a 16-week horizon. If one correctly calculates cumulative storage costs, one will find that buying on a weekly basis (option A) offers the least costly means of satisfying demand (the cost of storage is $60).

When asked to provide intuitive solutions to this problem, however, most (67 percent) subjects were inclined to pick the wrong option, B, even though they were given as much time as needed to perform the

163

required arithmetic. Why? In debriefings, most respondents who picked B confessed that they solved the problem by focusing on the large percentage discount offered in method B, and intuitively underestimating the cumulative impact of the costs of storage. In addition, many of those who picked the correct option, A, confessed that they did so more as a hunch than out of a reasoned expectation that it would be less expensive in the long run.

Another example of this can be seen in intuitive solutions to the following machine-replacement problem:

> You are a manager of a factory that produces a good at a rate of k units per period, and you are able to sell all you produce. Each month a new manufacturing technology becomes available that would allow you to increase your rate of productivity by l units per period. You may acquire this new technology at a fixed refitting charge C. How should you decide to refit your factory?

In a study of how individuals solve this problem about variations in speeds of improvement and replacement costs, we found a systematic bias to replace equipment less frequently than would be predicted by optimal replacement theory. In short, subjects tended to see the out-of-pocket costs of replacement as outweighing the opportunity costs of not replacing more often.[14]

What drives this apparent bias? The most likely explanation is one that initially arose in studies of intuitive mathematics. When asked to provide intuitive answers for such things as the sum or product of descending series, such as $960 + 850 + 750 + 650 + 300$, responses tend to be systematically greater than that for ascending series.[15] The explanation Kahneman and Tversky offer is that individuals solve such addition problems using a heuristic that sets the initial number in a sequence as a seed or anchor, which is then (insufficiently) adjusted upward or downward to arrive at a final answer.[16] In this case, intuitive computations of opportunity costs are naturally biased downward by the (usually small) single-period cost. Hence, the tendency to underappreciate the direct costs of cumulative storage, and undervalue the opportunity costs of failing to refit a factory.

Temporal Myopia. There is also evidence that suggests that the apparent tendency toward myopia is not simply a matter of individuals being poor intuitive arithmeticians. Rather, research in complex problem solving suggests that individuals are much more prone to focus on how a given action will affect immediate rather than long-run rewards.[17]

An illustration of this has recently been offered by Camerer, Johnson, Rymon, and Sen,[18] who examined the process by which individuals obtained intuitive solutions to "shrinking pie" negotiation games. Subjects were faced with a three-stage bargaining problem in which Party A was given a cash sum to share with Party B. If Party B rejected Party A's initial proposed division of the funds, the total sum was cut in half, and B was invited to make the next offer. This process continued for one more round, after which, if no division offer had been accepted, neither side received a payoff.

As in the centipede game discussed earlier, the problem of setting A's initial offer is optimally solved by backward induction; one should first decide what offer A should make in the last round, where Party B faces the choice of either accepting A's last offer or nothing, and then work backward. When actually faced with this task, however, most individuals attempted to solve it by *forward* induction, and then only over a short horizon: They imagined how Party B would react to differing initial offers, then tried to imagine how Party B would respond if the initial offer was too aggressive and rejected, and rarely proceeded beyond two stages of negotiation. By using forward induction, subjects overlooked the fact that by having the last move, they were, in fact, in an extremely strong bargaining position, so most initial offers were above what would be prescribed by the optimal policy.

WHEN IGNORANCE IS BLISS: THE FUNCTIONALITY OF DYSFUNCTIONAL REASONING IN GAMES

One might think managers pay a stiff price for this heuristic approach to problem solving. As shown by the examples, decision biases do sometimes lead managers to suboptimal results. What is the price of ignorance? In many cases, it is surprisingly small—or even nonexistent. As discussed, intuitive dynamic reasoning appears guided by a series of well-defined heuristic principles:

- Learning and judgment are driven by case-based thinking.
- There is an aversion to choosing actions that are seen as having downsides relative to a present position.
- Dynamic planning, when it occurs at all, is myopic and forward-looking.

While these heuristics, taken either jointly or in isolation, can be shown to yield damaging consequences for some decision problems, what is perhaps more remarkable is that most of the time they work remarkably well. For example, a standard result of experiments in job-search behavior is that individuals often come quite close to realizing optimal wages, even though few subjects could likely hazard a guess as to how one would begin to analytically solve such problems.[19] Similar findings of near-optimality in more complex tasks—such as stockpiling and scheduling replacement policies—have been reported by Meyer and Assuncao and Cripps and Meyer.[20]

Sometimes, particularly in noncooperative games, ignorance of optimal policies leads to results that are better than those predicted by natural models. For example, consider a study of how individuals actually play the competitive product-launch game described earlier.[21] Thirty-four pairs of subjects were asked to assume the role of R&D managers of a firm that was attempting to bring to market a new device that would greatly enhance the resolution of standard television transmissions. Subjects were told that their R&D department would periodically produce a new version of this device that would be assigned a quality score from 0 to 1,000, which were independent draws from a distribution (described in Table 6.1). In each period, each player was to decide whether to bring its new technology to market. The first player to enter received a profit payoff tied to the quality of its technology, and the lagging firm received nothing.

Subjects played six versions of the game with different speeds at which innovations were produced and different distributions from

Table 6.1
Actual versus Predicted Winning Innovation Values

Innovation Rate	Predicted by Game Theory	Actual	Net
Low	591	666	75
High	591	738	147
Distribution			
Uniform	666	701	35
Low–quality	365	627	262
High–quality	743	765	22

which quality levels were drawn. Subjects were given full information about the parameters of each game before the outset; and during the course of each game, they could observe both their own innovation stream as well as that of their opponent.

How close were subjects to the rational competitive equilibrium in entry decisions? In Table 6.1, we report the average quality of the first-to-enter innovation compared to the rational equilibrium threshold values predicted by theory. Across all variations of the experiment, actual implicit entry thresholds were consistently higher than those predicted by classic game theory, yielding higher average earnings. These results were quite robust and did not vanish through repeated play in any environment.

What explains the findings? First, we should note that this type of game outcome—with subjects performing better than the rational prediction—is hardly a new one. A common finding in repeated games with attractive cooperative outcomes (such as the centipede game) is that empirical equilibria almost always lie above the strict competitive solution.[22] The most well-known example is probably that of the finitely repeated Prisoner's Dilemma: Although the classic game-theoretic solution for this game predicts defection on all trials (by backward induction; since it is the dominant strategy for the terminal period, it is a dominant strategy for all earlier periods), uniform defection is rarely displayed by actual players. Rather, individuals display a type of "forgiving tit-for-tat"—a behavior only under the assumption that each player believes there is some chance on each trial that the other player will be altruistic and not choose the dominant strategy of defection.

While a number of explanations could be offered, perhaps the most simple is this: The superoptimal returns were a simple consequence of subjects failing to understand (or think deeply about) the true competitive nature of the task (e.g., the risk that they might be preempted). Although thinking deeply about the likely strategic behavior of one's opponent is commonly spoken of as a virtue in games, here is a case where ignorance has its benefits: Mutual myopic thinking leads to longer waits for R&D (as players wait to attain some aspired quality level), which, in turn, increases the joint returns of all players. Given satisfactory returns, there is thus little incentive for any player to revisit his or her play strategies (or lack thereof). Consistent with this, when subjects were asked after the experiment to describe the strategies they used, they said they employed a diverse mix of "nonoptimal" play heuristics—such as threshold rules with high threshold values and fixed waiting-time rules—which, when played against each other, *happen* to yield a quasi-cooperative outcome.

CAN NAÏVE PLAY BE EXPLOITED? WHEN INFORMED PLAYERS PLAY NAÏVE OPPONENTS

The preceding discussion leads to a natural question: To what degree can a highly informed player—one well trained in both the theory of games and strategic psychology—exploit this knowledge to obtain superior outcomes in games? The answer, unfortunately, is not as straightforward as one might think. On one hand, knowledge that one's opponents may be naïve in their approach to a game can be used to adjust the standard game-theoretic analysis of a game, as discussed by Ho and Weigelt. It thus may no longer be optimal to provide bargaining opponents extremely low offers in "split the pie" games, or even to defect in a single-round Prisoner's Dilemma. If one could know with precision the way the opponent would play the game, it should be possible to use that knowledge to advantage. But it is usually impossible to know with perfect certainty the likely short strategy to be used by the opponent. Perhaps more important, it is very difficult to assess the opponent's ability to learn or adapt play in response to the strategies used by the more informed player.

A Game Theorist Plays the Preemptive Innovation Game

To illustrate, assume two decision makers are playing the preemptive innovation game just described. One is well versed in the game's normative solution as well as the result of our experiments describing actual play, the other not. How should the informed player approach the game? If the informed player could assume that the opponent is unlikely to learn (such as if the game were being played over only a small number of rounds), the best strategy is easy to prescribe. Because the informed player knows that the naïve player will likely be more patient than game theory would predict, the informed player can take advantage of this knowledge by setting an innovation threshold that is also higher than that prescribed by game theory (so as to increase the expected size of the payoff given a successful innovation), while still being lower than that likely to be used by the naïve opponent (to increase the odds of moving first).

What if the informed player assumes that the opponent can learn? Here, an informed player might do even better, but the required strategy is a highly risky one. In particular, *both* players will be made strictly better off if the informed player can successfully teach the naïve player to cooperate; in particular, promote a tacit agreement that *neither* will move first until one of them develops an innovation that is nearest the highest possible. How should this best be done? Well, there's the rub. If it turns out that the opponent is naïve not just about the game *but also about reading cooperative signals,* the informed player who tries to initiate cooperation will be rendered strictly worse off. Given a high cooperative threshold set by the informed player, a naïve player will most likely end up launching first, learning only that one apparently does not need to know much about the game to do well in it.

Indeed, it turns out that it is this inability of opponents to learn and read signals that imposes the greatest limitation on the ability of informed players to exploit this knowledge in the marketplace. Competitors who are nearsighted, fail to learn from experience, and are poor at reading the cooperative signals of their opponents *are* at a disadvantage in the marketplace, as they can be exploited by more informed players. But, as the experience of the airline industry will attest, their presence can nevertheless make life miserable for more informed players, by precluding the possibility of coordinated play. Reflecting this, when real-world firms question the reasoning skills of their competitors, one is more likely to hear a wish that they would behave more rationally, rather than rejoicing over the exploitability their naïveté offers. Often, an informed competitor is the best competitor.

LONG-TERM PROSPECTS FOR LEARNING: NAÏVE STRATEGISTS ENGAGE IN A FARE WAR

Our discussion to this point leads us to what might seem a bleak portrait of the reality of competitive markets. For the most part, managers are endowed with few of the skills that would seem required to solve most complex business problems, and are poor learners from experience. To the degree that firms may often perform well in competitive situations, it is due more likely to the tendency of many game structures to forgive ignorance rather than superior ability in analytic reasoning. Taken to the extreme, one might suggest that the often-cited (and criticized) tendency for firms to underattend to competitors when making strategic decisions may have a positive evolutionary basis: Competitive markets where firms mutually ignore competition are rarely penalized, and moreover, firms that *try* to model—and outguess—their opponents will not always be rewarded, as their competitive conjectures (such as to try to initiate cooperation) are often just as likely to be wrong as right (or mostly wrong).

At the same time, however, speaking against this view is the simple observation that real markets are rarely marked by such myopic chaos. Consider, for example, the case of fare wars in the airline industry. While the on-again, off-again pattern of such wars may not be consistent with the rational theory of games, it is also inconsistent with a market containing completely naïve competitors who make no attempt to form conjectures about opponents. Specifically, in spite of the periodic incidence of fare wars, there is evidence that the industry is, with time, learning to be more cooperative, as evidenced by the decreasing frequency and intensity of such wars in the U.S. domestic market. Such behavior, in turn, is just what would be predicted by a game-theoretic analysis of rational, farsighted competitors.

Trial-and-Error Learning

How might these two views be reconciled? An increasingly dominant view among game theorists is a belief that while learning does take place in competitive markets, it is more as a trial-and-error process rather than a result of common rational conjecturing by players.[23] Such an account, for example, may be consistent with the pattern of "noisy learning," which marks fare wars: an oscillating pattern of price changes, overlain by a general trend toward rational cooperation.

To illustrate, consider the following simulation in which two naïve players in the airline industry choose pricing strategies at random and change them based on the outcomes of the preceding round. To keep things simple, assume that a given market is served by two, equally structured airlines that face the following common payoff matrix when deciding which of two fares to set in each of a number of periods (X,Y refers to the payoffs for airlines A and B, respectively):

| | | **Airline B** | |
		Price Low	*Price High*
	Price Low	50, 50	200, 0
Airline A	*Price High*	0, 200	100, 100

How might this Prisoner's Dilemma evolve over time if managers of the two airlines did not think as game theorists, but rather as limited decision makers who set strategies by trial and error? To model such a process, we start by assuming that both firms begin a series of fare decisions, not knowing which of a number of strategies for setting fares might be the best to use against the other.

The two players initially chose at random from among 10 strategies (including cooperation, defection, and tit-for-tat options) on the first round. If the outcome of that strategy was equal to or greater than the cooperative payoff, the player continued with the same strategy. If not, the player selected a new strategy at random.

What would happen to airline price patterns if firms followed such a pricing process? In Figure 6.1, we plot the average proportion of high-price postings over time, which arose when we simulated this process for 1,000 pairs of competing airlines over 60 decision periods. The figure yields two intriguing insights. First, it displays a general trend toward cooperative pricing behavior, even though we allow no mechanism for communication or deductive reasoning by firms. In

Figure 6.1
Average Market Prices for a Simulated Adaptive Duopoly

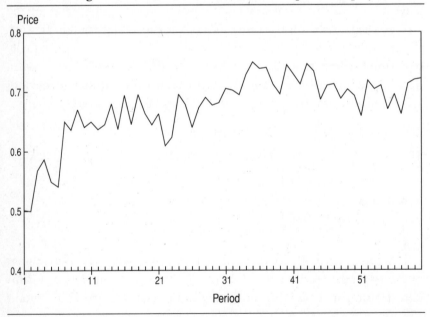

this case, it arises purely as a consequence of trial-and-error sampling of strategies by firms that share a common aversion to noncooperative profits.[24] Second, the general trend is marked by a pattern of oscillating price levels, suggesting that the move toward cooperative pricing is irregular, marked by periods of noncooperative pricing, even with this high level of aggregation.

Perhaps an even more interesting result of the simulation is that it reveals a well-behaved evolution of strategic rules that underlie these prices. In Figure 6.2, we plot the relative frequency with which the 2,000 simulated firms used each of the six classes of considered strategies in each pricing period. It reveals an interesting pattern of natural selection: Even though not permitted at the start, a simple tit-for-tat strategy quickly emerges as the dominant strategy hypothesis retained by firms. Although tit-for-tat is often described as an efficient rational play strategy for Prisoner's Dilemma games, its emergence here was by a simple process of trial-and-error.

Figure 6.2
Frequency of Strategy Survival for a Simulated Duopoly

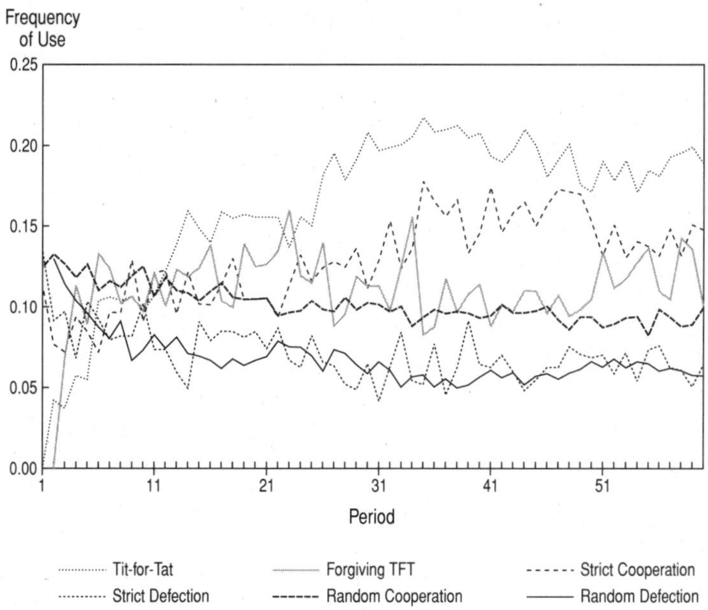

We should stress that this example describes an extraordinarily naïve learning process. A more complete treatment might include such things as a more complete strategy set, and, perhaps, a mechanism for allowing learning within the rule set itself (i.e., rule breeding). But the very simplicity of the example serves to underscore a point: *Nearly optimal market outcomes may eventually be observed in markets where firms never engage in complex reasoning and learning processes.* Indeed, as in our earlier example of the problem of product-launch timing, a case could be made that naïve thinking here helped rather than hurt, to the degree that hyperrational reasoning may have led to a strictly noncooperative pricing policy (joint defection) on all periods.

CONCLUSION: MANAGING IMPERFECT MANAGERS AND COMPETITORS

The discussion points out the danger of applying game theory without understanding the mind-set of competitors. The best players are not those who study game theory and always play predicted equilibria, but rather they are those who understand their opponents and design optimal response strategies in the light of these specific opponents. This often yields play that does not resemble what textbooks would prescribe.

Although we are currently quite far from anything like a formal positive theory of how individuals and firms solve strategic reasoning problems, there is an emerging picture that looks something like this:

- Problems tend to be solved using logical heuristics—such as pattern-matching—which are often remote from normative, decision-theoretic logic, but which do a reasonable job of approximating normative outcomes much of the time.
- The use of such heuristics often appears as something of an optimal adaptation; in some cases, the incremental benefits from engaging in more strictly rational reasoning are small relative to their cognitive costs, and in some noncooperative game settings, help in the realization of higher joint (quasi-cooperative) payoffs, given that the opponent could not be assuredly rational.

The second of these conclusions is worthy of some elaboration. First, it is important to stress that it is *not* the case that a manager's reliance on suboptimal decision heuristics will be universally harmless. As we noted earlier, the most serious consequence are the limits it imposes on tacit coordinated action, which requires a high level of informed reasoning among all players. Likewise, a failure to understand the limits to human decision making and inference abilities has occasionally had disastrous effects on firms, such as in failure to anticipate technological and stylistic obsolescence, and myopia in understanding the factors that drive success and failure.

On the other hand, it also seems to be the case that turning to more rational processes of inference may be of limited help in *competitive gaming scenarios,* where optimal solutions require rationality to be *mutual* among all players. Here, playing rational strategies against an irrational opponent may simply degenerate to an exercise in frustration. Moves that should rationally initiate cooperation may be overlooked or incorrectly responded to, with, paradoxically, the naïve player being left with the advantage. Alternatively, aggressive actions (such as price-cutting or early product launches) that presume that one's opponent will act aggressively may turn out to be unnecessary.

Are we thus to conclude that normative game-theoretic analyses have limited value as an approach in strategic management? This conclusion, too, would seem premature. The one thing that probably can be said almost without reservation is that one particular component of traditional normative analysis—rational equilibria—is probably of limited value either as a descriptive or prescriptive guide in strategy. In most cases, individuals do not have the intuitive ability to think as rational players when solving competitive dynamic problems, and as we have shown, in some cases are not the worse for it.

At the same time, the broader study of games and dynamic analysis can continue to provide an extremely useful framework for thinking about and modeling individual and competitive behavior, but with one caveat: For applications to be useful, it is critical that they be based on realistic assumptions about how individuals think about and plan for the future; and, in game applications, the assumptions players make about the psychology of other players.

The implication, therefore, is that if there is a calculus out there for helping firms accelerate the process of strategic learning, it may more closely resemble the type of strategic learning simulations illustrated here rather than the deductive calculus of traditional game theory. Although the emergence of tit-for-tat as a successful evolutionary strategy for Prisoner's Dilemma games illustrated here is a simple result that might well have been anticipated, survival patterns in more complex games—such as those with multiple rational equilibria—probably will not be as obvious.

In sum, the heuristics and biases that characterize human strategic reasoning define a set of very real and measurable constraints that firms need to explicitly consider when formulating strategy. Although it is common to speculate that, with experience, heuristic-based reasoning will naturally vanish among firms—causing markets to behave more as game theory would predict—there is strong evidence that this will not often be the case. The reason, simply, is that most strategic structures do not severely penalize—and at times even reward—firms that engage in nonoptimal play. The right competitive response for a given problem is thus not necessarily that prescribed by game theory, but rather, possibly, an apparently suboptimal rule that performs well with a particular nonoptimal opponent. Of course, since the exact nature of that rule will be uncertain, the best skill a firm can possess is both a willingness to experiment with strategic policies and an ability to learn from the experience of applying these policies.

CHAPTER 7

Coevolution: Toward a Third Frame for Analyzing Competitive Decision Making

ERIC J. JOHNSON
The Wharton School, Department of Marketing

J. EDWARD RUSSO
Cornell University, Johnson Graduate School of Management

Darwin is probably a better guide to business competition than economists are.
Bruce Henderson, Founder
Boston Consulting Group

Both the economic view (game theory) and the behavioral view, discussed in the preceding two chapters emphasize different aspects of competition. The perspective of economic theory emphasizes rationality and equilibria while the behavioral frame emphasizes biases in mental models and cognitive limitations. These two views or frames of strategy often seem to have little in common, and each casts its own light and shadows on competition. This chapter examines the strengths and weaknesses of each of these perspectives for analyzing competitive strategy. We conclude that both frames obscure significant issues related to the interaction of competitors, and present a third perspective—that of coevolution—which addresses issues ignored by both of the other frames. Coevolution focuses on interdependent adaptation, the race to adapt to new conditions, and the importance of initial advantages and conditions. While each frame has its shadows, the three together can increase the illumination on the dynamics of competition.

Based in part upon a paper prepared for the conference, Understanding Competitive Decision Making, and appearing in the proceedings of that conference published in *Marketing Letters*. Comments by the participants of that conference and Paul Schoemaker are gratefully acknowledged, as are discussions with Colin Camerer, Eldar Shafir, and Sharoni Shafir.

$\mathbf{T}$he senior vice president of a leading pharmaceutical firm must develop strategy in a changing competitive environment. These changes include managed care, price pressures, and competitors' mergers. As can be seen from even this simple summary, the strategic challenges presented to this manager are quite complex. The vice president must not only anticipate changes in the environment but also the actions of competitors, as summarized in Figure 7.1.

How do managers "wrap their brains around" such complexity? Where can our senior vice president turn for advice? A manager's personal understanding of the business environment is often called a *mental model*. Some of these individual internal models are tightly structured, having developed over years of experience, study, and discussion. Others are piecemeal and incomplete. Whatever the quality of executives' mental models, it is these understandings on which they base their strategic decisions.

Figure 7.1
Complex Competitive Challenges

	Continuous Change	Discontinuous Change
Environmental Changes	• Downward pressure on drug prices • Growth of managed care • Declining role of individual physicians and pharmacists	• Various potential health care reforms (federal and state levels) • FDA change in regulations for clinical trials (of a new drug in humans)
Competitive Changes	• Refocusing sales efforts toward managed care organizations • Increasing R&D budgets in selected therapeutic classes • Engaging more expertise from outside the company	• Pharma-PMB acquisitions • Entry into the generic drug market • The acquisition of biotechnology and the "top-down" development of new drugs • Comarketing alliances • Direct marketing to consumers

Managers develop and extend their personal mental models by turning to more general models of competitive interactions. These frameworks can come from strategy consultants and the discipline of strategy. Managers also draw upon established scholarly disciplines, including economics and psychological or behavioral research. These scholarly disciplines are the focus of this chapter. Whatever reservations managers may have about the practicality or currency of this approach, disciplines such as economics possess large, tested, coherent bodies of knowledge that are the external equivalent of general mental models.

This chapter examines two major approaches to strategic decisions, one based upon economic theory and the other upon behavioral science. After examining their strengths and weaknesses, we propose a potential synthesis or common ground. By doing so, we hope both to help decision makers appreciate and utilize appropriately the current approaches to strategic decisions, and to encourage decision makers and academics to attack the blind spots inherent in these approaches.

COMMON GROUND

We start with what is common to both descriptions. The two approaches share much, since they both originate in the study of risky choice, often typified by lotteries or gambles. The standard description of decision making consists of three elements: alternatives, states of the world, and outcomes. Decision makers select the one course of action that seems most appropriate given their beliefs about the world. For our executive, the alternative may be to acquire or not acquire a mail-order pharmaceutical business. The states of the world may depend upon whether governmental changes in the environment occur (or not); and finally, the outcomes might be an increase (or decrease) in profitability, with subsequent increases (or decreases) in stock prices, company reputation, and executives' compensation and future career prospects.

What makes this different from simple gambles? Competitive decisions are distinguished by the presence of an intelligent opponent or opponents whose own choice of actions influences the outcome for the decision maker. If other firms invest in direct distribution, the profitability of this action might decrease. In general, managers making decisions in a competitive environment must shoulder the burden of additional complexity. Uncertainty grows because competitors' actions are not perfectly predictable. Further, those actions may be deliberately designed to *create* uncertainty to confound competing managers. Since the consequences of a manager's actions now depend partly on competitors' responses, the evaluation of consequences and the selection of actions become much more difficult. Our executive must not only bet on the states of the world, but also guess what the competitors will do.

THE ROLE OF FRAMES

Our executive now turns to either economics or behavioral science for help in this task of guessing what competitors will do. But she may be reminded of the old Hindu fable in which six blind men touch different parts of the elephant and come to different conclusions about its nature. Different frames for viewing competitive decision making have largely determined researchers' theoretical assumptions, phenomena of interest, and tools employed. Hence, the choice of frames determines their recommendations to managers facing such challenges. In short, our understanding and prescriptions have been influenced more by where we stand than by the nature of the beast we are dealing with. In contrast, our manager is necessarily interested in the nature of the beast as a whole, even if that picture is only approximately right.

A frame is the structural core of the mental models we bring to a problem.[1] For instance, some product managers view their distributors as adversaries competing for an ever-larger share of the distribution channel's economic surplus.[2] Other managers view these same channel intermediaries as partners whose collaboration is the best way to increase the economic surplus available to all. Similarly, a competitor may be framed as an opposing military force,[3] or as a rival sports team in your league.[4]

In simple terms, any frame creates its own highlights and shadows in the decision environment. By a highlight, we mean the elements of the environment to which attention is naturally drawn. The manager of a new product launch that frames decisions as a military battle will highlight security and surprise, weaponry and his or her own role (as the general). Framing the launch group as a basketball team highlights coordination among the group's members, opportunism, and conditioning. A shadow is simply the opposite of a highlight, namely an element of the decision situation that is naturally overlooked, downplayed, or ignored as the frame draws attention away from it. For instance, where are the consumers in either the military battle or sports team frames? And the structure of a game like basketball, carefully regulated by rules and a clock, seems remote from new product launches. The basketball frame occludes introductions of newer technologies and other outside threats that often occur in new product development.

Research in competitive managerial decision making has been dominated by one frame and challenged by the emergence of another. The dominant frame has its general origin in economics, with its particular character drawn from game theory, as described by Ho and Weigelt in Chapter 5. The emerging alternative frame is based upon behavioral decision research, as discussed by Meyer and Banks in Chapter 6. At the moment, research in competitive decision making is a tale of one-and-a-half frames. Our goal is not to choose between them, though our own roots lie in psychology, but to convey the limitations of both. We then proffer a third frame that may be more suitable for understanding competitive decision making.

The Economic Frame

The extension of microeconomics to game theory dominates the study of competitive decision making. This frame draws unique coherence from economic assumptions of rational behavior. And it draws predictive power from strongly valid rules of influence that employ mathematical or logical operators.

This strength comes at a price. Because the decision must be represented in a way that is compatible with the rules of inference, great simplicity and structure are required. For instance, typical formulations required that the focal actor know a competitor's cost structure and its likely behaviors.[5] Because many researchers are troubled by the unrealistic strength of these assumptions, great effort has been directed toward relaxing them, while retaining the economic-logic frame's strongly valid rules of inference. For example, Weigelt and Camerer employ sequential equilibria in game formulations that tolerate incomplete information.[6] These partial relaxations of the individual assumptions of rationality seem like substantial conceptual gains. However, in comparison to the reality of managers' decision making, this can seem like a painfully small step. For instance, Jacquemin relaxes the assumption of prior knowledge of a competitor's cost structure, but requires the focal actor to be able to enumerate all possible competitor price structures, assign probabilities to each, and conjoin these with the probabilities of different pricing strategies.[7] Does this seem reasonable for our pharmaceutical executive? Probably not.

For all its restrictions, the economic frame offers an effective mechanism for producing new knowledge, and has been central to the study of competitive decision-making. It also has had its real-world application and impact: The 1995 FCC auction of frequencies for new communication services is one example.

What advice might the economic frame offer our pharmaceutical executive? Figure 7.2 summarizes some of the specific advice that might be drawn from the economic frame. The economic frame helps the executive analyze the potential payoffs of different strategies for the company and competitors. It examines how these payoffs lead to an expected equilibrium. The figure shows the central role of an assumption of rationality, especially by competitors. As a descriptive model, the economic frame seems to make heroic assumptions that may limit its usefulness for many strategic decisions. Is there an alternative?

Elements of the Behavioral Frame

Behavioral views of competitive decision making are neither as well articulated nor as complete as those of the economic frame. Still, the application of behavioral decision research to competitive decisions sheds new light on old biases and illustrates the need for new research. It also has highlighted some of the shadows of the economic frame. The behavioral frame emphasizes cognitive limitations and mental effort.

Figure 7.2
Advice from the Economic Frame

	Continuous Change	Discontinuous Change
Environmental Changes	• Calculate the equilibrium as competitive pressures drive down the price. If the equilibrium price is unsatisfactory (e.g., because a firm is *not* the low-cost producer), then plan to exit the market for the drug in question. • Frame customers as competitors and frame the buyer-seller exchange as a price-driven transaction, both of which lead to tough bargaining on price.	• With respect to changed FDA regulations to speed clinical trials and approval decisions, reanalyze the environment for the optimal plan of clinical trials given the new parameters.
Competitive Changes	• Calculate your optimal move in response to competitive downsizing to lower costs (e.g., also to downsize to remain competitive) and to their selective increases in R&D budgets. (Is it optimal to increase or decrease in the same areas as the competitors' increases if competitor rationality is presumed?)	• Under the presumption of competitor rationality, quickly seek to acquire one of the few remaining Prescription Benefit Manager firms.

These human shortcomings may be particularly relevant to competitive and dynamic decision making. In contrast to the rational approach of the economic frame, this frame acknowledges that players may define rationality differently. The behavioral frame seeks to determine the patterns of these biases and reveal what appears to an economist as "the method to their madness."

Perhaps the defining characteristic of the past 30 years of decision research has been a number of marked contrasts between normative and descriptive analyses. Almost shockingly, there has been very little application of these analyses to competitive decisions. The most notable exception has been in the circumscript realm of negotiation.

The decision biases highlighted by behavioral research include case-based reasoning, loss aversion, and other reference-based judgments and temporal myopia, as discussed by Meyer and Banks in Chapter 6. These biases can distort our perceptions of other parties, but the biases of opponents also may be exploitable in competition. These biases make the kind of rigorous competitive analysis proposed by the economic frame difficult, if not impossible.

For our pharmaceutical executive, the dangers of accepting the economic frame and its advice become clear. In a world of individuals, unable to achieve the economic paradigm's standards of perfection, our manager's guesses about what competition will do, and the decisions she bases on those guesses should deviate markedly from those suggested by the economic frame.

How might the behavioral frame address the challenges facing the pharmaceutical executive? The advice it offers is very different from that of the economic frame (see Figure 7.3). It is not that the two sets of advice conflict; they just address different elements of the same situation.

THE IMPACT OF GROUPS ON DECISIONS

One might point out, however, that most strategic decisions are made by groups rather than individuals. Won't these groups help eliminate some of the individual biases found in behavioral studies? Unfortunately for the economic frame, groups are often afflicted by the same biases as individuals. Consider the following examples of the way these group biases detract from the effectiveness of the economic frame.

Perceptions of Others

Because of false consensus or social projection,[8] we tend to believe that others, such as our competitors and customers, are more like us than they actually are.[9] Consequently, our pharmaceutical executive

Figure 7.3
Advice from the Behavioral Frame

	Continuous Change	Discontinuous Change
Environmental Changes	• Reference point. Offer the public guarantee that price increases will not exceed the rate of inflation (CPI). • Frame customers as part of a relationship. This requires a long-term "fairness" in pricing. For example, Lilly and Merck both maintained a single-price policy (to all buyers whether large or small; i.e., powerful or weak in negotiation price discounts) long after many industry analysts thought they should.	• False consensus. If you are currently ahead in a race to market a new drug, assume that your revised clinical trials plan for adjusting to new regulations is "safe" because your competitor(s) will probably make a similar adjustment.
Competitive Changes	• Anchor on a competitor's change and adjust for your firm's particular strengths or weaknesses. • Use a competitor's change in price, size of salesforce, etc., as a reference point.	• Frame biotech as "not us"; i.e., outside the boundary of the organization's self-frame.

might believe that customers share her view that pharmaceutical prices are justified by the high cost of research and development or that the competitors also have concluded that direct distribution at lower prices is important. This stands in stark contrast to the presumption in economic models that the executive has accurate, if not precise, beliefs about the opinions of consumers and competitors. Errors of false consensus may be exploited by competitors. An opponent who knows that we suffer from false consensus could make better predictions of our behavior than one who believes that we are motivated entirely by calculated self-interest.[10] Thus, if our pharmaceutical executive's false consensus is known to others, they may feign interest in an acquisition to increase its cost.

Do multiple decision makers eliminate or at least reduce false consensus? The answer seems to be no, in most cases. Groups show false consensus about members of their own group and even, although to a lesser extent, about members of other groups.[11] The exception is cases in which there are extreme in-group/out-group manipulations. While Hoch suggests such problems may not be large for marketing managers,[12] Mitchell, Adams, and Johnson provide evidence that marketing managers, even those with significant expertise, believe that their customers are much more like themselves than they really are, and that this hurts their predictions of market successes and failures.[13]

Perceptions of Probabilities

Decision makers also suffer from the bias of overconfidence.[14] Since managers' actions are predicated on their predictions about the behavior of competitors, overconfidence could result in, among other things, insufficient contingency planning and a lack of preparation for surprises. Our pharmaceutical executive might be much too sure that a competitor will enter the bidding for an acquisition and make an overly generous opening offer to "scare" off the competition, which is, in reality, uninterested. Conversely, if the executive is overconfident there will not be another suitor, she may not plan for its entrance into bidding.

When judgments are made by groups, overconfidence is reduced, but far from eliminated. Russo and Schoemaker report that when managers were asked for a 90 percent confidence interval, their rate of misses averaged 72 percent, far above the ideal of 10 percent.[15] When those same intervals were estimated in groups of three or four, misses were reduced to a smaller but still grossly overconfident 56 percent.

Ambiguity

Managers face ambiguity because probabilities are not precisely known, but instead can be described as a range. For example, our pharmaceutical executive surely had, at best, a range of probabilities that health care reform would emerge from the political process. According to economic theory, such ambiguity should have no effect upon the decision. An average probability is 0.5, even if from a range of 0.1 to 0.9, is fully equivalent to a coin toss with an exact chance of 0.5.[16]

Unfortunately, ambiguity may pose problems similar to overconfidence in competitive decisions. Because beliefs about competitors' behavior can rarely be reduced to a simple probability like a die roll or coin toss, economics' strong normative assumptions do not hold. An executive might benefit from knowing, for example, how averse to ambiguity are his or her competitors.[17] In a game theoretic study, Karajalainen and Camerer find that players typically pay significantly more for nonambiguous options.[18]

Perceptions of Outcomes

As discussed by Meyer and Banks in Chapter 6, the framing of information relative to a standard affects how it is perceived. For example, we might be able to describe a year's profits as either 20 percent greater than the industry average, or 20 percent down from last year. In both cases, we might be talking about the same profitability. A 12 percent profit looks great compared to an industry profit of 10 percent (an increase of 20 percent), but not so good when compared to last year's profit of 15 percent (a decrease of 20 percent). Of course, the outcomes are identical but appear quite different when "framed" relative to different standards. The standard analysis of economics, however, suggests that choices among the outcomes of a decision will be invariant across descriptions.

Again, we ask whether groups somehow correct individual biases. McGuire, Kiesler, and Siegel suggest that face-to-face groups suffer from the same framing effects as individuals.[19] Whyte also shows that groups are fully as likely as individuals to ignore sunk costs and to escalate commitment.[20]

In sum, groups cannot be relied upon to remove or even ameliorate all individual biases. Whether groups help at all depends on the bias itself and possibly other situational factors. We do not yet know the characteristics of biases or situations that are invulnerable to group amelioration and those that are reduced by exposure to the views of others. We do know, however, that organizations cannot assume that a group of smart, well-intentioned managers will automatically remove the biases of each individual member. Even with groups making decisions, managers rarely, if ever, achieve the rationality expected by the economic frame.

A BATTLE OF TWO FRAMES: POINT AND COUNTERPOINT

Given the fundamental differences between these frames, it is often hard for managers to reconcile them. Nor are these differences fully resolved within each frame. But there has been an ongoing debate between the two views, which we have summarized in the following point and counterpoint arguments that might be made by proponents of each frame. Consider, first, the economic frame's attack on the concerns of the behavioral frame.

The Economic Frame Attacks

The economic frame dismisses the concerns of the behavioral frame as irrelevant: Any individual-level biases will be limited, and especially unimportant in the aggregate. While individual-level departures from calculated rationality are not denied by the economic frame, they are deemed inconsequential since they will disappear in real-world settings of import.

How does this happen? At the heart of this logic are two distinct levels of analysis, which we will term *evolutionary learning* and *adaptive learning*. First, the evolutionary argument is that biased decision makers will be eliminated or selected out by competition.[21] This is actually a stronger argument than is necessary. Instead, biased players may not become extinct, but rather remove themselves from a competitive situation as a result of self-selection: Only those who have appropriate strategies choose to play a given game. Quasi-rational players will not necessarily disappear, but rather they will migrate to domains where their weaknesses will not hurt. As a society, efficiency occurs by matching roles with strengths and weakness of players. The key assumption of evolutionary adaptation is that selection erases the influence of any biased decision maker.

Second, the economic frame would argue that adaptive learning results from developing specialized heuristics or mental shortcuts that perform nearly as well as more complex normative processes, a process similar to views popular in cognitive psychology.[22] In contrast to the mechanism of selection among species, adaptive learning emphasizes the learning of appropriate strategies as a result of feedback.[23] With this mechanism, organisms do not die, rather they learn. The emerging body of work in experimental economics demonstrates in a rather large set of circumstances that people can come to a predicted equilibrium. The ultimate question is not whether normative economic models are descriptive of process, but whether they are predictive of outcomes—particularly in the long run. In many cases, the answer is rather comforting for the economic frame. Taken together, these arguments suggest that observations of individual departures from the economic ideal are of limited interest at best.

The Behavioral Frame Replies

An obvious reply from the behavioral perspective is that "in the long run we are all dead." The key concern for many managers concerns the speed with which the system arrives at equilibrium. Figure 7.4 represent the results of a fairly lengthy experimental market which, by round 190, settles down to approximately the equilibrium predicted by the economic frame.[24] An advocate of the behavioral frame might claim that this is a long time, especially in a simple classroom experiment. Moreover, most of the profit in this market, our behavioralist might note, occurs while the market is marching toward equilibrium, not *at* equilibrium. Someone who knows how to exploit this convergence path could "get rich getting to equilibrium."

We believe that there is substantial merit to this point. After all, the real world is often less stable than these experiments, and adapting to changing conditions seems to be a hallmark of viable corporate strategy.

Figure 7.4
Arriving at Equilibrium

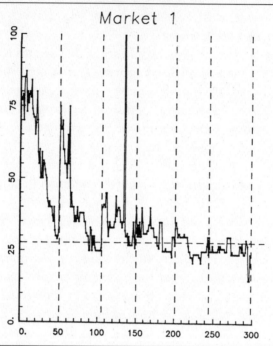

Jessica Goodfellow and Charles R. Plott, "An Experimental Examination of the Simultaneous Determination of Input Prices and Output Prices, *Southern Economics Journal, 56* (1990), pp. 969–983.

Certainly, as the market for personal computers changed in the beginning of the 1990s, IBM changed more slowly than Compaq, with obvious consequences.[25]

A second concern raised by the behavioral frame is the impact of transaction costs and other sources of friction in the market.[26] Costs of thinking, communicating and implementing, our behavioralist would reply, are all substantial barriers to adaptation, and should be included in any analysis. In fact, they must be included in an analysis of rationality, a goal that an advocate of the behavioral frame might argue is beyond the technical limits of most formal models.[27]

A final point concerns the "prizes" that are the goal of economic rationality. Even if we accept that the mechanisms can produce convergence to equilibria, there is still an important question: What is being maximized? Specifying what constitutes utility or personal value is complicated. Can considerations such as fairness be easily accommodated by rational models of utilization maximization? Even if they can, how can we, a priori, assess what should be in the utility function?

In summary, our behavioralist might quote Herbert Simon:

> The assumption that actors maximize subjective expected utility (economic rationality) supplies only a small part of the premises in economic reasoning, and that is often not the essential part. The remainder of the premises are auxiliary empirical assumptions about actors' utilities, beliefs, expectations, and the like.[28]

Caught between Frames

Where does all this squabbling leave our executive, with her need to make decisions? Even if she had an appetite for the esoteric, she must feel profoundly disappointed. Neither frame addresses the questions raised by the other. Looking at Figure 7.4, an economist might ask several reasonable questions of a psychologist: Why did this market take longer to converge than some others? When might it not converge? Why do people start with such high prices? Note that although the behavioral frame has a surplus of interesting and provocative constructs, it has little in its arsenal that would enable it to address these interesting, provocative, and appropriate questions.

On the other hand, the economic frame, which points proudly to its success at predicting prices starting at round 200, would have difficulty answering some of the behavioralist's questions: What is the cause of the variations we see in prices in these later trials? What would happen if the parameters of the market change? Would adding or subtracting agents affect the speed of convergence?[29]

For our executive, these questions are real and important. Translating Figure 7.4 into the questions that face her is easy, finding answers is not. She needs to know if the market for pharmaceuticals will converge given new realities. What will happen if different firms believe different things will happen? She needs to know the path of future prices: What prices will prevail and when? She can make money by knowing the path to equilibrium, but no matter how highly paid, her advisors cannot seem to help her, at least not within these two conceptual frameworks.

A Missing Piece

We offer, in Figure 7.5, our depiction of the overlap of the two frames, with what we believe to be a generous definition of the intersection. Each ellipse contains the highlights of a frame, that is, those foci, assumptions, or goals that comprise and define it. Without any one of them, the frame would be substantially different. Try to imagine economics without assuming managers' rationality to derive such prescribed behaviors as optimal prices, product introductions, and

Figure 7.5
Relationships among the Three Frames

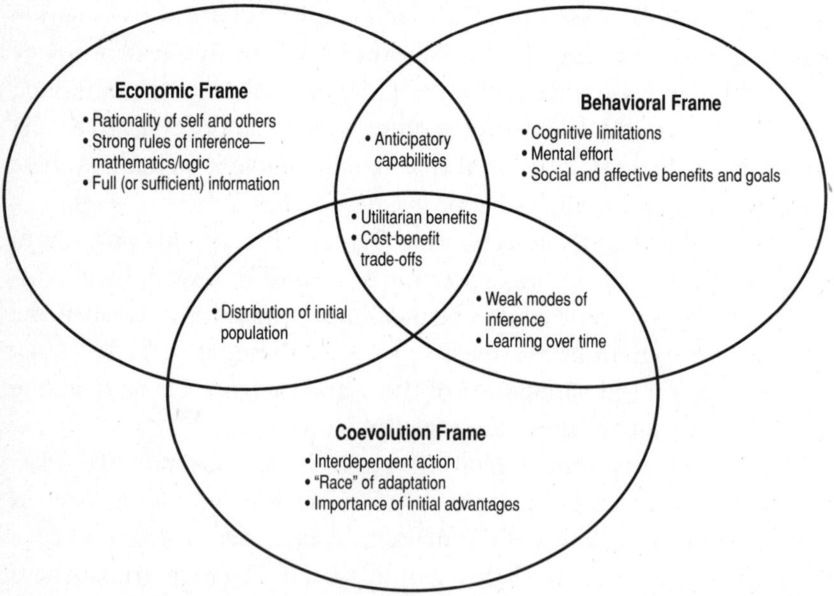

advertising levels. Similarly, what would be left of the behavioral perspective if learning over time were excluded?

We suggest that to both academics and our pharmaceutical executive what matters in Figure 7.5 is not so much what is included in each frame, but what is excluded. The danger of accepting frame-bound advice usually lies in the shadows that the frame casts. In making competitive decisions, managers are more frequently tripped up by shadows, that is, by what is overlooked, than by the highlights they have focused on. Consider the economic frame's focus on equilibria, with its occlusion of learning over time. A competitor less fixated on "equilibrium solutions" to its decision problems might "get rich getting to equilibrium" because of its focus on learning. Furthermore, in an evermore rapidly changing business environment, continuous learning may yield greater benefits than (optimal) equilibrium solutions to conditions that are never stable.

As one examines Figure 7.5, the narrowness of the overlap between the economic and behavioral frames is striking. Even here, we are more generous than Zeckhauser, who argues that the gap is greater than even "a Kuhnian struggle among paradigms" because the two camps cannot agree on a common set of phenomena to battle.[30] Instead, each camp selects phenomena that are well explained by its own paradigm and ignores those that are not. In the same conference volume, George Steigler notes "there have been several attempts to find and develop links between economics and psychology in the last 150 years. However, these have had little effect."[31]

Although we largely agree with our distinguished colleagues that the economic and behavioral frames exhibit frustratingly little overlap, we also feel that what is left out by both frames may be even more important. Even adaptive learning does not, by itself, identify unique equilibria if we abandon the assumption that competitors have common and mutual rationality. Not only are there many interesting questions at the intersection of the two frames, but there are many issues that neither frame addresses. For our executive, these questions are not just of academic interest, but painfully real, with clear implications for her decisions. And these issues fall between the cracks of the two frames.

COEVOLUTION: AN INTEGRATIVE PARADIGM?

What is this third frame of coevolution? Coevolution, a concept we borrow from evolutionary biology, points out that play is not necessarily against a rational opponent, or even against one capable of rationality. Instead, the adversaries may be single-cell organisms, for which common and mutual rationality is not an acceptable assumption. Coevolution has a 100-year history in biology, originating in the study of parasite-host relationships, and is employed in studying linked systems such as birds and the food they eat, and viruses and their effect upon those they infect.[32] The ideas have been applied broadly. For example, Durham presents an intriguing analysis of how genetics and the environment interact to produce diversity in human cultures.[33] We suspect that an analysis of strategic decisions in commerce can benefit from viewing them in the coevolution frame.

Any system in which the outcomes of behavior are interdependent can coevolve. Consider the classic coevolutionary case of bees, flowers, and their symbiotic relationship. Flowers provide food (nectar) for the bees, and the bees pollinate the flowers. Selection renders the flowers more attractive, because it increases their chance of pollination, while the bees who are more efficient pollinators of the flowers are also better foragers, increasing their probability of survival.

This type of coevolution can be seen in the development of the Internet. Netscape, which pioneered the market, gives away its most visible product—the Navigator browser. Like a flower designed to attract bees, the browser is only a means to an end. The estimated 40 million users of Netscape's browsers, help it carry its "pollen" into large organizations. The goal is to sell Web server products and Intranet consulting services to corporate customers. As Netscape CEO James Barksdale told *Fortune,* "The browser is a tactic, not a strategy. Our objective was to get known, get into corporate America, and then move up the food chain."[34] More important, bees (consumers) benefit from the free software, and the company benefits from the broader visibility achieved through this large user base.

Note that coevolution can tolerate departures from rationality, yet reach an equilibrium. Flowers (which in our allegory represent firms) compete for the attention of bees (consumers) by producing variations that the bees find the most attractive. Imagine, however, that the bees in this story suffer from a bias, judging the attractiveness of a flower relative to the immediately surrounding flowers provided by the plant, something akin to the attraction effect.[35] In this case, a successful adaptation on the part of the plant would be the introduction of a number of "decoy" flowers. These are purposely less attractive and thereby render the "target" flowers more attractive from the perspective of the bees. Note that the flowers would seem to adapt to the quasi-rationality of the bees, and that a flower that adapts will do better than one that does not. Further, note that this is an equilibrium.

Companies do this by offering a low-priced, stripped-down model of cars or other products. Once they attract the customer through these lower-margin products, they then try to move them to higher-margin luxury products that appear much more attractive in relation to the low-end models.

Recall that frames have both highlights and shadows. How does the coevolution frame shift the light? This analysis shifts our focus from the irrationality or rationality of actors to their interdependence. Rather than the actor/manager having to adapt to an unyielding environment or a rational opponent, the players coevolve. The outcome of this process could well be a stable equilibrium, but one that does not originate from assumptions of common knowledge and mutual rationality.

The important elements (highlights) of a (co)evolutionary analysis of competitive games are quite different from those suggested by either the economic or behavioral frame. For example, coevolutionary outcomes are very sensitive to the distribution of strategies in the initial population, the initial beliefs about this distribution held by the population, and the process of revising these beliefs. Neither the economic nor behavioral frame can, as currently constituted, address these issues in a complete or satisfying way. Yet these questions seem important: What do new entrants to a market believe about their competitors? What do they believe about their own capabilities? Are these beliefs accurate? What is the speed of learning among new entrants? Coevolution suggests that answers to these questions can help us understand some of the questions we raised when examining Figure 7.5. These answers depend upon an assessment of what the initial beliefs and strategies are (which might be of interest to a behavioral frame) and an understanding of the processes by which they are modified, abandoned, or refined.

The coevolutionary frame also highlights a race to adapt. Those organisms or firms that first recognize and take advantage of an opportunity in the environment—possibly an opportunity resulting from a recent adaptive move by competitors or customers—may win the race of adaptation. Being first with a superior strategy or capability may yield a defensible competitive advantage, at least until another actor's adaptation changes the environment once again. Although the evolutionary time scale is much, much longer than that granted to managers, it may be speedy, relative to the competition that is more salient. As Darwin himself noted, "[t]hough Nature grants long periods of time for work of natural selection, she does not grant an infinite period . . . if any one species does not become modified and improved in a corresponding degree with its competitors, it will be exterminated."[36]

Obviously, we feel that the coevolutionary frame offers many benefits for viewing competitive decision-making. At a minimum, it should be added to the current portfolio of frames that can illuminate the complex competitive decisions facing managers. Yet it, too, has its shadows, and these must not be forgotten. In adopting the coevolutionary frame, we sacrifice the power of mathematical inference that makes the economic frame so useful. And this third frame lacks the behavioral frame's recognition of the social and affective goals of managers, personal goals of recognition and satisfaction that are distinct from the "bottom line" survival of the organization. Finally, and perhaps most limiting to the coevolutionary frame's value to managers, is its reactive stance. It offers no capability for proactively anticipating changes in the competitive environment and preparing for various contingencies.

CONCLUSION

We have presented three frames through which managers can view competition. Which one should be used by the vice president in the opening example? She might be wise to view competition through each of these frames—to understand the nature of the beast more completely. Each frame casts it own light on different aspects of competition and each creates its own shadows. Managers should be aware of the strengths and blind spots of each approach.

We are reminded of the classic story of the drunk who has lost his keys. He is groping on the ground near a lamppost. When asked why he is looking there, he replies, "Because there's light here." Suspicious, his inquisitor asks where the keys were lost. "Down the block" is the reply. The two frames, economic and behavioral, help to remind us that if we restrict ourselves to one, the keys of knowledge may lie in its shadows. Certainly, each of these two alternative viewpoints has its fair share of shadows. Adding the third light of the coevolutionary perspective can help remove some of these blind spots.

How can these different approaches be enlarged and developed to shed more light on competition? Extending formal economic models to incorporate more realistic assumptions about human behavior would seem only to move us away from the light of strongly valid inference processes. Adding inferential power to more vertical behavioral representations of a decision maker's knowledge, including knowledge of the competition, is clearly a desired direction. But this is more like moving the lamppost down the block to where the keys are—a nice idea, but not very practical. Our very brief sketch of coevolutionary ideas suggests that notions of interdependence and mutual adaptation could provide at least a glimmer of moonlight upon our search.

CHAPTER 8

ANTICIPATING REACTIONS: FACTORS THAT SHAPE COMPETITOR RESPONSES

S. VENKATARAMAN

Rensselaer Polytechnic Institute, Lally School of Management and Technology

MING-JER CHEN

Columbia University

IAN C. MACMILLAN

The Wharton School, Department of Management

The preceding chapters have presented several theoretical frameworks for understanding and anticipating competitor reactions. This chapter discusses the results of an empirical study of actions and reactions in the airline industry. It addresses the question: If you initiate a given action, how will rivals respond? The authors identify three key factors that influence whether there will be a response and the characteristics of that response: the nature of the action, the nature of the actor, and the nature of the rival. These factors determine whether and how quickly the target firm is likely to respond.

The success of a given strategy very often depends upon the reactions of rivals, but these reactions can only be known after the fact. Even what appears to be an effective strategy can turn out to be a disaster if competitors react in the wrong way. What is it that makes competitors ignore one move while responding aggressively to another?

This chapter discusses insights into the factors that influence competitive reactions. The findings are derived from the results of a recent large-scale study of actions and reactions in the airline industry. As part of the study, we conducted an extensive eight-year analysis of articles in *Aviation Daily* to catalog reported actions and reactions among the major airlines. In all, we looked at more than 800 actions and more than 200 responses. Although individual firm and industry characteristics will have an impact on the nature of the competitive response, this study provides important insights into the key factors that affect the responses of rivals.

The results confirm the obvious observation that rivals will react more strongly to attacks "closer to the jugular." Companies fight more fiercely for their lives than they do for an unimportant market. But the study also provides finer insights into the nature of competitive interactions and offers a set of guidelines for anticipating the responses of competitors in developing your own strategies.

The approach to this study is meant to capture the naïve reasoning that is often used by managers. As noted by Meyer in Chapter 6, managers rely heavily on simple heuristics to reduce the complexity of decisions or facilitate choices. This study uses the behavioral theory of the firm to capture the ways managers actually think about the complex situations involved in competitive actions and reactions.[1] This approach is particularly useful in industries that have many competitors who vary in size, age, resource endowments, strategy, market and product focus, and so on, and who are therefore affected very differently by the same actions. In real-world competition, this is a situation in which many managers find themselves.

THREE DIMENSIONS THAT DESCRIBE THE PICTURE

Before turning to the airline industry, consider the predicament of John Doe, the director of fixed income funds at a large investment company. He is debating a variety of alternative strategies in his quest to gain a larger share of the bond funds market and increase the management fees obtained by his firm. Among his options: He could decrease the load on the company's funds, raise management fees, maximize operating efficiencies, increase advertising, or acquire other boutique firms. All of these choices could potentially have the impact of increasing share, increasing operating fees, or both. But the crux of John Doe's problem is that the success of his action depends on his rivals' reactions, and he cannot be sure whether or how they will respond. Depending on the responses, any action he takes will have different consequences for the profitability and market share of his firm.

If Doe were operating in a perfectly competitive industry, then he would have to make only one decision: What quantity of his product to supply (where to cap the funds) at the prevailing price that the market is willing to pay for such funds (over which he has no control). Essentially, there are just two variables that he has to worry about: price and quantity.

If, on the other hand, the industry and the products were sufficiently differentiated, Doe would have to worry about only a handful of competitors similar to his company. Then, he could usefully and practically employ a variety of analytical techniques (for example, game theory) to decide on the optimal competitive moves.

But Doe's predicament is particularly troublesome because he operates in an industry where he faces numerous competitors that are quite heterogeneous in their capabilities and preferences, and each of which, like him, faces numerous choices of its own. Before he makes his move, Doe would like to know, for example:

- Which types of competitive actions elicit responses and which do not?
- To which actions are competitors most likely to respond?
- Which firms are most likely to respond?
- Are there differences in the speed of reactions depending on the nature of the action, the nature of the actor, and the nature of the affected rival?

Although analytical techniques can be employed in such complex situations, the techniques become so complex that managers generally do not have the time to employ them, nor do markets behave according to the normative solutions these techniques suggest. The question then is whether we can discover some predictable patterns in interactive competitive behavior that would facilitate choice, or at least reduce complexity to allow a more meaningful use of sophisticated techniques.[2]

Facing this complex competitive picture, managers such as Doe can economize their time and attention by reducing the uncertainty and ambiguity of actual events to a few simple dimensions. In effect, managers can work off a line drawing of the competitive situation. It lacks many of the details and richness of the original situation, but it also is much easier to sketch and to grasp. In creating this image of competition—and planning their response—managers need to focus on three key dimensions of competition:

1. The characteristics of the competitive action that has been taken.
2. The characteristics of the initiator of that action, or the actor.
3. The characteristics of the affected rival.

This framework is illustrated in Figure 8.1. Using this framework, John Doe can analyze each of his planned actions from his competitors' perspectives. By determining the characteristics of his company and the rival, as well as the nature of the competitive action in relation to the rival, he can better anticipate the likely reactions that will be evoked. He can better understand which competitive actions are most likely to elicit responses, which are not, and how quickly a response

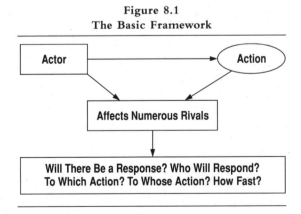

Figure 8.1
The Basic Framework

201

will be made. But he also needs to know *how* the three factors affect the potential for response. The following study of the airline industry provides such insights. After examining this study, we will return to John Doe's challenges at the conclusion of the chapter.

COMPETITIVE FLIGHT PATHS IN THE AIRLINE INDUSTRY

To understand the combinations of the nature of the action, the actor, and the affected rival that have the highest (and lowest) probability of response, and the quickest (and slowest) response times, we examined interactions in the U.S. domestic airline industry between the years 1979 and 1986. This is an intensely competitive industry with a large number of diverse rivals.

We reviewed every issue of the trade journal *Aviation Daily* over an eight-year period, identifying the most significant and prominent competitive actions and reactions in the industry.[3] The total sample consisted of 816 actions (103 of these actions provoked at least one response, while the remaining ones did not) and 203 responses. We developed a database of competitive actions, defined as moves that have the potential to take market share at the expense of rivals, or to reduce the anticipated returns of rivals. Actions that have no demonstrable impact on market share, such as organizational restructuring, were excluded.[4] One article, for example, is headlined "United Airlines and Frontier Responded to Continental's 35% price cuts."[5] The action—the price cut by Continental—provoked a price response from its rivals.

This population of competitive actions and their responses contains 13 types:[6]

1. Price cuts.
2. Promotions with travel agents.
3. Promotion campaigns.
4. Feeder alliances with commuter.
5. Cooperation with other airlines.
6. Service improvements.
7. New service introductions.

8. Increases in daily departures.
9. Route exits.
10. Route entries.
11. Frequent flier promotions.
12. Mergers or acquisitions.
13. Hub creations.

Table 8.1 presents a detailed account of all competitive actions studied and their corresponding responses. At first glance, the table reveals that price actions relative to other actions are most likely to be responded to with very little delay. Before we jump to conclusions, though, we must remember that our objective here is to discover the combinations of the nature of actions, actors, and affected rivals that have the highest or lowest likelihood of response and quickest or slowest response time. This table just looks at actions. Before we discuss how all three of these factors affect responses, first we must examine the relevant characteristics of action, actor, and affected rival that are salient from the behavioral theory point of view. We will then highlight the most interesting combinations of these three properties.

Nature of the Action

The first question we considered is whether there are unique properties in the actions that would provoke a response from rivals. Two properties of actions are significant in the behavioral theory of the firm: The first is the visibility of the action, and the second is the logistical complexity of the action.

Visibility of an action is important for two reasons. First, time and attention are scarce resources. Managers have a limited span of attention and time, so they will attend only to certain competitive actions, while ignoring others. Actions that draw great attention in the market will have a greater probability of attracting competitors' attention, a necessary condition for response to occur. Second, firms are inherently political. The attention of managers is most likely to be focused on those issues that are receiving the scrutiny of the key stakeholders and of other institutions that control valuable resources required by

Table 8.1
Summary of Action and Response Characteristics

Action	Number Observed	Percent Responses	Average Time for Response (In Days)	Percent of Actions Matched
Price Cut	124	75%	5.7	98%
Promotion with Travel Agents	48	69	11.4	100
Promotion Campaign	103	37	18.2	74
Feeder Alliance with Commuter	9	33	46	100
Cooperation with other Airline	24	17	13	100
Service Improvement	24	12.5	10.7	100
New Service Introduction	23	8.7	NA	NA
Increase in Daily Departures	153	3.3	45	100
Route Exit	33	15	22	0
Route Entry	172	4	41	43
Frequent Flyer Promotion	29	17	22	100
Merger & Acquisition	18	11	55	100
Hub Creation	17	17.7	28	33

the firm. The greater the attention drawn to an action, the more the marketplace (transactional, competitive, financial, and others) is alerted to the particular challenge that the action poses to the affected firm. Thus, there is pressure on the affected firm to respond to that action. Interestingly, it may not even be in the incumbent firm's best interests to respond to those challenges to which resource controllers and stakeholders have been alerted. But regardless of whether the decision makes rational economic sense, there is a high probability that a firm will choose to react to rivals' actions that are highly visible in the environment.

To examine the role of visibility, we performed two types of analyses. First, we divided all actions into price and nonprice actions. Price actions are a special category of competitive move because they impart much more information than other moves. Since price changes directly affect a business's bottom line, it is much easier to estimate their impact on the profits of both an actor and on the affected rival. Because of their immediate visibility and the ease with which market share can be determined, price actions tend to be more provocative than others.

Second, we pooled all the actions and then categorized them as high-visibility and low-visibility to examine the likelihood of response and response time. High-visibility actions were those that, in the opinion of industry experts, (a) were most likely to receive great industry publicity; (b) were most likely to be announced publicly by top management; (c) required top-management approval; and (d) created strong obligations to major stakeholders such as unions and travel agents. Visibility and complexity of a move were assessed through a mail questionnaire survey of 312 senior airline executives and other industry experts.[7]

We next looked at the complexity of the action. We considered actions to be highly complex if, in the opinion of industry experts surveyed, the actions would: (a) require substantial relocation of staff and equipment; (b) meet with stronger resistance from stakeholders to reversing the move; (c) make the redeployment of resources (other than aircraft) to other purposes difficult; (d) disrupt staff, systems, and/or procedures during implementation; (e) require extensive interdepart-mental coordination; and (f) impose high financial cost to reverse.

Complexity of an action is important for two reasons. First, a com-mon feature of organizational activity is its programmed character—the extent to which behavior in any particular case is the enactment of preestablished routines. Most procedures are "standard," and therefore are not easily adaptable to particular situations. Consequently, organi-zations have a greater tendency to respond to those actions or stimuli that evoke standard responses and procedures and *ignore those that do not evoke such standard routines.* Highly complex competitive actions are pre-sumably relatively rare in the experience of any organization, compared to more routine competitive ones. Moreover, such complex actions may take a variety of forms, and the precise scope and nature of these actions may not be easily estimated. More important, routine responses to highly complex actions may not be sufficient; such actions may there-fore require nonstandard responses. The parochial preferences of dif-ferent coalitions, the need to coordinate numerous stakeholders, as well as bounded rationality all make departure from standard procedure dif-ficult and tend to result in inertia rather than in response.

Second, complex actions also typically involve high commitment on the part of the actor. An actor's commitment has two important implications. First, in the absence of the ability to estimate potential payoffs for actions and responses, and in an environment where there is ambiguity about causality and interpretation, an actor's commit-ment to its action has important informational value. Because the costs of abandoning the action are very high, the initiator of a highly com-mitted action is unlikely to back down. As noted by Thomas in Chap-ter 13, greater commitment makes it more likely the incumbent will not withdraw. In addition to the obvious economic costs of with-drawing after making a commitment, several academic studies have found that there are also psychological and organizational costs to backing down from an action.[8]

These costs surrounding a committed action make it clear that the actor would defend its position if the affected rival counterattacked. Thus, the greater the commitment by the actor, the less chance the re-sponder has of forcing it to back down.

Nature of the Affected Rival

The second question we considered is whether there are particular characteristics of affected rivals that would make them predisposed to respond to a given competitive action? Behavioral theory draws attention to two aspects of the organization affected by a competitive action: incentive to react and ability to react. Since the predominant character of any organization is inertia, or the propensity to follow preestablished routines and procedures, there must be an incentive to respond that has crossed the attention threshold of managers. Second, given the presence of such an incentive, the company must also have the ability to respond.

Because of the constraints of time and attention, and an aversion to changing standard operating procedures, organizational actions and reactions are thought to be triggered by two characteristics of organizations: organizational performance and slack availability. While performance provides the incentive to react to a given action, slack availability determines the ability to react to this action.

To measure organizational performance, we looked at two dimensions: (1) the potential impact of a given action on the future performance of a rival and (2) the past performance of the affected rival.

The effect on future performance is captured by the rival's dependence on the affected market(s). The greater the dependence on the market(s) affected by an action, the greater the incentive on the part of the rival to respond to that action. To examine the effect on future performance, we divided the affected rivals into two types: those airlines that were highly dependent on the markets affected, and those airlines that were not highly dependent on these markets. This variable was determined according to the airports affected by the given action; the number of passengers affected in each airport by the action; the airlines serving the affected airports; and the estimated proportion of each rival's passengers affected by the action. This procedure allowed us to separate the affected rivals into those highly dependent on a market affected by an action and those not affected.

Poor past performance also increases the incentive to respond. Behavioral theory predicts that poorly performing firms will have a greater incentive to respond, or at least will respond more quickly than better performing firms. The poorly performing firm is often searching for solutions to its problems, so its managers pay more attention to actions of competitors. Indeed, firms with decreasing performance are expected to be more responsive to competitive actions because such actions may pose a further threat to these firms' already inferior performance. Hence, with lower performance, there is greater likelihood of reacting, and reacting more quickly, to a competitive action.

We measured past performance using a weighted index of four performance variables: profit margin, operating revenues per revenue-passenger-mile, operating profits per revenue-passenger-mile, and S&P's stock rating. Each company had a specific performance index for each year of the research period.[9]

Organizational slack also affects the ability of an affected rival to respond. Slack exists when a firm contains a pool of unexploited resources, in the form of excess liquidity or underutilized assets, which may be used either to deal with nonroutine events or to search for new profit-making or threat-reducing opportunities.

Slack can be viewed as a firm's resource reservoir, allowing the firm to adapt to unanticipated and uncontrollable changes. The size of an organization is often used as a measure of its slack. Larger organizations often have redundancies and excess resources of human capital, liquidity, facilities, equipment and services, or other resources, which may be redeployed to combat a new competitive threat. Thus, larger organizations in general should have greater ability to respond to competitive actions than smaller organizations. Accordingly, we used the size of an organization as a proxy for slack availability. We measured size by classifying airlines into two types: major carriers (e.g., United Airlines) and national carriers (e.g., Midway Airlines), with major carriers representing large airlines and national carriers representing small airlines.

Nature of the Actor

The final question we considered is whether certain characteristics of the acting firm will especially predispose rivals to respond to its actions. We think that the size of the actor will tend to have an effect on response behavior. Organizational size has long been considered one of the most significant variables in the organizational theory literature.

Size of the actor is important for two reasons. First, actions of larger firms are more visible than actions of smaller ones. This visibility is important in a world of limited time and attention, as we discussed. Smaller firms, given the disadvantage of their size, are more likely to adopt covert tactics and indirect or subtle attacks to avoid widespread recognition. In contrast, the need to meet the diverse obligations of a wide variety of stakeholders, and the pressures to signal their commitment to a particular action (in hope of intimidating competitors and deterring responses), larger firms are apt to make their competitive challenges as visible as possible. This difference in relative visibility suggests that actions of larger firms are more likely to induce responses and quicker responses than actions of smaller firms.

Second, actions of larger firms provide greater incentive for affected rivals to respond, because, given their size, larger firms pose greater threats to the market share of affected rivals. If left unchecked, there is the grave danger that the larger firm may be motivated to escalate its challenge to acquire an even greater share. In contrast, smaller firms pose a relatively smaller threat, at least in the short run.

As before, we measured size by classifying airlines into two types, major carriers and national carriers.

Price Actions, Size of Rival Are Most Important Factors

Which were the most important factors in eliciting a competitive response? The single most significant dimension that determines whether an action will elicit a response and, in the event of a response, the speed of response is the price/nonprice dichotomy of the action. Figure 8.2 shows the result of such an analysis. Of all the actions we observed, 16 percent of the actions were price actions, and the rest nonprice.

While price actions have a very high probability of eliciting a response (0.75 probability), nonprice actions had a very low probability (a mere 0.17 probability). Although there is not much difference in whether these actions elicit a matching response (where the response is

Figure 8.2
Action Type and Response Characteristics

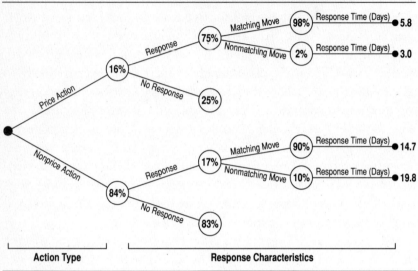

the same as the original action), price actions tend to have significantly quicker responses (average time to respond, less than 5.8 days) than nonprice actions (average response time, over 14.7 days). Thus, whether an action is a price action or not is one of the most important indications of the likelihood and the speed of the response.

The second most important dimension was the size of the affected rival.[10] Although size of the actor was also a useful discriminator, it was not as pronounced as the size of the affected rival in eliciting response. Table 8.2 shows that major carriers affected by an action are much more likely to respond to it (0.20 probability) than are national carriers (only 0.037 probability of responding). Similarly, actions of major carriers are much more likely to elicit a response (0.10 probability) than are actions of national carriers (0.026 probability).

Surprisingly, this difference in the propensity to react persists even when we divide the actions into price and nonprice actions, as Tables 8.3 and 8.4 indicate. The propensity of affected national

210

Table 8.2
Probability of Any Given Affected Competitor Responding to Action

		Responding Airline		
		Major Carrier	National Carrier	
Actors	Major Carrier	.27	.038	.10
	National Carrier	.125	.035	.026
		.20	.037	

carriers to respond is uniformly low, regardless of whether the action is a price action.

Visibility and complexity of an action also turn out to be reasonably good discriminators when it comes to predicting likelihood of response, but only when the affected airlines are major carriers, not national airlines.

Visibility of the action has no clear impact on response time, as shown in Figure 8.3. But low-complexity actions, as shown in Figure 8.4, elicit significantly quicker responses than high-complexity ones.

Table 8.3
Impact of the Nature of the Action

Probability of Responding to	Rival Is Major Carrier	Rival Is National Carrier
Any Action	.20	.037
Price Actions	.24	.034
Nonprice Actions	.17	.039
High-Visibility Actions	.23	.04
Low-Visibility Actions	.16	.03
High-Complexity Actions	.12	.02
Low-Complexity Actions	.23	.04

Table 8.4
Probability of Response

Nature of Actor	Any Action	Price Action	Nonprice Action
Major Carrier	.10	.10	.10
National Carrier	.026	.10	.06

Further, the highly complex actions of major airlines elicit quicker responses than those of national airlines.

The last dimension that was somewhat significant in predicting likelihood of response was the extent of the rival's dependence on a market affected by an action. Rivals with a high dependence on markets affected are significantly more likely to respond than those with a lower dependence. Here again, the discrimination is more pronounced in the case of major carriers as actors than in the case of national carriers.

Figure 8.3
Action Type, Actor Type, and Response Characteristics

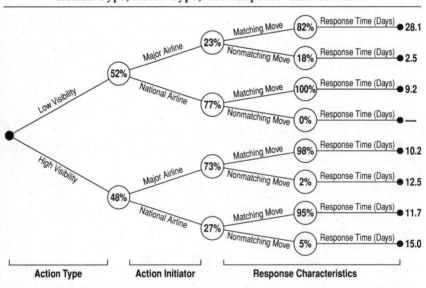

Figure 8.4
Action Type, Actor Type, and Response Characteristics

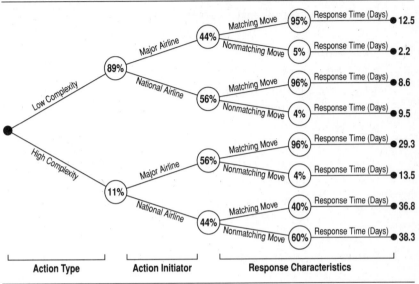

| Action Type | Action Initiator | Response Characteristics |

Past performance of the affected rivals was found to have no effect on responses. Both high performers and low performers have equal likelihood of response, although actions by major airlines are more likely to elicit a response. The results remain the same even if we introduce other dimensions into the analysis, such as price, visibility, and complexity of actions.

To summarize, the most significant factors in shaping a competitive response, in order of importance, seem to be: price/nonprice dichotomy, size of the rival, size of the action initiator, visibility of the action, and, finally, complexity of the action.

The Impact of Each of the Three Dimensions

In summary, let us revisit the three dimensions of the framework we considered to see how each contributed to explaining action-response dynamics in the airline industry:

1. *Nature of the Action.* Given limits on the managers' span of attention and the political nature of the firm, we suggested that the visibility and complexity of actions may influence competitor response and response speed. Indeed, our results show that visibility of actions, particularly price/nonprice dichotomy, is the single best predictor of competitor response. Similarly, more complex actions were better predictors of response and response speed than less complex actions, while less complex actions elicited quicker responses than more complex actions.
2. *Nature of Rivals.* The ability to respond, as represented by the size of the affected rivals, is the second best predictor of competitor response after the price/nonprice dichotomy. Surprisingly, incentive to respond, as measured by past performance and dependence on the market under attack, was not useful in predicting competitive responses.
3. *Nature of the Actor.* The size of the actor is an important factor in predicting responses. Larger actors were more likely to attract responses, particularly from other large companies.

John Doe's Challenge

In the light of these findings, let us now return to John Doe's predicament and see what guidance these analyses provide as he contemplates his moves for his firm. The first inference that Doe can make, using a behavioral perspective, is that all three dimensions—namely, nature of the action, nature of the affected rival, and the nature of the actor—will affect the likelihood of response and the speed of response. At a more detailed level, John Doe can infer that because his company is a major player, any action he takes will in all likelihood be met with a response. In particular, if he contemplates a price action, he can expect a quick response from rivals. While it is not always clear what is the price equivalent in the financial services industry, one might speculate that the load that a fund charges and its operating costs determine the cost, or equivalently the price to the customer to own that fund. Thus, actions taken by John Doe to change either the load charged by a fund and/or its annual operating expenses may have the greatest likelihood of attracting a response and a quicker response.

John Doe should pay close attention to his large rivals. The results show that his firm's actions are much more likely to be responded to by other large organizations than by smaller organizations. Thus, John Doe can expect greater reaction and quicker reaction from fund groups such as Vanguard, Dreyfuss, T. Rowe Price, or the Franklin/Templeton group. While not all of these organizations may respond, there is a very high probability that at least one of them will respond fairly rapidly. Further, the smaller the rival, the less likely will be a response from that organization. Thus, in planning and executing price moves, John Doe can safely ignore a whole segment of the competitive market. (It is interesting to note here that price actions taken by smaller organizations are as likely to be responded to as price actions of larger organizations.)

Those actions of John Doe that are highly visible and less complex are much more likely to elicit a response, especially if those actions directly affect larger rivals. Although not every affected rival may react, there is a high probability that at least one of them will react. In contrast, John Doe has the least to fear in cases where he takes less visible, nonprice actions that have a greater impact on the smallest rivals in the market.

Conclusion: Avoiding Response

What are the best ways to avoid drawing fire from a competitor? By combining the previous findings, Tables 8.5 and 8.6 show the combinations that are most likely and least likely to attract a competitive response. Tables 8.7 and 8.8 show the combinations that are most likely and least likely to draw a speedy response. Although not all of these strategies will be possible or desirable for a given firm in a given market, they offer a good starting point for discussing ways to avoid provoking a competitor.

Analyzing the nature of the actor, action, and affected rival can provide important insights into the likelihood of a competitive response and the speed of that response. This approach is particularly useful in

Table 8.5
Combinations with the Highest Likelihood of Response

#	Action Type	Actor Type	Responder Type: Size	Responder Type: Performance	Responder Type: Dependence
1	Price	Large	Large	High performer	High dependence on affected market
2	Price	Large	Large	Low performer	High dependence on affected market
3	High visibility	Large	Large	High performer	High dependence on affected market
4	High visibility	Large	Large	Low performer	High dependence on affected market
5	Low complexity	Large	Large	High performer	High dependence on affected market
6	Low complexity	Large	Large	Low performer	High dependence on affected market

contexts in which there are numerous players having numerous choices, and where the firms are quite heterogeneous in their attributes, but where the customer market does not reflect the same variety as the suppliers. In such situations, the manager faces significant uncertainties about the nature of day-to-day competition.

The behavioral perspective focuses on underlying conditions in which the manager operates, and the likely influence of these conditions on competitive dynamics. In contrast to calculating payoffs and optimal responses, the behavioral perspective examines characteristics of

Table 8.6
Combinations with the Lowest Likelihood of Response

#	Action Type	Actor Type	Responder Type: Size	Responder Type: Performance	Responder Type: Dependence
1	Nonprice	Small	Small	Low performer	Low dependence on affected market
2	Nonprice	Small	Small	High performer	Low dependence on affected market
3	Low visibility	Small	Small	Low performer	Low dependence on affected market
4	Low visibility	Small	Small	High performer	Low dependence on affected market
5	High complexity	Small	Small	Low performer	Low dependence on affected market
6	High complexity	Small	Small	High performer	Low dependence on affected market

actions, of actors, and of affected rivals, and how these characteristics themselves shape responses. First, some actions, by their very nature, will attract attention and provoke responses while others will not. Second, actions of certain firms are more likely to elicit a response than actions of others, and finally, some affected rivals are more likely to respond than others.

Table 8.7
Combinations with the Most Immediate Response

#	Action Type	Actor Type	Responder Type: Size	Responder Type: Performance	Responder Type: Dependence
1	Price	Large	Large	High & low performer	High dependence on affected market
2	Price	Small	Large	High & low performer	High dependence on affected market
3	High visibility	Large	Large	High & low performer	High dependence on affected market
4	Low complexity	Large	Large	High & low performer	High dependence on affected market

Table 8.8
Combinations with the Slowest Possible Response

#	Action Type	Actor Type	Responder Type: Size	Responder Type: Performance	Responder Type: Dependence
1	Nonprice	Small	Small	Low performer	Low dependence on affected market
2	Nonprice	Small	Small	High performer	Low dependence on affected market
3	Low visibility	Small	Small	Low performer	Low dependence on affected market
4	Low visibility	Small	Small	High performer	Low dependence on affected market
5	High complexity	Small	Small	Low performer	Low dependence on affected market
6	High complexity	Small	Small	High performer	Low dependence on affected market

CHAPTER 9

UNDERSTANDING COMPETITIVE RELATIONSHIPS

JAGMOHAN S. RAJU

The Wharton School, Department of Marketing

ABHIK ROY

The Hong Kong Polytechnic University

In addition to defining the arena and relative advantages of competitors, it is important to understand the patterns of relationships that govern competition in a given market. For example, does one competitor always lead and the others follow? Although many managers assume that relationships among competitors are independent and self-maximizing, there are actually a variety of possible relationships among firms in a market or industry. This chapter discusses three distinct relationships: independent, leader-follower, or collusive. It also examines tools for determining which relationship characterizes a specific market. For managers entering a new market or contemplating a strategic move, determining the relationship of current players is crucial to success. These relationships determine how competitors are likely to respond to actions in the market.

Consider the challenges that face managers at a U.S. corporation planning to enter a foreign market. A key element in their decision process is to understand the nature of competitive relationships among the current local players. Is one of the firms the price leader? Do local players act competitively or in collusion? The answers to these questions are essential to understanding the new market and the best approach to entering it. This chapter discusses various types of competitive relationships among competitors in a market, and describes several techniques for identifying the relationships that prevail in a given market. We also discuss a few of the industry dynamics that could change the prevailing relationships in a market.

THE PRICE OF IGNORING COMPETITIVE RELATIONSHIPS

While the field of economics has long understood the significance of *competitive relationships,* business strategy has not yet fully recognized their importance and implications for competitor analysis. A careful understanding of the existing pattern of competitive relationships in a market can result in a number of benefits for practitioners, the most important of which is helping to understand how competitors might react to a given move.

Consider the case of Signode Corporation, a manufacturer of steel strappings, which faced an important pricing decision in the mid-1980s. Major steel producers decided to raise the price of steel, a significant cost item for Signode, by nearly 7 percent. During more favorable times, Signode had passed on all cost increases to its buyers. Now, however, it faced intense competition from lower-priced rivals. Signode wondered whether a price increase on its part would be followed by price increases by the six smaller competitors.

If its competitors treated Signode as the price leader and raised their prices following Signode's example, the move could have a positive impact on profits throughout the market. But if Signode raised its prices and its competitors held theirs steady or cut prices, it would further erode Signode's position in the market. How could it tell how its rivals would react?

Another instance that these relationships are very important is when a company is entering a market. The potential entrant might be interested in knowing the prevailing mode of competition among the major incumbents. For example, if there is evidence of leader-follower patterns in a new market, the entrant might choose to become one of the followers. Alternatively, the entrant could try to impose its own price leadership on the market. Such battles are common in the U.S. airline industry as airlines enter new market segments. An entrant into a market where there is (implicit and legal) collusion among the existing players might opt to join the colluding group, or act independently. In the global oil industry, new oil-producing nations have such strategic options available to them—whether to join OPEC or operate outside the cartel. In each case, the prevailing competitive relationships have a direct bearing on the profit potential of the new entrant.

THREE TYPES OF COMPETITIVE RELATIONSHIPS

Competitive relationships are probably described best by a continuum of possibilities. However, three distinct types of competitive relationships are key milestones on this continuum:

1. Independent.
2. Leader-follower behavior.
3. Collusive behavior.

These three relationships are illustrated in Figure 9.1. To understand the distinctions among these three, consider the following hypothetical market with only two major players. Each player wants to maximize its profits. Furthermore, each knows full well that the industry demand as well as its market share (and the resulting profits) will depend not only on what price it charges, but also on the price charged by its competitor. In this context, consider the following three possible types of market conduct:

Scenario 1. Each player independently decides what price to charge. The market demand is determined by the prices of both players. Their relative prices determine how the industry demand is split between the two players. This is an *independent* or *Nash* relationship. In this mode, competitors recognize that the actions of one affect all. Each assumes that the other will act in its own self-interest and selects its strategy to maximize profits, assuming the other's strategies as given externally.

Figure 9.1
Competitive Relationships

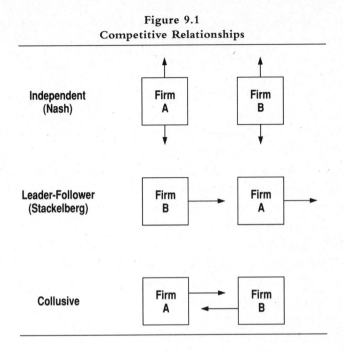

Scenario 2. One player decides its price first and announces its plans. Based on this information, the second player decides the optimal price to charge. The market demand depends on prices of both players. How the market is split between the two depends on their relative prices. This is *leader-follower behavior.* One firm acts as the leader and the other firms follow. (This is also known as *Stackelberg behavior.*) While leader-follower behavior is a specific and well-defined mode of competitive relationship, the extent to which one firm acts as the leader and the others follow, varies from coexistence to cooperation.

Scenario 3. The two producers collectively decide their prices to maximize their joint profits. The market demand depends on the prices of both players; the market share of each player depends on their relative prices. This is *collusion.* Firms act to maximize joint profits. While collusive decisions are less likely to occur among competitors, they do result in higher profits for each firm than any other structure. Such systems might develop if a few dominant players arrived at an implicit understanding about the mutual benefits of collusive behavior.

The key feature to note is that the degree of coordination increases as one moves from Scenario 1 to Scenario 3. We recognize that real-world markets are quite different from the market characterized in the stylized two-firm example here. Although Scenario 1 assumed the firms had no information about what price the competitor was likely to charge, competing firms may have some—although very limited—knowledge of what price the other firm is going to charge. Scenario 2 assumed the first firm announced exactly what price it was going to set, whereas in real competition, the company may provide some limited information about what it intends to charge. Scenario 3 assumed managers of competing firms sat down together, whereas real competitors might achieve price coordination through signaling their intent over a number of years.

These three scenarios are not intended to capture the actual complexities of competition but rather to illustrate conceptual benchmarks with which we can compare real markets. The key question one should ask is not whether a particular market is exactly like one of the three scenarios described, *but which one of the three scenarios it most resembles.*

Examples of Competitive Relationships

Although real competition may not be as tidy as our stylized examples, these three patterns can be seen in a variety of real-world examples. How would one classify competition in the following markets:

- U.S. automobiles?
- Soft drinks?
- European airlines?
- Photographic film?
- Laundry detergents?
- Japanese flat glass?

- U.S. cigarettes during the 1920s and 1930s?
- U.S. steel industry before the 1960s?

To determine the relationships in these industries, researchers have used a variety of statistical methods, which are presented next. They found the following results:

- Although an early study of the U.S. automotive industry uncovered collusive pricing patterns,[1] a more recent study found that the pricing behavior in the midsized sedan segment of the U.S. automobile industry was closer to a leader-follower type of relationship.[2] Overall, the researchers found that Ford seems to act as the price leader with Chrysler as the follower in this particular segment of the market. The researchers used nonnested model comparisons to arrive at these conclusions, a technique described later in this chapter.
- In soft drinks, one study found that Coca-Cola appears to act as the price and advertising leader while another found evidence of collusion. A number of empirical studies have examined competitive interactions involving advertising spending, spending on product quality improvement, or R&D expenditures. Gasmi, Laffont, and Vuong[3] found evidence of price and advertising leadership in the soft drink industry. Using a number of models of price and advertising competition between Coca-Cola and Pepsico, Inc., they found a model that assumed Coca-Cola as the price and advertising leader with Pepsico as the follower provided the best fit to the data. In a follow-up study, they also found a pattern of collusion in advertising between the same two firms.[4]
- The airline industry shows evidence of leader-follower relationships. Hanssens[5] examined competition between three major airlines on a city-pair route in Europe and found evidence that one of the airlines was an advertising leader in this market. Interestingly, the advertising leader was the smallest share airline in the market. Hanssens conducted a similar analysis for another important strategic variable in this market, namely, the number of

flights offered, and found evidence of leadership behavior there, too. Competitive reaction was unidirectional—the flight schedule of one particular airline was influenced by changes in the flight schedule of another airline in this market, but not the other way around.

- In the photographic film industry, Kadiyali[6] found some evidence of price and advertising collusion, with Kodak accommodating the entry of Fuji into the market. Prior to entry, Kodak appeared to have engaged in a limit pricing strategy, but after Fuji entered the U.S. market, the incumbent changed to an accommodation strategy in pricing and advertising.

- In laundry detergents, Kadiyali, Vilcassim, and Chintagunta[7] found that Procter & Gamble's Tide and Unilever's Wisk were the price leaders, and Unilever's Surf and P&G's Era Plus were the followers, respectively. In other words, each firm had a follower (its subpremium brand) to the other firm's leader (their premium brand). The interdependent pricing behavior is explained in terms of the firms competing in a number of segments of the same market, thus resulting in a strategic mode that is "softer" than Nash competition. This begins to show the complexity of these competitive relationships as we move from the stylized examples to actual markets.

- In an early empirical study of the Japanese flat glass industry, Iwata concluded that Nash competition was the norm in that industry.[8]

- A study of the cigarette industry in the United States during the 1920s and 1930s characterized its relationships as leader-follower, with the big three manufacturers selling Camel, Lucky Strike, and Chesterfield brands as price leaders.[9]

- The American steel industry is another example. U.S. Steel acted as a price leader for decades, until the early 1960s when confrontations with the federal government and a well-publicized price war with the number two firm, Bethlehem Steel, led to the price leadership role rotating among industry members, some of them small.[10]

- The breakfast cereal market—a tight oligopoly in the 1960s and 1970s—implemented a joint movement to higher prices through a system of price leadership.[11]

As shown in these examples, studies of relationships among companies in an industry tend to focus on leader-follower and collusive relationships. This should not be interpreted as a sign that these relationships predominate. Actually, independent behavior (Nash competition) is considered the norm, so most studies of competitive relationships focus on exceptions to it.

STATISTICAL TECHNIQUES FOR DETERMINING COMPETITIVE RELATIONSHIPS

How can you determine the prevailing competitive relationships in a given market? Most managers assess these relationships through observation and experience. But the biases inherent in intuition and observation often make these approaches unreliable. Managers commonly misperceive the true intentions of their rivals and the relationships in the market.

Our suggestion to those interested in uncovering the competitive relationships is that *it is best to let the data tell the story.* In other words, we recommend that readers use one of three primary statistical methods described next to infer competitive relationships in the industry. These techniques for uncovering competitive relationships in a market require access to historical data on prices and sales in the market of interest. But much of this data will already be gathered for other purposes. For example, a new entrant in a market may be collecting data for estimating market potential and growth.

As discussed in Chapter 1, one traditional approach for capturing competitive effects based on market response is the cross-elasticities method.[12] A high cross-price elasticity between a pair of brands implies that the two are *close competitors*. Because cross-elasticities may turn out to be asymmetric, we may conclude that one firm has a more dominant influence over the other. However, cross-elasticities alone cannot identify whether one brand is a leader and the other is a follower. Furthermore, *closeness* of competition does not reveal whether the firms are colluding, or if indeed their decisions are independent of one another. The following methods go beyond what can be achieved through the cross-elasticities approach.

The Three Methods

The following three methods for determining competitive relationships can be used in concert or independently:

1. Granger causality.
2. Conjectural variations.
3. Nonnested model comparisons.

The choice among the three depends on the availability of data and the depth of insights needed. Granger causality is the simplest approach, requiring less data than the other two methods. It requires only market input data such as pricing and advertising spending. The latter two methods also require output data, such as sales and profits.

Granger causality, based on the work of C.W. Granger, uses a time series approach to relate the actions of one firm in a previous period to the action of a second firm in the current period.[13] If Firm 1's actions lead to action by Firm 2, and the reverse is not true, then Firm 1 is a leader and Firm 2 is a follower.[14] The study of the airline industry cited uses a similar approach.

This is the easiest of the three approaches to implement, but also has the most limitations. Although this approach requires less data, a positive result only indicates the *possibility* of a leader-follower relationship. It does not explain the exact nature of the relationship. The time frame used also affects results. If quarterly price observations are used, the test might reveal causality. However, with annual price data, the causal pattern might not be detected. One way to ensure this does not happen is to use a level of aggregation consistent with the timing of the decisions. If price changes are typically implemented in an industry once a year (as in the automobile industry), then annual price data are appropriate. With frequently purchased grocery products, quarterly (or even finer level) data may be required. The Granger causality method, while it provides a test of the independent decisions hypothesis, does not provide a good test of collusive behavior.

Conjectural variations (CV) approach estimates how the marketing decision variables of one player are affected by the decision variables of competitors. The study of the Japanese flat glass market cited used this approach. If the companies appear to select their best strategies independently, then an independent (Nash) relationship prevails. If they act in concert to maximize joint profits, this is an indication of a collusive relationship; and if one company's decision variables have an effect on the other, but not the reverse, then there is a leader-follower relationship. This method produces a CV estimate for each firm on a scale of 0 to 1 (although it can also be negative). If one firm had a measure of 1 and the other had a measure of 0, the first firm is acting as the leader. If the two measures are equal to 0, this implies that neither firm is leading, so there is an independent relationship. If the measures both are equal to 1, this implies that both are leading equally, so there is a collusive relationship.

A disadvantage of the CV method is that it is sensitive to the assumptions about the demand function and the firms' objectives. If these assumptions do not reflect the *true* demand structure and objectives, then the equations that provide estimates of the CV parameter are not correctly specified, and the estimate of the CV parameter will be biased.

Nonnested model comparisons (NNMC) are based on examining equilibrium sales and price outcomes. Each of the three competitive relationships discussed previously leads to a distinct pattern of outcomes. This approach provides a mechanism for matching the patterns of data in the market with the fingerprints of the different competitive relationships.

The NNMC method can distinguish between independent decisions, leader-follower competition, and collusion. It also can be adapted to reflect the impact of carryover effects and other factors on the demand structure.[15] The price of this scope and flexibility is the complexity of the model. While the conceptual foundations of the NNMC test seem straightforward, its implementation is not. The first step is to estimate a model from sales and marketing mix equations. Often, this involves using constrained simultaneous equation regression. The next step is to test which of the three competitive relationships best fits the data. These different models are distinct, or not nested within one another, thus the name of this approach. There are a variety of statistical approaches that can be used to compare nonnested models.[16]

The choice of methods depends upon the nature of the market and data availability. When information on sales outcomes is not available, as may be the case in some industries, but only the data on the marketing decision variable(s) are available, there is no alternative but to use the Granger causality approach. If there is little evidence of demand carryover effects, and the objective functions of firms are well understood, then a static conjectural variations approach might work well. If it appears that dynamics are important, then either a modified CV method or NNMC is more suitable.[17] Uncertainty about the specification of demand or firms' objectives would make NNMC the best choice.

CHANGES IN RELATIONSHIPS OVER TIME

Although these three statistical approaches describe the dynamics of the relationship between firms in a market, they do not show how these relationships might change over time. All these methods rely upon historical data, so they actually show *past* competitive relationships. Markets usually exhibit stable patterns of competitive relationships. Changes do occur, but a change in competitive relationships is often a very slow process. Hence, we believe that using past data to infer the future is usually appropriate, at least in this context. Nonetheless, it must be kept in mind that any inference drawn from past data is not likely to be useful if the market has undergone a discontinuous change.

The actions of firms within the market and the evolution of the market can sometimes change the competitive relationships. For example, the arrival of new entrant into a leader-follower market can upset the relationships in the market. If the new player doesn't also follow, firms in the market could be forced to adopt a more independent stance. Research suggests that as the number of players increases, the competitive relationship in a market is more likely to be closer to Nash competition.

On the other hand, research suggests that the presence of a dominant market share firm shifts the competitive relationships in an industry toward one of greater coordination. The dominant firm is often accepted as the price leader. So this achievement of a dominant position by one firm might shift the relationships from independent to leader-follower.

Differences in information about the market can change competitive relationships in an industry. The development of the SABRE online reservation system has often been cited as the reason for American Airlines becoming the price leader in the airline industry. SABRE provides American Airlines with up-to-the-minute information about market demand. Similarly, the adoption of scanner technology may have helped supermarkets assume the leadership role from major packaged goods manufacturers in the United States. Scanner technology allows the retailer to obtain detailed information on how consumers respond to new products and changes in marketing strategy, giving the retailer a far superior access to knowledge about consumer behavior. Just as the presence of a higher market share firm, a firm with a lower cost position, or a firm with a superior access to raw materials can affect the nature of competitive relationships, so can the presence of a firm with vastly superior information about the market.

If your market is undergoing shifts in information, the emergence of a player with dominant market share, the entry of new players, or other changes, you should examine how these changes might influence the relationships in the market. You should also examine how the strategic moves you make could affect the current competitive relationships. We recommend that managers begin by understanding the prevailing relationships in the market. The approaches discussed in this chapter can help identify these relationships. In environments of discontinuous change, these methods can still help track changes in relationships mong firms. At the minimum, they can provide a baseline for current observations and future projections.

CONCLUSION

The ability to understand how competitors react to one another is essential to the formulation of a successful strategy. The three patterns of competitive relationships discussed in this chapter—independent, leader-follower, and collusive—represent varying degrees of coordination among the competing firms in an industry. The three statistical techniques presented here are important tools in determining which competitive relationships prevail in the market. Our recommendation to managers is that they use one or more of the suggested techniques to infer competitive relationships in a market. The choice depends on their needs and the data available.

Prior to the availability of the techniques summarized in this chapter, researchers often attempted to infer competitive relationships from market structure and other industry characteristics. While this is no longer the sole method available to infer competitive relationships, an understanding of the link between industry characteristics and the nature of competitive relationships is useful.

By default, practitioners often assume Nash competition as the mode of competitive conduct in an industry. We hope that this chapter has highlighted that other types of relationships do exist, and techniques are available that allow one to reliably uncover these relationships from market data. It is important to recognize the possibility of the existence of alternative competitive relationships. Practitioners are urged to identify these competitive relationships, and use this information carefully while formulating and implementing competitive strategy.

PART III

FORMULATING DYNAMIC COMPETITIVE STRATEGIES

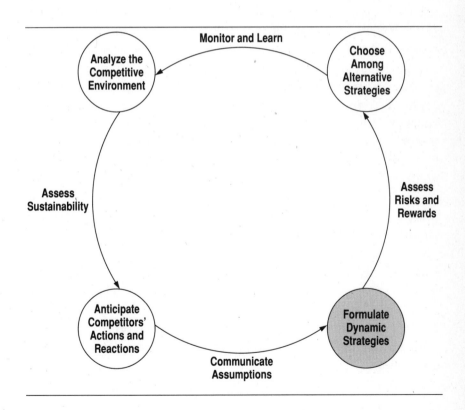

Nations Air, an upstart airline, moved into the prime Philadelphia market of USAir. The newcomer offered much lower fares. How should USAir respond? Should it accommodate this new player or move aggressively against it?

Sony anticipated high future growth in the market for 3.5-inch disks. How could it move to preempt IBM and other rivals in this market?

Texas Instruments wanted to control a new market for digital watches. How can it let its rivals know how serious it is about the market and discourage them from entering?

General Motors and Ford are locked in a bitter price war, eroding profits through the extensive use of end-of-year rebates, cash-back, and dealer discounts. How can GM use commitments to get Ford to charge a higher price so GM can price higher?

Time Warner and Turner had formulated a strategy to merge their corporations, but after months of negotiations, the final judgment on the deal had to be passed by the Federal Trade Commission. How can companies anticipate the impact of antitrust regulations during the process of formulating strategies?

This section examines these and other issues related to the formulation of competitive strategies. Chapter 10 discusses USAir's reaction to Nations Air and examines a wide range of options for developing competitive reactions. Chapter 11 examines how Sony built capacity to preempt rivals, and other strategies for preemption. Chapter 12 describes how Texas Instruments used price announcements to discourage other companies from entering the digital watch market. It examines a variety of ways such signals can be used in competitive strategies. Chapter 13, which explores the competitive use of commitments, discusses how General Motors used its new credit card to defuse the price wars. By making this commitment, it reduced competition over rebates and other discounts. Finally, Chapter 14 examines the impact of antitrust rules on mergers and other competitive activities and helps managers anticipate these effects during the strategy process.

FORMULATING DYNAMIC COMPETITIVE STRATEGIES

Given the competitive environment identified in Part I and your understanding of competitors from Part II, how should you design your own strategies? This section examines a variety of important factors that should be considered in developing competitive strategies, including reactions, preemption, signaling, commitment, and antitrust constraints.

The first chapter in this part explores the challenge of responding to the move of a competitor. There is a much wider range of possibilities than many managers consider. For example, instead of responding to a price cut in Market A with a similar move, you might consider an increase in the salesforce in Market B. The chapter explores five dimensions of reactions, indicating the range of creative possibilities for responding to the moves of competitors.

But why wait for competitors to move? Sometimes the best move is a strong offense. The next chapter explores the uses of preemptive strategies. These are strategies designed to knock out the rival's planes while they are on the ground or move first into a new market. To do this effectively, however, you have to know where your rival will move next. Chapter 11 points out that many moves, such as line extensions, are fairly predictable. Even new product introductions are in the labs for years before they reach the market. By assessing where the rival might move next and your own capacity for preemption, you can develop strategies to beat your competitors to the punch.

Preemption, however, often requires a significant resource commitment for an uncertain result. Signals, discussed in Chapter 12, sometimes offer a more economical alternative. By preannouncing a new product, for example, you can test the waters and preempt competitors before the product is even created. But preannouncements are just one aspect of signaling. The chapter explores a wide range of types and uses of signals—from both announcements and actions—and discusses how they are interpreted. Just as gestures often convey essential information in conversations (either confirming or contradicting the words of the speaker), signals also provide and convey essential information in competitive interactions. In formulating strategy, managers should explicitly consider these signals.

CONSTRAINTS ON STRATEGIC OPTIONS

The last two chapters in Part III examine constraints on strategic options. Chapter 13 discusses the uses of commitment in competitive strategy. In contrast to the view that companies benefit by keeping many options open, this chapter shows how companies can sometimes improve their positions by narrowing their options. For example, by committing to build excess capacity, companies can make it unprofitable for rivals to enter a market. In formulating your competitive strategy, it is important to consider how much flexibility you need and whether there are times when commitments can improve your competitive position.

Finally, the closing chapter in this part examines another external constraint on your strategies—antitrust. Most strategists leave antitrust to the legal department. As discussed in Chapter 14, this could be a mistake. Mergers and other strategic moves often face intense scrutiny by regulators, who can ultimately scuttle or fundamentally alter the plans. This chapter offers insights into the differences between how regulators and judges view competition and how managers see it. It helps managers think through the antitrust implications during the process of formulating strategy.

Collectively, the chapters in Part III offer insights into several key considerations in formulating strategy. While not exhaustive, they help you think through the diverse options for reacting, preempting, and signaling. They also help you consider the constraints of commitment and antitrust considerations. While there are many other issues to consider in formulating strategy, these are among the most important considerations in developing dynamic strategies.

CHAPTER 10

CREATIVE STRATEGIES FOR RESPONDING TO COMPETITIVE ACTIONS

HUBERT GATIGNON
INSEAD, Department of Marketing

DAVID REIBSTEIN
The Wharton School, Department of Marketing

When a competitor moves into your market, how do you respond? Many firms respond by fighting fire with fire, making a similar move in the same market, matching a price move with a price move, for example. But there is actually a wide range of options for responding to the moves of a competitor. You could fight a price move with a new product launch or salesforce expansion. You could react by moving in a different market of your rival. You could react aggressively or choose to accommodate. You could react immediately or bide your time. This chapter explores the range of options for responding to new entrants and other competitive moves. It examines a full spectrum of choices about where, what, how, and when you respond.

Nations Air, an upstart airline, moved into the Philadelphia market in late 1994. To lure customers, Nations Air offered round-trip flights between Philadelphia and Boston for just $118. This was about one-third of the fare charged by USAir, the leading carrier in the market. This move could represent a major threat to a key USAir market. How should it respond?

It could choose to ignore this new challenge on the Philadelphia-to-Boston route, focusing instead on identifying new markets to attack. On the other hand, because USAir has invested in building a presence in the Philadelphia market, it may want to find a way to defend that turf. While new markets may help it avoid a war with Nations Air, it would probably find other firms already in or entering those new markets. Because of the investments in customers and infrastructure in a market, it is often more efficient to defend existing markets than to aggressively pursue new ones.

Often, the first impulse of established players is to meet fire with fire. If an entrant slashes price, as Nations Air did, the incumbent also cuts price in the same market. Would this really be the best move for USAir? With its high market share, a price cut could hurt it much more than its smaller rival.

There are also other long-term consequences. When a company matches or responds directly to a competitive attack, it often leads to a protracted war, as competitors engage in a volley of tit-for-tat actions, or worse, an escalating battle. In contrast, responding in other markets or by using other marketing instruments is often seen as less aggressive, even though the move may have the same impact on customers. This chapter explores the many different combinations of responses that can be developed when a firm is attacked by another player in the market or a new entrant.

KEY COMPETITIVE QUESTIONS

In shaping its response, USAir must answer five key issues, as illustrated in Figure 10.1:[1]

1. Competitive stance. Should the incumbent bother to respond at all? If so, how aggressively?
2. *Magnitude.* What should be the relative magnitude of the response compared to the reaction? Should the incumbent match the moves of competitors or outdo them?
3. *Speed.* How quickly should the firm respond to the actions of the competitor? Should it adopt a "wait and see" stance or make an immediate response before the competitor puts its stakes in the ground?

Figure 10.1
Decision Model for Determining Response to a New Entrant

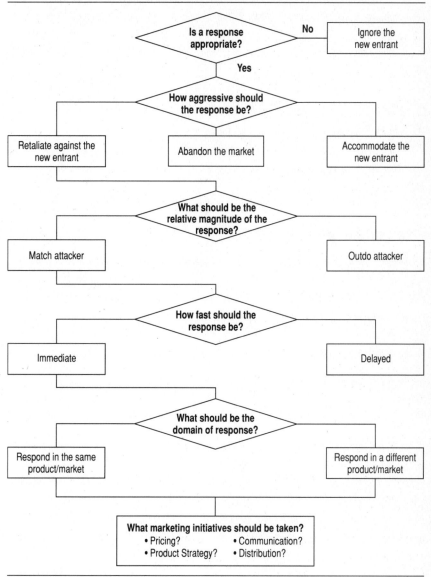

4. *Domain.* Where should the firm respond? Should the respond-ing company always move in the market in which it was at-tacked, or does it make sense to respond in other markets?

5. *Weapon.* What marketing instruments should the firm use to respond? How does the firm decide which instrument to use?

COMPETITIVE DEFENSIVE STRATEGY DECISIONS

Each of these dimensions of response offers the manager a variety of choices in shaping a competitive reaction. We examine the choices in each of these five areas next.

Competitive Stance

The first issue to consider in developing a response is whether to re-spond at all. Should the incumbent fight fiercely or give ground to the new competitor? If it decides not to retaliate, there are a variety of ways it could give ground. Its primary choices are:[2]

Ignore the move.

Accommodation.

Abandonment.

Retaliation.

Ignore the Move. The first choice is to ignore the competitor's move. This means the firm decides to take no action at all. For exam-ple, when GM introduced credit cards with a 5 percent rebate on pur-chases of cars, Chrysler did not respond. It didn't retaliate. It didn't accommodate. It did nothing. In the case of an entry into the market, the decision to ignore means that the established firm does not change its strategy after the entry. This could be due to the lack of significant impact of the entry on the firm's performance, but it could also reflect a "wait-and-see" attitude that gives time for the firm's managers to gather information about the newcomer and the market's reaction.

Accommodation.   A more active stance is to make way for the new-comer by decreasing marketing effort. This decision to accommodate is appropriate when there is enough business for all competitors, including an aggressive one, or when the increased competition could serve to increase the overall size of the market. Some cooperative behavior among the players would be in the best interests of all parties. By reducing the likelihood of a destructive competitive battle, accommodation could minimize losses in profits for both firms, and signal a desire for cooperation and sharing of the education tasks and resulting "larger pie."

The risk of any accommodating move is that while it signals a desire for peaceful coexistence, it may also be interpreted as a sign of weakness. This could invite the competitor to become even more aggressive, creating bigger problems down the road. Even if the current competitor decides to cooperate, other rivals or potential rivals may read the accommodation as a sign that the incumbent will not fight to defend its territory. This may embolden them to attack, creating more risks for the accommodating company. Thus, while the accommodating move may be intended to avoid confrontation, there is the risk that it might stimulate even more aggression. Thus, it is generally desirable to indicate the purpose of the accommodation so as to reduce the risk of being misunderstood.

Abandonment.   The most extreme stance to take in response to a new entrant is to abandon the market. The decision to exit the market should be considered only if the market is undesirable or the attacker has a large competitive advantage over the responding firm. In some circumstances, the superiority of the attacker because of a better product, resources, size, or other factors is so overwhelming that staying in the market (with or without fighting) would result in greater losses than exiting the market. In this case, "discretion is the better part of valor."

Retaliation.   Finally, the incumbent firm may choose to fight the incursion by the new entrant by increasing its expenditures and pushing its sales through a stronger marketing effort. Retaliation corresponds to a declaration of war, wherein the firm wants to signal to the attacker and to the other competitors its intention to fight back. A study of industrial markets found that 60.2 percent of the companies in the PIMS database chose to retaliate in response to salesforce expansions, for example.[3]

Retaliation may not be the best strategy because, with increased marketing activities, prices and profits often fall. However, retaliation may signal commitment to the market, which may deter future aggressive actions by the competitors. While deterrence could be more effective when leading rather than reacting, a strong retaliation may provide an opportunity to demonstrate the will of the firm and, hence, might prove to be more profitable in the long run.

Magnitude: How Aggressively to React

If managers decide to retaliate, they need to decide how forcefully to respond. Should they give the upstart a slap on the wrist or attempt to drive it out of the market by force? There are two key options for the magnitude of the competitive reaction:

- Match the attacker's move, thereby not allowing it to gain any competitive advantage in the customers' eyes.
- Outdo the competitor's move, in an effort to fight back with enough intensity to directly hurt the attacker's chances of success.

The matching strategy is a strong signal to the attacker that the competitor is unwilling to allow the attacker to gain any ground. It should discourage any further moves, because the attacker will recognize that any move will most likely be matched again.

One advantage of the matching strategy is that it may be a peacemaking approach. Given the signal that the incumbent is unwilling to be outdone, the entrant may elect to stop trying to outdo the incumbent. Of course, this may not always be the case. For example, when MCI entered into the telecommunications industry, AT&T—after delaying for a while—eventually chose to match MCI's price.

Given MCI's only point of differentiation was lower price, MCI had no choice but to retaliate, in turn, by further lowering its price. Thus, a matching strategy led to escalation of the price war.

A radical reaction could be necessary early on to prevent the entrant from building a strong position in the market or to deter further attacks. In the best of cases, a strong reaction unanticipated by an entrant could lead the newcomer to exit before it commits too much of an untenable position. In other circumstances, a minor signal could be sufficient to cause the attacker to back down.

If the attacker does not back down, however, this becomes much more of a "warring" strategy. Here, the signal is that share will not be yielded without a major fight. The choices for the new entrant are either to retreat because it did not realize how difficult the confrontation would be, or to respond in kind with either a matching move of its own or an even more aggressive move. The more aggressive step is not unusual, given it reestablishes the relative positions intended with the initial entry move.

The detrimental effects of such exchanges can be seen in the battle between Johnson & Johnson and Schering Plough in the market for vaginal yeast infection creams. Johnson & Johnson, with its brand Monistat, had been the dominant player. When the category made its transition from prescription medicines to the over-the-counter market, Schering Plough introduced a rival brand, Gyne-Lotrimin, at what was deemed to be an aggressive price. Johnson & Johnson responded not only by lowering its price to match Gyne-Lotrimin, but outdid Schering Plough by dropping its price even further. The war was on, with prices continuing to plummet, each brand chasing the other throughout the entire year. This battle escalated beyond the pricing dimension, as similar iterative, aggressive one-upmanship transpired on the advertising and promotional fronts.

If a new entrant stays in the market, it often is forced to become a follower or an alternative provider. Many times, customers are seeking a second source of supply, just to keep the primary source of supply "on its toes," as well as to provide some safeguard in case the primary source of supply falters in its ability to deliver.

Speed: How Fast to React

In addition to the size of the reaction, managers also need to consider the speed of the reaction. The primary choices are:

- *Immediate reaction.* The incumbent reacts as soon as it learns of the competitor's move.
- *Delayed reaction.* The incumbent adopts a wait-and-see attitude to gauge the impact of the move and the seriousness of the competitive threat.
- *Preemptive strike.* The incumbent reacts in anticipation of the competitor's move before it happens.

The primary reason to react quickly is to reduce the potential impact of the competitor's move as quickly as possible. To wait and see might be too late. The damage would have already been done. It is much harder to remove a competitor once it is already entrenched than to prevent it from ever gaining successful entry. Once a competitor has gained a spot on the retailer's shelf or with the distributor, it will be a while before the retailer (distributor) is willing to remove the product from its inventory. In this case, the product has every opportunity to demonstrate its acceptance to the final consumer. If the response had been quick enough, the defender might have prevented the retailer (distributor) from even opening a spot for the new competitor.

The reason for adopting a wait-and-see attitude is that it avoids overreacting to the move, which can waste resources or draw the competitors into a brutal war. A study of competitive reactions found that, of those that react to rival moves, 22.3 percent respond within the first six months of the competitor's new product introduction, 52.2 percent within a year, and 47.7 percent take more than a year to respond.[4] This means that nearly half of the reacting firms wait for more than a year before making their moves.

The fastest move is to react *prior* to the competitor's move. Companies often increase their advertising, increase promotional activity (either at the trade or consumer level), or lower price in order to build up inventories at both the trade or customer level to make the entry all the more difficult for the new entrant. The purpose is to prevent the competitor from even entering the market. This preemption strategy is discussed in Chapter 11.

Domain: Choosing Where to Respond

The next issue to consider is where to respond. This decision can impact the effectiveness of the response, as well as how the response is viewed by the rival. The responding firm can react in:

The same market or segment in which the attack occurred,

Another market or segment of the rival, or

A neutral market or segment.

Standing and Fighting: Responding in the Market of Attack. The most common response is to react to an attack by fighting back in the same market. Companies usually dig in their heels and try to defend the market in which they are already established, changing the marketing mix of the brand or product in the segment or segments under attack. For example, the predictable response for Nations Air would be for it to react to USAir in the Philadelphia market.

The most natural reflex is to attempt to defend the territory one already owns. Given the company has already made an investment in establishing awareness, customer relations, distribution, and so on, it makes sense to protect one's investment. Further, because of this previous investment, or "head start," it might be easier to protect an established position rather than making new investments in other markets.

In the case of the attack by Nation's Air, USAir already had invested in gates, sales offices, brand awareness, and local customer loyalty (through its frequent flier programs). Many of its connecting flights travel through both Philadelphia and Boston, even though neither is a USAir hub. USAir had a significant amount to lose because of its considerable fixed expenses. It makes sense for it to choose to fight in this market where it has a strong position (high brand awareness, convenient and plentiful gates, numerous connections, customer base with already developing frequent flier accounts, and more).

Another reason a company may choose to defend its home market is that it may feel a retreat would be a sign of weakness. This may make competitors more bold in attacking the company in other markets. In essence, an indirect confrontation might be begging for subsequent aggression. If not here and now, then when and where? It may also signal to other competitors or potential competitors that the company is an easy target.

Shifting Domains: Responding in the Competitor's Market. The most effective reaction strategy may be to move to a different market or segment rather than counterattacking in the same one. It may be much more effective and less costly to fight on someone else's turf. For example, USAir may find it easier to respond to Nations Air on another route where USAir is not such a large player. For example, it might compete with Nations Air on some of its routes to Florida, which were not as well "owned" by USAir.

This cross-parry into another market may be most appropriate if the competitor is vulnerable in another market. Such a move can be particularly effective if the responding firm has an opportunity to move into a core market of the rival, particularly if this market is supplying resources for the company's attack. By attacking the opponent's base of strength in this second market, the responding company cuts off the resources for the rival's attack in the original market. This pins down the company there, preventing it from reassigning resources to the new entry (which typically is costly to begin with).

Rockwell used this approach to fend off an attack by Schlumberger. The European rival had entered the residential gas meter business in the U.S. market, where Rockwell had long been a major player. Rather than respond aggressively in the U.S., Rockwell acquired a small company in Schlumberger's European stronghold and threatened to compete aggressively there. Schlumberger, in an uncharacteristic move, backed off any significant marketing activities in the U.S. market. Its European market was too important to risk this kind of attack by Rockwell.

When the relatively new Southwest Airlines started offering half-price fares on the Dallas–San Antonio route, Braniff chose to shift the domain of its response. It cut its price on the Dallas-Houston route, which was the only profitable route for Southwest Airlines at the time.

Because price moves hurt the large-share incumbent more than the low-share attacker, it is often more effective to respond to the low-price attacker in its own core market. In such a case, none of the responding firm's existing margins has to be sacrificed. Any inroads come at the expense of the attacker.

In moving into other markets, it is important to keep an eye on the competitors in the periphery of the action. The move against the attacker in another market could also be threatening to other players in that market. This could lead to unexpected and unpleasant reactions to the move.

Stepping Aside: Responding in a Neutral Market or Segment. A third option for response is to get out of the way. The responding company can avoid the attacker completely and invest in markets where this competitor is not present. This could occur if the new entrant is too powerful to compete with (for example, if its resources were largely superior or the competitor was too well established). Renault, for example, abandoned the U.S. car market in reaction to the Japanese aggressive marketing in the region to focus on trucks (with MAC) in the European market. Renault knew it would have a tough time competing against them. Similarly, Barco was an innovator in producing videotape projection equipment for the airline industry, but moved aside when Sony entered the video projection market. After the entry of this powerful rival, Barco shifted its focus to the projection of data, and subsequently to graphics. At each stage, Barco was prepared, perhaps out of necessity, to get out of the way of the giant, to migrate to a new market opportunity rather than attempt to confront Sony and its powerful resources head on.

Which market a firm chooses to compete in depends on the strength and size of the firm and the strength of its competitors. A large company with significant resources compared to the attacker's is much more likely to stay and fight. On the other hand, as described in the Barco example, if the attacker has a large arsenal, it might make sense to step aside and seek other markets in which to pursue prosperity. This approach also should be considered if a new entrant has a powerful advantage. If the competitor enters with a truly superior technology or product or at a lower price backed by significantly lower cost structure, it may not be wise to try to fight the new entrant head-on.

Note that this stepping aside is not a complete withdrawal from the market, but rather moving to another segment or portion of the same market. The abandonment of the market is an option discussed under the choice of stance previously.

Weapon: How to Respond

The final issue to consider is which element of the marketing mix to use in the responses. More often than not, firms respond to a competitive move by using the same element of the marketing mix as the one used in the attack. If the rival initiates price reductions, the firm responds with a price reduction of its own. If the competitor steps up advertising, the firm responds with its own increase in advertising. While this approach is often the first impulse for managers, it is often not the best move. In fact, companies can shape their response to an attack by using any combination of the following elements of the marketing mix:

- Price.
- Awareness advertising (to enhance the consumers' knowledge about the brand's existence).
- Image advertising (to persuade consumers that the brand possesses certain attributes).
- Distribution.
- Salesforce.
- Promotions.
- Repositioning of existing products.
- The introduction of new products.

Which is the best method? The choice depends on the capabilities of the responding and attacking firms as well as the market. The relative strengths and weaknesses of the competitors along the different dimensions of the marketing mix are important to consider in shaping a response. Not surprisingly, firms usually react with their most effective marketing instrument, that is, the one with the greatest elasticity.[5] In other words, they fight with their best weapons. They also choose to attack with a weapon that plays to their competitor's weaknesses.

The responsiveness of the market should also be considered. The best weapon is the one that draws the strongest response from the market. A very price-sensitive market, for example, would respond much more readily to a pricing move. Thus, a company should not simply use its strongest weapon, but also the one that has the most impact on the particular market.

Responding with a Different Element. There is an advantage in responding with a different element of the market mix than the one used in the attack. When the response is made using a different dimension, the attacker sometimes doesn't even view it as a response (although it feels the effects). The attacker believes it has been able to take an aggressive act without a response from the competitor, when in reality the response was simply on a different dimension. This asymmetric response helps avoid needless head-to-head wars.

One negative side effect of responding on price is that it can help shape customer expectations of lower prices for future purchases. For example, customers of bedsheets or linens know to expect a "white sale" every fall. Thus, many normal purchases are delayed in anticipation of the sale period.

New entrants often compete on price. Because the new player has low share in the market, the total impact of its price cuts are much smaller than for a high-share incumbent. To reduce prices, the incumbent must cut prices for all its customers, even those who might be willing to pay a higher price. In addition, the more price-sensitive consumers who might be attracted by a low price are usually also more likely to abandon the established provider for the low-priced competitor. Thus, the incumbent gains by shifting away from price competition or changing the domain.

Which weapons do firms use most often? A study of the effectiveness of different defensive strategies against new product introductions found that 56 percent of incumbent firms responded using a communication variable, either personal communications via salesforce changes or via mass media; 27 percent responded by cutting price; and 82 percent repositioned or introduced a new product themselves.[6]

Even though using the introduction of a new product as a response may appear to be a difficult strategy to implement, it is a relatively common reaction, which can be very successful. For example, Procter & Gamble's introduction of specific diapers for boys and girls was successful in regaining market share from Huggies and Luvs, which had concentrated on product quality improvements related to absorption and fit.

Complex Reactions. The percentages in the study just cited add up to more than 100 because firms often respond with "complex reactions," using more than one element of the marketing mix. Companies can also use different weapons in the different domains discussed. The firm can react with one marketing variable in the market where the attack is made and with another marketing instrument in another market, either where the attacker competes or where it does not. For example, an airline might match a price cut on a route where the attack started and increase advertising on a route where that attacker enjoys a comfortable position.

Awareness versus Image Advertising. In presenting the elements of the marketing mix, awareness advertising is considered separately from image advertising. Under certain conditions, the reaction can be different for awareness and image advertising.[7] For example, if the size of the market does not increase after a competitive entry, the optimal defensive strategy is to decrease the budget for awareness advertising. This is because there are smaller potential sales for each of the competitors that must share the market, reducing profitability after the entry.

However, if consumer tastes are uniformly distributed, and the new competitor attacks on one attribute, profits increase if the incumbent increases advertising spending in order to reposition its brand along a different attribute.

FACTORS INFLUENCING REACTIONS

Given the diverse competitive options just discussed, which factors should managers consider in designing their competitive reactions? Research on competitive reactions has identified three that tend to influence the speed and intensity of reactions:

1. The importance of the business to the responding firm,
2. The ability of the organization to respond, and
3. The size of the threat posed by the rival.

In general, managers tend to react more quickly when the market under attack has great strategic importance, when their organizations have low organizational inertia, and when the move poses a great threat.[8] Although research is fairly limited on this issue, these studies can help managers identify key issues in planning their reaction and provide them with benchmarks in making their decisions. (To consider how these and other factors influence the reactions of competitors, refer to Chapter 8.)

Importance of the Business

The first issue to consider in developing a response is the importance of the market to the firm. There is obviously no point in aggressively defending a market that is of little financial or strategic importance. But what makes a market important? The long-term importance of a market corresponds to the perceived potential profits that the firm expects from that market. This is determined by both the industry characteristics—such as market growth and customer-switching costs—and the organization's market share and competitive position (relative advantages).

Market Growth. As indicated earlier, competitors will react more quickly if they view the market as highly attractive. One measure of attractiveness is the growth potential. There are two views on the impact of market growth on the reaction of the firm. On the one hand, it could be argued that companies should react less aggressively to market share erosion when sales are growing at a satisfactory rate, particularly when the new product itself increases primary demand.[9] Since the market is growing, all competitors may adopt a live-and-let-live attitude. On the other hand, because a new entrant threatens the incumbent's performance,[10] the firm may react to minimize this shortfall. Also, share gains in growing markets are worth more than in mature markets because the return will grow through time as the market grows.[11] This may be why empirical studies have found that reactions to new entrants tend to be larger and more rapid in high-growth markets than in low-growth ones.[12] Growth markets are important, and competitors likely feel the need to take hasty action in response to a new entrant.

Market growth also appears to affect the method of response. A study of industrial firms found they tend to retaliate more with salesforce actions in high-growth markets than in low-growth markets; but price wars tended to be avoided in high-growth markets.[13] This is probably because price moves are counterproductive in growth markets, where customers are less price-sensitive. The focus of competition is on reaching new prospects fast, which makes salesforce moves the most appropriate approach.

Customer-Switching Costs. If the company has high customer-switching costs, the one-time costs buyers face in switching from one supplier's product to another, this may reduce the need for a rapid and aggressive reaction. Researchers have found that firms in markets with high customer-switching costs have marginally more delayed responses to rival actions.[14]

Market Share of the Reacting Firm. If the firm has a high market share, the market will usually have high strategic importance, and the firm will move to defend it more forcefully and quickly. Studies have found that competitors with a higher market share tend to react more quickly than lower-share firms.[15] In the highly competitive photographic industry, new product introductions, quality, and cost control are the keys to strength. Fuji has been the leader in the area of new product introductions, including 400 and 1600 speed film and a disposable 35mm camera. Kodak, with a higher market share has always been quick to react to these new products using a variety of tactics.[16] When firms have a high market share within their served market, which typically follows from a strong relative advantage in this market segment,[17] they are expected to react more quickly and intensely. Therefore, firms that have a vested interest in maintaining the sales of their present successful product should defend their position strongly by responding quickly.

Another important consideration that may temper the aggressiveness of the response is the danger of cannibalization The high-market-share firm has the most to lose from introducing a new product or cutting prices. Managers of these firms should carefully consider this threat in crafting their response to a move by a competitor. They can mitigate cannibalization effects by choosing other elements of the marketing mix—for example, responding to a new product by increasing the salesforce.

Market Concentration. Firms in highly concentrated markets can be expected to react more quickly and aggressively to new brands that pose a threat to industry profitability. Companies in these markets are constantly monitoring the competition, making it more likely they will notice and respond to moves of rivals. Market concentration also appears to affect the type of reaction. A study of industrial markets found that salesforce retaliations are much more likely in concentrated markets, and price retaliations are far less likely.[18]

Organizational Abilities of the Reacting Firm

Sometimes, the organization itself creates constraints on its ability to react quickly and forcefully to a rival's move. If the organization is not designed for rapid responses, it may be difficult for the company to marshal its resources to create a strong and rapid reaction to a competitive threat. For example, an advertising agency cannot develop a new advertising campaign overnight. It is clear that some marketing activities are easier to react to than others. Product moves might take a considerable time in which to react, depending on the complexity and propriety of the new product introduction. In contrast, the time required to implement a price change is usually very short. The only time lag is in the communication of the change. This ease and speed of implementation is probably the reason many competitive battles are fought on the price dimension.[19]

The complexity of the move can slow the firm's response. More complex and radically different products generally take longer to develop.[20] Complex products require "extensive reorganization of interdependent procedures and/or the coordination of many skills and multiple departments."[21]

Environmental instability, in which there are many and often unpredictable changes and competitive actions, may increase the ability of competitors to respond quickly. One study found that in industries in which firms change all or part of their product line frequently, firms respond more quickly to new product introductions.[22]

Threat Posed by the Action

Of course, one doesn't have to respond to just any competitive activity unless it truly is a potential threat. How strong is the firm introducing the new product in the served market? Is it committed and does it have the resources to fight off a competitive attack? The speed and magnitude of reaction to the introduction of a new product depend on how these questions are answered. Researchers found shorter response times when competitor actions were perceived as being more threatening.[23]

If the attacker's move is irreversible, it may be more threatening.[24] The threat is also greater if the attacking firm has a large market share, giving it the resources to fight aggressively. Companies often fail to see this threat when the moves are very radical. It generally takes more time for companies to gather information or formulate a response in these cases. Managers should carefully assess the threat of a given move to avoid either overreacting or underreacting to it. It is also important to be aware of small firms or small moves that might represent a threat but not be recognized as one.

CONCLUSION

USAir, thus, had many options in responding to the entry by Nations Air. USAir could move in a different market. It could use a different element of the marketing mix. It could ignore the move, accommodate, abandon the market, or retaliate. It could move quickly or adopt a wait-and-see approach. It could match the pricing moves of Nations Air or up the ante by making even deeper cuts. It could respond in Philadelphia or another market. It could respond to the pricing move by launching new flights or making other changes in service.

Each option leads to a very different outcome in the competitive arena. USAir elected to stand pat and fight in the Philadelphia market. It dropped its price aggressively to defend the existing market, giving customers little or no reason even to try Nations Air.

By exploring all the possible reactions, and considering some of the factors discussed here, you can select the best overall strategy for responding to a competitor's move. A careful analysis of the options will lead to more effective strategy. Rather than simple, knee-jerk reactions of fighting fire with fire, you can develop more effective response strategies, ones that will have the desired impact on rivals and the market. This can help you make appropriate responses and avoid turning a simple response into a protracted conflagration.

CHAPTER 11

PREEMPTIVE STRATEGIES

JERRY WIND
The Wharton School, Department of Marketing

Beyond simple responses or offensive actions, preemptive strategies act against a competitor before the competitor makes its move. Effective preemption may be one of the most difficult strategies to formulate and implement, but it is also among the most powerful. This chapter describes preemption and presents a process for understanding opportunities for preemption by analyzing the potential moves of competitors. It then presents a framework for formulating preemptive strategies.

When it is possible, preemption is perhaps the most powerful form of a competitive maneuver. A reactive move tries to stop, slow, or limit the damage of a rival's action after it has been initiated. A simple offensive maneuver is designed to attack a competitor or move in a new direction. In contrast, preemption is focused on attacking the future moves of a competitor, *before* they have been made. Preemption attacks the competitor's *intention* to attack. Defensive maneuvers might be compared to firing an antimissile barrage in response to an attack. Offensive maneuvers are like launching your own attack. Preemption is tantamount to knocking out your rival's missiles while they are still on the ground. Or, to take the analogy of a chess match, preemption is seizing control of key squares on the board, thus preventing competitors from moving into those positions. It is a very powerful attack that can slow or stop competitors or pin them down before they have had a chance to act.

The author wishes to acknowledge the helpful comments of Dave Reibstein, George Day, and Robert Gunther.

Consider a few examples:

- *Locking up capacity.* Anticipating growth in the market for 3.5-inch disks in 1984, Sony announced a fivefold increase in production capacity. It made this move before IBM had made clear its intention for the next generation of personal computers. This extensive capacity discouraged would-be rivals from setting up their own plants.
- *Locking in markets.* Gillette moved Sensor into 19 countries almost simultaneously, and P&G introduced Pampers Phases into 90 countries in less than a year. This rapid propagation of new products made it difficult for rivals to create a toehold in global markets.
- *Locking up minds.* A software company announces a product that is more than a year from reaching the market. Customers wait for this promised "vaporware," which is repeatedly postponed or never produced. Meanwhile, competitors' products that are on the shelves today are ignored as customers wait for the promised new product. The software company has preempted its rivals.
- *Blocking a competitor's intended action.* In the summer of 1990, Kellogg was planning to launch a new whole grain shredded wheat. The fortified cereal, whose packages described it as the "most nutritious shredded wheat you can buy," was due to arrive at retailers on August 6, and Kellogg had produced 7,800 cases with the claim printed on the box. On July 26, lawyers for rival Nabisco sent a letter to Kellogg accusing it of "false and misleading" claims on its packaging and threatening to sue if Kellogg did not withdraw its claims. In its letter, Nabisco revealed that it would be introducing its own spoon-size shredded wheat that would also be fortified and would invalidate Kellogg's claims. Nabisco used the launch of its own cereal to preempt Kellogg's positioning as the only fortified whole grain shredded wheat cereal.

A Process for Preemption

To develop preemptive strategies, managers need to engage in three levels of analysis:

1. Determine where the market or competitors are moving or might move.
2. Identify potential strategies for getting there first or for blocking these moves.
3. Determine whether these strategies are feasible and consistent with the firm's current strategic goals, and whether they are likely to affect the competitor's objectives, actions, and reactions.

Although preemption can be a powerful competitive strategy, it is not always possible or recommended. Preemptive moves are complex because they require managers to decide where their markets and rivals are headed and act quickly. Preemption also is risky because companies could make a mistake about the future of competition and seize a potential market that never materializes. This can be an extremely costly mistake.

If Sony had not accurately predicted that 3.5-inch drives would be the standard in personal computing, its increase in capacity would have been a liability rather than an asset. However, by assessing where the market was heading and getting there first, it effectively blocked other competitors from building their own capacity. Gillette, which did little test marketing before its rapid global launch of Sensor, took the risk that its success in the United States and Europe might fail in other markets.

In situations in which the moves of competitors or the market can be predicted with relative assurance—for example, when rivals have signaled their intentions or the market is evolving along a certain trajectory—the risks of preemption are greatly reduced.

This chapter describes a process for identifying and analyzing potential preemptive moves, as shown in Figure 11.1. The process begins with identifying the intended or possible moves of competitors by examining the market. Managers then generate potential preemptive strategies for "getting there first." Next, each strategy is analyzed to determine whether it is likely to achieve its objectives, and whether it is feasible and consistent with the preempting firm's own capabilities and strategic goals. Finally, the framework examines the dynamic interplay between a preemptive move and the rival's response.

Figure 11.1
Planning for Preemption

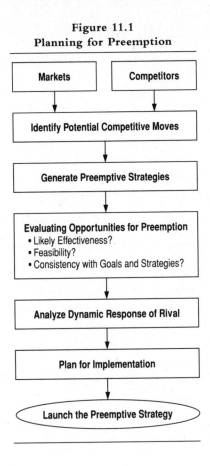

DETERMINING WHERE THE MARKET OR RIVALS ARE HEADED

The key to preemption is to determine where competitors or the market are headed. To preempt a move, a manager must first be aware of the possibility for the move. How can this be done? Often, there are patterns of market development that lead to logical next steps. There are also signals or patterns of behavior by competitors that offer clues to their possible moves. This information can provide insights into opportunities to preempt. Understanding the evolution of markets provides the opportunity to lock in future markets. Understanding the possible moves of competitors provides the opportunity to lock them out.

Understanding the Expected Trajectory of Markets

The trajectory of markets is often quite clear. By carefully observing market changes and trends, managers can predict the next stage in the evolution of the market. They also can identify opportunities to shape the future evolution of the market—for example, through shifting the business paradigm. There are several market patterns that offer opportunities for preemption:

- *Natural line extensions.* Customer trends such as the move toward "healthier" products clearly suggest natural line extensions for large numbers of products—lower- or nonalcoholic beers, lower- or nonalcoholic wines, lower- or nontar and nicotine cigarettes, lower- or noncalorie soft drinks, and so on. Similarly, expansion of colors, flavors, sizes, type of packages, strengths, and other *varieties* are often predictable, especially when linked to demographic and sociocultural or economic trends. By determining what the next extensions of the product lines might be, companies can preempt their rivals by moving to these new extensions first. For example, if potato chips have expanded to include sour cream and onion, and barbecue flavors, a producer of tortilla chips might move before rivals to expand to these new flavors that have been accepted in the market. Or, if the current product offerings are a high-priced, luxury product and a low-priced generic product, a company might preempt by introducing a moderately priced product that offers many features of the luxury product.
- *Next-generation products.* Most products, regardless of their success are likely to be replaced sometime in the future by a new generation of products. Consider, for example, the evolution of records from the 45 to long-playing vinyl records to cassettes to CDs, or the evolution of pocket cameras from 110 to 35mm. As

Figure 11.2
Multiple Generation Diffusion Functions

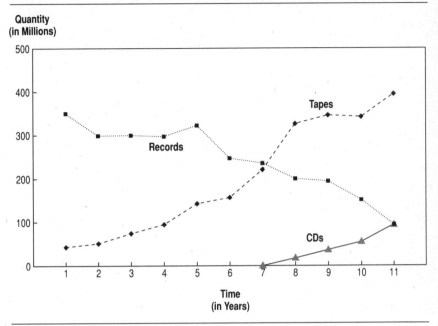

Source: J. Norton & F. Bass, "The Law of Capture: Substantive Findings of an Investigation of a Model of Diffusion and Technological Substitution."

shown in Figure 11.2, the decline of records was correlated with the rise of the next generation, tapes, and these were correlated with the rise of CDs. These patterns have been shown in many different markets. By determining what this next-generation will be, as Sony did with 3.5-inch computer disks, companies can pre-empt their rivals by moving first to the next-generation product. These shifts also give companies the opportunity to establish the standard for the new generation of products—as Matsushita did with VHS in videotapes.

• *Innovative products.* Innovative products significantly affect consumer behavior and change the way consumers perceive a given market. This often leads to the creation of a new dimension in consumers' perceived assessment of the market map. Consider, for example, the addition of voice to the traditional movie camera market (Kodak's introduction of the "talkies"), the introduction of the video camera that changed dramatically the traditional movie camera market, or the introduction of digital cameras to replace traditional chemical films. Innovative products are often driven by technology. As such, consider, for example, the enormous impact the emerging interactive industry is starting to have on consumers, with 1995 sales of over $11 billion dollars split among video games (3.8 billion), home shopping (2.8 billion), CD-ROMs (2.5 billion), commercial online services (795 million), interactive 800 numbers (425 million), Internet (366 million), kiosks (292 million), virtual reality (116 million), and interactive TV (37 million).[1]

Is it possible to identify new-to-the world technology that doesn't follow a predictable "next-generation" trajectory? The identification of the next innovative product is fraught with uncertainty. But there are two facts that make it possible:

• The technology for most of the new products that we are likely to see in the next decade have already been invented. In fact, the average time from the issue of a patent for an invention to the time a product based on that patent is introduced to the market is about 10 years, as shown in Figure 11.3. The dishwasher was invented in 1889 and introduced 23 years later in 1912. The microwave oven was invented in 1945 but brought to market a decade later. The

Figure 11.3
Mean Values for Incubation Time

Product Category	Number of Products	Mean Incubation Time	Mean Time to Peak Sales
Major Appliances	10	9.2 years	23.6 years
Housewares	11	6.1	18.2
Consumer Electronics	11	9.6	16.3
Grand Mean	32	8.3	19.6

Source: Kohli, Rajeev, Donald Lehmann, and Jae Pae, "New Product Forecasting: The Extent and Impact of Incubation Time." Paper presented at the *JMR* Conference on "Innovation in New Product Development: 'Best Practice' in Research, Modeling and Applications," May 1995.

cellular phone was invented in 1970 but didn't make it to market until 1983. It is clear that there is often plenty of margin for pre-emption between the time an invention is created and when the re-sulting new product is launched.[2]

• Most successful innovative new products respond to or help shape the changes in consumer needs. Thus, understanding the changing market needs could help identify likely new products. Consider, for example, the trends toward value, health, exercise, environmental protection, two-career families, working at home, and the nu-merous products that are being created to address these trends.

This combination of understanding the technology in the labo-ratories and the changes in the market can offer insights into new innovations that will reshape future markets. These insights could provide opportunities to preempt by moving into these new mar-kets ahead of rivals.

• *Customer analysis.* Understanding customers' satisfaction and dis-satisfaction with the products and services of the firm and its competitors, along with changing customer needs, problems, ex-pectations, and behavior is key to the design of any strategy.

• *Emerging new business paradigm.* Recent years have witnessed a dramatic shift in the business paradigm of an increasing number of firms in various industries. The major shift is from a focus on a product and its price (a "pill" at discount price in the case of pharmaceutical firms) to its benefit to consumers (total health care solutions such as wellness, in the case of pharmaceuticals) *and* the associated business solutions (not just to provide a discount but to help the client—hospitals, managed care organizations, physicians or patients—achieve their financial objectives). This can lead to value-based pricing, help in increasing the efficiency of the operation or in generating new revenues, and so on. The movement to this new paradigm for a pharmaceutical firm is il-lustrated in Figure 11.4. Similar paradigms, focusing on the two dimensions of industry solutions [the domain of activity of the given industry such as telecommunication solutions (for firms such as Northern Telecom and AT&T), financial solutions (for

Figure 11.4
A New Business Paradigm for a Pharmaceutical Firm

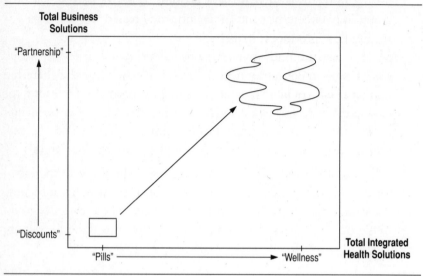

financial services), interactive integrated communication solutions] and business solutions, have been found in a number of other industries.

In each of these market trajectories, the preemptive company can focus on accurately reading the direction of the market. The company also can work to shape that direction, by forcefully introducing the next-generation product or by introducing a new market paradigm. In reading the market, the company is viewing signals that also may be apparent to attentive rivals. But in shaping the market, the company may have an even greater capacity to preempt because the future direction of the market may not be at all clear to competitors. For example, when Craig McCaw began developing his cellular network, many others underestimated the potential of the cellular market. By moving quickly and forcefully, McCaw took a huge risk, but he also was able to preempt rivals in building a national cellular system.

Understanding the Intended Trajectories of Rivals

The goal of preemption in reference to the plans of rivals is to head them off at the pass. If a rival is test marketing a certain product, a competitor could then introduce its own product quickly before the test marketer has time to bring its final product to market. The test marketer, unless it is bluffing, has signaled its intention to move into a market. This opens the opportunity for preemption. Microsoft's bid to purchase Intuit clearly showed its intent to move into financial services. Its rivals then had an opportunity to preempt. (This case illustrates that knowing *how* to preempt is not the same as having the *ability* to preempt. Few rivals were in a position to match this move. But many banks across the country accelerated their move into electronic banking to reduce the opportunity for a firm such as Microsoft to erode their relationships with customers.)

Managers also must identify potential moves of competitors. A rival may have no apparent intention to enter a specific market, but by recognizing that the rival has the opportunity to enter that market, the preemptive firm can act first to limit that opportunity. Thus it preempts the rival's strategy before the strategy is even formulated. It is not necessary for the preempted company to even know that it can move in a certain direction. It can be preempted even if it has the potential to move but is not yet aware of that potential.

How can you tell where competitors are headed or could head? The intentions of competitors are often deliberately shrouded in mystery. But sometimes their intentions are quite clear.

- *Competitive signals.* As noted, test marketing or acquisitions often provide information about competitor's intended strategies. The key is to accurately interpret the signals of competitors (which is discussed in Chapter 12). Also, a patent search can provide insights into the potential moves of competitors by showing technologies currently under development. Similarly, a competitor's hiring and firing actions and planned strategic alliances can provide useful signals for planned strategic moves.

- *Competitive analysis.* Understanding how competitors have behaved in the past and what moves they could make based on their strengths and weaknesses provides insights into possible future moves. This, at the minimum, includes a careful analysis of each competitors' objectives, strategies, historical strengths and weaknesses, and competitive actions and reactions. The analysis should also include the personality and actions of key decision makers and an analysis of their successes and failures. This analysis identifies potential moves that could be preempted.
- *Distribution channels.* A SWOT (Strengths, Weaknesses, Opportunities, Threats) analysis of the current and emerging distribution options such as megastores, category killers, new electronic distribution, and other channels for reaching the target segments is key to understanding potential competitive moves. It also helps identify potential opportunities to seize new distribution channels.
- *Environmental analysis.* What changes in the environment create opportunities for rivals, and how can these opportunities be preempted? Fundamental in this area is an understanding of the socio, cultural, political, legal, economic, and technological forces and trends that may affect the behavior of customers and other stakeholders. A critical aspect of this analysis is the assessment of the impact of these forces on the emergence of new competitors.

GENERATING PREEMPTIVE STRATEGIES

The ability to preempt often requires companies to think creatively. In fact, creativity is often a key resource in preemption. It allows companies to see the unexpected opportunity and to rethink competition. There are a variety of approaches for generating creative ideas that can be applied to the challenge of developing preemptive strategies. These include:

- *Brainstorming sessions.* Using a selected group of experts can help introduce new perspectives. In its most common format, a brainstorming session involves a relatively small number of participants (usually under 15), who are encouraged to think of the wildest ideas possible, generate the most number of ideas, and suspend all criticism and judgment. Brainstorming is often aided by other approaches and tasks such as constructing and reacting to future scenarios.

- *Analogies.* The analysis of analogous situations in other industries and countries can be expanded to include analogies to sports, chess, politics, military, and other domains of human behavior involving preemptive strategies.

- *War games and simulations.* By using one team of managers in the role of competitors and another team presenting the company's position, managers can gain new insights into the potential mind-set and moves of rivals. Simulations also can help predict the likely moves of competitors. (A more detailed examination of simulations is presented in Chapter 17.)

- *Morphological analyses.* Given that creativity is often defined as the combining of seemingly disparate parts into a functioning and useful whole, morphological analysis seems to be of great value in the generation of new ideas. To use these approaches to generate new product ideas, for example, see things as they are, then ask why they cannot be combined, used in new ways, modified, magnified, minimized, rearranged, reversed, and so on. One process for using morphological approaches to generate new ideas is the following:

1. Identify of all "relevant" factors that could be associated with a preemptive strategy.

2. Identify as many alternative options as possible for each factor.

3. Generate new ideas by understanding all possible combinations of factors, examining these combinations and identifying the more interesting ones.

Figure 11.5 presents such a preemptive option generation grid, which can also be used to organize and summarize in one place the results of all the other approaches for generating creative options. The major advantages of this and other morphological approaches are that they are: systematic, capable of encompassing a very large number of alternative new ideas, flexible with respect

Figure 11.5
An Illustrative Preemptive Option Generation Grid

Market Segments	Positioning	Pricing	Sources of Supply/Production
• Our loyal customers	• Premium	• Long-term contract	• Secure critical sources
• Our vulnerable customers	• Cost savings	• Bundled	• Vertical integration with key suppliers
• Our former customers	• Quality	• Discount	
• Prospects	• Value added	• Change pricing formula	
	Promotion	**Distribution/ Logistics**	**Legal Action**
Timing	• Frequent buyer programs	• Exclusive arrangements	• Patent infringement
• Immediately		• Loading the channel	• Trademark
• Near Future	**Preannouncement**	• Strategic alliance (M&A)	• Deceptive advertising
• Few Months	• No preannouncement		
• A Year or More	• Preannouncement of new product entry		**Misinformation**
Geographic Scope	• Preannouncement of price changes	**Advertising/ Communication**	• Send misleading signals
• U.S.		• Endorsements by clients	
• Selected regions U.S.	**Product and Service Offerings**	• "Capture a positioning"	**Key Leverage**
• Selected regions of the world	• Add new services	• Exclusive media	• "Capture the client"
• Global	• Expand the product line		• Tie up distribution
• The competitor's home	• Introduce a new generation product		• Distract competition in its key country
• Country			

to the selection of relevant attributes, simple and relatively fast and inexpensive to use.[3]

EVALUATING OPPORTUNITIES FOR PREEMPTION

Once you have examined the potential changes in the market or moves of competitors, you should be able to identify a list of expected competitive moves or potential moves based on market changes. Each of the items on this list is then a target for potential preemption.

Using this list, you can then create specific preemption strategies for each expected or potential move by a competitor. In determining the objective(s) of preemption, it is important to determine not only the desired magnitude and duration of impact on the competitor's ability to implement its strategies, but also the impact on other stakeholders. For example, with regard to the *customer,* the preemptive move may be focused on establishing the standard for the industry, locking in customers or to attain a first-mover advantage (be the first to capture a position in the customers' minds). Similarly, one can establish specific objectives for *distribution* (such as tie up shelf space), *suppliers* (lock in sources of materials), the *competitors* (to signal seriousness in defending the markets; to create barriers to entry), *security analysts* (to attain a first-mover innovative image or create the perception of a decisive management team), and others.

Once the specific objectives are determined for the strategies of each of your key competitors, you need to ask: How could this strategy be preempted? The grid in Figure 11.5 provides a framework for developing these strategies. For each potential move by a competitor, the grid can be used to generate specific strategies for preemption by selecting among choices in each category. For example, a company might respond to the extension of a product line by selecting a move focusing on loyal customers and acting immediately in the United States; by initiating legal action; or by undertaking a strategic alliance with another competitor. For each potential move, managers can identify a number of specific preemptive strategies.

Do You Want to Preempt? Can You?

So far, the analysis of markets and competitors has generated opportunities for preemption, but has not yet suggested a strategy. This analysis leaves two important questions unanswered:

- Does the company want to preempt? Is a given preemptive strategy consistent with the company's own competitive goals?
- Can it preempt? Does the company have the capabilities to make preemption feasible? And can the preemptive strategy achieve its intended objectives?

These questions can be analyzed using the table shown in Figure 11.6.

269

Figure 11.6
Initial Evaluation of Preemptive Options

The Likely Competitor's Move _____	Criteria			
Preemptive Strategies	Consistency with Our Objectives and Strategy	Feasibility	Likely Effect on the Competitor	. . .
A				
B				
C				
D				
E				

First, list each of the strategies as rows on the left-hand side and then evaluate them based on the criteria in the columns. (You can add criteria based on your own particular concerns or situation.) The first criterion considers whether the move is consistent with the firm's current objectives and strategy. If the preemptive move is not consistent with the strategy and objectives, it may still be a good move. But the key question is how far astray does it take the company? Is it an irreversible commitment or is it easy to backtrack?

If the preemption is consistent with the firm's objectives and strategy, then the next question is whether the company can preempt. It may have developed a great strategy that is not feasible. The company may not have the resources or capabilities to pull off the preemption. For example, if it is planning to preempt by introducing a next-generation product, the company might lack the R&D capabilities to do this. On the other hand, feasibility can be changed by shifting resources. The firm might be able to acquire or ally with a partner that has the capabilities needed for the preemption. Such an alliance may be a preemption in itself. For example, when domestic U.S. carriers allied themselves with European airlines, this rapidly preempted the choice carriers for later entrants.

Finally, managers need to consider the magnitude and duration of the preemptive move on the competitor. Will it prevent the competitor from moving? Slow it down? How will the competitor react to the preemption? What options does it have? Do these reactions make the preemption more attractive or less attractive? There are variations in the magnitude and duration of the impact. Sometimes, the preemption creates a long delay; other times, just a temporary delay; sometimes, it stops the competitor cold. In evaluating the likely impact, it is important to assess both the *magnitude* and *duration* of impact. The range of preemptive strategies on these two dimensions is illustrated in Figure 11.7. Whereas the "ideal" outcome of preemption is a permanent maximum impact, other outcomes are possible and should be planned for.

Figure 11.7
The Range of Preemptive Outcomes and Associated Objectives

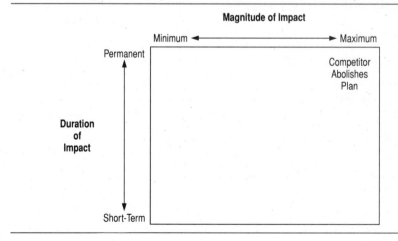

A DYNAMIC PROCESS

Thus the development and implementation of preemptive moves is an interactive process between the company and its competitor. The rival's potential and actual strategies create the opportunities for developing the firm's own preemptive moves. But these preemptive moves change the possible moves of the competitor and thus lead to a new set of strategies. The manager then needs to reshape the company's preemptive strategy to reflect this new set of competitive moves.

One way to think through this dynamic process is to use the Analytic Hierarchy Process (AHP).[4] The AHP, which has been used in analyzing issues from nuclear arms agreements to new product launches, creates a structured model for the decision process. It is a system for breaking down complex decisions into a series of side-by-side comparisons. For example, the strategic decisions of our company can be represented as a set of decisions about its mission, a set of possible scenarios it perceives for the future, a set of objectives for the firm, and finally, a set of choices about specific strategies, as shown on the left-hand side of Figure 11.8. Decisions at each level affect the decisions at the level below. This hierarchy and the particular choices at each level are developed by a group of key decision makers in the organization who represent diverse functions and experiences. This group process allows the integration of "objective" market data with subjective management judgment.

This is merely a brief overview of the Analytic Hierarchy Process. The formal process of developing the AHP would involve a careful structuring of the hierarchy and the evaluation of each element on a nine-point scale. Finally, it would involve a weighing algorithm to determine the importance of a set of options based on the group's judgment. This process is facilitated by a software package called Expert Choice.[5]

To examine the dynamics of preemptive strategies, the company would develop a second hierarchy representing the decision choices and processes of its rival. This can typically be done based on analyses of the competition and by having a group familiar with the competitor *role-play* its management. This hierarchy is represented on the right-hand side of Figure 11.8.

Figure 11.8
A Dynamic AHP

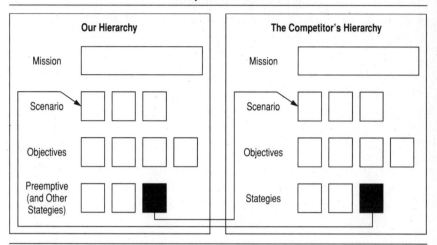

Note: The firm's hierarchy and the competitor's hierarchy will most likely be different since each should reflect its unique decision process.

The next step is to link these two hierarchies, as shown by the lines in the figure. Our proposed preemptive strategy thus becomes the input for our competitor's scenarios. Its strategies in response to these moves then become the inputs for our scenarios. After several iterations of this process, the best strategies for preemption and the ultimate impact of these strategies after multiple rounds of competition will become apparent.

The AHP is just one approach for examining the interactions among competitors, and assessing the impact of preemption strategies. Part IV of the book presents several other useful ways for thinking about dynamic interactions among competitors, including conjoint analysis, scenario planning, war games, and computer simulations. In particular, the final chapter on simulations presents a more thorough examination of methods of simulating competitive interactions.

What are the characteristics of organizations that are well positioned for preemption? To successfully implement preemptive competitive strategies requires a competitive mind-set, speed, a process for ongoing collection and analysis of relevant data, a process for generating and evaluating preemptive strategies, an implementation process, and an organizational architecture that facilitates the design and implementation of preemptive strategies.

- *A competitive mind-set.* This mind-set is critical since preemptive strategies may lead to intensified competitive battles. It is also required if one is to assure the attention and resources required to put in place a process for preemptive strategies.
- *Speed.* By its nature, preemption depends on speed. The window for preemption is often very narrow. It is the time between recognizing a potential move of a competitor and the competitor moving upon that opportunity. The organization must be able to act quickly to seize these opportunities.
- *An ongoing process for collecting and analyzing data.* The development and evaluation of preemptive strategies requires a fair amount of information and analysis. Given the dynamic nature of the business environment, one cannot rely only on a onetime analysis; rather it is critical to develop ongoing processes for data collection and analyses and the creation of *knowledge bases* for each key competitor, customers, prospects, and other stakeholders affected by the changing business environment.
- *A process for generating and evaluating options.* The design of processes such as those described for generating preemptive strategies is critical. There are numerous possible preemptive strategies, and it is desirable to spend the time and effort to identify timely, creative preemptive strategies. Having generated a large number of options, it is important that the selection of strategy for implementation be done in a systematic way. Hence, the need, as discussed, for explicit evaluation of the various options on an explicit set of criteria.
- *A process for implementation.* Having selected a strategy, an implementation plan should be developed. The plan should address explicitly how to overcome the obstacles to successful implementation. It should also address confidentiality issues. The

development of the implementation plan should receive as much attention as the development of the preemptive strategy itself.

• *Organizational architecture.* The preemptive strategy should be consistent with the firm's vision, objectives, and overall strategy, as well as the corporate culture. In addition, it should assure that the firm has in place the necessary processes, people, competencies, and resources. It is extremely important to have performance measures and associated reward and incentive systems consistent with preemptive strategies.

CONCLUSION

Preemption requires an understanding of the planned and potential moves of competitors as well as strategies for slowing or blocking those moves. The success or failure of a preemptive strategy depends upon how competitors react to it. The opportunities for preemption are not found in a single strategy, rather in the interactions between your own actions and those of your competitors. Preemption requires that you understand the payoffs, mind-sets, and potential reactions of rivals, as discussed in Part II of this book.

The approaches described in this chapter, including the dynamic AHP, have been used by two firms to design preemptive strategies. In both cases, the approaches generated preemptive strategies that were not identified in an initial brainstorming session; and in both cases, the strategy resulted in the desired objectives.

Preemption is not always advisable. As discussed, preemption has its risks. You could be walking into a land mine or off a cliff. It also could elicit an unanticipated—"wrong"—response from the target rivals or other stakeholders such as customers, suppliers, distributors, government or new entrants. You need to consider how aggressively the competitor might respond to a preemptive strike. There also are times, particularly when the total market is expanding, when you might choose to cooperate rather than to race to beat the rival to the market.

Even with these potential risks, preemption should be considered as part of planning for any competitive strategy. If there are risks of preempting, there are also risks of *not* preempting. Passing up the chance to preempt could leave you vulnerable to preemption by a rival. It is, therefore, vital to recognize opportunities to preempt your competitors and to recognize how they might preempt you. As in a gunfight in the Old West, each company is attempting to preempt the other by being the quickest draw. And like these gunslingers, the company that misses its first shot at preemption may not get a second shot.

CHAPTER 12

SIGNALING TO COMPETITORS

OLIVER P. HEIL

Johannes Gutenberg—Universitat Mainz, Department of Marketing

GEORGE S. DAY

The Wharton School, Department of Marketing

DAVID J. REIBSTEIN

The Wharton School, Department of Marketing

Strategic actions or public statements send signals to competitors. By under-standing how these signals are generated and interpreted, managers can use them as an integral part of their competitive strategies. This chapter explores the uses of signals to influence the actions of rivals. It also explores how moves can be misinterpreted and how the signals of competitors can be decoded.

Every action and every statement of the firm sends a signal to competitors. Some of these signals are inadvertent, tipping the company's hand to rivals. Others are deliberate, serving as a warning or a challenge to rivals. They all have important strategic implications. By understanding how actions or announcements are interpreted and signals are generated, managers can become more adept at sending signals and interpreting the moves of competitors.

THE POWER AND PERIL OF SIGNALS

Signals can be highly effective in shaping the actions of competitors. For example, at the time that digital watches were being developed for introduction onto the market, Texas Instruments (TI) announced plans to offer a watch at $19.95. Upon learning this, Gillette and several others that were working hard to develop the technology for entry were quickly dissuaded, convinced margins would not be high enough to make the market profitable.

Interestingly, after others decided not to enter the industry, Texas Instruments discovered that it, too, could not effectively operate at a price point of only $19.95, and ended up entering the market at a higher price point. As is always the case with such announcements, it is impossible to know whether TI sincerely thought it could enter at that price or was deliberately trying to dissuade competitors. In any case, the move was very effective in keeping out other would-be entrants.

On the other hand, actions can lead to the wrong signal (i.e., the motives behind the action may be misunderstood by the reacting competitor). In the tire industry, one firm offered an end-of-year volume discount of $2 and a marketing allowance of $1.50, on a $35 tire. This firm then heard that a major competitor was selling a similar tire at an invoice price of $32. In response, it lowered its own invoice price from $35 to $32. Only later did it realize that the competitor was not offering any discounts or allowances, so the relevant price for comparison purposes was actually 50 cents higher.

The purpose of this chapter is to harness the power and avoid the perils of signaling. We first explore the many ways signals can be used to shape the actions of rivals. Then, we examine why moves can be misunderstood and lead to unintended signals, as in the case of the tire manufacturer. This understanding should allow managers to better use signals themselves and avoid misinterpreting the moves of competitors.

THE STRATEGIC USES OF SIGNALS

The primary motive for signaling is to shape competitors' behavior in ways beneficial to all or at least one firm in the industry. There are a variety of ways signals can be used, including the following:

Discouraging Attack

Signals can be used to discourage competitors from initiating attacks on your markets. For example, for years Procter & Gamble has been able to discourage frontal attacks on its core products. P&G's signals carry a lot of weight because of its strong market presence, its ability to retaliate strongly and quickly against entrants, and frequent public reminders that the company's first priority is holding share. Similarly, Intel has repeatedly announced it would sue anyone violating its microprocessor patents, and followed through with a legal challenge to Advanced Micro Devices.

Blocking Entry

A competitor may announce major capacity additions to dissuade others from adding capacity lest they create excess capacity.[1] For example, Marriott Hotels announced its intention to add a new major convention hotel in Philadelphia long before a brick was laid. This was done not to encourage guests to begin booking rooms, but as a clear message to competition that Marriott had already moved to gain a stronger foothold in the Philadelphia market. Any addition by competition would result in a nonprofitable venture, since it would create too much hotel capacity in the area.

Beyond just overcapacity threats, announcements can also discourage competitive entry by showing the rival the cost of the battle, as Glaxo intended in 1988 when it announced it had made "massive investments in buildings, equipment, and human resources," for its new drug colony-stimulating factor.

Disciplining an Errant Competitor

Another use of signals is to show unwillingness to accept belligerent or uncooperative behavior by rivals. If a price leader has announced that a price increase is in order, and some competitor breaks ranks and keeps its prices steady, a signal may be sent to punish the insubordination. This can be accomplished by rescinding the announced price increase, or instituting a sizable "temporary price reduction." The price cut may signal to the deviant competitors that they will not be allowed to gain a competitive advantage in the marketplace. The only way they will benefit is by getting in line with the rest of the industry. It is often argued that to be an effective price leader, it is necessary to be able to punish those who do not follow.

When Southwest Airlines entered the Chicago market, it sent a strong message to all carriers that this upstart was not going to continue to be a small competitor focusing on travel in the southwestern states but a national carrier instead. Although some of the markets Southwest Airlines targeted were not of prime importance to either United Airlines or American Airlines, these incumbents responded aggressively, sending a clear signal to Southwest Airlines about how difficult it would be to enter future markets "belonging" to those two, and what the likely responses might be.

Influencing Codes of Conduct

The intensity of competitive behavior in any industry can range from peaceful coexistence to all-out combat conditions.[2] Signals may be beneficial in reinforcing desirable norms of conduct and discouraging dysfunctional behavior to improve overall industry profitability. These codes of conduct can be established through signals that expose one's assumptions about current conditions, price levels, capacity requirements, and future prospects. Often, the signal contains implicit pleas for price discipline or avoidance of debilitating promotional spending, or perhaps is a call to maintain a united front in dealing with regulators. For example, when software vendors found themselves in a "service war," in which the cost of service escalated with extended hours, toll-free services, and so forth, Microsoft then scaled back. Whether its action was intended to serve primarily as a signal to competition on the "appropriate" level of industry behavior, or merely a cost-cutting measure may never be known. Nonetheless, this move served as a clear signal to other providers in the industry that a reduced level of customer service would be tolerated by the lead firm. It served as a strong lead which everyone else could follow.

Dividing Up the Market

In some markets, signals may be sent to gain acceptance of a *de facto* partitioning of the market that will ensure peaceful coexistence. The message is that there are certain markets that are "hands off" to competitors. These markets can divide by geography; that is, we operate in the Northeast while you occupy the Southwest, but any form of segmentation is a logical basis for "market allocation." The mere fact that an incursion is not made into the competitors' market is a *signal* of desired peaceful coexistence. If one of the competitors decides to extend its boundaries and starts to enter other markets, it sends a considerably different signal to the competitors. How each of the incumbent competitors responds is a strong signal, in turn, to the aggressive firm. A nonresponse, for example, could be a signal of weakness or unwillingness to fight to defend.[3] This might serve as an invitation to the aggressive firm to enter other markets of this competitor because resistance is not likely.

Each of the Regional Bell Operating Companies (RBOCs) had peacefully coexisted in the territories they had inherited with the divestiture of AT&T. As soon as the first RBOC started to offer cellular service in one of its sibling's territories, the sanctity of territorial exclusivity started to disintegrate. It is only now starting to fully evolve into open confrontations with private lines, local loops, and even "plain old telephone service" (POTS) being contested in *other's* markets.

Companies also use signals to avoid head-to-head competition. For example, a firm may announce a new technology that would allow it to significantly reduce price. A competitor may then react by announcing plans for an advertising campaign aimed at repositioning its brand. As a result, competitors may be able to select new market positions and avoid competing head-to-head. Announcing plans is particularly effective when it is conducted outside the public eye (in a trade journal, for example). This way, the announcements will not delay consumers' purchases or damage consumers' willingness to pay.

Sending Up Trial Balloons

Announcements and other signals are often used to test the competitive reaction in advance of a product launch. There often is nothing that binds the firm to fulfill what was promised. Thus, if the competition offers another feature, there still is the opportunity to delay entry and offer an enhanced product, as well. Or, if competition does not follow the price lead, the opportunity to come in at a lower price is still available. It is a well-known practice in the airline industry for price increases to be announced prior to posting to the public, and then to be reneged whenever competition does not follow.

Bluffing

In addition to testing the waters, a firm may signal an action without any intention of following through. A bluff can often confuse customers and put the company's credibility at risk, thus deliberate and clear bluffs are undertaken with great caution.[4]

But most signals—even those that are known to be bluffs within the firm—are usually more ambiguous to outsiders. There is good "vaporware," which occurs when a software house begins releasing details of a program under development to customers who need to be advised because it is critical to their business or to those who are enlisted to help improve the software. Bad vaporware is a prerelease of information with the intent to hurt a rival. This issue was at the heart of the antitrust case against Microsoft Corp.[5] The characteristics of the signal and competitors, as discussed next, can give clues as to whether the signal is true or a bluff.

The likelihood of bluffing may also be affected by the type of signal. A recent study of bluffs in competitive market signaling found no evidence of significant bluffing in new product signaling, but significant bluffing activity in price increase signaling.[6]

TYPES OF SIGNALS

Signals arise from a variety of actions and announcements. Most actions are directed toward the firm's customers, but are clearly viewed and reacted to by both the channels of distribution and rivals. Other actions are primarily designed to influence the channel itself to either carry more of the product, alter the price, or take some other desirable marketing action. Finally, some actions and statements are specifically directed toward competitors.[7]

Actions

Some actions are very public, such as a change in a price schedule, the launch of a new product or a new ad campaign, or the breaking of ground for a new plant. These actions may be accompanied by a clarifying explanation, just to ensure the proper message is received. Other actions are just as real, but may be deliberately obscured, such as a price concession to a major account or a technology licensing agreement that signals a change in strategy. We offer additional important details about actions when we discuss price cuts later.

Announcements

In addition to actions, announcements are used to prevent a competitor's action, or to signal to customers what is to come. This often leads the customer to defer purchases of what is on the market today in anticipation of what is expected to be on the market in the future. A company that is lagging in technology has the motivation to announce its product launches well ahead of time. The announcements today of new high-definition televisions or the "soon to the market" merger of televisions and computers has the potential to create pent-up demand from customers deferring their purchases in fear of making purchases that will soon be obsolete.

In addition to its impact on customers, the announcement could also shape the form of competitive response. Beyond the product announcement there is often a price announcement as well. This might serve to alert competition as to what the appropriate price levels should be in this category. Without this announcement, competitors might have entered the market too low, destroying the profit potential for everyone. On the other side, it is also possible to announce a low price, discouraging competition from entering the market at all, as in the case of Texas Instruments cited previously.

New Product Preannouncements

The preannouncement of a new product well before it is launched is a signal to both customers and competitors. The message for customers is that they should either prepare for the new product or delay buying a rival's product because a superior alternative will soon be available. (This use of this strategy to preempt competitors is considered in more detail in Chapter 11.) Of course, there is always the risk that the customers will stop buying the firm's existing products as well. These signals are also directed at competitors, to discourage them from entering the market.

A recent study of U.S. marketing managers found that 51 percent of their firms had preannounced their last new product or service an average of three or four months before availability.[8] Preannouncement becomes more desirable as more of the following conditions are satisfied:

- The firm has a low market share (so the risk of cannibalization of its sales is low) and the competitors are not likely to react.
- The new product has strong patent protection, which provides some immunity to retaliation.
- The firm's image will be enhanced by taking the initiative and demonstrating market leadership.
- The buyers need advance warning, because the product requires substantial learning; and/or they have lengthy decision processes.
- The sale of the new product requires the participation and commitment of distributors or sellers of complementary products such as software. An early preannouncement of new computer systems is necessary to encourage the development of application software.

To Act or to Announce?

Actions and announcements exhibit very different signaling properties. In the following table, we contrast the signaling properties of these two bases of signals. As noted, compared to actions, announcements offer exceptional speed and flexibility. For example, when a car manufacturer announces that prices for its cars are likely to increase several percentage points in the next model year, competitors can react using similar announcements. The price that will finally be implemented will, if the announcements and counterannouncements have worked, in all likelihood lie somewhere in between the initial proposals. The prices have evolved rather quickly and without involving consumers or affecting consumer perceptions and loyalties. The price-finding process was rather fast in execution and low in cost for the companies.

However, since announcements are so easy and inexpensive, bluffing is more likely. As a result, a manager needs to choose between the fast, low-cost announcement or the slower, more expensive but often more credible action.

Basis of Comparison	Action	Announcements
Costs	Expensive	Inexpensive
Speed to implement	Slow	Fast
Commitment	Difficult to reverse	Easy to reverse
Believability	High	Low
Precision	Moderate to tailor to intentions	High ability to tailor to intentions

GETTING THE MESSAGE ACROSS: THE CHALLENGE OF INTERPRETING SIGNALS

Since the signals are not usually direct communications from the sender to the receiver, there is often a lot of room for misinterpretation.[9] Companies don't have the option of saying to competitors: "I'm raising my price, and if you follow, we can all enjoy higher margins." Instead, they must simply raise the price and hope the competitor interprets the move properly. The challenge is that a single statement or action can be interpreted in many different ways. For example, when a firm raises its price, it might be interpreted as:

- A weakness by the acting firm, indicating it cannot make money at the existing prices. This could lead to an aggressive "go for the kill" response by an opportunistic competitor.
- A signal to all competitors to raise their prices so that everyone can establish wider margins.
- No signal at all, resulting from internal considerations without any anticipated reaction by the competition.

Because each move can be interpreted in many ways, it is important to understand and manage the signal so that the desired competitive reaction is elicited. It could be disastrous to try to gain a cooperative increase in prices by raising them only to initiate a price war, because the move was misinterpreted as one of desperation (the first option). On the other hand, the ambiguity of signals can sometimes be used to the company's advantage if it wants to keep rivals guessing about its true intentions.

Attributes of Signals and Signalers

The interpretation of signals is affected by the clarity, aggressiveness, and consequences of the signal, and the perceived commitment of the sender. It is also affected by the similarity of the sender and the receiver.

Clarity. A move that has a clear cause can be read quickly, resulting in a clear signal. A clear signal indicates the sender's desire to encourage an immediate response, such as following an industry price increase. Conversely, a noisy signal leaves room for alternative explanations and creates uncertainty. This may lead to a delay in the receiving firm's reactions. A noisy signal may also be used to gain information from competitors. For example, a firm may be interested in expanding its market presence (by region or by segment) but have limited capacity. Its goal, therefore, is to expand first where it will encounter the least competitive resistance. Vague announcements of market expansion may be made to assess how vigorously competitors will signal their intent to defend particular markets. Thus, noisy signals may encourage competitors to reveal possible future reactions.

Aggressiveness. Signals are viewed as aggressive if they threaten the competitor's performance. Thus, Pizza Hut viewed McDonald's new pizza product as a very threatening move. Similarly, price reductions in an airline's hub by a rival are often viewed as signaling aggressive intent because the move can bring prices down at the hub, harming the high-share hub airline much more than a smaller aggressor. Competitors are much more likely to respond aggressively to an aggressive signal.[10]

Research in game theory suggests that cooperative behavior elicits cooperative behavior and that competitive behavior elicits competitive behavior.[11] In a comparison of diverse competitive strategies, a "tit-for-tat" strategy on average outperformed all other strategies. Tit-for-tat starts with a cooperative move and matches a competitor's move afterwards. One implication of a tit-for-tat strategy is that initial compliance with a cooperative move can sustain cooperation throughout the interaction and benefit all participants. In turn, not complying with initial cooperation can lock the competitive interaction into a noncooperative mode, harming all rivals.

Commitment. This reflects the perceived willingness of the sending firm to stick to its market action, either because some of the costs associated with the signal are nonrecoverable, or it has major strategic or legal ramifications. Commitment to an announcement will be high when there is a certainty of legal action if the promises are not kept. Thus, commitments are decisions that limit the options of a manager after the signal is sent, making it more likely the firm will act as signaled.

Consistency. Signals are often interpreted not only from a single action, but from a series or history of actions. The more consistent the historical behavior, the easier it is for the signal to be heard, understood, and correctly responded to. MCI Telecommunications has sent a very clear signal to AT&T by consistently pricing itself under AT&T. Every time AT&T has lowered its prices, MCI has immediately responded with a corresponding price decrease. Similarly, as AT&T has dared to raise its prices in a few categories, MCI has not let the gap grow, but has been right there on AT&T's heels. Many managers believe it is desirable to "keep competitors guessing" as to what their next move might be. If your intent is to signal to competition to gain cooperation, it is best to be consistent and easily predictable. If you are trying to lead competition, they have to know where you are going.

Similarity of the Sender and Receiver.   The accuracy of the generation of signals increases with the increasing similarity of the sender and the receiver. When rivals follow similar strategies, use similar structures, and the managers have similar backgrounds, they understand each other and usually make correct attributions of each other's moves. Difficulties arise with new competitors that go unrecognized because they are members of a divergent strategic group. For example, for many years the competitors in the traditional securities industry ignored mutual fund marketers (such as Fidelity, Vanguard, and Dreyfuss) and refused them membership in the Securities Industry of America trade association. As a result, they tended to disregard their activities and failed to recognize their growing strength.

LISTENING: SIGNALING IS A TWO-WAY STREET

Managers who recognize the importance of signals often overemphasize *sending* competitive signals instead of reading the signals of their competitors. Thus, although messages are constantly hitting the competitive airwaves, very few are heard. Listening for competitors' signals and accurately interpreting them is every bit as important as sending signals effectively.

Experiments with senior executives in a simulated competitive environment have revealed an often-fatal attraction to sending signals rather than attending to those of competitors. During the simulations, managers are asked to make a series of pricing decisions, under the belief that they are competing against two other managers in the simulated environment. In reality, the competitors are a preprogrammed set of computerized responses that are very consistent in their behavior: One always undercuts the manager's last price by a slight amount, while the other holds price relatively constant. Thus, if the managers would raise their prices over time, one of the competitors would follow upward. Because they fail to recognize this pattern in the competitive signals, participants usually get involved in a price war. When asked why, the most common response was that they were busy trying to send a message, which was not being heard, and so had no idea that a very consistent message was being sent to them.

Effectively interpreting signals depends on understanding all the issues discussed from the sender's perspective. When receiving a market signal, managers should consider the signal and sender characteristics just noted. They should also examine possible motives for signaling, both sinister and benign, as discussed at the opening of the chapter. Finally, they should conduct consistency checks to assess signal meaning and credibility. Signal senders tend to disseminate multiple signals during any given period of time, such as impending price changes, proposed new products, proposed new plant capacity, and others. Although some of the sender's signals may have no immediate relevance to the receiver, they can be used to perform signal consistency checks. In other words, a receiving firm uses seemingly unrelated competitive market signals of the sender to cross-validate meanings inferred from signals that are of direct concern. The degree of similarity, or correlation, between the meanings affects the degree to which the manager feels competent to judge the new signal. This implies that the reacting manager should develop other sources of information to increase the chances of accurate signal interpretation.

To avoid missing or misinterpreting signals, managers should carefully analyze the potential strategic message of every action or announcement. For example, if a rival initiates a price cut, a manager should consider the following issues:[12]

- *The scope of the price reduction.* In how many markets or market segments will the price cut take effect? Is this unusual?
- *The timing of the price reduction.* Why was this particular time of the year or season selected? Does the acting firm face internal pressures (e.g., too much inventory) or external pressures (e.g., threat of competitive entry, obsolescence of current technology)?
- *The duration of the price reduction.* How long will the price cut last, and how does this duration compare to price cuts normally observed? Is the price cut unusual?
- *The degree of irreversibility of the price reduction.* Does the price cut harm or change consumer loyalty or brand equity? Is the change likely to be permanent, (e.g., consumers might become more price-sensitive)?
- *The competitors' ability to react, in response to the price reduction.* Are there competitors who cannot react; for example, because of commitments to a certain production technology, or because their products are already priced in, say, a catalog?
- *The size of the price reduction.* What are the absolute and relative levels of the price cut? Are such price cuts frequently observed in the industry, or could the cut be based on a new production technology or new insights about consumer preferences?

Each of these questions will help sharpen the manager's understanding of which signal is intended.

CONCLUSION: MESSAGES FOR MANAGERS

This chapter highlights some of the competitive uses of signals and the factors that influence their interpretation. There are several key points managers should consider when sending and receiving signals. We have framed these lessons from the vantage point of the recipient of a signal, but they apply equally to a firm thinking about sending a signal:

Invest in understanding the reasons behind a competitor's move. If what the competitor is doing doesn't seem sensible, it is likely that you don't understand it well enough to react wisely. At the same time, the signal must be put into context. This is especially important for price cuts, where it is crucial to have a full picture of all the price changes (and nonprice changes) being made by the competitor. The cost of a delayed reaction is probably lower than the cost of a misinterpretation that launches a competitive battle.

Avoid overreaction. Once the competitive signal has been derived, and sensible motives have been imputed, it is important to follow a tit-for-tat logic to avoid escalating the competitive battle. Remember that managers who look at their competitor's signals are biased to view them as a threat even if one wasn't intended. If aggressive motives are imputed, strong reactions may be triggered by seemingly innocuous competitive moves or announcements.

Attend to the periphery. If managers pay too much attention to their immediate rivals, they often overlook the signals from competitors in adjacent markets or low-visibility niches because there is no immediate threat and the signal itself may be weak. The lack of shared understanding appears to lead managers to discount any threats from peripheral players.

Communicate carefully. Many missteps can be avoided by taking the competitor's point of view before signaling. If there are doubts as to how they will react, be very careful to provide careful explanation of why the move was made, along with appropriate qualifiers and limitations.

Weigh the risks. Just because announcements and other signals require little resource commitment doesn't mean they are without risk. Well-conceived signals may sometimes be counterproductive, and inadvertent signals are very risky. If too much is revealed to competitors about your plans and intentions, they may be impelled to accelerate their new products in response, or initiate spoiler tactics such as loading retailers with inventory before the launch of the planned product. Meanwhile, consumers may delay or cancel their purchases of your current products and wait for the announced new product, rebate, or price cut. Furthermore, as Yao discusses in

Chapter 14, signals may be interpreted as collusive acts and may trigger antitrust action. For every planned signal, it is important to assess the possible risks of the move.

Manage the competitive interaction. Managers should not take for granted that rivals will respond to signals as expected or recognize a competitive interplay that is beneficial for the firms in an industry. For example, a firm's price cut at the wrong moment may be viewed by competitors as a signal of the firm's desire to steal market share from others. Such an aggressive signal will prompt strong reactions and may lead to a downward price spiral. Conversely, cooperative signals may alter the course of a competitive interaction that is heading in the wrong direction. In other words, the competitive interaction is "made" by the competitors themselves and should be managed.

Once a signal has been generated, the reacting firm can countersignal through an appropriate action or an announcement. A countersignal may be used to seek further information, to propose an alternative or seek cancellation of the vote implied by the signal. If the countersignal doesn't work, then the firm has to decide whether any reaction is warranted; and if so, how quickly to take action, in what markets, and how strongly to act. These issues were explored in the earlier chapter by Gatignon and Reibstein.

This dynamic interaction of signal and response provides an added dimension to competition—like the voice track of a motion picture. It is often as difficult to interpret these competitive gestures as it is to unravel gestures and comments in conversation. Signals add greatly to the complexity of competitive interactions and create additional opportunities to influence the behavior of rivals. The interplay between actions and signals, the give-and-take of signals and responses shapes competition and affects the way future signals can be developed and how they will be interpreted. Effective competitive strategy cannot ignore the importance of this aspect of competition.

CHAPTER 13

COMMITMENT: HOW NARROWING OPTIONS CAN IMPROVE COMPETITIVE POSITIONS

LOUIS A. THOMAS
The Wharton School, Department of Management

Many managers believe that in developing a competitive strategy, it is important to keep their options open. Can narrowing competitive options be a good strategy? The commitment of resources affects not only the company's position, but also the positions and behavior of rivals. For example, commitments to building high capacity can forestall entry by other players. Large commitments to brands and advertising also can block moves by rivals. Commitments to customers (such as frequent flier programs) or to industry standards can raise profits for all players—if they are accepted. This chapter examines the impact of commitment on competitive strategy. It explores "tough" commitments that decrease rival profits, and "soft" commitments that increase the profits of rivals. Finally, it presents a matrix for deciding when to use one approach rather than another.

$\mathbf{A}$t first glance, it would seem strange to believe that managers can actually improve their performance by limiting their options through commitment. Many management theorists emphasize the idea that firms need to be flexible. But sometimes, making a commitment that is impossible or difficult to reverse can be a very effective way to block or preempt competitors. The benefits of commitments that decrease the profits of rivals are apparent. But, as will be pointed out in this chapter, commitments that increase the profits of rivals also can be part of an effective strategy.

BURNING BRIDGES

To grasp how narrowing options can improve a firm's competitive position, consider the following military example. Two armies are on opposite sides of a river. There is an island in the center of the river that each army wishes to occupy, as shown in Figure 13.1. The island is connected to the banks of the river by two bridges. Each army can march across the bridge and take the island, but the intense fighting would be too costly for each side. Army A comes up with the following plan: It decides to march across the bridge and occupy the island and burn the bridge behind. Army B now surveys the situation and realizes that Army A is committed to fighting because it has no way to retreat. Army B decides the fight is not worthwhile, and thus Army A captures the island. By limiting its options, A makes itself better off.

Similarly, commitment can play an important role in competitive interactions. As in the military example, rival companies often move in on the same market. By making a commitment—for example, building excess capacity in the market—a company can force rivals to back down. This is just one way resource commitments can be used in competitive strategy, and it is a fairly simple one. In this chapter, we examine a variety of potential commitments and their impact on competition. In particular, we look at commitments that reduce rival profits (make a company tough) and those that increase rival profits (make a company soft). We also introduce a matrix for deciding when the various types of commitments are most appropriate.

Figure 13.1
Limiting Options Can Improve Your
Competitive Position

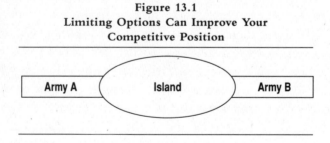

COMMITMENT AS A STRATEGIC WEAPON

Commitment has become a subject of increasing interest in strategic management.[1] If managers are able to commit to certain strategies, rivals will take this into account when determining their best actions. This suggests that managers with foresight then could choose strategies and resources so as to influence rival responses to their advantage.

Ghemawat describes commitments as resulting in lockin or lockout. The firm is said to be locked in if the resources deployed to implement a strategy are difficult to redeploy for some other purpose. This commits the firm to a certain strategy. Resources that meet this criterion are durable, specialized, and nontradable. The mirror image of lockin is lockout, when the commitment locks the firm out of certain options. If a firm is locked in to a certain strategy, it is often locked out of other strategies.

Consider the issue of building excess capacity in a growing industry. If an incumbent expands its capacities beyond the needs of the market, this could discourage competitors from building capacity. The excess capacity in the industry would mean that if a rival also built plants, it would drive down prices for all players and lead to a surplus of production. But what if the incumbent isn't locked in, if it could reduce its capacity in response to the rival's entry? The rival might then be encouraged to build the plant, hoping the incumbent would back down or accommodate the new entrant as a small player. The incumbent, with its large market share, has the most to lose from an all-out price war or a saturated market.

If the company makes an irreversible commitment to this capacity, it will be absolutely clear to competitors that the incumbent would find it very costly to back down. Like the army burning the bridge at its back, the firm has eliminated the option of reducing its capacity. (One way it could safely commit to this strategy is if it had lower costs than rivals.) By committing to the capacity, the incumbent will make it much less likely that the competitor will decide to build capacity. This shows why commitment is important in shaping rival behavior. Without this commitment, the rival could force the incumbent to reverse its strategy.

TOUGH AND SOFT COMMITMENTS

Commitments can either be tough or soft based on their impact on the profits of rivals. Some commitments, such as building excess capacity, reduce the profits of rivals, and thus are tough. Other commitments, such as preferred customer agreements, can actually increase the profits of rivals, and thus are soft commitments. Companies usually only make such soft commitments if they increase the profits of the industry as a whole (the firm and its rivals). To better understand the uses of tough and soft commitments in competitive strategy, this section describes a few examples of each.

Tough and soft commitments will elicit different responses from competitors. Obviously, tough commitments are far more threatening and so could be expected to draw a more forceful and aggressive response. But tough commitments can be used in ways that evoke an accommodating response from rivals (as will be discussed in the discussion of the matrix presented later).

Tough Commitments

Commitments that make companies tough—reducing rival profits—include capacity preemption and commitments to brands and advertising. These commitments tend to block the moves of potential new entrants by raising the costs of entering an industry or reducing the likelihood of returns.

Capacity Preemption. As noted, capacity preemption is a common tough strategy. Firms in the semiconductor industry preempt one another by building new fabrication facilities (fabs) in advance of expected increases in demand. This strategy has helped Intel remain dominant in microprocessors, the Japanese to displace American firms during the 1980s, and Korean firms to displace many Japanese firms during the late 1980s. Building fabs early allows Intel to preempt competition, decreasing rival profits. Thus the strategy is tough.

Figure 13.2 shows evidence of capacity preemption in new fab construction in the DRAM market from 1980 through 1990. One would expect that as the market size grows relative to the number of fabs,

Figure 13.2
New DRAM Fabrication Facilities

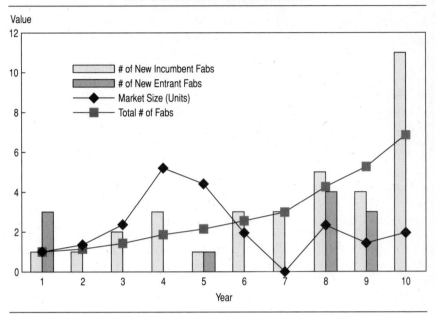

Source: Dataquest

firms would find it profitable to introduce new fabs. Companies should not be opening new fabs faster than the growth of the market unless they want to preempt rivals. The figure suggests the latter is true. From the mid–1980s, the number of fabs grew relative to the market size, but incumbent firms continued to open new fabs. This is unlikely to be profitable in the short run, but if it forecloses subsequent entry opportunities, incumbents may be able to preserve industry profits. Most of the firms building during this period were Japanese, and as a result they were able to capture substantial market share from the American firms, many of whom had to exit the industry.

Commitments to Brands and Advertising. Sunk investments in advertising are another example of commitments that make a company tough. One feature of advertising-intensive industries, particularly for those in the food and drink group, is the market share persistence of leaders. Kellogg's, Coca-Cola, and Budweiser have been market share leaders in their respective industries for long periods despite rapid market growth and evolving consumer tastes, all of which should have made outside entry profitable. Table 13.1 illustrates the point for other industries.

By spending large sums on advertising, managers build a stock of well-known brands or "brand capital."[2] If consumers are more likely to try brands with which they are familiar, the firm with the largest stock has an advantage in bringing new products to market. The observed market share persistence in Table 13.1 can be explained using this

Table 13.1
Brand Leaders of 1923

Share Leader in 1923	1983 Rank
Swift's premium bacon	1
Kellogg's cereals	1
Kodak cameras	1
Del Monte fruit	1
Hershey's chocolates	2
Crisco shortening	2
Carnation milk	1
Wrigley chewing gum	1
Nabisco biscuits	1
Eveready batteries	1
Gold Medal flour	1
Life Savers candies	1
Sherwin Williams paint	1
Hammermill paper	1
Prince Albert tobacco	1
Gillette razors	1
Singer sewing machines	1
Manhattan shirts	5
Coca-Cola soft drinks	1
Campbell's soups	1
Ivory soaps	1
Lipton teas	1
Goodyear tires	1
Palmolive soaps	2
Colgate toothpaste	2

Source: *Advertising Age*

notion of brand capital. As an industry evolves, new market segments open as a result of changes in consumer tastes or new consumers entering the market. Some of these new segments are large while other smaller segments can only profitably support a small number of products. The firm with the largest stock of brand capital has an advantage because it can affiliate its new product with one of its existing brand names. Because consumers are more likely to try such a product, the managers of high-capital firms will find early entry to be more profitable.

In fact, data from the U.S. beverage and ready-to-eat cereal industry shows that the firm with the greatest brand capital is the most likely early entrant in new market segments, while those with less brand capital enter only if the expected segment size is large.[3] Thus, high-brand-capital firms enter both small and large new market segments, while low-capital firms enter only large ones. This would help to explain the market share persistence in these industries.

As discussed by Jerry Wind in Chapter 11, companies use line extensions to preempt competitors. By making a commitment to the new extension before rivals, competitors secure this new market space for themselves. This commitment makes the company tough by shutting out rivals. The line extension strategy allows companies to keep their lead even in the face of market growth and changes in consumer tastes. Companies with high brand capital, which have already spent large sums to build brand names, face lower costs in introducing new line extensions.

Preemptive commitments to line extensions have helped Kellogg's control nearly 45 percent of the ready-to-eat cereal market since World War II. As shown in Table 13.2, there has been very little entry. In the raisin and chex cereal segments, with the exception of two products, all new introductions were extensions, and these extensions were introduced when the gap between the market size and number of products was small. This new product investment strategy suggests firms are entering prior to anticipated market growth, thus making rival entry less profitable. This is true in the chex segment where all of the extensions were introduced by Purina, the sole incumbent. By introducing extensions before the market became large enough to profitably support more brands, Purina, was largely able to block entry.

Table 13.2
New Product Introductions

Cereal	Year	Firm	New Name or Extension	Market Size less Products
		Raisin Segment		
Honey Nut Crunch	1981	General Foods	Extension	−0.51
Low-Sodium Raisin Bran	1984	Kellogg's	Extension	−0.97
Raisin Nut Bran	1986	General Mills	New Name	−1.25
Amazin Raisin Bran	1987	General Foods	Extension	−1.71
Total Raisin Bran	1988	General Mills	Extension	−2.14
Nutri Grain Raisin Bran	1989	Kellogg's	Extension	−2.41
		Chex Segment		
Raisins & Wheat	1980	Purina	Extension	−0.07
Crispix	1983	Kellogg's	New Name	−1.39
Crispy Oat	1984	Purina	Extension	−0.99
Honey Graham	1986	Purina	Extension	−3.07
Oat	1989	Purina	Extension	−3.89

Source: L. Thomas, "Brand Capital and Entry Order," *Journal of Economics and Management Strategy,* Vol. 5, No. 1 (Spring, 1996), 107–109.

The only successful outside entry was Kellogg's Crispix. In the raisin segment, Kellogg's and General Foods, the incumbent firms, were also able to block entry by introducing extensions when the number of products was large relative to the market size. The only successful outside entry was an extension, Total Raisin Bran, introduced by General Mills. Thus, entrants may only find profitable ways of entering by using brand extensions themselves.

Sunk investments in advertising may also explain the evolution of industry structure. Sutton offers both theoretical and empirical evidence that managers can use increased investments in advertising to keep the industry concentrated even as demand grows.[4] Sutton points out that certain industry and firm characteristics are determined by forces outside management control. For example, the output level of a plant which minimizes cost is determined by the underlying production technology. Other characteristics, such as advertising and R&D, are determined by managers. Thus managers can change the cost of entering an industry by increasing their investment in advertising or R&D. Rival firms and potential entrants must now meet the new hurdle to remain or exit. Thus, even if the industry becomes large enough to allow several profitable firms to exist, incumbents can increase the entry hurdle, thus denying entry and forcing small firms to exit. This, in turn, keeps the industry concentrated.

Figure 13.3 helps make the point. Let's say we have an industry where the average cost (AC1), marginal costs (MC1), and demand (d) are related, as shown. With this level of demand, there are a few firms that could profitably operate in the industry. Now suppose demand rises to D. At AC1, many firms could operate in the industry, and the structure would become very fragmented.

Figure 13.3
Effect of Advertising Industry Structure

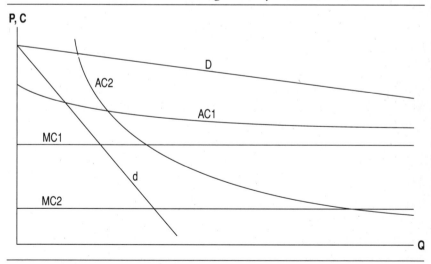

Suppose, however, that at some point, one firm increases the level of advertising needed to succeed in the industry. Advertising makes it more likely consumers will try a product, thereby lowering the cost to market a new product. The advertising thus increases the fixed cost but lowers the marginal cost. The average cost curve moves from AC1 to AC2. Now, far fewer firms can operate profitably in this industry. The dominant firms can use advertising to prevent the industry from becoming highly segmented and unprofitable.

Soft Commitments

So far, we have considered strategies that make a firm tough. We will now consider a few strategies that make the firm soft, increasing the profits of rivals. Why increase rivals' profits? These commitments should be made only when they increase industry profits (the size of the pie). In these cases, they can be effective strategies to create win–win situations. In environments in which soft commitments increase rival profits at the expense of the firm, they are important to recognize as strategies *to be avoided*. Among the soft commitments made by companies are: most-favored customer clauses, meet-the-competition clauses, frequent flier programs, and the development of industry standards.

Most-Favored Customer Clause. Most-favored customer clauses (MFC) guarantee the buyer that if the seller ever cuts the price, the seller will rebate the buyer the difference. These types of contracts make price cuts very costly. Because they commit the firm to a higher price level, rivals can also raise prices without fear of retribution. Thus MFCs are examples of strategies that makes a firm soft.

Meet-the-Competition Clause. With a meet-the-competition clause (MCC), the seller commits to match any lower price received by the buyer. These are common in many retail industries. On the surface, these contracts would seem to benefit consumers, but they actually allow manufacturers to enjoy higher prices because the profits from a price cut are less attractive if competitors are committed to matching.

Thus an MCC would allow your rival to enjoy higher profits, so again this is a commitment that makes a firm soft.

Frequent Flier Programs. Frequent flier programs have a similar effect. For example, if you live in a city where American Airlines is the dominant carrier, you are most likely to want to accumulate as many frequent flier points as you can with American because it has the most flights from your city; and when you decide to use your points, you will have the most destinations from which to choose. You are more likely to want to book a flight with American than any other airline. This allows American to price higher at airports where it is dominant, which, in turn, allows rivals to price higher. Thus these contracts raise rival profits and make the firm soft. As shown in Table 13.3, the hubbiness (percentage of traffic that is moving through the airport on the

Table 13.3
Hubbiness of Airports

Airport	Percent Changing Planes	Airport Herfindahl*	Airport Fare Premium (%)
Charlotte	75.7	0.579	18.8
Atlanta	69.0	0.347	17.2
Memphis	67.7	0.355	27.4
Dallas/Ft. Worth	65.8	0.386	20.5
Pittsburgh	62.1	0.529	15.9
Salt Lake City	61.3	0.430	19.1
St. Louis	56.2	0.354	−4.0
Chicago-O'Hare	55.7	0.270	14.8
Denver	54.1	0.272	15.3
Minneapolis	51.0	0.418	31.5
Houston	49.5	0.423	15.6
New York–Kennedy	47.3	0.202	2.9
Detroit	43.6	0.296	−0.7
Baltimore	40.5	0.299	9.1
Phoenix	33.1	0.205	−28.4
Miami	31.0	0.171	−14.3

* Market share of top four airlines.

Source: S. Borenstein, "The Evolution of U.S. Airline Competition," *Journal of Economic Perspectives*, Vol. 6, No. 2 (Spring, 1992).

way to other cities) and price premium are positively correlated; therefore, airlines at hubs are able to charge higher prices.

Incentives to build customer loyalty, such as branded credit cards that offer customers rebates on cars, gasoline, and other products, are similar to the frequent flier program. One example, the GM credit card, will be discussed in more detail later.

Compatibility.   Compatibility can also be a soft strategy, because it raises the profits of all the companies in a given industry. For example, manufacturers of stereo components must decide whether to make their receivers and compact disc players fully compatible with components of rival manufacturers. There are many reasons to make systems compatible; most notably, it increases product variety and thus consumer demand across the industry. If a manufacturer makes its components incompatible and then cuts the price of one component, it increases the demand for its other products. If the components are compatible with rivals, a price cut for one component will stimulate demand for rival components as well. This makes the price cut less attractive. Thus, compatibility makes the manager less likely to cut prices, allowing all firms to enjoy higher prices and profits.

In many high-technology industries, firms compete on product standards (e.g., OS/2 versus Windows). Companies must decide whether to create their own proprietary standards (a tough strategy) or to adopt a common standard (a soft strategy). Creating a tough proprietary standard could lead to fierce price competition with rival standards unless the firm has the power to keep them out. Adopting a rival standard, a soft commitment, would avoid this competition but would mean sharing the market.

Risks of Commitments

Because commitments limit options, every commitment carries a risk. The rigid computer disk industry illustrates some of the risks of commitment. Computer disk drives come in several sizes: 14″, 8″, 5.25″, 3.5″, 2.5″, and 1.8″. Large sizes are primarily used in mainframe or mini-mainframe computers. Smaller sizes (less than 5.25″) are used in desktop personal computers. Because there has been a great deal of turnover in market leadership, those firms that dominated in large drives failed to introduce smaller drives that appealed to other market segments. Some of these market segments grew, allowing entrants to capture share.

Managers in this industry must decide what types of new technologies to bring to the market and when to introduce them. New products would tend to lower profits to rivals. Thus these strategies would tend to make the firms tough. Consider a manager whose firm is a potential entrant and has little or no current market share. The manager must decide which technologies to bring to market and when to introduce them. Price competition hurts large share firms more than smaller entrants. When a new product is launched, the large-share firm also loses revenues from its existing line of products.

Seagate, and later Conner, developed technological and marketing capabilities that allowed them to introduce new drives for different segments of the market. They were the first with the 5.25″, 3.5″, and 2.5″ drives, which opened the desktop and portable computer segments. As these segments grew, so did the market shares and profits of these firm. Why should Seagate have delayed the introduction of the 3.5″ disk and left an opening for Conner? If Seagate had jumped into the 3.5″ game, it would have meant immediate lower prices for 5.25″ drives. Since most of Seagate's profits come from these drives, this strategy would have seriously hurt Seagate's bottom line. If Seagate had jumped in immediately after Conner, this would have meant that the prices for the 3.5″ drives would have fallen rapidly because of the price competition. This would have put 5.25″ drives under even more pressure. Thus it was in Seagate's best interest to hold back because of its commitment to the previous standard.

Herein lies the risk of commitment: The payoff to Seagate was lower than to Conner if it introduced radical (obsoleting) technologies. On the other hand, the payoff to Seagate was higher than to the entrant if the innovation was incremental.

Another risk is that competitors may not react as expected to a given strategic commitment. For example, consider American Airline's adoption of a new price strategy in 1992. American set up a four-tier pricing structure and pledged to maintain the structure even in the face of price cuts by rivals, so it was similar to a most-favored customer clause. If American lowered its price for any part of the structure, it would have to lower all prices. This strategy would make American reluctant to cut prices. Rivals could thus be expected to raise their prices without fear that American would undercut them. This should have been a soft strategy, allowing rivals to raise profits. Unfortunately for American, Northwest Airlines decided that, rather than enjoy higher prices, it would start a price war. This forced American to cut its prices across the board. Eventually, American had to abandon the pricing scheme. This is an example of how important it is to understand how your competitors think; they may not always value profitability.

TOP DOGS AND FAT CATS: WHEN TO BE TOUGH AND WHEN TO BE SOFT

When should a company be tough, and when should it be soft? These decisions depend upon the competitiveness of the market, as measured by price competition, and the goal of the company in initiating the strategy. Industries with high price competition are characterized by frequent price wars and low margins. The ease with which consumers are willing to switch among rival sellers determines the level of price competition, because managers tend to find price-cutting more attractive in markets where small price cuts lead to large increases in demand. In industries in which price competition is low, managers should try to capture as much market share as possible. In this case, rival managers are unlikely to find it useful to respond by cutting prices. Since the size of the pie is increasing, one should go for the largest slice.

The last element in determining the kind of commitments to make is the goal of the strategy. Does the firm want to be accommodating (A) to the rival or to attempt to deter or block entry (D)? Usually, unless a firm has a cost advantage or a reputation for superior products, most managers would find it more profitable to be accommodating (i.e., live and let live) rather than attempt to deter entry.

General Motors Credit Card

To examine these challenges, consider the situation of competitors in the U.S. automobile industry. Because of flat demand and competition from foreign manufacturers, the three major U.S. car manufacturers had substantial profit losses during much of the late 1980s and early 1990s. In 1992, GM alone lost $4.5 billion. Part of the problem was the extensive use of end-of-year rebates, cash-back, and dealer discounts. As soon as one manufacturer used incentives to clear excess inventory at year-end, others had to follow. Worse still, car buyers came to expect these incentives, so they waited, and by waiting, forced manufacturers to offer them earlier in the year, too. Both Ford and General Motors could choose either a high-price strategy or a low-price strategy. The outcomes of these moves, however, differ based on the moves of their competitors, as shown in Table 13.4.

Because of flat demand and high competition, each firm was charging the low price and thus suffering losses. But it would have been very costly for GM or Ford to attempt to drive the other out of the market (i.e., induce exit). In addition, because of the substantial costs to enter, neither firm had to worry about new entry. Instead, each needed to find an accommodation strategy to get to the high-price level and thus enjoy higher profits. This would result in a win-win situation for both firms. The problem was that if one firm unilaterally raised its price while the other stayed at the low price, the former

Table 13.4
Auto Industry Pricing Game

		Ford	
		High Price	Low Price
General Motors	High Price	Win-Win	Win-Lose GM Loses
	Low Price	Win-Lose Ford Loses	Lose-Lose

would lose market share and profits. This was a win–lose situation. How could GM get Ford to charge a higher price so that GM could price higher?

General Motors introduced the GM credit card in 1991, allowing customers to earn rebates toward the purchase of a GM car or truck. At first glance, it might seem that this commitment would reduce GM's profits, unless it could substantially increase its volume. But this commitment actually created a win–win situation for GM and its competitors. Let's say that the average size of the rebate was r and the industry was currently pricing close to cost, c. With the rebates, GM could now raise its price to $c + r$ and not lose customers. The higher price for a GM car would allow Ford to raise its price to $c + r$. GM could now raise its price to $c + 2r$ without losing any consumers. Thus the rebate program allowed the firms to move to the high-price square in the matrix.

Top Dogs and Fat Cats

In the case of General Motors, it wanted to be accommodating, and price competition was high. The commitment to customers through rebates raised rival profits, so it made the firm soft. The following generalized matrix, shown in Table 13.5, presents four possible strategies for accommodation, depending on the intensity of price competition and whether the commitment makes the firm tough or soft.

If price competition is low and the resource commitment makes the firm tough, the best strategy is a top dog strategy, as shown in the lower left of Table 13.5. This strategy raises firm profits at the expense of rivals by capturing a large market share. It is a win–lose strategy.

Table 13.5
Strategies for Accommodation

	Commitment Makes Firm Tough	Commitment Makes Firm Soft
High-Price Competition	Puppy Dog	Fat Cat
Low-Price Competition	Top Dog	Lean and Hungry

When price competition is low, a top dog strategy will be unlikely to elicit a strong rival response. But when price competition is high, competitors will very likely respond aggressively to a top dog strategy, because it threatens their own profits. In this case, it may be better to scale back the strategy so as not to evoke such a powerful response from rivals. We call this a "puppy dog" strategy. Rival profits are still hurt, but not enough to make it worthwhile to launch a counterattack.

Similarly, if the resource commitment makes the company soft (increasing rival profits), the company also has two choices for strategies to pursue. In high-price competition, companies should adopt a "fat cat" strategy, a win–win option that allows competitors to adopt strategies that raise industry and firm profitability. Since the size of the pie is getting bigger, the company allows rivals to increase profits while increasing profits of its own. In environments of low-price competition, companies should use a "lean and hungry" strategy, whose approach is to deliberately avoid making soft commitments. This is a situation where the manager doesn't have to worry about pricing moves by competitors, so the goal is to grab as much profit or market share as possible.

To summarize the four generic strategies:[5]

- *Top dog.* A strategy that increases firm profits but lowers those of rivals.
- *Puppy dog.* A top dog strategy that is scaled back to avoid an aggressive rival response.
- *Fat cat.* A soft strategy that raises firm profits and industry profits, including those of rivals.
- *Lean and hungry.* A strategy of avoiding making soft commitments to prevent raising rival profits.

The preceding discussion focuses on strategies of accommodation. What if the company, because it has a cost or reputation advantage, wants to drive out competitors? The firm's strategic choices would be slightly different. If the industry is characterized by high-price competition and the commitment is tough, the firm should choose a top dog approach to drive out competitors. In this case, the rival is most likely to respond by cutting prices, but a price war is to the firm's advantage since it is trying to drive out the rival and has a cost advantage.

If the industry is characterized by low-price competition, then the goal is to capture as much market share as possible, leaving one's rival with insufficient residual share to make staying in the industry profitable. Again, this calls for a top dog strategy. If commitments make the firm soft, then in either a high- or low-price competition regime, the firm's best strategy is lean and hungry (i.e., don't pursue strategies that make the firm soft).

Applying the Matrix

Consider a manager faced with the challenge of entering a new market with a new brand or a brand extension. Entry into the market is tough because it lowers the profits and market share of incumbent firms. Incumbents could thus be expected to respond aggressively to the new entrant. A puppy dog strategy is more appropriate because it is less likely to draw a rival response. By choosing a new brand name rather than an extension, the manager may reduce the severity of the competitive response.

This is the approach used by General Mills in the ready-to-eat cereal industry. Quaker has long enjoyed a dominant position in the oatmeal segment. Its market share has remained close to 67 percent for several years. There have been several attempts by rivals both inside and outside the hot cereal segment to challenge Quaker's position. General Mills launched the most serious challenge to Quaker with its introduction of Total Instant Oatmeal in 1987, the only hot oatmeal cereal that was fortified with 100 percent of nine of the USDA-recommended daily allowance of minerals and vitamins. Quaker responded by boosting its 1987 advertising spending on its oatmeal line by 33 percent to $35 million and increased the fortification of its oatmeal. In addition, it rolled out its own Quaker Extra, which matched the fortification of Total Instant Oatmeal. General Mills initially gained 12 percent of the instant market, but by 1989, that figure had fallen to 3.1 percent.

General Mills tried again with a very different strategy, using a new brand (a puppy dog strategy) instead of a brand extension. In 1988, it introduced Oatmeal Swirlers, which came with packets of instant oatmeal and a packet of fruit-flavored jam to spread on the oatmeal. Quaker did not respond with a counterproduct, and its advertising level of its instant oatmeal cereals did not change significantly from the preceding year. In 1990, General Mills introduced another instant oatmeal cereal called Undercover Bears. Again, Quaker did not launch a counterproduct.

In this case, managers responded more aggressively to a brand extension than to a new brand. The additional commitment of advertising invested in the brand name made the move tougher and more of a threat. By choosing a puppy dog strategy instead of a top dog strategy, General Mills was able to elicit a more accommodating response from Quaker.

Although discretion is often the better part of valor, companies do not always want to accommodate. In the rare cases when they have the strength or cost advantage to block or drive out rivals, they often choose to use this capability. For example, consider Du Pont's decision to build preemptive capacity in the titanium dioxide industry in the late 1960s. The strategy would have allowed it to substantially increase its market share in the industry. We can use the matrix to evaluate Du Pont's decision. Because it would reduce rival profits, so it was a tough strategy. Because of the growing level of imports, there was some price discounting in the industry, so intensity of price competition could have been characterized as high. According to the matrix, Du Pont should have considered the puppy dog option if it wanted to accommodate. But it may not have wanted to accommodate. As discussed, it should have chosen the top dog strategy if it wanted to drive rivals out of the market. So the question was: Could it drive its rivals out of the market? Two factors favored the top dog strategy. The first was that Du Pont had a cost advantage owing to superior technology and learning curve effects. This raised the possibility that Du Pont would have been able to drive some of its competitors out of the market. The second was that, while the industry was characterized by intense price competition, Du Pont's rivals had high levels of capacity utilization. Thus it was unlikely that they would have been able to retaliate by lowering prices. This suggested the top dog strategy, and that is the strategy Du Pont successfully pursued.

CONCLUSION

Clearly, the choice of commitments has a significant effect on the success of competitive strategy. Commitments—soft and tough—have an influence not only on the future direction of the company's own strategy but also on the action of rivals. By understanding the way commitments influence the firm and its competitors, managers can better choose the commitments that will best advance their strategic positions.

The framework developed in this chapter reconciles two competing views in the strategy literature. The resource-based view (RBV) suggests that firms have hard-to-imitate resources from which they derive economic rents. This view is unclear, however, as to how these resources give a firm an advantage in a competitive product market where firms can acquire resources. The competing view, the structure-conduct-performance (SCP) paradigm, argues that industry profitability depends on the structural characteristics of the industry.[6] But this view fails to recognize that companies can often alter the structural characteristics of the industry. This is often done by investments in resources—in other words, making commitments.

The framework developed here shows that resources do matter, but only those that commit a firm to certain strategies have an effect on competitive advantage. Through the use of commitments, companies can create barriers to entry and affect actions of rivals to their advantage. Commitments to advertising or R&D, for example, can force rivals and potential entrants to match those commitments, making it far more expensive for them to enter. Rather than accepting the structure of the industry as a fixed characteristic, companies can use commitments to reshape it.

CHAPTER 14

ANTITRUST CONSTRAINTS TO COMPETITIVE STRATEGY

DENNIS A. YAO
The Wharton School, Department of Public Policy and Management

Will your strategy provoke an antitrust action from regulators or rivals? The focus of competitive strategy is gaining advantage, but some means of gaining advantage can attract government investigations or lawsuits. Increasingly, strategy has focused on cooperative moves such as alliances and joint ventures, but collaboration may be viewed as anticompetitive if it reduces competition too much. The best-designed strategies can be delayed or derailed by an antitrust challenge. In this chapter key principles of antitrust regulations and the differences in perspective between business strategists and regulators are described. We examine possible antitrust responses to collaborative moves, including information exchange, signaling, patent licensing, and joint ventures or mergers. Finally, we consider when and how antitrust actions can be used as a competitive weapon.

ANTITRUST CONSTRAINTS TO COMPETITIVE STRATEGY

When Time Warner and Turner finally hammered out a plan for a $6.2 billion merger in 1996, the two sides had forged an agreement that would have tremendous impact on their strategies and on the cable industry. But there was still one last hurdle, and it proved to be a significant one: The deal could not be completed until it received the approval of the Federal Trade Commission (FTC). This became a serious challenge, threatening to reshape or even scuttle the deal that had been so painstakingly crafted.

Sharis Arnold Pozen assisted in the preparation of this chapter.

It was only after months of intense negotiations between the companies and the FTC that a settlement was reached. Because the deal would consolidate about 40 percent of the nation's cable systems and programming revenues, the FTC made Turner and Tele-Communications, Inc. (TCI) (which had a 21 percent stake in Turner) agree to concessions to prevent the entertainment giants from squeezing out smaller rivals. These concessions included divestiture of certain interests, cancellation of some existing long-term contracts, and various restrictions on future contracts, pricing and product offerings.[1]

The merger was viewed as a cornerstone of CEO Gerald M. Levin's strategy for Time Warner's future. As an analyst at Cowen & Co. told *BusinessWeek,* "If the deal had not gone through, it would have been seen as a failed strategy."[2] Yet its success or failure was significantly dependent upon antitrust considerations.

Antitrust considerations are often given insufficient attention in the early and middle stages of formulating and implementing strategy. When antitrust implications are recognized late in the game, it is sometimes difficult or impossible to retrofit the strategy to avoid antitrust actions. Some strategies, like the Time Warner-Turner deal, survive but in a different form. Others are blocked by antitrust actions, or they are delayed or changed so much that one of the partners pulls out of the deal. (The latter possibility was a focus of speculation in the Time Warner-Turner deal.)

This chapter explores some of the ways antitrust laws affect competitive strategy. It will help managers recognize when and how to identify and address antitrust constraints. It will also help them to better understand the differences in perspectives between managers with business training and regulators and judges with legal training.

It is impossible to do justice in a short chapter to the wide variety of ways antitrust policy can affect the choice of business and corporate strategy. This chapter will, therefore, focus on a small, but important, set of business strategies that illustrate important principles about antitrust policy. These strategies involve cooperative arrangements between two (or more) firms—from formal alliances to more informal relationships such as information exchanges.

A Primary Goal of Strategy Is Often the Target of Antitrust

Achieving or maintaining market power is frequently a goal or direct consequence of successful business and corporate strategies. To the extent that market power is created by superior performance (e.g., increased efficiency), antitrust law may permit it; but when the power is created deliberately, for example, by use of existing market power (e.g., an exclusionary practice) antitrust concerns are raised.[3] Thus, antitrust regulations ultimately constrain the set of strategies legally available to the firm. Rather than considering the antitrust implications during the strategy formulation process, many managers do not recognize these constraints until *after* their strategies are developed or implemented.

The antitrust process may introduce delays, reshape agreements, derail planned mergers or other actions, or add downstream risk into the implementation of a strategy. As in the case of the Time Warner-Turner deal, mergers of a certain magnitude involving a U.S. firm cannot be consummated until U.S. antitrust agencies have been given time to examine the proposed merger. While the vast majority of these mergers are cleared in a very short time, when there is an overlap of product lines in a concentrated industry, the review will sometimes take several months.

More important, resolution of antitrust concerns can involve a modification, or in some cases, abandonment of current practices. Mergers and joint ventures can be enjoined or approved subject to remedial actions such as partial divestiture or mandatory licensing. Antitrust actions will often lead to constraints on future business actions as well, through, for example, regulatory prior approval requirements imposed on a firm's future acquisitions.[4] And, the threat of antitrust enforcement is a deterrent to anticompetitive action. In fact, the bulk of the impact of antitrust policy is not in the observable actions but in the invisible effect of that policy in constraining business behavior.

Consider Antitrust at the Outset

There are many instances when examining antitrust after strategic choices are largely decided would be a mistake. The relevance of antitrust considerations in the early stages of strategy formulation depends on a number of factors:

- The likelihood that one's strategy has anticompetitive effects; this, in turn, is partially dependent on the structure of the industry and on the actions contemplated.
- The impact on strategy formulation and implementation of an antitrust challenge either from the government or a private party.
- Potential downstream remedies to anticompetitive problems.
- The decision-making process of the organization.

Antitrust law and enforcement procedures constrain both firm conduct and, particularly with respect to acquisitions or joint ventures, the speed and certainty with which these actions can be consummated. To the extent that these are critical considerations, strategists should consider modifying the plan, creating contingency plans based on various regulatory/judicial strategic scenarios, and obtaining consent provisions to avoid litigation. Such considerations can go to the heart of one's competitive strategy and may not be appropriately left to the end of the strategic choice process.

Knowledge of antitrust constraints is also helpful for understanding constraints faced by one's competitors. These insights can be used to formulate defensive strategies based on private antitrust challenges and to predict future alliances that one's competitors might undertake.[5] Managers are then better informed when they assess their options to deal with potentially dangerous alliances that may be entered into by a competitor.

U.S. ANTITRUST INSTITUTIONS AND LAWS[6]

To understand the strategic implications of antitrust laws, it is important to understand their purpose and the institutions that create and enforce them. U.S. antitrust laws are designed to preserve the benefits of competitive markets for consumers by protecting competition, not competitors. The United States Supreme Court has described U.S. antitrust laws as the "Magna Carta of our free enterprise system."[7] The laws are based on the principle that competition, when allowed to flourish unimpeded by anticompetitive practices, generally results in greater choice, more innovation, higher quality, and lower prices for consumers.

To preserve competition, the antitrust enforcement programs of the Department of Justice, the Federal Trade Commission, and the states are aimed at preventing or eliminating unlawful restraints on competition resulting from anticompetitive mergers or acquisitions. Enforcement agencies also focus on restraints on competition from collusion, monopolistic and other anticompetitive single-firm behavior, and other activities that distort the workings of a free and fair marketplace.[8] These laws provide businesses an opportunity to offer their products and services to consumers, and to have their success or failure determined by consumers' choices, uninhibited by the market power of other competitors.

Deterring Conspiracy and Monopolization

Two primary concerns of the antitrust laws are conspiracy in restraint of trade and monopolization.[9] The Sherman Act, which was enacted in 1890, is the most fundamental antitrust law. Section 1 of the Sherman Act prohibits all conspiracies or agreements that unreasonably restrain trade. The law is not aimed at all conspiracies or agreements, just those that *unreasonably* restrain trade. Its language is purposefully general; it prevents businesses from engaging in a number of activities that have little or no redeeming consumer benefit and that may lessen competition. These include conspiring to fix prices, to divide marketing territories or groups of customers, to boycott other firms, or to use coercive tactics with the intent or effect of injuring competitors to gain a competitive advantage.

Conspiracies involve agreements among competitors to act collectively to lessen competition among themselves or to suppress competition from some firm outside the group.[10] Proving a conspiracy does not necessarily require the production of a signed agreement or videotaped conspiratorial meetings. An implied agreement, or agreement shown by circumstantial evidence, can be sufficient as long as it has, or is intended to have, the requisite effect on competition.

Monopolization is another area of concern of the antitrust laws and is prohibited by Section 2 of the Sherman Act. Monopoly power is the power to raise prices or restrict output (along with lowering quality) without having competition undermine the profitability of the actions. Some monopolies are the natural result of innovation or a firm's ability to please consumers. Thus, merely having a monopoly is not illegal in the United States; but obtaining a monopoly through improper conduct is considered illegal. However, if a firm has monopoly power and it engages in unfair or unreasonably exclusionary practices to obtain or maintain a monopoly, then it may well be accused of monopolization. American courts have generally viewed monopoly power to exist when a firm has a market share of 70 percent or more, but courts may find monopoly power when smaller market shares are involved.

Preventing Anticompetitive Market Conditions

Antitrust law also is designed to prevent certain market conditions from developing that might foster anticompetitive outcomes. To do this, mergers and joint ventures above a certain size are required by law to be reported to the federal antitrust agencies prior to consummation. The agencies are then given an opportunity to review the potential alliance before it can be concluded. The idea of preconsummation intervention is that once the merger has occurred, it often is difficult or impossible to "unscramble the eggs" and return a market to its previous level of competition.

If the proposed acquisition, joint venture, or merger is likely to substantially lessen competition, it is illegal under Section 7 of the Clayton Act. The concern may be that the merger could create a monopoly. With a merger that stops short of creating an absolute monopoly, but nevertheless reduces the number of competitors, a primary concern is that the competitors could increase their ability to coordinate their market activities.

Which Cases Are Likely to Be Pursued?

While the law dictates the types of behavior that will be found to be antitrust law violations, not all potential cases will be pursued by the government or a private party. Thus, the likelihood that antitrust action or investigation will be initiated is another critical feature to consider in weighing its impact on strategy.

Because enforcement agencies have limited resources, many potential law violations are not fully investigated.[11] The agencies focus their efforts on cases that may involve substantial consumer injury (and in which they have a reasonable chance of prevailing in court). Potential injury is assessed on the basis of preliminary evidence, experience with related cases, economic theory, and other factors.

The choice to pursue or not pursue cases is termed the exercise of "prosecutorial discretion," whose use, subject to constraints of courtroom viability, allows the agencies to, within reason, weigh various factors that may or may not be given significant weight by the courts. For example, many believe that the enforcement agencies, in deciding whether to bring a case, give a heavier weight to efficiency arguments than would a court in deciding on liability. Similarly, in the last decade, there has been a marked decrease in the number of vertical and price discrimination cases that have been brought by the agencies largely because of an increasing sense by agency officials that such cases, in general, provide consumers with limited benefit and may involve costs. How an agency weighs these merits is also likely to vary with the policy views represented by the leadership in the enforcement agencies.

Private parties—including customers and competitors—could also decide to file antitrust suits. The decision of a private party to bring an antitrust suit involves a different cost-benefit calculation because private parties can obtain treble damages for antitrust injuries. Antitrust suits can be brought under most antitrust laws by "any person . . . injured in his business or property by reason of anything forbidden in the antitrust laws."[12] In addition to more merit-based suits, many suits have been brought as part of delaying actions or to signal displeasure to one's competitors. It is important for managers to be aware of this as a potential reaction by competitors to their moves and to make sure they have as good a defense as possible against such a tactic.

REGULATORS AND JUDGES DON'T THINK LIKE MANAGERS

In addition to the differences in the goals of antitrust and competitive strategy, there is also a difference in approach and training between managers and regulators or judges. These differences in viewpoint can lead to unpleasant shocks for managers who fail to understand them. Many managers, especially before they spend time with legal counsel, think that once business realities are explained to the antitrust law enforcers or to the judge, that their actions will be found innocent of antitrust liability. Sometimes they are right, but often they are not. The law has not fully embraced many ideas generally accepted by economists, much less the ideas from management strategy. Management strategy is not part of an antitrust lawyer's education (with little presence in case law or in the classroom), nor is it studied by most antitrust economists. The perspectives of managers and regulators on the same issues are often quite different, as illustrated in Table 14.1.

Table 14.1
Examples of Differences between Strategic and Regulatory Perspectives

What a Manager Might Contend Is:	An Antitrust Regulator Might See as:
Information exchange, benchmarking, avoiding price wars	Collusive behavior to fix prices or reduce competition
Strategic advantage	Monopoly power or anticompetitive behavior
Merger, cooperative strategy	Reduction of competition

Lack of specialized knowledge is offset in the legal decision-making process through evidence provided by business documents, including strategic and marketing plans, affidavits and testimony, discussions with business decision makers, and the use of experts. However, even the Supreme Court has acknowledged that: "Courts are of limited utility in examining difficult economic problems . . . [They are] ill-equipped and ill-suited for such decision making [and cannot] analyze, interpret, and evaluate the myriad of competing interests and the endless data that would surely be brought to bear on such decisions."[13]

While the courts and regulators have become increasingly sophisticated over time, differences in perspective and vocabulary persist and can affect the weight that management concepts have in a legal decision-making process. Many cases turn on "hot documents" in which mid- and senior-level managers discuss the business merits of proposed actions in terms that make their antitrust counsel cringe. For example, some documents—apparently written to persuade top management of the value of the merger, but without any consideration of how the same document would play in an antitrust merger review—have indicated that a merger will allow the new merged entity to raise prices.

Antitrust agencies have well-trained industrial organization economists on staff, but it is rare to find personnel with significant private-sector business training or experience. As economics has become more important for antitrust law, antitrust practitioners have become increasingly conversant with economics fundamentals. Similarly, day-to-day contact with business documents and businesspeople has led to a basic understanding of business. Nevertheless, this understanding is filtered through legal and economics-oriented training, and not through a general business policy conceptual framework.

Strategic versus Economic Perspectives

One can get a sense of this state of affairs by examining the differences between an economist's and a business strategist's explanations for market outcomes in various industries. Economists have historically focused on industry outcomes rather than on individual firm outcomes, so many of the models began with perfect competition. Strategists have focused on individual firm strategies. Economists use an optimization approach to solve problems, which produces a best strategy for given circumstances but, for tractability reasons, keeps the number of "circumstances" to a manageable number. Strategy scholars have often been trained in an organizational behavior-organizational management perspective where managerial and strategic problems are seen as situation-specific and very complex. These differences have led to rather disparate perspectives and interests and, therefore, different learning.

Professor Richard Nelson notes that economists have, for the most part, failed to get away from the starting point that, given the same conditions, all firms will do the same thing.[14] Strategy literature, in contrast, is often replete with references to blind spots, competitor tendencies, competitor reactions to your actions, political constraints on action, leadership, and so on. One current management perspective, the resource-based view of the firm, focuses on the importance of specialized, difficult-to-imitate resources as the source of sustainable supernormal profits. Such an approach is not inconsistent with the classical microeconomics approach to firm and industry performance, but the management perspective's starting assumption is different: Firms are intrinsically different and face different choice sets.

ANTITRUST IMPLICATIONS OF SPECIFIC TYPES OF COLLABORATIVE STRATEGIES

The differences in the purpose of antitrust law and competitive strategy, and the differences in perspectives between regulators and managers, naturally complicate the strategic decisions of managers. Managers will benefit from the ability to view their potential strategies through the eyes of antitrust regulators and to anticipate antitrust objections and constraints.

To examine how antitrust actions affect strategic initiatives, this chapter focuses on one important aspect of antitrust laws, those affecting collaborative arrangements. The discussion is meant to be illustrative rather than exhaustive. These actions include the process of deal making, facilitating practices and signaling, contracts involving

Table 14.2
Antitrust Implications of Collaborative Activities and
Possible Defensive Strategies

Collaborative Activity	Antitrust Implications	Defensive Strategies
Exchanging information through signaling, deal making, or other activities	If the information could facilitate collusive behavior, even if it is not used for this purpose, it could attract antitrust actions.	Ensure there is a strong competitive rationale for all information exchanged and be aware of anticompetitive implications.
Licensing of intellectual property	Although patents give exclusive use, they do not grant an economic monopoly. Patent protection that is leveraged to extend market power could attract antitrust actions.	Avoid contract provisions that appear to be designed to extend the leverage of the existing intellectual property. Ensure that borderline provisions can be justified as procompetitive.
Mergers and joint ventures	Mergers and joint ventures can increase the ability of firms to coordinate actions and engage in anticompetitive behavior.	Large mergers will be reviewed prior to consummation. Partners should also look for ways to structure the ventures and information flows to avoid the appearance of and opportunity for anticompetitive actions.

intellectual property, and mergers or joint ventures. Table 14.2 summarizes several of these collaborations, their antitrust implications, and defensive strategies for reducing the risk of antitrust actions.

When Does Collaboration Begin to Look Like Collusion?

In recent years, strategic alliances and other forms of cooperation have become an increasingly important part of business strategy. "Collaboration between competitors is in fashion," note Gary Hamel, Yves Doz, and C.K. Prahalad.[15] Such strategies allow quick responses to rapid market and technological changes, which are characteristic of the global competitive environment.[16] But collaborative arrangements often attract the scrutiny of regulators. Anticompetitive problems can arise out of innocent actions that may have accompanying anticompetitive effects. Other problems may be rooted in knowing actions (e.g., to rationalize industry capacity, avoid ruinous competition) with direct anticompetitive overtones.[17] Because collaborative strategies are more likely to facilitate collusion than "unilateral" strategies, antitrust considerations would appear relatively important in this arena.

For example, in the 1990s, antitrust enforcement attention has been focused on signaling by airlines through a fare reporting clearinghouse; licensing agreements and renegotiations involving patented products in the chemical and pharmaceutical industries; information sharing among competing hospitals; and alleged exchange of advertising and marketing plans by infant formula manufacturers through an industry trade association. In addition, many mergers have received scrutiny, and many preliminary merger discussions have been terminated once antitrust concerns were identified.[18]

Where is the line between acceptable cooperation and unacceptable collusion? It has been difficult for regulators and the courts to draw. A primary object of many competitive and collaborative strategies is to gain market power or leverage with respect to buyers or suppliers, or to create mobility barriers. Market power created by superior performance, (e.g., increased efficiency) is generally permitted, but when the power is created deliberately, say by the use of existing market power, antitrust concerns are raised.

Exchanging Information among Competitors

The exchange of information—even in informal discussions—sometimes attracts unexpected antitrust attention. This can happen when businesspeople get together to talk about other things and inadvertently exchange information that they should not. For example, in one case, the court upheld the criminal price-fixing conviction of several realtors after one realtor announced a commission rate change at a dinner party, after which informal discussion of rates followed. Within months, each realtor present at the dinner party adopted similar rates.[19] In another example, the FTC alleged that a respondent's representative met with officers of a competing firm and invited them to fix prices on certain products that both companies produced. The managers' defense was that they only went to their competitor's plant to see their competitor's low-cost production processes. It was not their intent to discuss prices. However, the complaint alleged that these discussions quickly turned to discussions about price.[20] The intent of the information exchange is less relevant than its impact on competition in determining whether antitrust action will be pursued.

Exchanges of information can be direct or indirect (through signaling). Direct exchanges occur between the informed principals (including benchmarking), through joint ventures or other alliances between the principals, or through third parties such as associations. In direct exchanges, information such as costs for various manufacturing operations, historical prices and sales, forecasts of demand, information about processes, and other competitively valuable information may be exchanged. Firms are generally loathe, of course, to provide information that involves their core competencies and technologies, and will not typically provide information unless reciprocated information is also valuable.

The antitrust concern is that these exchanges will sometimes make collusion more likely. Exchange of information can be seen by antitrust officials as reducing uncertainty about a rival's plans or past actions, making it easier for participants in a collusive scheme to detect and punish deviators and to reach a tacit (or explicit) agreement.

The exchanged information itself is less the problem than what the information does for the ease of creating and maintaining a collusive scheme. Such information exchanges are called *facilitating practices*. "A facilitating practice is an activity that makes it easier for parties to coordinate price or other behavior in an anticompetitive way. . . . The vice of a facilitating practice is its anticompetitive tendency in the circumstances rather than a proved anticompetitive result in the particular case."[21]

The indirect exchange of information through signaling or through other facilitating mechanisms will be more likely to attract antitrust attention if no apparent legitimate justification exists. For example, the Department of Justice alleged that eight airlines that operate a computerized fare exchange system have unreasonably restrained price competition in the $40 billion domestic air travel industry.[22] The complaint alleged a *per se* violation of the Sherman Act in that the airlines used the Airline Tariff Publishing Co. (ATP) to: exchange proposals and negotiate fare changes; trade fare changes in certain markets for fare changes in other markets; and exchange mutual assurances regarding the level, scope, and timing of fare changes. The complaint further alleged that the defendants' agreement to maintain, operate, and participate in the ATP system was an unreasonable restraint of trade under a rule-of-reason analysis. Specifically, it alleged that certain aspects of the ATP fare dissemination system facilitated coordination of fare increases and eliminated discounts. An important consideration in this case was the DOJ's concern that no credible efficiency justification appeared to exist for many of the alleged anticompetitive practices.

There have been only a few consents or successfully litigated cases focused primarily on signaling as a facilitating practice. But these few cases have been recent. In addition to the airline price case, the 9th U.S. Circuit of Appeals reversed a district court summary judgment dealing with the oil industry, holding that exchange of price information might be sufficient to infer an agreement; and an FTC complaint involving the infant formula industry alleged, among other things, that Wyeth signaled its bidding intent to the other manufacturers.[23]

Information Released through Deal Making or Strategic Alliances

Discussions between or among competitors will often occur in the normal course of business through existing interfirm relationships such as joint ventures involving the competitors, or because competitors are considering a merger or other formal relationship. Thus, managers contemplating the structuring of information flow and responsibility within an organization need to consider how antitrust considerations constrain organizational design possibilities; and managers attempting to negotiate a relationship with a competitor must be careful about what information is released, when it is released, and to whom it is released.

The New United Motors Manufacturing, Inc. (NUMMI) joint venture for subcompact automobile production provides a good example of how antitrust considerations can affect information flow between the joint venture partners and NUMMI. Here, because the FTC believed that the joint venture would create the opportunity for nonventure-related, sensitive, competitive information to be exchanged between GM and Toyota, the FTC insisted, and obtained through a consent order, a number of restrictions on information flow and procedural safeguards to minimize information exchange risks to competition.[24]

Predeal discussions with potential partners and suitors are another setting in which antitrust considerations can be important. The potential problem arises when such discussions take place between horizontal competitors, reach a relatively advanced stage, but do not ultimately result in consummation of a deal. In such cases, competitively sensitive information may have been exchanged that might facilitate collusion. The tension is created because information is needed to determine fit and price, but most deals don't go through.

Firms can take a number of actions to reduce their antitrust vulnerability in these circumstances. Information is released only when it can be justified (much of the information is exchanged after some form of commitment to an acquisition is made during due diligence) and care is taken to isolate the information from those who don't need it, but could use it in anticompetitive ways. For example, operational personnel are often kept out of the loop in the early stages; instead third parties are relied on. In addition, the buyer receives information from the seller, but not necessarily vice versa.[25]

There has been little antitrust action in these settings, perhaps because firms are very careful in conducting the negotiations (there are more legal problems than just those associated with antitrust) and because the agencies and courts recognize that some level of information exchange is absolutely necessary to facilitate efficient mergers and acquisition activity.[26] For example, former Assistant Attorney General James F. Rill remarked, "To suggest that this analysis has to be done in an abstract way, where there is not an exchange of useful, often sensitive, information, could have very far-reaching consequences that might deter the formulation of mergers and joint ventures. So I would be very concerned about overreaching in that area." He goes on to note a concern with sham deals that might mask cartel activity,[27] a concern shared by the FTC.[28]

Patents and Licensing Intellectual Property

Control of intellectual property and a strategy to exploit that property is a critical driver of profitability in many industries. Such property provides asymmetries that can lead to superior performance. Because intellectual property is often easy to copy or steal, ownership and use is protected through patents, copyrights, and other legal institutions such as trade secret law. Understanding the limits of these legal protections is therefore central to developing an effective technology business strategy.

Antitrust considerations limit the extent of the competitive leverage provided by ownership of intellectual property. There are limitations on which competitors can be licensed, which licenses can be exchanged, and which provisions can be written into license contracts.[29]

According to DOJ/FTC IP guidelines, licensing one's major competitor (or the major potential competitor) could sometimes be viewed as a reduction of competition that would not be permissible under the antitrust laws. On the other hand, using patent power as a lever to dominate the market could also be viewed as anticompetitive. Patent policy allows the patent holder exclusive use, but does not give the patent holder an economic monopoly. Often, this is because there are other equally attractive products that compete with the patented product for sales. In the absence of such substitutes, managers need to be careful not to use the patent to dominate competition.

Patent holders often try to use their current patent advantage to create barriers to the erosion of the patent holder's dominance. For example, the patent holder might try to take actions to extend the "effective" duration of the patent or to reduce the amount of R&D on technologies that might displace the patented technology.

A recent Department of Justice complaint against Pilkington with respect to its licenses of patented float glass technology illustrates some of the (alleged) anticompetitive implications of such actions.[30] The DOJ's complaint stated that the combined effects of territorial and use restrictions Pilkington placed on licensees, "prevented competitors from using or developing competing float glass technology" and that Pilkington (among other things) had "continued enforcement of the territorial, use, and sublicense restrictions indefinitely, even after no further licensing royalties were payable and the patents had expired."

The regulatory and legal responses to anticompetitive practices associated with intellectual property have included mandatory licensing of the patent, sometimes royalty-free, and required transfer of know-how.

Mergers and Joint Ventures

Mergers and acquisitions can raise antitrust concerns because they increase the ability of firms in the relevant market to coordinate actions (thereby raising prices), or because they increase the ability of a single firm to raise prices. Conventional merger analysis involves first defining the appropriate product and geographic market, then examining the possible competitive effects in that antitrust market, and finally looking at offsetting aspects of the merger, such as merger-specific efficiencies or whether one of the relevant parties is a failing firm.[31] The starting point for assessing competitive effects is determining concentration and change in concentration in the antitrust markets affected by the merger. The importance of concentration, however, is greatly undermined when entry is easy.

Joint ventures also raise similar issues, but as a looser form of inter-firm relationship, they have typically drawn less attention than horizontal mergers. Joint ventures or similar strategic alliances have been less susceptible to antitrust challenge for a number of reasons. Joint ventures generally have a clear efficiency purpose and do not involve extensive integration among the parent entities. Such ventures will often be in a market in which neither parent is involved or in which only one of the parents is involved. The goals of the venture partners are likely to differ, so that the implementation of anticompetitive coordination through the venture is less likely.

There are a number of reasons why a joint venture might nonetheless draw antitrust scrutiny. Most have to do with the effect of the venture on the actions of the parent entities, for example:

- If the parent entities currently compete with each other, the joint venture could lead to less intense competition between the parents.
- If, in the absence of the venture, one or both parents would enter on their own (or at least pose a serious threat of entry), a joint venture might reduce potential competition (*United States v Penn Olin Co.*[32]).
- The joint venture may lead to spillovers, such as exchange of information, that could facilitate collusion as discussed (GM/Toyota[33]).
- A joint venture could create a barrier to entry through control of an essential input (Home Oxygen & Medical Equipment Co.[34]).

In some instances, joint ventures that are clearly anticompetitive in a conventional sense will be permitted because the joint venture creates a "new product" that would not exist without the venture. For example, ASCAP and BMI sold marketing rights to copyrighted songs under a blanket license to radio stations, television stations, and restaurants. CBS argued (in *BMI v CBS, Inc.*) that these blanket licenses amounted to price-fixing among the copyright holders (and the clearinghouse organizations) and should be condemned as a per se violation of the antitrust laws. The Supreme Court disagreed, noting that, "Here the whole is truly greater than the sum of its parts; it is, to some extent, a different product. The blanket license has certain unique characteristics . . . . ASCAP, in short, made a market in which individual composers are inherently unable to fully effectively compete."[35] Ultimately, these arrangements were allowed to stand.

More generally, joint ventures are justified because of their efficiency aspects under the rule-of-reason balancing of the potential benefits and potential harms. Similarly, in the European Union, "cooperative" joint ventures that are found otherwise to restrict competition can be exempted because of the efficiency-enhancing aspects of the venture.

Postmerger Antitrust Actions

Although large mergers and joint ventures are subject to antitrust review prior to consummation, they can and have been challenged after consummation as well. It is therefore important in the negotiation stage of a potential venture that managers be aware of the potential antitrust actions that may occur, because antitrust actions are sometimes an important downstream source of unanticipated restrictions on actions.

For example, Brunswick Corp. established a joint venture to manufacture and market outboard motors.[36] The joint venture allocated territories for the sale of the joint venture motors and limited Yamaha (a parent company) to marketing its own motors in Japan. Because this latter restriction was viewed as interfering with the potential entry of Yamaha into the North American market, the joint venture was ordered to be dissolved.[37] In many cases, specific provisions of joint ventures, rather than the venture as a whole, will be challenged. This will occur, in particular, when the allegedly anticompetitive provision is not seen as central to the purpose of the joint venture.

FACTORS THAT SHAPE ANTITRUST DECISIONS

How do regulators and courts analyze whether the actions are innocent competitive strategies or antitrust violations? A variety of factors shape that decision. In particular, competitive benefits of the action are weighed against its potential harm. Next, we consider a few of the factors considered in cases involving the exchange of information.

Rule of Reason: Weighing Benefits against Harm

In analyzing information exchanges, the courts and antitrust agencies use a rule-of-reason analysis that balances the potential benefit of the exchange against the potential anticompetitive harm. If there is a legitimate business justification for the exchange of information, regulators have generally avoided antitrust actions. This approach contrasts with the per se legal analysis that identifies certain types of conduct such as price-fixing and market allocation agreements as illegal without an in-depth balancing analysis.

Several other factors affect whether an information exchange or other collaborative behavior will be viewed as an antitrust violation:[38]

- The parties' competitive positions and the competitive structure of the market in which the exchange takes place.
- The competitive significance of the information exchanged.
- Frequency and timing of the exchange.
- The efficiencies or business justification for the exchange.

Competitive Positions. Exchanges among parties that do not (and are unlikely to) compete in the same market raise minimal antitrust risk. Thus, the vast majority of benchmarking of functional activities that go on between firms in different industries are unlikely to cause antitrust concern.[39]

For parties in the same industry, the first concern regarding competitive position and competitive structure is whether the exchanging parties have market power. There are a number of issues about market definition, ease of entry, ease of coordination within the industry in question, and others that are critical components of the market power/market structure analysis. Without market power, economic theory suggests that no anticompetitive harm will occur.

How is the product market defined for the purposes of antitrust analysis? An antitrust product market generally is defined as all products that compete with the product at issue.[40] Based on these market definitions, the antitrust agency will then attempt to determine the types of competitive effects that will occur given the transaction being reviewed (depending on factors such as concentration, heterogeneity of products, and so on). If a product market is defined broadly (e.g., all dog food rather than puppy food), then the market will generally be found to be less concentrated and less prone to collusion. This is because the interacting parties are less likely to jointly have a significant market share in a broad versus a narrow market. However, if the product market is defined narrowly, there may be no overlap between the parties exchanging information (e.g., ship-launched antiaircraft missiles versus missiles) and, hence, less anticompetitive potential.

Significance of Information Exchanged. Antitrust officials are also concerned with the competitive significance of the information exchanged; that is, whether the information can lead to reductions in the competitiveness of the market. The significance of the information is best understood in light of the anticompetitive theory that is being considered. Generally, however, certain types of information are considered more dangerous, that is, more competitively significant, than others. For example, the "exchanges of current price information . . . have the greatest potential for generating anticompetitive effects, and although not per se unlawful, have consistently been held to violate the Sherman Act."[41] The same holds true for future prices and future competitive plans.[42]

Historical information, particularly that which is publicly available, is of lesser concern. Exchange of cost information has some potential to be anticompetitive especially when part of a larger effort to restrain competition.

Timing of Exchange. The more frequent and timely the exchange, the more dangerous it becomes from an antitrust perspective, because such information will possess greater utility for coordinating pricing actions or for detecting cheating by members of a cartel. On the other hand, antitrust liability can be avoided more easily if information is exchanged through third parties or associations, and is aggregated information.

Procompetitive Justifications. Finally, the agencies and courts will examine whether there are procompetitive justifications for the information exchange and whether the same goals can be obtained through a different, less potentially anticompetitive approach. For example, the courts and agencies have been relatively lenient on information exchange that is viewed necessary for setting industrywide standards, such as interface standards between different kinds of software.[43]

The 1994 DOJ/FTC health care antitrust policy statements provide a good example of how the agencies have recently applied these criteria. One of the nine statements deals directly with exchanges of price and cost information among health care providers. In it, the agencies say that they "will not challenge, absent extraordinary circumstances, provider participation in written surveys of (a) prices for health care services, or (b) wages, salaries, or benefits of health care personnel," if certain conditions are met broadly—the survey must be managed by a third party, the data must be more than three months old, and various other criteria (e.g., number participating, relative size)—so that no individual provider's costs or compensation paid can be determined.[44] The statement warns that exchanges of information as to planned prices or compensation are likely to be considered anticompetitive.[45]

When there appears to be no anticompetitive effect from an information exchange, then the antitrust agencies will not challenge it. In many cases, as suggested, however, the exchange of information may entail some anticompetitive risk. Thus, a strong case for the procompetitive aspects of the information exchange in question is important to establish.

ANTITRUST AS A STRATEGIC WEAPON

Until now, we have considered defensive actions to anticipate the antitrust concerns raised by competitive strategies. But there are also important *offensive* uses of antitrust actions against competitors. In closing, we consider how antitrust can be used as a competitive weapon.

Successful antitrust suits often end in substantive changes: mergers are prevented, plants are divested, licenses are mandated, various competitive practices are enjoined. The indirect effects of suits—especially in large cases—may also be important: Additional uncertainty is introduced into a competitor's business environment, substantial delays may be caused, a company's public image may be affected, and management attention may be diverted. Further, companies that are most powerful—those with market power—are also most susceptible to successful antitrust suits. Outcomes that cannot be achieved through market action can sometimes be achieved through legal action.

While the antitrust weapon can be powerful, its effectiveness depends on there being at least a serious question as to whether the target has violated the antitrust laws. Suits lacking any merit are subject to dismissal by the court; suits that get past this summary judgment hurdle can lead—via settlement or litigated judgment—to changes favorable to the plaintiff. In the early 1980s, there were on the order of 1,000-plus private antitrust suits each year, compared with approximately 100 government antitrust suits. Refusals to deal were the most common type of case, followed by horizontal price-fixing, tying or exclusive-dealing cases, and price discrimination (less than 20 percent). Cases involving vertical relationships outnumbered horizontal cases, and the vast majority were settled. Excluding one outlier case, the average award in 1984 dollars was about $450,000, and the average length of a case was about two years.[46] Many of these private antitrust suits were follow-on suits to those brought by the government.[47]

A Double-Edged Sword

Assuming that there is some chance of prevailing on an antitrust action, does it make sense for a company to pursue antitrust litigation? Is there anything to lose? In addition to potentially large legal bills, there are two significant dangers associated with legal weapons—particularly with large cases. First, an effective legal strategy will generally place substantial burdens on management. Second, the litigation process is partly, and in some cases substantially, out of a company's control.

If the object of the suit is to effect a change in the defendant's market behavior, the outcome of the suit is likely to impact the attractiveness of various competitive strategy options available to the plaintiff. For example, Advanced Micro Devices (AMD) had to decide whether to copy Intel's microcode (rather than create a "clean room" microcode), and this decision was made while litigation over AMD's legal right to use that microcode was in process. If AMD copied Intel's microcode and then subsequently lost its suit, the court might prevent the sale of the relevant AMD microprocessors.[48] In these kinds of cases, competitive strategy and legal strategy dovetail.

Antitrust cases also create burdens for managers, a problem that is exacerbated by another feature of the legal system. Absent a settlement, courts and juries, not the companies involved, determine outcomes and remedies. Countersuits can be brought, and enforcement agencies may find related cases to bring that may not be desirable.

Companies have more control over private actions than government actions.[49] A private action can be terminated, or a mutually beneficial settlement may be reached (one that may not even resolve the antitrust issues in the original suit). On the other hand, governmental actions are pursued depending on governmental objectives (e.g., protecting competition, not competitors), and solutions to antitrust concerns must, at least in theory, resolve the problem. In addition, in the process of investigating the matter at hand, other information concerning competition in the industry is likely to come to light. This information may lead the agency to pursue a different antitrust action that might have negative consequences for the firm that desired the original antitrust action.

Another risk of antitrust actions is that they are not taken kindly by the target, so upstream or downstream firms risk considerable goodwill with the target firm if they initiate or support an antitrust action. Perhaps it is not that surprising, therefore, that the number one category of antitrust action involves a refusal to deal where the business relationship is already bad.

CONCLUSION: THE UNSEEN PLAYER IN DYNAMIC INTERACTIONS

Most businesspeople have a limited understanding of law and legal processes, while their lawyers generally lack business training and rarely have full access to the full range of business information needed for strategic decision making. If the legal strategy is complex and if it dovetails with business strategy, considerable coordination may be called for. But this coordination is required by personnel who may have considerable difficulty even asking the right questions of their counterpart, much less making appropriate decisions in an unfamiliar environment.

In most antitrust cases, tight coordination between business strategy and legal strategy is probably not needed. For example, if the object of the suit is damages in compensation for past anticompetitive actions, the legal and the business concerns may be decoupled. But even in those cases, both plaintiffs and defendants should be aware that current strategies (and outcomes) often provide material evidence influencing litigation outcomes. Managers should be aware of antitrust implications of strategies during their development and implementation.

Regulators and the courts are often the unseen third force in competitive interactions. While managers focus on customers and competitors, they sometimes fail to see how this third force can upset the dynamics of the interactions among competitors. As the discussion illustrates, ignoring the impact of regulators and the courts can be just as dangerous as neglecting a current or potential competitor. A good strategy in theory will only be good in practice if it can survive a run through the gauntlet of antitrust.

PART IV

CHOOSING AMONG ALTERNATIVE COMPETITIVE STRATEGIES

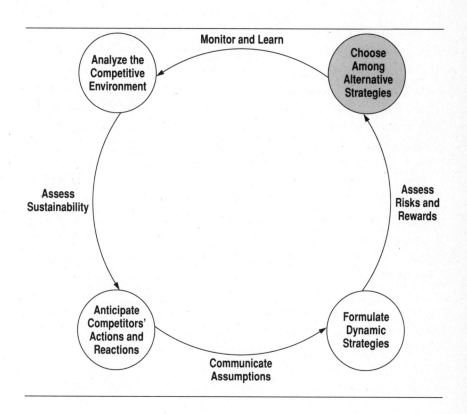

A cellular telephone manufacturer is considering changing its product offerings. It could change prices, its warranty, or the weight of the phone. But what happens if competitors match its features? And how will the market respond to the resulting chain reaction of moves and countermoves?

An international leader in providing economic information services to businesses is facing a radical shift in computing technology. Since its products are all computer-based, this could have a dramatic impact on its business, but the exact course of the technological change is uncertain. Given this uncertainty, which key corporate assets and capabilities should it develop for the future?

A major oil company is considering launching a new set of self-serve mini-pumps that would greatly expand its locations and redefine competition in its region. But how will customers respond to the new format? And will competitors match the move?

The following chapters examine these and other management challenges, and offer different approaches to analyzing the outcomes of specific strategies. The phone manufacturer analyzed its product changes using a form of conjoint analysis, as described in Chapter 15. The economic information provider employed a "strategic assets" framework, built around scenario planning, as described in Chapter 16. The oil company used a competitive simulation to evaluate the long-term impact of the new minipumps, as described in Chapter 17.

These three chapters offer approaches for evaluating the diverse set of strategies generated by the preceding parts. These tools and approaches help managers assess which of all the options is best to pursue, given the competitive environment discussed in Part I, the mindsets of rivals discussed in Part II, and the competitive strategies considered in Part III. These final chapters draw together many of the insights of the preceding chapters. These approaches allow you to examine the outcomes of different strategies, given different scenarios for the competitive environment and diverse moves and responses of rivals.

If the tools and perspectives presented in the preceding chapters are compared to setting, casting, and acting skills, this part is concerned with understanding the full drama of competition. It offers approaches that can be used as dress rehearsals, that can examine strategies across multiple futures and that can simulate complex competitive interactions over time.

ANTICIPATING THE END GAME

A given strategy usually results in a chain reaction of moves and countermoves by competitors. It is often only by playing through to this "end game"—like successive moves in a chess match—that the wisdom or foolishness of a given strategic direction at the outset becomes apparent. Most chess players and strategists think only a few moves in advance. But the masters think ahead many moves and examine many different combinations.

This part presents three approaches for building a coherent view of competitive dynamics over time and across multiple futures. These frameworks explore the impact of possible strategies, either through multiple product iterations, multiple scenarios, or multiple rounds of competition across time.

Chapter 15 presents a market-based approach, using conjoint analysis, a marketing research tool that captures the perceptions of the market about competing products. The authors show how this approach can be used to model a series of competitive product introductions. This can help managers anticipate the reactions of rivals to their products and think forward to develop a more optimal product for the market, given the likely moves of competitors.

Chapter 16 presents a strategic assets framework, that allows companies to integrate an analysis of industry characteristics, firm capabilities, and scenario planning. Whereas most firms focus on the capabilities that are needed to succeed today, these key capabilities and resources often shift over time. The most important challenge is to determine the ones that will be valuable in the future. Chapter 16 examines the key capabilities and resources that will be needed under various future scenarios. What resources and capabilities will be most valuable in the future, given changes in the environment and the current resources and capabilities of the firm?

The closing chapter examines the use of competitive simulations. Like flight simulators, these business strategy simulators allow managers to experience and experiment with strategy without the risk of crashing and burning in actual competition. These simulations help managers to explore the moves and countermoves of competitors and determine the probable outcomes of given strategies. Chapter 17 examines a range of uses of strategy simulations and options for designing them.

These simulations can incorporate conjoint analysis, scenario planning, and a wide array of other approaches. In fact, virtually all the perspectives and approaches in the book can be incorporated into a simulation. Either through formal computer modeling or more informal "war gaming," simulations offer the opportunity to actually "experience" the dynamics of competitive interactions over time, before investing the time and money to execute them.

THE STRATEGIZING ORGANIZATION

These three chapters offer managers a way to integrate the learning from the preceding chapters of the book. They also begin to address the challenge of how to incorporate the perspectives presented in this book into the strategic thinking of the organization.

The approaches in this part form a focal point for drawing competitive perspectives from many parts of the organization. They also help to diffuse strategic perspectives throughout the organization, ensuring that all employees understand the company's strategies.

Finally, the emphasis on changes over time makes these approaches a natural part of an on-going learning process. As organizations repeatedly examine outcomes and scenarios, or engage in simulations, they continue to learn. It is this learning process and this broad awareness of strategic issues that can help companies respond quickly and effectively to changing competitive realities. This ensures that strategy is held not only in the upper levels of the firm, but understood throughout the organization. Strategy is not merely the domain of one department but part of the overall mission of a strategizing organization.

CHAPTER 15

USING CONJOINT ANALYSIS TO VIEW COMPETITIVE INTERACTION THROUGH THE CUSTOMER'S EYES

PAUL E. GREEN

The Wharton School, Department of Marketing

ABBA M. KRIEGER

The Wharton School, Department of Marketing, Operations and Information Management, and Statistics

Conjoint analysis is a powerful tool for measuring consumer attitudes and choices. For more than 25 years, it has been helping marketers meet the needs of the market by analyzing customer values for product attributes. This chapter examines how conjoint analysis can be extended to examine competitive actions and reactions to new product or service launches and extensions. When one firm launches a new product or changes product attributes, its competitors will often respond with their own changes. By outlining a series of moves and countermoves by competitors, the model examines how competition moves toward an equilibrium. As an illustration, the model is used to examine the addition of new features to a cellular phone system and subsequent rival reactions.

The Alpha Company, a cellular telephone manufacturer supplying the southwestern United States, is considering changing its product offerings. Among its options, it could change prices, its warranty, or the weight of the phone. It could add features such as a cigarette lighter battery charger, larger memory,

The authors would like to acknowledge the support of the Goldberg Fellowship from the Sol C. Snider Entrepreneurial Center, Wharton School, University of Pennsylvania.

speed-dialing, and a high-strength battery. But which set of features should it offer?

The first question it faces is: Which combinations of attributes do customers want? The second question is: If Alpha creates new offerings, how are its key competitors—Beta and Gamma—likely to react to Alpha's changes?

To address these questions, Alpha employed a marketing tool called conjoint analysis. Although conjoint analysis has been used for more than a quarter of a century to answer the first question—consumer reactions to product attributes—it has only recently been extended to examine the second question, competitor reactions.

Whereas traditional conjoint analysis looks at customer reactions to products of a company and its competitors, this expanded approach looks at both reactions of customers *and* potential reactions of competitors. This process begins by developing an optimized product for one company. Then it shifts perspective to examine the best competing product that could be created in response by a rival. By simulating responses and counterresponses, the model explores a series of competitive interactions, until the design of the product settles into an equilibrium: an optimal product, *given optimal competitive responses*. This is usually different from the initial product developed by considering only customer inputs.

This chapter begins with an overview of conjoint analysis and its development, particularly the use of buyer-choice simulators to forecast how consumers choose among competing suppliers. We then discuss how this approach can be extended to study dynamic competitive interactions in the marketplace—viewed through the eyes of the consumer. Finally, we return to the challenges facing Alpha Company to examine in more detail how this method can be applied to an actual strategic challenge.

THE FUNDAMENTALS OF CONJOINT ANALYSIS

Conjoint analysis addresses a central issue in formulating product and market strategy: the question of *why* consumers choose one brand or service supplier over another. This issue affects decisions from product design through after-sale service. Over the past 25 years, marketers have conducted thousands of conjoint analysis studies. Conjoint analysis is generally believed to be the most popular approach to measuring consumers' attitudes and understanding the reasons underlying their choice of brands or suppliers.

The central idea of conjoint analysis is that products and services can be described by a set of attributes. For example, cellular telephones can be described in terms of price, weight, battery life, features, and so on. Consumers attach different values to the levels of these attributes. They make trade-offs among the attribute levels characterizing the various competitive offerings. How important is a warranty of one year versus a warranty of three years? Is a lower price more important than a longer battery life?

Consumers choose the offering that has the highest total value (or utility) across all the attributes. Since different consumers have different attribute-level values—called part-worths—their trade-offs vary. Hence, different brands can appeal to different consumers. Conjoint analysis measures these part-worths.

The Key Concepts

To illustrate the basic concepts of conjoint analysis, assume that a pharmaceutical firm that sells liquid dietary supplements (for use in hospitals) wishes to modify its current product. One of the first steps in designing a conjoint study is to develop a set of attributes and levels that sufficiently characterize the competitive domain. Focus groups, in-depth consumer interviews, and internal corporate expertise are some of the sources used to develop the sets of attributes and levels that guide the rest of the study.

Conjoint analysis is a very efficient methodology. Table 15.1 shows nine attributes employed in an actual study. Note that the number of levels within an attribute range from 3 to 4, for a total of 32 levels. However, the total number of possible combinations of levels is 82,944. This is far too many for a single customer to consider explicitly, and far too many for a researcher to test efficiently.

Table 15.1
Attribute Levels for Liquid Dietary Supplement Study

Source of protein

1. Amino acids
2. Meat, eggs (natural)
3. Casein
4. Soy/caseinate

Percent calories from protein

1. 24
2. 18
3. 12
4. 6

Caloric density (calories/milliliter)

1. 2.0
2. 1.5
3. 1.0

Incidence of diarrhea, cramps (side effects), percent of patients

1. 5
2. 10
3. 15
4. 20

Percent of patients disliking taste

1. 5
2. 15
3. 25
4. 35

Flavor base

1. Fruit juice
2. Chocolate-flavored milk
3. Unflavored

Convenience of preparation

1. Ready-to-use liquid
2. Powder to be mixed with water
3. Powder to be mixed in blender

Health professionals' endorsement

1. Most recommend
2. Most are neutral
3. Most are neutral to negative

Therapy cost per patient per week ($)

1. 40
2. 50
3. 60
4. 70

Conjoint analysis, using highly fractionated factorial designs, can test these choices using a small fraction of the total.[1] A set of just 64 profiles (less than 0.1 percent of the total) is sufficient to represent the main effects of all 82,944 possibilities on an uncorrelated basis. In the study of liquid dietary supplements, the designers used a hybrid conjoint design, so that each subject received only eight (balanced) profile descriptions, drawn from the 64 profiles.[2] The respondents dealt with a manageable set of eight options, while the researchers were able to use this information to examine a far larger set of product possibilities.

Figure 15.1 shows two illustrative prop cards, used to present options to respondents in the study. The respondent is first asked to sort the prop cards in terms of preference, then to rate each on a 0–100 scale based on likelihood of acquisition. In small conjoint studies (e.g., six or seven attributes, each at two or three levels) the respondent receives all of the full profiles, generally ranging in number from 16 to 32 prop cards. In these cases, the prop cards are sorted into four to eight

Figure 15.1
Illustrative Full-Profile Prop Cards

1	2
Protein Source ▶ Casein	Protein Source ▶ Amino Acids
Cash rebate ▶ 6%	Percent Calories ▶ 24%
Caloric Density ▶ 2.0 calories/ml	Caloric Density ▶ 2.0 calories/ml
Incidence of diarrhea, cramps ▶ 20%	Incidence of diarrhea, cramps ▶ 10%
Percent disliking taste ▶ 25%	Percent disliking taste ▶ 5%
Flavor Base ▶ Fruit Juice	Flavor Base ▶ Unflavored
Convenience ▶ Ready-to-use liquid	Convenience ▶ Powder mixed with water
Endorsement ▶ Most recommend	Endorsement ▶ Most are neutral
Therapy Cost ▶ $50	Therapy Cost ▶ $70

ordered categories and ranked within group before likelihood-of-purchase ratings are obtained for each separate profile, within group.

Types of Conjoint Data Collection

The use of prop cards is just one way to collect data on customer preferences for a conjoint analysis study. There are five major types of data-collection procedures:

- *Trade-off tables.* Each respondent sees a sequence of tables, involving two attributes each. The respondent is asked to rank the cell descriptions of each two-way table based on preference; other attribute levels are assumed to be equal across the options of interest.
- *Full-profile techniques.* Each respondent sees a full set of cards, as illustrated in Figure 15.1. After initial sorting into ordered categories, each card is ranked and then rated on a 0–100 likelihood-of-purchase scale.
- *Compositional techniques, such as the CASEMAP procedure.*[3] Strictly speaking, this is not a conjoint analysis technique since preferences are collected by having each respondent rate the desirability of each set of attribute levels on a 0–10 scale and then rate each attribute's importance on a similar 0–10 scale. CASEMAP uses a compositional technique where the value of an option is computed as the sum of each attribute-level desirability, times its attribute importance. (This approach is also called self-explicated preference data collection.)
- *Hybrid techniques.* Each respondent receives *both* a self-explicated evaluation task and a small set of full profiles for evaluation. The resulting utility function is a composite of data obtained from both tasks.[4]
- *Adaptive conjoint analysis.*[5] This technique is also a type of hybrid model in which each respondent first receives the self-explication task, followed by a set of partial profile descriptions, two at a time. The respondent evaluates each pair of partial profiles on a graded paired-comparisons scale. Both tasks are administered by computer.

These data are then entered into preference models to determine part-worths for each attribute. Figure 15.2 shows illustrative (averaged) part-worths for each of the attribute levels for the dietary supplement described in Table 15.1. As noted, part-worths are often scaled so that the lowest part-worth is zero, within each attribute.

Strictly speaking, part-worth functions are evaluated at discrete levels for each attribute. However, in most applications, analysts interpolate between levels of continuous attributes, such as price. Note that the scale (vertical axis) is common across all attributes. This enables the researcher to obtain the overall utility of any possible product combination by adding the appropriate part-worths of the product attribute levels.

Figure 15.2
Average Part-Worths from Hybrid Conjoint Model

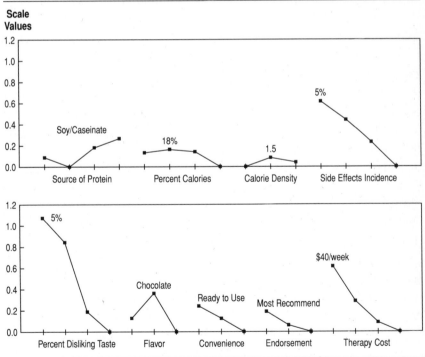

FURTHER ADVANCES IN CONJOINT ANALYSIS

Since its introduction to marketing,[6] the theory and practice of conjoint analysis have continued to advance.[7] These advances include the development of buyer–choice simulators, computer packages, and the move of conjoint analysis from the research department to the boardroom. The next step in this evolution, as discussed in this chapter, may be the use of conjoint analysis to simulate dynamic competitive interactions.

Buyer-Choice Simulators

Among the most important of the early advances in conjoint analysis was the development of new product/service consumer choice simulators, which allow managers to forecast buyer adoption rates or market shares for new or restaged products.

The sophistication and versatility of these buyer-choice simulators has continued to increase. They have been extended to include sensitivity analysis, which can be used to determine how market share and return are affected by changes in the levels of product attributes, buyer background profiles, decision rules, attribute importance changes, and the like. Table 15.2 describes some of the sensitivity analyses that can be easily programmed into current choice simulators.[8] In this way, the researcher can systematically explore the implications associated with one or more changes in the simulator's inputs.

Today's choice simulators are considerably more versatile. Table 15.3 shows a list of various features that current conjoint simulators may display, but it is not meant to be exhaustive. As noted from the table, three kinds of simulations can be provided: single–product; multiple (competitive) products; and a "bundle" of the firm's products, against a backdrop of competitive products. Choice rules include the max utility, Bradley-Terry-Luce (BTL), and logit-transformation rules. Output can be organized by respondent background characteristics; and limited sensitivity-analysis capabilities are sometimes included.

The next advancement in choice simulators was the development of product and product line optimizers. Instead of researchers testing

Table 15.2
Illustrative Outputs of Sensitivity Analysis Simulator

Preliminary detail—proportion of sample that selects each attribute level as displaying the highest part-worth, by attribute

Sensitivity analyses (assuming a bundle of two or more new products): Compute bundle share (and individual item shares), given:
- Deletion of each item of bundle, in turn.
- Change levels of each attribute of each product, holding all others fixed at initial levels.
- Fixing or restricting range of levels of each attribute across all items in the bundle.
- Raising or lowering of all status quo utilities by a fixed (user-supplied) percentage.
- Selection of a specified segment (based on background-variable categories or cluster-based segments).
- Random selection of K bundles (up to 1,000) where random bundles can be constrained to include user-specified profiles and/or restricted attribute-level variation.

Additions to basic sensitivity analyses
- Inclusion of attribute-level returns to the user's product line.
- Inclusion of price versus utility relationship for adjusting respondent utilities to price increases/decreases.
- Inclusion of effect on firm's existing products (cannibalization) due to new product(s) introduction.

specific options, these optimizers explore the whole space of potential options to find the product (or product line) that maximizes the firm's market share or profits.[9]

Moving into the Mainstream

Until the mid-1980s, conjoint analysis applications displayed an aura of the arcane. Several consulting firms offered their particular version of the methodology, often accompanied by strident claims of superiority over others. The introduction of microcomputer software packages changed this, placing conjoint methodology into the hands of nonspecialist analysts, those working for marketing-research supplier firms and in industry research departments. (Several leading packages are discussed later in the chapter.)

Table 15.3

Characteristics of Consumer-Choice Simulators

Product simulation flexibility
- Single product (versus status quo)
  - Likelihood of purchase (average response)
  - Proportion of respondents whose predicted likelihood of purchase exceeds a user-supplied criterion level
- Multiple products (sponsor and competitors): share received by each
- Sponsor's product bundle (versus competitors' products): share received by bundle and its separate components

Choice rules for the multiple-product and bundle cases
- Max-utility rule
- Share of utility (BTL) rule
- Logit rule

Other substantive features of choice simulators
- Interpolation of part-worths
- Base-case entry with adjusted current-product comparisons
- Confidence intervals around output measures
  - Parametric intervals
  - Nonparametric (bootstrapped) intervals
- Frequency tabulations and histograms of responses
- Replicated cases in a single run
- Inclusion of price and cost parameters
- Brand-switching matrices
- Derived attribute-level importances (based on choice data)

Consumer characteristics
- Respondent background data for market segment summaries
- Respondent importance weights
- Respondent perceptual distributions
- Individual/respondent output file (for additional analyses)

Sensitivity features
- Runs through all levels of a single attribute
- Flexibility for fixing attribute levels at user-present values (in all runs)

Cosmetic features
- Menu-driven
- Graphics output
  - Pie charts and histograms of market share; part-worth graphs
  - Averaged part-worths for total sample and segments

Another major trend, which also started around the mid-1980s, has been the "upward mobility" of conjoint analysis applications. In its first 15 years of application, most studies were initiated for tactical reasons; for example, to determine whether a price change should be implemented, or what set of benefits to promote in a new ethical drug. Studies were done by marketing research suppliers, and results were typically presented to corporate marketing research managers.

Times have changed. For example, over the past few years, McKinsey and Company has sponsored over 200 applications of conjoint analysis. The results are being used in high-level marketing and competitive-strategy planning.[10] Recently, McKinsey used a conjoint study (on behalf of AT&T) as evidence for seeking legal redress from foreign producers' incursions on the U.S. business-communications market (through alleged price-dumping practices).

Nor is McKinsey the only general management-consulting firm becoming interested in conjoint analysis. Booz-Allen, Arthur D. Little, The Boston Consulting Group, and Bain & Company are some of the large, general-line consulting firms that have added conjoint analysis to their research toolbox. We expect the trend to continue, particularly as the implications of conjoint analysis for strategy are recognized.

A Dynamic Approach to Conjoint Analysis

One drawback of product and product line optimizers is that they assume competitors maintain their current product or service profile throughout the forecast period. In fact, competitors are very likely to modify their products in response to the company's changes. Until now, however, these competitive reactions have not been explicitly considered in the model.

The following discussion shows how these static product and product-line optimizers can be extended to deal with dynamic conditions where competitors may react to an initiating firm's changes in product features or price with changes of their own. Some of the questions explored are:

1. What happens to market shares and individual supplier returns as a result of a sequence of competitive actions and reactions?
2. Does the time path of shares and returns settle down into some type of stable situation, that is, an equilibrium in which further changes are not attractive to any competitor?
3. How do long-term strategy outcomes relate to short-term strategy?
4. What happens when some firms stand pat and refuse to change their product/price strategy in response to others' competitive moves?

These research questions and others are all part of the next phase in the development and growth of conjoint analysis, one that attempts to model the interaction of competitors' initiating and retaliatory moves *over time*.

The SIMOPT and SIMDYN Models

The dynamic simulation model used in the remainder of this chapter is based on the static SIMOPT (SIMulation and OPTimization) model, an optimal product-positioning model that can be used for either the single-product or the product-line case.[11] Its principal inputs are a matrix of buyers' part-worths and set of competitive product profiles. The part-worths may come from any conjoint procedure, including commercial software programs. In particular, part-worths obtained from hybrid conjoint models are appropriate.[12] Moreover, the part-worths may contain two-way interaction terms as well as main effects.

In addition to input matrices of buyer part-worths and competitive-supplier profiles, the model has options for including:

- Buyer "importance" weights (reflecting buyers' frequency and/or amount of purchase);
- Demographic or other background attributes;
- Demographic weights for use in market-segment selection and market-share forecasting;

- Current market-share estimates of all supplier (brand) profiles under consideration (used in model calibration); and
- Cost/return data, measured at the individual-attribute level.

The model's outputs consist of market shares or dollar contributions to overhead and profits for each supplier. In the latter case, direct (or variable) costs and returns have to be estimated at the individual-attribute level for each supplier—a daunting task in most real-world settings.

In any given run of the model, the user obtains market share (return) for each supplier on both an unadjusted and adjusted (for initial share) basis. Outputs can be obtained for both the total market and for any segment defined by the user from the available demographic variables.

The user is then able to perform four types of analysis:

1. *A sensitivity analysis.* This shows how shares (returns) change for all suppliers as one varies the levels within each attribute, in turn.

2. *An optimal attribute-level analysis.* If this option is chosen, the model computes the best attribute profile for a given supplier, conditioned on specified attribute levels for all competing suppliers.

3. *A cannibalization analysis.* The user can also specify one or more ancillary products. If so, the model finds the optimal profile that maximizes share (return) for the set of chosen products (that can include the firm's existing products). This profile can be compared to the best product for a given supplier that does not take into account interactions with the firm's existing products.

4. *A Pareto frontier analysis.* In most real-world problems, the marketing strategist is not interested only in finding the best return but also wishes to get some feel for the trade-off between financial return and market share. SIMOPT provides a capability to trace out the (Pareto) frontier of all financial profiles that are undominated with respect to return and share. The user can then find out what the potential value may be in giving up some amount of return for an increase in market share.

Through a sequential series of new-product additions, the user can also examine the cumulative effect of adding/deleting products in the firm's line.

SIMDYN's Features

The SIMOPT model is basically a static optimizing model where competitors' product profiles and consumers' tastes (i.e., part-worths) are assumed to remain fixed over the firm's planning horizon. SIMDYN (SIMulation via DYNamic modeling) extends this model to explicitly consider a sequence of competitive moves and countermoves.

In addition, SIMDYN allows the user to input differential attribute level costs, by competitor, and to fix certain attribute levels (e.g., brand name). SIMDYN maintains a running record of each competitor's optimal profile (when it makes a move) and associated market shares and returns (i.e., contributions to overhead and profits) for all competitors at any stage in the sequence.

Nash Equilibrium. How can conjoint analysis of two or more competitors be brought together into a model of competitive interactions? The key is the concept of Nash equilibrium. To understand Nash equilibrium, imagine two or more competing suppliers, each independently trying to formulate its competitive strategy to maximize its own profits, given a specific set of competitive products, market strategies, and consumers' preferences. Since the market shares of competing products would usually be affected by a given firm's strategy, we could expect their attribute levels to change in response to the initiating firm's actions. The Nash equilibrium represents a market situation (perhaps unattainable) where no individual firm can make further gains for itself by *unilaterally* departing from the Nash equilibrium.

There are two iterative procedures available for finding a Nash equilibrium: simultaneous and sequential.[13] In the latter case, players (competitors) select strategies, in turn, in a predetermined order. We believe that the sequential approach is a more realistic portrayal of real action/reaction sequences; this is the approach considered here.

ANSWERING THE CALL FOR DYNAMIC CONJOINT ANALYSIS: THE CELLULAR PHONE CASE

To demonstrate this dynamic use of conjoint analysis, let us return to the challenge of Alpha company (a fictitious name for a real company) described at the opening of the chapter. As Alpha considers how to change its current cellular phone products, it needs to anticipate how competitors Beta and Gamma will respond.

The Study

Alpha's management commissioned a hybrid conjoint study among potential cellular phone buyers in the southwestern United States. Prospective buyers were defined as those who expressed interest in purchasing (primarily for personal use) a cellular phone during the next six months. Interviewing was conducted via a telephone-mail-telephone procedure. Initial screening of qualified respondents was done by telephone and followed by a mailing of questionnaires and conjoint materials. This, in turn, was followed by the main telephone call in which the conjoint exercise was conducted and responses were recorded. A total of 600 questionnaires were completed.

Color photographs and detailed descriptions of each telephone feature were included with the questionnaire booklet. The list of 15 attributes and their levels is shown in Table 15.4. Respondents' self-explicated desirability ratings on each attribute's level were obtained, along with a constant-sum importance point assignment across the 15 attributes.

Following the self-explicated tasks, each respondent received eight profile cards drawn from a master orthogonal design of 32; each set of eight cards represented a balanced block from the set of 32. After examining all eight cards, the respondent sorted them into three graded piles: least desirable, neutral, most desirable. Profiles were then ranked within subgroup. Starting from the top-ranked profile, the respondent rated each of the ranked profiles on a 0–100 likelihood-of-purchase scale. The respondent then answered some demographic questions.

Table 15.4
List of Attributes and Levels in Cellular Phone Application

Initial Price	Level	Features (Absent = 1 or Present = 2)
$125	1	High-strength battery (15 hours)
$175	2	9-number speed dialing
$250	3	Programmable for two different numbers
		Cigarette lighter battery charger
		Large-size (100 numbers) memory
		Portable car-roof antenna
		Low-battery warning beep
		Electronic lock
		Missed-call counter
		Mute function (for privacy)
		Extra (rechargeable) battery included
Brand		
Alpha	1	
Beta	2	
Gamma	3	
Warranty		
3 years	1	
1 year	2	
Weight		
7.5 ounces	1	
8.5 ounces	2	
9.5 ounces	3	

Conjoint part-worths were obtained from an individually based hybrid model; their average values are shown in Figure 15.3.

Experimental Assumptions

There are many factors that could influence competitive responses. In this experiment, we focused on two key variables: the cost structure of competitors and their participation in the market. For each of these variables, we examined two different assumptions:

1. Cost Structure
   a. All competitors are assumed to have the same variable costs for the attribute levels shown in Table 15.4.

358

Figure 15.3
Part–Worths for Convex Combination Model
(See Table 15.4 for Full Attribute-Level Descriptions)

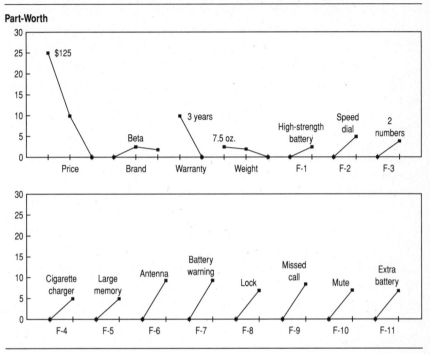

b. Competitors are allowed to have different attribute level costs.

2. Active versus Passive Participation
   a. All competitors are assumed to be active, that is, participate in the action/reaction sequence.
   b. One (out of three) competitors is assumed to be passive and does *not* change its product–price profile in response to others' moves.

Table 15.5 shows the cost/return structure for conditions 1a and 1b. Costs were estimated (crudely) by the sponsoring firm. As noted

Table 15.5
Estimated Attribute–Level Cost Structures

	Levels		
Attribute	Alpha Levels	Beta Levels	Gamma Levels
Net Price	75; 105; 150	75; 105; 150	65; 95; 140
Brand	0; 0; 0	0; 0; 0	0; 0; 0
Warranty	−10; 0	−15; 0	−5; 0
Weight	−20; −10; 0	−30; −15; 0	−15; −5; 0
Battery	0; −2	0; −2	0; −2
Speed dialing	0; −2	0; −2	0; −2
Program numbers	0; −4	0; −2	0; −2
Battery charger	0; −5	0; −2	0; −4
Larger Memory	0; −5	0; −5	0; −5
Antenna	0; −8	0; −7	0; −5
Low–Battery Beep	0; −5	0; −7	0; −5
Lock	0; −5	0; −7	0; −10
Missed call	0; −9	0; −8	0; −10
Mute function	0; −5	0; −2	0; −10
Extra battery	0; −10	0; −5	0; −15

Note: For equal cost case, Alpha's cost structure is assumed to apply to all three suppliers.

in Table 15.5, net prices per unit for each firm are shown first, followed by variable costs per unit for each attribute level. Under the equal cost condition, Alpha's cost data were assumed to apply to all three competitors.

Nash Equilibria under Equal Costs and Active Participation. The SIMDYN model was first applied to the equal costs and active participation case. There are six different sequences by which competitive moves can be initiated and reacted to, that is, six permutations. We started with the sequence: Alpha, Beta, Gamma, and continued through the remaining five sequences. A Nash equilibrium was achieved when three moves in a row resulted in the same shares and returns.

A Nash equilibrium was found in all six sequences, although the number of moves required to reach equilibrium varied from as few as 6 to as many as 11. By sequence, the number of moves required for equilibrium are:

Sequence	Number of Moves
Alpha, Beta, Gamma	7
Alpha, Gamma, Beta	6
Beta, Gamma, Alpha	6
Beta, Alpha, Gamma	8
Gamma, Alpha, Beta	11
Gamma, Beta, Alpha	9

As noted, when Alpha initiates the sequence, equilibrium occurs with as few as six moves. When Gamma initiates the sequence, as many as 11 moves are needed before equilibrium is reached.

Table 15.6 shows the history of the equilibrium process for one sequence: Alpha, Beta, Gamma. (In all cases, we permit all attributes to vary, except brand name.) We first examine the initial conditions and note that shares for Alpha, Beta, and Gamma are, respectively, 20.4 percent, 33.7 percent, and 45.9 percent, with associated unit returns of $6.73, $17.52, and $13.31.

These results correspond to the initial profile conditions of:

Alpha	11231
Beta	22112
Gamma	13231

where 11231 denotes $125, Alpha, one-year warranty, 9.5 oz., and no high-strength battery, as shown in Table 15.4.

We next optimize Alpha's profile, conditioned on fixed profiles for Beta and Gamma. As Table 15.6 shows, the best levels for Alpha for the first five attributes are 31132, which, respectively, are $150, Alpha, three-year warranty, 9.5 oz, and high-strength battery. As it turns out, in all cases, the optimal levels for attributes 5 through 15 are the *presence* of the feature (coded 2). We also note that when the Alpha profile is optimized, the share for Alpha increases to 61.1 percent, with an associated return of $48.90.

We next shift from Alpha's perspective to Beta's. Given Alpha's newly optimized product, how should Beta optimize its own product? The process is updated as the sequence continues. Finally, we note that at

Table 15.6
Equilibrium History Based on the Alpha, Beta,
Gamma Sequence (Equal Costs)

Move Initiator	Brand	Profile: First Five Attributes	Market Shares	Returns	Sum
Initial	Alpha	11231	20.4%	$ 6.73	
Conditions	Beta	22112	33.7	17.52	
	Gamma	13231	45.9	13.31	37.56
Alpha	Alpha	31132 (best)	61.1	48.90	
	Beta		15.1	7.84	
	Gamma		23.8	6.90	63.64
Beta	Alpha		34.2	27.39	
	Beta	32132	44.1	35.30	
	Gamma		21.6	6.27	68.96
Gamma	Alpha		26.2	20.95	
	Beta		29.5	23.63	
	Gamma	33122	44.3	31.01	75.59
Alpha	Alpha	31112	38.6	23.13	
	Beta		25.0	19.99	
	Gamma		36.5	25.52	58.64
Beta	Alpha		33.0	19.81	
	Beta	32112	37.8	22.67	Equilibrium
	Gamma		29.2	23.35	
Gamma	Alpha		33.0	19.81	
	Beta		37.8	22.67	Equilibrium
	Gamma	33132	29.2	23.35	
Alpha	Alpha	31112	33.0	19.81	
	Beta		37.8	22.67	Equilibrium
	Gamma		29.2	23.35	

move 5, the Nash equilibrium is initiated; and at moves 6 and 7, the solution has stabilized with returns of $19.81, $22.67, and $23.35, respectively, for Alpha, Beta, and Gamma.

It is worth noting that at equilibrium, all three brands are charging the highest price ($150). All three brands also offer a three-year warranty, but Alpha's and Beta's weight is 7.5 oz. while Gamma's optimal weight is 9.5 oz.

Note that the optimal profile after competitive interactions are considered is different from the initial optimal profile. As shown in Table 15.6, Alpha's short-term optimal profile (31132) changes to 31112 at equilibrium, where the weight changes from 9.5 oz. to 7.5 oz. We also note that Beta's initially optimized profile (32132) moves to 32112 at equilibrium, and Gamma's initially optimized profile (33122) moves to 33132 at equilibrium. Hence, optimal weight appears to be sensitive to the sequence of moves.

We conclude for these conditions that each competitor should offer all 11 features, a three-year warranty, and a $150 price. However, optimal phone weight still varies by brand. It is also worth noting that at initial conditions, the returns vary relatively widely, with a low of $6.73 (Alpha) to a high of $17.52 (Beta). However, at equilibrium, the returns are much less varied; Gamma is now highest at $23.35.

The Unequal Costs Case

A similar analysis was run for the unequal costs case (see Table 15.5). Starting conditions were the same as before; the only characteristic that varied was the assumption of different attribute-level costs across brands. Again, a Nash equilibrium was reached over all six sequences of moves. Table 15.7 shows the results for the sequence Alpha, Beta, Gamma.

As noted in Table 15.7, equilibrium was reached after six moves. In comparing Table 15.7 to Table 15.6, we note that under initial conditions, the returns for Beta and Gamma differ from the equal costs case (Table 15.6) because of the different cost structure assumptions. Although not shown in the table, we found as before that it was optimal to have all 10 features. The equilibrium profile for Alpha (31112) is the same as it was in the equal costs case of Table 15.6. The equilibrium profile for Beta (32132) differs, however; the optimal weight is now 9.5 oz. (rather than 7.5 oz.). The equilibrium profile for Gamma (33122) also differs in that the optimal weight is now 8.5 oz. (rather than 9.5 oz.). We also note that the initially optimum profile for Alpha changes from a weight of 9.5 oz. to a weight of 7.5 oz. at equilibrium.

Table 15.7
Equilibrium History Based on the Alpha, Beta,
Gamma Sequence (Unequal Costs)

Move Initiator	Brand	Profile: First Five Attributes	Market Shares	Returns	Sum
Initial	Alpha	11231	20.4%	$ 6.73	
Conditions	Beta	22112	33.7	15.17	
	Gamma	13231	45.9	8.26	30.16
Alpha	Alpha	31132 (best)	61.1	48.90	
	Beta		15.1	6.78	
	Gamma		23.8	4.28	59.96
Beta	Alpha		34.7	27.39	
	Beta	32122	44.1	35.95	
	Gamma		21.6	3.89	67.13
Gamma	Alpha		26.2	20.95	
	Beta		29.5	25.39	
	Gamma	33122	44.3	26.13	72.47
Alpha	Alpha	31112	38.6	23.13	
	Beta		25.0	21.49	
	Gamma		36.5	21.52	Equilibrium
Beta	Alpha		38.6	23.13	
	Beta	32132	25.0	21.49	Equilibrium
	Gamma		36.5	21.52	
Gamma	Alpha		38.6	23.13	
	Beta		25.0	21.49	Equilibrium
	Gamma	33122	31.5	21.52	

Finally, we again see less disparity in returns across the three brands when the Nash equilibrium returns are compared to those associated with the initial conditions. It is also interesting to note that at equilibrium, Alpha's return is the highest of the three, even though it was lowest at the initial conditions stage.

The Passive Products Case

Suppose one competitor does not actively respond to the moves of its rivals? Companies sometimes choose to ignore moves of competitors or, if recognized, fail to respond to them. The analysis was repeated with the assumption that two companies were active and one was passive. We looked at both the equal cost and unequal cost conditions. Again, Nash equilibria were obtained.

Table 15.8 shows the results for active products Alpha and Beta, and passive product, Gamma, under the unequal costs condition. An equilibrium is reached after only four moves. In general, the players converge to equilibrium more quickly if one player is passive. The profile of products may also differ. Starting conditions are the same as those shown in Table 15.7. At equilibrium, Alpha's profile (first five attributes) is the same as that shown in Table 15.7. Such is not the case for Beta. In Table 15.8, Beta's optimal weight is 8.5 oz. while in Table 15.7 its optimal weight is 9.5 oz. Apparently, the passivity of Gamma has an effect on the optimal profile for Beta (but not on Alpha).

Table 15.8
Equilibrium History Based on the Alpha, Beta Sequence
(Gamma Passive, Unequal Costs)

Move Initiator	Brand	Profile: First Five Attributes	Market Shares	Returns	Sum
Initial	Alpha	11231	20.4%	$ 6.73	
Conditions	Beta	22112	33.7	15.17	
	Gamma	13231	45.9	8.26	30.16
Alpha	Alpha	31132 (best)	61.1	48.90	
	Beta		15.1	6.78	
	Gamma		23.8	4.28	59.96
Beta	Alpha		34.2	27.39	
	Beta	32132	44.1	37.95	
	Gamma		21.6	3.89	69.23
Alpha	Alpha	31112	41.5	29.04	
	Beta		38.2	32.84	
	Gamma		20.3	3.66	Equilibrium
Beta	Alpha		41.5	29.04	
	Beta	32122	38.2	32.84	Equilibrium
	Gamma		20.3	3.66	

SOFTWARE FOR CONJOINT ANALYSIS

For managers seeking to use conjoint analysis, commercial computer programs can be a relatively inexpensive way to start. Two principal conjoint software packages are currently available for applications researchers:

Bretton-Clark's package of Conjoint Designer, Conjoint Analyzer, SIMGRAF, LINMAP, and Bridger.

Sawtooth Software's Adaptive Conjoint Analysis.

Bretton-Clark's and Sawtooth's packages play an increasingly important role in utilization of conjoint. Their appearance has served to define the state of conjoint practice (which is not far different from the kinds of studies carried out in the mid-1970s). More recently, a bigger player in the marketplace, SPSS, Inc. (1990), has introduced a PC software package that is virtually identical in design to Bretton-Clark's. Similarly, another software developer, Intelligent Marketing Systems (1991), has designed a package that also utilizes the full-profile approach found in the Bretton-Clark software.

Bretton-Clark's and Sawtooth's software have played a critical role in diffusing conjoint methods throughout industry. However, neither package has incorporated optimal product or product-line design models. Their software limits users to simulating outcomes related to a relatively small set of new-product candidates in a buyer-choice simulator. Commercial software packages all include some type of choice simulator that incorporates consumer part-worths and competitive product profiles.[14]

CONCLUSION

As illustrated by the case just discussed, recognizing the potential moves of competitors can have an impact on optimal product design. In the cellular telephone case, when competitor moves are considered, the optimal products are often different from the initial optimization. In addition, the model allows managers to optimize the product under a variety of assumptions, allowing them to anticipate a variety of competitive situations (such as different cost structures) or competitive moves (such as a passive competitor). For this case, the interactions among competitors did, in fact, converge to Nash equilibria. The speed of convergence, however, depends on the order in which companies make their moves.

In the complex and dynamic world where consumer preferences do change, where individual competitors may not try to optimize their strategies, and where new firms may enter and old firms may exit, it should be realized that the Nash equilibrium is essentially a theoretical concept, not a practical reality. Still, as many theoretical concepts have demonstrated, the Nash equilibrium can provide a useful way to study real competitive behavior by providing a rational norm and framework for examining a firm's strengths and weaknesses, under the concept's assumptions. (Indeed, the laws of physics are idealizations as well; their predictions of empirical phenomena are always subject to statistical fluctuations.)

In addition, the cost of making attribute-level changes, internal constraints on which attribute levels can be changed, and the difficulty of accurately measuring attribute-level variable costs present serious research challenges. Also, more study is needed of the so-called first-mover advantage and the possible muted effect of "me-too" followers that try to emulate innovative product designs.

Even with these limitations (many of which apply to any model), this dynamic approach to conjoint analysis can offer a powerful tool for developing strategy. At the minimum, it can point out those components of one's current brand profile that are most resistant to competitors' retaliations. Just as earlier work in conjoint analysis has proved very valuable to marketers, this extended model offers an important tool to strategists by allowing them to view competitive interactions through the customer's eyes.

CHAPTER 16

THE COMPETITIVE DYNAMICS OF CAPABILITIES: DEVELOPING STRATEGIC ASSETS FOR MULTIPLE FUTURES

PAUL J.H. SCHOEMAKER
The Wharton School, Department of Marketing

RAPHAEL AMIT
University of British Columbia,
Faculty of Commerce and Business Administration

To succeed in the future, managers must develop the resources and capabilities needed to gain or sustain advantage in the emerging competitive environment. Managers tend to address this issue either by looking from the inside out (focusing on internal capabilities and resources) or from the outside in (focusing on key success factors in the external competitive environment). This chapter offers a framework that joins these two perspectives and focuses them on the future. The authors use an integrative framework based on scenario analysis in order to identify those strategic assets that are robust across multiple futures.

What are the key resources and capabilities necessary for competitive success? This question, which underlies the success or failure of firms in the marketplace, has been a key focus of recent strategy research and practice. To address this

Professor Jerry Wind and Wharton's SEI Center for Advanced Studies in Management are gratefully acknowledged for the initial support of this research project, including the organization of a workshop. We are also grateful to the Peter Wall Foundation for its generous support of this research.

368

issue, strategy theorists have developed the resource-based view of the firm and such concepts as core competencies, key success factors (KSF), dynamic capabilities, leverage points, and barriers to competition. These concepts, particularly when applied, tend to be internally focused or identify capabilities that were important *in the past* rather than those that may be needed in the future. In a rapidly changing environment, identifying and building future capabilities is vital to sustaining profitability.

The capabilities that contribute to competitive success in an industry shift over time. Competitive moves and environmental changes undermine the importance of specific capabilities. Mainframes give way to personal computers and then to distributed processing. A product focus is superseded by an emphasis on service. Mass production gives way to microsegmentation and customization. Today's capabilities may provide about as much advantage as buggy whip craftsmanship in an automotive age.

This chapter presents a framework for identifying and building *future* capabilities. It combines scenario analysis with a structured examination of the firm, its customers, and competitors. This approach incorporates key concepts from research on capabilities, but offers a broad, multidimensional view, addressing the issue of how to identify and build the capabilities that will be needed in the future.

CHANGING THE FORMULA FOR SUCCESS

In the mid-1960s, the U.S. infant formula business enjoyed secure and stable markets. A few companies, led by Ross (a division of Abbott) and Mead Johnson (part of Bristol Myers Squibb), controlled over 80 percent of the American infant nutritional market. Because infant formula is viewed by the Food and Drug Administration (FDA) as a medical food, strong ties to hospitals along with a cozy relationship with pediatricians were the keys to high margins. In the 1980s, the situation began to change. The Infant Formula Act was enacted in 1980 to assure high standards for infant formulas. The act assured consumers that all formulas were safe, and consequently weakened claims of product differentiation. Then, the Women, Infants, and Children (WIC) program was launched by the U.S. government, providing low-cost access to infant formula for many families, and WIC soon accounted for over 50 percent of domestic sales. Eventually, companies had to compete on price (generally winner-takes-all bids, state by state) to qualify for the government's program. Furthermore, the increasingly powerful La Leche League extolled the virtues of breast milk over infant formula and cow's milk, reducing demand for formula. Last, the international food and pharmaceutical giant, Nestlé SA of Switzerland, entered the U.S. market in 1988 by purchasing the Carnation company. Nestlé decided to target parents directly in its marketing, bypassing the pediatricians who had gradually lost power due to fundamental changes in the U.S. health care sector.[1] Nestlé's direct marketing approach was in part possible because the United States was not a signatory to the World Health Organization's (WHO) guidelines for the marketing and selling of infant formula (following Third World abuses). Ross needed to develop a new set of capabilities to succeed in this transformed market.

As illustrated by this example, the dimensions of competition can shift dramatically in a short time. Ross had competed by offering a differentiated product (with high margins) to pediatricians and hospitals in a domestic market, but then had to offer a low-cost formula directly to customers, and compete against global players. The forces that brought about this change were both external (such as globalization, health care restructuring, and governmental regulation) as well as endogenous to the industry (low-cost formulations, lobbying, possible collusion, and new entrants).

The Need for an Integrative View

Managers and theorists traditionally have approached strategy from one of two perspectives. They either have looked at strategic situations from the outside in—focusing on key competitive factors in the external environment—or from the inside out—focusing on the internal core competencies that lead to competitive success.

The outside-in perspective emphasizes the requirements for success as dictated by the demands of a particular competitive environment.

Key success factors (KSFs), for example, are based on the intuitively appealing idea that certain activities, resources, or capabilities are much more important to success than others in a particular industry, and that senior managers should focus on those that are key.[2] Although popular, this notion has long lacked a clear definition and solid theoretical underpinning.[3] It is also unclear whether industries (as opposed to strategic segments therein) exhibit distinct KSFs,[4] how long they last, and whether they are the result of foresight or luck. After all, if many firms pursue the same KSF, it may no longer be a discriminating factor of success.

In contrast, the inside-out perspective examines the internal resources, competencies and capabilities that have made the company successful.[5] The firm's resources are assets that it owns or controls, and that are externally available and transferable. They include such things as know-how that can be traded (e.g., patents and licenses), financial and physical assets (e.g., property, plant, and equipment) and human capital. Capabilities are the organizational processes used to deploy resources. They are information-based, tangible or intangible processes that are specific to a firm, having been developed through complex interactions among the firm's resources. Capabilities might include highly reliable service, repeated process or product innovations, manufacturing flexibility, responsiveness to market trends, and short product development cycles.

Capabilities and key success factors examine two parts of one competitive picture. Capabilities usually focus on the company's internal workings, with little explicit attention to competitor actions or the external environment. Yet actions of competitors or shifts in the environment can radically alter the organizational capabilities needed for success. Key success factors (KSFs) are determined by focusing on industrywide success, often overlooking the importance of organizational factors within the company. Further, most discussions of capabilities examine them separately when, in fact, they often work together synergistically as bundles. Managers need a way to bring these two perspectives together and develop a more complete view of competition. We introduce next the concept of *strategic assets* to join these two perspectives.[6]

Strategic Assets

Strategic assets (SAs) are the set of firm-specific resources and capabilities that bestow a company's competitive advantage in the future. As illustrated in Figure 16.1, strategic assets are identified by combining the inside-out and outside-in perspectives.

The right-hand side of the figure represents the outside-in perspective. It shows the industry forces that shape the competitive environment. All of these forces shape the industry-specific factors that are required for success, which we call *strategic industry factors* (SIFs). These SIFs are determined, at a market level, as the result of complex interactions among competitors, exogenous shocks, customer

Figure 16.1
An Integrative Strategy Perspective

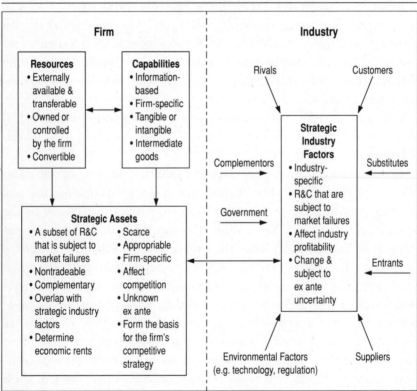

preferences, regulators, the nature of the technology, and so forth. When examined ex post, they have become the primary determinants of economic performance for industry participants. It is important to recognize that SIFs are industry- or segment-specific. Furthermore, the relevant set of SIFs changes and cannot be predicted with certainty in advance.

SIFs are the capabilities and resources that are necessary for successful performance in an industry or strategic segment. Some of these will be easy to obtain, such as receiving a government license to sell insurance in a given region, whereas others may be extremely challenging, such as being a true innovator. Hence, there are "must" SIFs, without which a firm cannot be a credible player, and "discriminating" SIFs that underlie differences in profit performance. Thus, SIFs possess both an absolute character (e.g., the need to be licensed for an insurance company) and a relative character (e.g., to meet a minimum quality standard dictated by consumers and common practice). At their heart, SIFs revolve around market failures, that is, the inability to purchase the requisite SIF overnight from outside vendors. The fact that they must be developed by firms over time makes them potentially enduring dimensions of competition. It is important that firms generate a tentative list of SIFs and then apply some of the criteria enumerated next to narrow down the list to those factors that are truly strategic (i.e., not easy to develop, relevant to customers, and crucial to the firm's internal operations or external image).

But this is only half of the picture in Figure 16.1. The upper left-hand side of the figure reflects the inside-out perspective. The firm has a set of resources that are either externally available or controlled by the firm, which give rise, over time, to a set of capabilities or processes that lie at the core of the firm's functioning. Combining these two perspectives, we can ask: Which of these various capabilities and resources (alone or in combination) provide an advantage (and, thereby, generate economic rents) given the specific characteristics of the industry? The subset of resources and capabilities that meets the industry tests of the right-hand side of the figure constitutes the firm's strategic assets. Examples of strategic assets are Wal-Mart's information technology and distribution systems; Frito-Lay's or Procter & Gamble's brand management; IBM's installed base of computers and research reputation; Merck's R&D capability; or Hewlett-Packard's innovation ability.

Characteristics of Strategic Assets. The preceding discussion describes how strategic assets are identified. In this section, we identify their distinctive characteristics. These are:[7]

- Difficult to trade or imitate.
- Scarce, durable, and not easily substituted.
- Complementary to one another (that is, one asset's value increases as another asset's value increases).
- Specialized to the firm (hard to transfer).
- In line with the future strategic industry factors.
- Create value for the firm's shareholders (appropriable).

In general, strategic assets are more valuable the more difficult they are to buy, sell, imitate, or substitute. For example, "invisible" assets such as tacit organizational knowledge or trust between management and labor cannot be traded or easily replicated by competitors since they are deeply rooted in the organization's history and culture. Such assets accumulate slowly over time. Further, they are often specific to a single firm or to a particular industry. This idiosyncrasy makes them difficult to imitate, especially if their development time cannot be easily compressed, as when building a strong R&D team. Consider, for example, Lincoln Electric's management system that made it the low-cost producer in the electric utility industry. Many companies have tried to copy it, but few have succeeded.

The more firm-specific, durable, and scarce SAs are, the more valuable they may be. The more firm-specific they are, the harder they are for competitors to imitate. The more durable the assets are, the smaller the investment required to offset their depreciation.

Finally, the asset must return surplus profit or "rent" to the firm, as opposed to selected individuals within the firm. For example, if an advertising agency is successful because of the work of one outstanding account executive, then the agency will not reap the rewards—the executive will. This question of rent appropriability is most crucial in talent markets such as professional sports, entertainment, Wall Street executives, and CEOs.

THE IMPACT OF DYNAMIC CHANGES

The strategic assets shown in Figure 16.1 are a snapshot of the competitive situation at a given point in time. These assets can shift due to changes in the firm or the competitive environment. For Ross, in our opening example, its good relationship with pediatricians was a strategic asset before the changes of the 1980s. Its investments in a salesforce and advertising or promotions directed toward physicians were very valuable in an environment in which health professionals largely determined the choice of formula for their patients. When that environment changed, however, these capabilities were no longer strategic assets. Faced with the changes of the 1980s, Ross needed to develop a new set of capabilities or reshape its existing capabilities and resources to meet the new challenges.

Changes in strategic assets can come from the outside in or the inside out. Consider the situation of a major worldwide distributor for a heavy equipment manufacturer. One of its most important strategic assets had been a global branch network that allowed it to install any spare part for its customers within 24 hours. With the advent of express delivery services, this capability suddenly ceased to be a strategic asset (literally overnight). Customers were willing to sacrifice some service for the reduced costs of express delivery. Suddenly, the company's extensive network of branch offices around the world was a potential liability rather than an asset. It needed to find new ways to use its current resources and capabilities to build new strategic assets to meet the needs of this transformed competitive environment.

Similarly, change can come from the inside out. A firm may develop new resources or capabilities that can transform the environment. For example, at one point in the steel industry, economies of scale and a large local market were major SIFs. But the onset of mini-mills, which used a different set of plant processes and furnace capabilities, reduced the importance of scale. The development of new capabilities within the firms transformed the strategic industry factors.

These changes may be easy to understand in retrospect, but the real challenge managers face is to *anticipate* these changes. Firms need to strengthen and build strategic assets today that will lead to competitive success in the future. Managers must ask: How can we leverage our capabilities in the multiple futures that may lie ahead? What new capabilities should we develop, and which ones will form the basis for our competitive advantage in the future?

All organizations must look for ways to take widely available resources such as labor, capital, and technology and create competitive advantage by turning them into something that cannot easily be developed, copied, or purchased. This challenge becomes increasingly pressing as markets globalize, giving more firms access to the same resources. It becomes easier, for example, for organizations to search the globe for labor that is low in cost (e.g., in Mexico) or highly specialized (e.g., in Silicon Valley). Recall Nestlé's entry into the U.S. market via an acquisition. Only firms that can use their resources in unique ways—say, by developing an organizational culture that stimulates software developers to higher productivity—will have a real chance of long-term success.

The following framework provides a step-by-step process for analyzing the strategic assets that are most important to develop across a range of possible future scenarios and competitive responses.

THE STRATEGIC ASSETS FRAMEWORK

The strategic assets framework presented in this section involves two main phases. The first phase examines the strategic situation from the outside in, identifying possible SIFs for different competitive scenarios in the strategic segments in which the firm may have to compete in the future. The second phase addresses competitive interactions among competing firms, specifically how quickly and easily the firm and its competitors can develop new strategic assets.

We will illustrate this process with StratCorp, a technology-based, wholly owned division of a leading business information company. Historically, StratCorp (a pseudonym) enjoyed rapid growth and profitability. It became an established international leader in providing high value-added, computer-based, and electronically distributed economic information services to businesses. Its rivals include several relatively small competitors who service well-defined vertical markets and one large company that has a broad product line similar to StratCorp's. Since 1969, StratCorp relied on the evolution of mainframe computer technology and telecommunications to gather, process, and distribute time-sensitive business information to its Fortune 1000 clients. Most of StratCorp's revenue came from recurring computer usage and from on-line processing of over 70 different information products.

In the early 1980s, StratCorp faced a serious strategic challenge. It was the dawn of the personal computing age, and IBM had just introduced the PC. The acceptance of PCs and their impact on businesses such as StratCorp were far from certain, but the rapid proliferation of personal business computers presented a major threat to StratCorp since its customers' needs for online processing and storage capability on a remote and expensive computer system were likely to decline significantly. The rapid spread of personal computers could make StratCorp's production and distribution technology obsolete, and lead to substantial excess capacity of its main technological resources as client usage rapidly declined. Thus, StratCorp's management had to formulate a practical business strategy for a proposed new venture that would turn this threat into an opportunity for continued growth and profitability. The problem was how to enter and compete effectively in a new market segment for business information disseminated on personal computers, while continuing to build on its existing strengths.

Some StratCorp managers thought the firm should invest in cost leadership to meet the challenges of the new environment. Others advised building up its technological base. Alternative choices for developing assets included strengthening brand awareness and reputation or expanding its network of offices. Where should StratCorp place its bets in a very uncertain future?

Phase A: Identifying Strategic Industry Factors

The first challenge for StratCorp was to identify strategic industry factors, both in its current environment and across a range of different future scenarios. The first step of the analysis is designed to identify this set of SIFs.

Step A1: Understand the Past.   Start by identifying strategic industry factors that were important in the past. Managers can use their own experiences to construct a set of plausible SIFs that best explain past successes in their industry. Then they can use a statistical analysis to validate these beliefs; for example, by running a multiple regression. Does the regression model indeed reveal that a few factors explain most of the variance in profitability? This exercise will help managers involved in the process identify some of their own biases and establish a firmer foundation for their future predictions.

For StratCorp, the past SIFs in its industry included access to a time-sharing computer system, low cost operations, marketing capability, a highly skilled group of economists trained in modeling, regional consulting teams, reputation, and high brand awareness.

Step A2: Imagine Possible Futures Using Scenario Planning.   The next challenge is to examine how these SIFs may change in the future. Scenario planning is a disciplined method for imagining possible futures. The art and science of scenario construction have been described and analyzed in a number of papers, so only its essence is outlined here.[8] The process identifies key uncertainties for the industry and then examines a set of broad outcomes for each uncertainty. These outcomes are then combined into a limited number of internally consistent scenarios.

One way for managers to approach this is to list the key questions they would ideally like answered about the future, such as issues regarding technology, regulation, or the economy. Next to the questions, they list the possible outcomes, like this:

Technology breakthrough?	yes/no
More regulation?	yes/no
Health of economy?	good/medium/bad

They then arrange the possible outcomes into conceptually different scenarios, and work with them, weeding out implausibilities and inconsistencies, until they have several scenarios that bracket a wide range of possible futures. These scenarios should be thought of as weather conditions—strategically relevant conditions that are beyond the firm's control.

For StratCorp, one key uncertainty it faced was whether mainframes or personal computers would dominate. A second key uncertainty was whether changes in technology and customer demographics would change the type of product demanded by customers. These two dimensions and their boundary outcomes are shown in Figure 16.2.

The Mainframe Dominates scenario is essentially the status quo, with large mainframes continuing to be the primary technology used by StratCorp's clients, and existing products continuing to be in the highest demand. The PC Dominates is a scenario in which the personal computer is widely accepted, although the primary products demanded by customers remain unchanged. In the Product Evolution scenario, there are new products and services, but they are delivered on existing mainframes. The Revolutionary Change scenario postulates the rapid spread of PCs and a demand for new products.[9]

Figure 16.2 provides a starting point for further scenario development. To be most compelling, a scenario needs to incorporate contextual detail the way a good story or movie does. To add this detail, we must consider other key uncertainties that might also matter, such as the state of the economy, trade restrictions on information flow,

Figure 16.2
Scenarios Facing StratCorp in the 1980s

| | | Computing Environment | |
		Centralized	Distributed
Customer Preferences for Information Products and Services	Existing	Mainframe Dominates	PC Dominates
	New	Product Evolution	Revolutionary Change

development of revolutionary new hardware or software, and so on. Depending on the length of the planning horizon (10 years in the case of StratCorp), these additional uncertainties may feature prominently or tangentially in any given scenario theme. The basic idea is to make assumptions about the remaining key uncertainties that best fit a given scenario cell in the matrix. For example, the Mainframe Dominates scenario can be bolstered by assuming a weak economic climate (which inhibits expenditures on new technologies), trade barriers (to prevent an influx of new Japanese computers into the U.S. market), or an abysmal failure of new hardware or software introductions. In contrast, the Revolutionary Change scenario is enhanced by making exactly the opposite assumptions. For ease of exposition, we will keep the scenarios two-dimensional, although they should in practice be much richer than the skeleton outline of Figure 16.2.

How do you know if your final scenarios are appropriate? The first criterion is relevance. To have impact, your scenarios should connect directly with the mental maps and concerns of the users (e.g., senior executives, middle managers, and so on). Second, the scenarios should be internally consistent (and be perceived as such) to be effective. Third, they should be archetypal, describing generically different futures rather than variations on one theme. Fourth, each scenario ideally should describe an equilibrium or a state in which the system might exist for some length of time, as opposed to being highly transient. It does an organization little good to prepare for a possible future that will be short-lived. In sum, the scenarios should cover a wide range of possibilities that highlight competing perspectives (within and outside the firm), while focusing on interlinkages and the internal logic of each future.

Step A3: Identify Strategic Segments. The next step, after scenario analysis, is to identify the significant strategic segments the firm is or might be competing in. This is important because recent research suggests that, on average, profitability varies far more across businesses within an industry than across industries.[10] The focus of analysis, therefore, should be on each strategic business unit of the firm, within its industry context. For example, Apple Computer might segment its business into the home, office, and educational sectors. The Canadian

Imperial Bank of Commerce might segment its wide range of financial services into retail banking, corporate banking, insurance, and brokerage.

The segmentation task can be approached intuitively or systematically. In the latter case, multidimensional scaling and cluster analyses may be useful tools to distill the relevant bases of segmentation and to identify the major segments.[11] Whatever procedure is used, the analysis should yield a limited number of business segments (from two to eight) that differ fundamentally in their strategic nature. These strategic segments need not be pure, such as product groupings or customer segments, but can be hybrids of product, market, technology, distribution, region, and pricing features. In deciding whether two segments are strategically different, you should examine: each segment's market size, both present and future; customer and product differences; the kind of competitors and strategies encountered; the distribution channels used; and the differences in technologies, suppliers, regulators, unions, and so on. Unless two segments are different in at least two of these criteria, they are probably not truly distinct strategic segments, although they might be very different from just a marketing or manufacturing perspective.

Each strategic segment must be understood in the context of its particular industry. Traditional industry analysis focuses on assessing the attractiveness of an industry, that is, on the potential profitability of the industry, in light of the structural factors depicted by Figure 16.1. However, industry analysis can also include softer analyses such as those dealing with the attitudes, reputations, and past interactions among the players in terms of retaliation, coalitions, commitments, and so on. The nature of the industry partly determines the number of firms (e.g., fragmented versus oligopolistic), their scope (e.g., single- versus multiproduct or domestic versus global), and their strategies (low-cost versus differentiation, or innovation versus imitation). Also pertinent are the competing firms' unique histories and evolutions, as these determine what kind of resources and capabilities they have at their disposal. After developing possible scenarios and identifying segments (Steps A2 and A3), the two can be cross-referenced in the Strategic Industry Factor Matrix shown in

Figure 16.3 for the case of StratCorp. This matrix shows the distinct strategic industry factors needed for a specific segment and scenario.

In the case of StratCorp, its segments were the traditional Fortune 1000 corporations and an emerging segment (that would become increasingly important with the spread of the personal computer) for small and midsize enterprises. Figure 16.3 shows how these two segments can be cross-referenced with just two of the possible scenarios. For each of the four boxes of the matrix, the company would determine the necessary SIFs, as discussed in step A4.

Figure 16.3
The SIF Matrix

		Scenarios	
		Mainframe Dominates	PC Dominates
Segments	Fortune 1000 Firms	**SIFs** • Access to a Specialized Time-Sharing Computer System • Low Cost Process • Regional Consulting Team • Highly Trained Staff of Economists • Reputation • Brand Awareness	
	Small and Medium Enterprises (SMEs)		**SIFs** • Technology Base • Brand Awareness • Reputation • Cost Position • Retail Marketing • Product Development

Step A4: Determine SIFs for Each Segment and Scenario. For each cell in the SIF matrix (Figure 16.3), managers must list the SIFs for that segment, given that scenario. Since different competitors, distribution channels, customers, technologies, regulations, and so on may operate in different segments, the applicable set of SIFs is likely to differ across cells within a column. For the conglomerate Textron, for instance, access to retail distribution channels and brand-name recognition by consumers are likely to be SIFs in its lawn mower segment (Homelite); yet these particular resources and capabilities are unlikely to be SIFs in Textron's helicopter manufacturing business (Bell Helicopters). For the Royal Bank of Canada, for example, the branch networks and automatic tellers that are important in its retail banking segment are unlikely to be important in its investment banking business. There, reputation and relationships are far more important.[12]

Likewise, the sets of SIFs may differ across scenarios. For example, consider an industry in which the life cycle of a particular technology is important. For a scenario that assumes a short life cycle, the capability for fast product development could be an SIF. For a scenario that assumes long product life cycles, the same capability may not be an SIF.

Some SIFs, such as customer service, may appear in multiple cells. These are the ones that managers may want to focus on, as their robustness across alternative scenarios may yield the "best bang for the buck." If no common SIFs are found across columns, the firm's exposure to environmental and structural changes in the industry is high. Also, if no SIF overlap occurs across rows, little synergy among a firm's business segments can be expected.

For StratCorp, we have depicted the SIFs for just two of the cells in Figure 16.3. For example, in the Mainframe Dominates scenario in the Fortune 1000 firm segment, the SIFs would remain the same as those identified in the past (in step A1). But for the scenario of distributed computing and the segment of small- to medium-size firms, the SIFs would be very different. They would include technology base, brand awareness, reputation, cost position, retail marketing, and product development. Note that reputation and brand awareness are common across these two cells.

The SIF matrix in Figure 16.3 is a simple but practical tool to test for such resilience and potential synergy. However, this analysis, which is performed at the industry and/or segment level, does not directly determine which capabilities to invest in most heavily for any given firm. The insights obtained from the industry and segment analyses have to be extended to a firm-specific strategy. For each cell of the scenario-by-segment matrix, managers must select some assets as the basis for developing their competitive advantage. The particular resources that will be targeted depend on firm-specific benefits and costs associated with investment in particular assets. The choice also depends on competitors' decisions about their particular SAs, and the importance consumers attach to various SAs. The second phase of our analysis reflects these firm-specific considerations.

Phase B: Selection of Strategic Assets

For StratCorp to survive and succeed in the PC Dominates or Revolutionary Change scenarios, it clearly needs to develop new strategic assets. But which ones? By definition, StratCorp cannot instantly create the new strategic assets it needs. Many of these assets are difficult, expensive, and time-consuming to develop. Its competitors are also engaged in this process of developing assets, so we need to consider their strengths and potential moves, because they might negate an advantage derived from developing StratCorp's assets. Finally, StratCorp needs to consider how important improvements in these assets are to its customers. Is it worth the effort?

Whereas the first phase of this analysis examines the competitive situation at the industry level, the second phase of this process starts from the firm level. The first phase develops a view of what is needed to succeed in the industry across multiple segments and scenarios. The second phase addresses which strategic assets should be developed or strengthened for a particular firm in the future. The first phase can be thought of as a macro view, identifying strategic industry factors, and the second phase as the micro view, identifying specific strategic assets to strengthen and develop for a particular firm. This second phase is focused on identifying the most important strategic assets for the firm based on the SIFs identified in the first phase and an analysis of the relative positions of competitors and the anticipated reactions of customers.

Step B1: Identify Strategic Assets.   The first step is to identify all relevant assets in which change could enhance the firm's competitive advantage in a particular cell of the scenario-segment matrix. Managers should consider both tangible and intangible assets that may bestow competitive advantage; for example, by influencing customers' decisions to purchase the products of a particular vendor. If this step reveals that there is little or no match between the firm's present set of SAs and the SIF for that particular scenario and business segment, the firm may not have any advantage over other players, and consequently may have to pursue alternative segments.

The identification of the SAs to be included in the analysis stems from the presumed SIFs for the scenario/segment cell considered, and any other current SAs that the firm already has. For illustration, we next consider a set of five SAs relevant to the PC Dominates scenario for smaller firms. The first four correspond directly to the first four SIFs in the bottom right cell of Figure 16.3. We also include one existing SA of the firm, namely its network of regional consulting teams (which we refer to as location). This is an existing SA that becomes less important under the new PC Dominates scenario. Thus, the five SAs we consider in the following analysis are:

(a1) *Technology Base.* In the market for electronic distribution of high value-added business information, StratCorp was a technology leader when time-sharing computing began to proliferate. Further, it had built its own telecommunications network, an asset considered essential in linking both large and small businesses to its value-added information products. A world of distributed processing would require a very different technology base.

(a2) *Brand Awareness.* There was substantial awareness among Fortune 1000 companies of StratCorp's range of information products and among smaller companies of StratCorp's parent activities in related information markets.

(a3) *Reputation.* StratCorp had an excellent reputation for timely delivery of reliable business information and for responsive on-site client support by skilled professionals.

(a4) *Cost Position.* StratCorp was not a cost leader because it focused on providing high-quality, high value-added information products to the high end of the market; in addition, its staff included a large number of high-cost professionals.

(a5) *Location.* StratCorp had an established network of regional offices and consulting teams that facilitated on-site customer-support programs and provided a base for its large, knowledgeable, and very effective direct salesforce.

Step B2: Assess Customer Reactions to Change. How would customers react if StratCorp began to invest in strengthening one of these strategic assets within the scenario postulated? This assessment could be based on market research (such as conjoint analysis), on the judgment and views of managers (using a Delphi method), or on information about the firm's existing and potential customers. An asset is judged to be of high importance if an improvement is likely to yield a strong, positive customer response (for a given scenario and segment).

This assessment is illustrated for StratCorp in Table 16.1. StratCorp determined that changes in the technology base (a1), reputation (a3), and cost position (a4) were of highest importance in the emerging market for electronically distributed information on desk-top computers. Brand awareness (a2) was classified as an asset of medium importance, and location (a5) as an asset of low importance. We will return to these

Table 16.1
Customer Reaction to Improvements in StratCorp's Strategic Assets

	Low	*Medium*	*High*
Technology Base (a1)			x
Awareness (a2)		x	
Reputation (a3)			x
Cost Position (a4)			x
Location (a5)	x		

assessments in step B5. Our focus from here on is on the bottom right cell of the scenario-segment matrix.

Step B3: Assess Investments Required.   No matter how important they may be to customers, developing new strategic assets requires an investment of time and resources by the firm. Is it worth it? The next step of the analysis examines the following issues: How difficult and time-consuming is it to improve or create assets? Will competitors simply match these moves? This step assesses the pace and cost of developing the strategic assets, both for the firm and for rivals. As shown in Figure 16.4, StratCorp classified each of the strategic assets based on the investment required and the pace at which they could be developed or strengthened. It then proceeded to perform the same analysis for each of its major competitors, one example of which is shown in Figure 16.5.

The last part of this stage of analysis is to determine which of the strategic assets are attractive for StratCorp to develop (i.e., requiring a relatively small investment of money and time). Those assets that are fast and inexpensive for the firm to develop are the most attractive, as shown in the upper right cell of Figure 16.5. Those that are slower and more expensive are less attractive, as indicated in the lower left of the

Figure 16.4
Determining the Speed and Cost of Building Assets (StratCorp)

		Pace		
		Slow	Medium	Fast
	Small	Neutral		a4 Attractive
Investment	Medium		a3 Neutral	a1 a5
	Large	Unattractive	a2	Neutral

Figure 16.5
Determining the Speed and Cost of Building Assets (StratCorp's Rival)

		Pace		
		Slow	Medium	Fast
Investment	Small	Neutral	a3	a4 Attractive
	Medium	a5	a2 Neutral	
	Large	Unattractive	a1	Neutral

matrix. Those along the middle diagonal are neutral. For StratCorp, its cost position (a4) can be improved quickly with a very small investment. Changing brand awareness (a2) is a longer process with a higher investment, so this would be unattractive.

Step B4: Comparative Evaluation of Assets. Those assets that are cheap and fast for the firm (attractive) but slow and expensive for rivals (unattractive) are the best to pursue. By changing these assets, the firm can move in a way that is difficult for competitors to match. The next step, therefore, is to compare the attractiveness of strategic assets for the firm relative to the attractiveness of those same assets for competitors. This comparison for StratCorp is shown in Figure 16.6.

The most appealing assets for StratCorp are those classified as attractive for itself and unattractive for the competitor (a1 and a5). This competitor will probably not react aggressively to the firm's investment in them. This area should be the focus of offensive moves, as shown in Figure 16.6, if this were the only significant competitor. The more assets that fall into this group, the more ways the firm has available to establish its competitive advantage vis-à-vis rivals.

Figure 16.6
Comparison of Asset Development for StratCorp and Competitor

		Competitor		
		Attractive	Neutral	Unattractive
StratCorp	Attractive	a4		a1 **Offensive** a5
	Neutral	a3	**Equal**	
	Unattractive	**Defensive**	a2	

An asset located in the bottom left corner is attractive to the rival but not to StratCorp. Investments in these assets are likely to be used by the firm's competitors in formulating their offensive strategy. It thus may be prudent for the firm to include in its competitive strategy a defensive plan that will reduce the effectiveness of competitors' likely actions (and consider how they would respond).

Finally, some assets are about equally attractive to StratCorp and its rivals. Note that cost position (a4) falls into this category. An investment by StratCorp in this asset could very well lead to a destructive competitive battle because its rival could invest in the same asset equally well.

Step B5: Select Strategic Assets. Our analysis thus far does not recommend any one SA as the basis for StratCorp's strategy. The final step is to combine the assessment of competitors above with the previous assessment of customer reactions from step B2. Which of the offensive moves identified in the preceding step are most important to customers?

As shown in Figure 16.7, of StratCorp's two primary choices for offensive moves, developing its technology base (a1) is far more important

Figure 16.7
Selecting Strategic Assets

		Importance to Customers		
		Low	Medium	High
	Offensive	a5		a1
Types of Asset	Equal			a4
	Defensive		a2	a3

to customers than expanding its branch offices (a5). As a result of the cumulative analysis of steps B1–B4, developing this asset (for the particular segment and scenario considered) would result in a strong positive customer response; could be done relatively quickly with a relatively low investment; and would be difficult for the competitor to neutralize.

Conversely, blocking the competitor's moves in strengthening its reputation (a3) should also be a central focus of StratCorp's defensive strategy since a change in this strategic asset is very important to customers and attractive for the competitor. StratCorp should seek to develop a strategy to block the rival's moves in this area, even if it requires substantial investment or perhaps a strategic alliance.

For the cells that are equally important to customers, such as cost position (a4), the best strategy is to develop the capacity to respond quickly if the competitor moves. Since initiating a move in these areas will likely lead to a destructive war, the best approach is to adopt a matching strategy (tit–for–tat) and signal this ahead of time.

The above analysis led StratCorp's to identify several hardware and software development programs for leveraging the company's existing technologies to sustain its competitive advantage. It included developing computer systems for massive multiuser access to the information tanks on its mainframes and augmenting its proprietary telecommunications network. Moreover, StratCorp comprehensively repackaged its products and services, and established an innovative repricing program. In addition, the firm undertook a variety of activities to enhance its reputation. These took time and effort, but they were necessary in light of the main competitor's strength on that asset.

Contrary to management's initial inclination, improving its cost position (a4) was not the most attractive strategy because it would not lead to a sustainable state of asymmetry. Both StratCorp and its competitor could have reduced costs quickly and inexpensively to produce an equally strong customer response. Investments in new locations and building brand awareness were rejected for other reasons. Location was attractive but unimportant in the emerging market where geography was less relevant. Enhancing brand awareness was of only medium importance to customers, and change would be more costly and time-consuming to StratCorp than to its competitor.

As the personal computer did, in fact, come to dominate the market, StratCorp became an attractive supplier of high and low value-added information services to both small and large businesses. Some corporate revenues were cannibalized by implementing this strategy; however, the strategy opened new revenue sources that more than offset the losses, which would eventually have occurred anyway. It developed new assets and strengthened old ones to respond to a changing competitive environment.

CONCLUSION

This analysis, summarized in Figure 16.8, is a simplified version of a complete analysis. The classification method presented would have to be applied to *all* the firm's major competitors, including pairwise comparisons among the rivals themselves.[13] For example, with three competitors, A, B, and C, a total of six pairings must be considered and then averaged. For instance, it may be the case that a given strategic asset is offensive for A in comparison with rival B, but equal or

Figure 16.8
Summary of Basic Steps

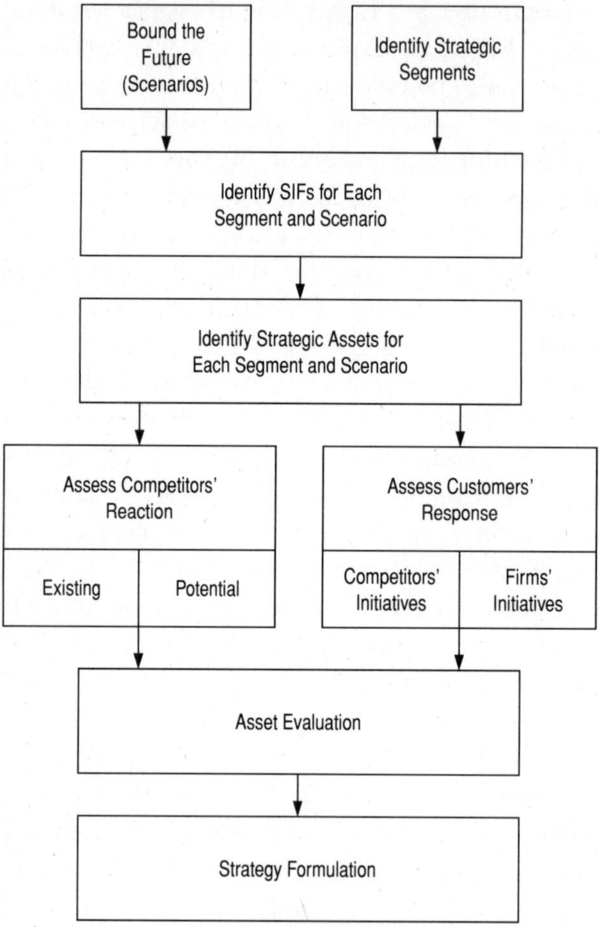

```
┌─────────────────┐        ┌─────────────────┐
│   Bound the     │        │Identify Strategic│
│    Future       │        │    Segments     │
│  (Scenarios)    │        │                 │
└─────────────────┘        └─────────────────┘
         │                          │
         └──────────┬───────────────┘
                    ▼
      ┌──────────────────────────────┐
      │     Identify SIFs for Each   │
      │    Segment and Scenario      │
      └──────────────────────────────┘
                    │
                    ▼
      ┌──────────────────────────────┐
      │  Identify Strategic Assets for│
      │   Each Segment and Scenario  │
      └──────────────────────────────┘
         │                          │
         ▼                          ▼
┌──────────────────┐      ┌──────────────────┐
│Assess Competitors'│      │Assess Customers' │
│    Reaction      │      │    Response      │
├────────┬─────────┤      ├─────────┬────────┤
│Existing│Potential│      │Competitors'│Firms'│
│        │         │      │Initiatives│Initiatives│
└────────┴─────────┘      └─────────┴────────┘
         │                          │
         └──────────┬───────────────┘
                    ▼
      ┌──────────────────────────────┐
      │      Asset Evaluation         │
      └──────────────────────────────┘
                    │
                    ▼
      ┌──────────────────────────────┐
      │     Strategy Formulation      │
      └──────────────────────────────┘
```

defensive in comparison with rival C. Further, it matters how rivals B and C stack up in regard to this asset. Although we did not illustrate the case of three or more rivals, the same process and logic apply.

Organizationally, this process should be undertaken first by senior management and then by the management teams of each division and Strategic Business Unit (SBU). It may require extended analysis by staff or external consultants. Parts of this process were implemented within Royal Dutch/Shell[14] when this firm still had a complex matrix structure organized around functions (e.g., exploration versus refining), regions (Europe versus North America), and business sectors (oil/gas versus chemicals). It is doubtful that the process we propose could succeed without strong support from the top, since it raises fundamental questions about the strategic direction and future design of the firm. In our experience, strong facilitation is needed in the early sessions to keep the process on track, as well as to deal with any intellectual or political challenges. Also, prior research on future trends, competitors, and changes in the marketplace (consumers, channels, new products, etc.) is highly recommended.

Since multiple perspectives are needed, SA analysis is best conducted in small groups. In our experience, management teams need no more than two or three days to apply the process at a qualitative, broad-brush level to their own situation. Especially when managers have done prior work on competitive analysis and understand past SIFs, the process can proceed quickly once sound scenarios have been developed. Flexible facilitation, including techniques that encourage creative, nonlinear thinking, is essential to the successful application of this process in management teams.

Once strategic assets have been selected for each SBU under each scenario, the challenge remains to integrate them in view of multiple SBUs and multiple futures. There is no optimal way to do this realistically, so we offer a heuristic procedure. First, identify any overlap among the selected SA investment programs across SBUs and scenarios. Those SAs that are robust over scenarios are safer to focus on than those that fit just one scenario. Likewise, SAs that are crucial to several SBUs (such as a strong R&D capability) will add complementarity and inimitability at the firm level.

Apart from the overlap of assets, the question of risk attitude must be examined. At least three postures can be identified: hedging, gambling, and staying flexible. Some firms may be able to pursue the robustness route[15] and invest only in those SAs that are necessary under multiple scenarios. Others may prefer, and be able to afford, to bet extensively on one scenario or SBU, thus taking a calculated risk. Or perhaps a middle ground that retains flexibility is possible. In essence, each asset bundle offers a unique risk/return profile that can be assessed only in light of future scenarios, SBU synergies, current asset endowment, competitive forces, and existing organizational constraints. Once these profiles are drawn, the final choice may be relatively easy, either by computing net present values[16] or by performing a formal trade-off analysis.[17] The real challenge is to imagine different SIF scenarios, as well as the corresponding SAs in which to invest as the basis for the firm's strategy.

The assessment of strategic assets is an ongoing process. The firm has to keep its SA evaluation current because environmental changes may have an impact on the assessment of the asset. The desirability of any business strategy may change over time, as industry conditions change, customers' preferences shift, or competitors take new initiatives.

In closing, we emphasize that the goal of performing the SA analysis is to create shareholder value. The process outlined allows managers to assess in a more rigorous way which assets to invest in. Our process explicitly considers whether the SA investments: fit the future scenarios; truly matter in a given strategic segment; are likely to bestow sustainable competitive advantage; and attract customers to buy the firm's products or services. As such, this chapter has sought to integrate various crucial pieces of the overall strategy puzzle.

CHAPTER 17

PUTTING THE LESSON BEFORE THE TEST: USING SIMULATION TO ANALYZE AND DEVELOP COMPETITIVE STRATEGIES

DAVID J. REIBSTEIN
The Wharton School, Department of Marketing

MARK J. CHUSSIL
Advanced Competitive Strategies, Inc., Portland, Oregon

Military strategists have long used simulation to plan campaigns, and airlines have long used simulation to polish pilots' skills. Now managers are using simulation to understand and anticipate the dynamics of their competitive strategies. These simulations range from multimillion-dollar formal computer models to brief, informal war games in which teams of managers and consultants play the parts of rivals and customers. In this chapter, the authors discuss the value and uses of simulation to understand the dynamics of competition in their markets and to explore their competitive-strategy options.

When the astronauts of Apollo 13 were making their perilous voyage home in their damaged capsule, mission control placed an astronaut on the ground into a flight simulator to work out the delicate maneuvers needed to return the mission safely to Earth. The controllers in Houston had to balance and assess many complicated issues and options, and they knew they had only one chance to get it right. They knew there was no substitute for experience, but, as the old saying goes, "experience is a hard teacher because she gives the test first, the lesson afterward." The astronaut in the simulator gave them the experience they needed to make their tough decisions, *before* they risked the lives of those in the real capsule.

Companies are often in a similar situation. They may have only one shot at launching a new product or making another competitive move. They have some sense of how competitors may react to their strategies but often have not worked out the complex "chess game" of competitive interactions. Usually, managers think only one move in advance, if that. But it is the combination of a whole series of moves and countermoves that determines the outcome of the game. They need to be able to think like chess champion Bobby Fischer, who is reputed to have planned *11* moves ahead in a game.

Competitive simulations offer managers a way to gain the experience they need before taking the test. They enable companies to "live through" the competitive consequences of a particular strategy or set of strategic options before committing real money and effort. As competition becomes more complex—with more potential players and smaller windows of advantage—it becomes increasingly important to make sure a strategy works the first time out of the box. As with the Apollo 13 astronauts, when the "oxygen supply" becomes more constrained, missteps are increasingly dangerous.

This chapter explores simulation in the business world: how it works, what options are available, and how they help strategists make decisions. We examine the benefits of strategy simulations, different types of simulations, when managers should use simulation, and how simulations can be structured. We begin with two examples that illustrate real-life uses of simulations, one to assess the impact of a planned strategy, another to block the strategy of an opponent.

$133 MILLION BELOW EXPECTATIONS: ASSESSING A STRATEGY'S LONG-TERM IMPACT

The Shell Oil Company recently was contemplating a major shift in its strategy in the U.S. market. It was considering building many unstaffed service stations requiring self-service operation. These stations could be set up in numerous new locations, significantly expanding the company's presence and providing the customer with easier access (more availability) and 24-hour service.

In the short run, this expanded presence seemed certain to give Shell a great advantage over its rivals. The move was based on an understanding of the market; many consumers want convenience. But one question worried managers: How would the market and competitors react?

Shell, with the help of a strategy consulting firm, Advanced Competitive Strategies (ACS), customized a version of ACS's competitive-strategy simulator, ValueWar™, to realistically simulate customer response in 10 market segments, as well as the cost structures and other factors influencing the moves of competitors. The result of the simulation was that Shell's move would be very successful—unless competitors chose to respond rather than to sit idly by as Shell captured market share at their expense. The managers' conclusion: Probable success for Shell in the short run (it takes time to react); probable failure in the long run (competitors don't like to lose).

Why would the move fail? Because, Shell managers discovered, the only logical reaction for their competitors would be to match Shell's strategy. Shell's short-term gains would quickly vanish as competitors built their own pumps. Consumer demand would not grow (people don't drive more because there are more gas stations), so the same market would be spread more thinly. Meanwhile, the battling suppliers' fixed capital costs would increase because of the new pumps. Bottom line: Costs would rise, revenue would not, and profits would suffer.

The simulation did more than give a general sense of competitive reactions; it attached numbers to the result. By not implementing the strategy, the company would have earned a projected $211 million in one geographic market over five years. Implementing the strategy appeared to offer $315 million in additional profits. But after allowing for the likely competitive reaction, Shell would make only $182 million. In other words, rather than adding $104 million in profits, the strategy would ignite a firestorm that would consume $29 million, and so it would come in $133 million below expectations.

Shell decided to back off on the initiative, although currently it is poised to respond quickly if a competitor launches a "pump war." The simulation was able to take the company to this point five years earlier and $133 million more efficiently than actual experience. Shell gained the experience without the expense of taking the test.

Preventive Medicine: Anticipating Competitors' Moves

In addition to assessing the value of managers' own strategies, companies use simulation to anticipate competitors' strategies. For example, Sterling Health Latina, a Mexico City-based unit now part of SmithKline Beecham PLC, discovered that a major competitor was planning to launch a new over-the-counter painkiller in a Latin American market to challenge Sterling's leading brand. Led by Adrián Cruz, senior vice president for Latin America and the Caribbean, Sterling executives and ACS organized a ValueWar "war college" to anticipate the competitor's moves and to develop a defensive—or offensive— strategy of their own.

A team representing the competitor came up with a devastating advertising concept, focusing on the fact that U.S. doctors prescribe the company's painkiller more than any other. The simulation demonstrated that the campaign would undermine Sterling's position in the market.

Having identified a serious threat, Sterling ran additional simulations, during which the Sterling team came up with an antidote: an advertisement touting that Sterling's drug was the most prescribed in the particular market. The simulation showed that the ad, used preemptively, would keep customers loyal. Sterling rolled out the advertisements before the rival's launch, successfully blocking its new product.

Sterling found out later that the rival had, in fact, planned to use the reference to U.S. doctors in its ads, but scrapped the idea when Sterling's preemptive advertising appeared.

ANALYZING COMPETITIVE STRATEGIES

Managers face a variety of challenges that they can address with simulation or other approaches. Many of these strategic decisions involve big stakes, hard-to-reverse investments, and significant uncertainty, such as:

- How should we position our new product?
- Is this dip in our profits just a little turbulence or the start of a nosedive?
- Should we cut price before our competitors do, or should we react to their moves?
- Will a costly customer-loyalty program help? What if our competitors respond? Will we have gained anything?
- Our smallest competitor was acquired by a big, aggressive firm. What should we expect?
- We hear that a competitor is about to double its advertising. What should we do?
- How do I get my management team to think like strategists?

In answering these questions, managers want to assess how a given strategy might play out in the future. They use approaches ranging from simple trend-line extrapolation and brainstorming to more complex scenario planning, war games, and computer simulations. These options differ in how they leverage the information and creativity of the organization, as shown in Figure 17.1 and Table 17.1.

Each of these approaches has its strengths and weaknesses. *Trend lines* are easy to understand, require little data about the future, and (by definition) reflect real experience. However, extrapolations of the past can inject serious analytic errors if used thoughtlessly, and they encourage neither creative nor critical thinking (e.g., *why* will sales continue to grow at their historical rate?). Simple extrapolations can lead to unrealistic inferences, especially if changes occur (or might occur) in the forces underlying past trends.

Most types of *forecasting,* such as regression and econometric modeling, take into account multiple factors that might influence the dependent measure (future sales, size of market, interest rates, and so on). Forecasting offers a major improvement over trend lines because it may use multiple (and possibly causal) factors. In addition, it allows

Figure 17.1
Assessing the Future

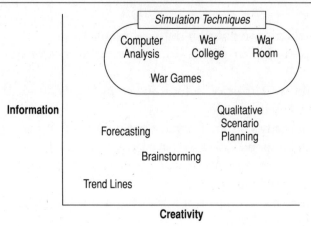

Adapted from "Competitive-Strategy Simulation: Using Virtual Competition to Get the Jump on Real Competitors," *Advanced Competitive Strategies White Paper,* 1995.

the user to test the impact of changes in the factors. A drawback, shared with trend lines, is that forecasting methods rely on the premise that historical relationships will hold true in the future. Also, if managers apply forecasting to come up with a single precise number—that is, if they try to determine what the future *will be*—then they can blind themselves to other possible futures.

Brainstorming can identify important issues and spark creative ideas but offers little opportunity to include detailed data in the process. It is best used to identify the ideas managers need to test. *Qualitative scenario planning* is a more formal and rigorous form of brainstorming. Scenario planning focuses on imagining possible futures and on fleshing them out in sufficient detail to think through what it would feel like to live (and compete) in those futures. It provides internally consistent, high-level views of possible scenarios for the future. However, it does not always capture the impact of competitive dynamics (the give and take of competitive decisions) within these scenarios.

Strategy simulations can incorporate insights from brainstorming, forecasting, scenario planning, and other nonsimulation approaches. The resulting model of competition, a simulation of competitive

Table 17.1
Nonsimulation Techniques for Analyzing Strategy

Technology	Example	Major Strengths	Major Weaknesses
Trend lines	Historical analysis	Fast, easy, inexpensive	Assumes the future will look like the past
Brainstorming	Idea-generation teams	Fast, easy, creative	Qualitative, judgmental
Forecasting	Econometric models	Quantitative, rigorous	Usually ignores competitive reaction or multiple scenarios for the future
Qualitative scenario planning	Scenario planning	Creative, can be quantified, proactive	Hard to evaluate desirability of scenarios or test competitive dynamics.

Adapted from "Competitive-Strategy Simulation: Using Virtual Competition to Get the Jump on Real Competitors," *Advanced Competitive Strategies White Paper,* 1995.

reality, can then test specific strategy options, including competitors' counterstrategies.

What Is a Simulation? From the Game Room to the Boardroom

What is a simulation? Formally defined, a simulation is a facsimile of reality. It is intended to display what would transpire if the assumed conditions were to occur in reality.

Simulation has long been used in many areas of life. The U.S. military simulates warfare to evaluate strategies before committing soldiers' lives. Lawyers simulate the courtroom with mock trials so they can test how their prosecution or defense might work and to find weaknesses in the opposition's case. Pilots practice in flight simulators.

Simulations in video games such as SimCity, Doom, Mortal Kombat, and Joe Montana Football allow participants to engage in activities that would not be possible (or advisable) in real life. They allow them to risk virtual life and limb, to build a city in a short period of time, and to test different strategies for offense or defense in the major leagues.

Among the most popular simulations on the market today are flight simulators. Why are they so popular? Partly because they allow amateurs to satisfy their instinctive craving to fly under the Golden Gate Bridge or to buzz the occupants of the Sears Tower. Perhaps more important, flight simulators give players—and real pilots—the chance to experience something far too risky to do in real life.

Try this experiment: Ask a group of people with access to computers whether they have ever used a flight simulator; many or most will answer yes. Then ask them if they've ever crashed in the simulator. Those who have flown will also have crashed (it turns out there's not much room between the bridge and the bay). Then be thankful that real pilots learn how to deal with dangerous situations in their simulators, rather than waiting for a real emergency to pop up at 30,000 real feet.

Managers are often criticized for being too conservative, for being unwilling to do something risky. Well, perhaps they're being rational: They don't want to risk adopting a strategy that only *might* fly high. In these days of accountability, they can't afford the possibility that they could actually "crash and burn." Simulation offers them an opportunity they don't get in real life: to try different approaches and to crash a few times as they build the skills to reach loftier heights.

Competitive-Strategy Simulation

The use of simulation has only recently become feasible and acceptable in business. As shown by the examples that opened this chapter, simulations offer a powerful way to think through and develop strategies. Competitive-strategy simulations include war games and war colleges, test marketing, and computer analysis. A variety of consulting companies have developed competitive simulations for commercial applications, including Advanced Competitive Strategies, Arthur D.

Little, Booz Allen, Mantis, Mercer, and Monitor. Simulation has been a growing business for all of these firms.

Managers can use simulations for rehearsing a specific strategy or for exploring multiple strategy options. *Rehearsal simulations* move through progressive quarters of competition with teams representing the home company and various competitors. Most competitive-strategy war games fall into this category. Conceptually, managers in such war games are like actors who hold dress rehearsals to simulate the actual production. The rehearsal simulation provides two key benefits: It raises familiarity and confidence with the situation, and it uncovers snags or bugs before going public.

War games use teams of managers to represent the home company and its rivals, and sometimes a control team represents other players such as regulators. A market team or a computer model assesses demand, sales, and market shares; financial feedback comes from anything from a simple spreadsheet to a rigorous model, showing teams the profit-and-loss impact of their moves. The teams use this feedback to determine their moves for their next decision (usually the next quarter). The game usually lasts for several days.

Because rehearsal simulations can take a day or more to simulate competition for a 5- or 10-year horizon, managers have little opportunity to roll back the clock and try different approaches. However, the detail possible in these rehearsals helps managers uncover pitfalls and unexpected problems in implementing a strategy. Rehearsal-style simulations can help managers make go/no-go decisions, and they can help them assess how a market might evolve, thereby allowing them to develop plans to support or defend desired outcomes. Rehearsal simulations are less useful for testing multiple strategies or for experimenting to formulate a new strategy.

Test marketing is another form of rehearsal simulation. Consumer package-goods businesses consider it de rigueur to conduct test markets prior to actually introducing a product to a larger market. In general, running a test market means selecting a limited geography, introducing the product there, and observing the results. If results are sufficiently attractive, managers roll out the product to the broader market.

Marketers sometimes run test markets simultaneously in several communities to avoid being led astray by the idiosyncrasies of a particular market. This practice improves the quality of decisions and sometimes saves time, but it also raises costs. In another test-market variant, marketers test multiple ways to go to market. This version gives marketers more than just a go/no-go decision; instead, they can choose from a set of alternatives.[1]

Exploration simulations, in contrast to rehearsals, can be run repeatedly using different strategies or different starting assumptions. They enable managers to test diverse strategies and to develop new strategies. These simulations generally use a computer model to calculate the results of moves managers nominate. First, managers select an existing model or build a new one; next, they gather data and assumptions to put into the model; finally, they use the simulation to test a wide range of competitive strategies and dynamics over time. The key is the interplay between managers and the model: They use their insights and creativity to think of strategies, then use the simulator to do the (generally complex) math, then revise their strategies based on the model's feedback; and they go through that process as often as desired.

As discussed by Green and Krieger in Chapter 15, managers can use conjoint analysis to experiment with different product attributes in the face of competitive reactions, and so it is a form of exploration simulation. The conjoint simulation leads to an optimal set of product characteristics, given likely responses by rivals. It doesn't take much of a conceptual leap to extend simulations beyond product attributes to include other competitive factors such as competitive position, market characteristics, loyalty and switching costs, and cost structures. Some competitive-strategy simulators do exactly that in a "war college."

The war college is a new technique that's proving very useful in conducting exploration simulations. In a sense, the war college is to exploration simulations what the war game is to rehearsal simulations.

As in a war game, the war college splits managers into teams to role-play competitors. Unlike the war game, however, the teams in a war college do not come up with a single strategy for a given quarter. Instead, each team actively and repeatedly experiments with a variety of different strategy approaches. These strategy alternatives, as well as those of rival teams, are entered into a computer model, so the teams receive direct feedback on the results of their strategies. Where war games focus on rehearsing strategy, the war college (as its name suggests) is concerned with learning, as each team experiments with various strategies to develop better alternatives. Managers in the Shell and Sterling cases discussed earlier used war colleges in their simulations.

Another new technique that extends the usefulness of the simulation over time is the "war room." The war room, in this instance, is more than a room where companies store data and gather for debates as they track their rivals' moves. It is, instead, a place where teams of managers in the organization can come together periodically (or as needed, as real-time events demand) to engage in an ongoing simulation. Each simulation builds on the insights gained from the previous one and on regularly updated data. Thus, managers' knowledge about competitors and the impact of various strategies accumulates over time. In addition, the war room becomes a learning environment for managers new to the business.

Some companies further extend the robustness of their simulations by engaging in simultaneous simulations. They create two or more parallel universes of competitors. Groups of managers in Universe A play the company and the different competitors. A separate group of managers creates companies in a parallel Universe B. Often, the home team in Universe A finds a good strategy, only to discover that the home team in Universe B has created a strategy that leads to significantly different results. These experiences help managers look beyond existing paradigms and demonstrate that there are no absolutes in strategy or simulation. There are bad options, there are good options, and then there are even better ones.

WHEN TO SIMULATE?

When should managers consider simulation rather than simpler alternatives? In general, it makes sense to simulate when the decision maker must choose among numerous alternatives and when it is not clear which alternative would yield the best results.[2] Simulations that can rapidly test many dissimilar alternatives can help a great deal. This is particularly true when the situation is very complex, when the problem is unfamiliar, or when the cost of errors is very high. We will now examine each of these situations.

Complex Situations

It may seem counterintuitive that simulation could help in complex situations; after all, if the situation is so complex, doesn't that make it especially hard to simulate? Yes, especially if the decision makers must invent a new model for their situation. (Well-established simulators have encountered many complex situations and are often able to analyze them thoroughly.) Nonetheless, simulation can help in complex situations by clarifying the problem and rigorously analyzing each component. In addition, personal intuition, experience, and assessment are *least* reliable precisely when the situation is complex, which means that the alternative to simulation is less attractive.

Unfamiliar Problems

Simulation can also add value when the problem is unfamiliar to the decision maker or when the relationship among different components of the problem is unfamiliar. For example, imagine competing in one of the many markets in which the rules of the game are changing due to shifting technology or regulations. Such industries—including telecommunications, electric utilities, consumer retailing, and pharmaceuticals—are among the heaviest users of competitive-strategy simulation.

High Cost of Errors

Finally, simulation can add value when the cost of errors is very high. When making high-stakes decisions, managers understandably retreat to very conservative behavior and avoid anything other than the tried and (presumably) true. Of course, this "safe" position may forgo tremendous benefits of more aggressive action, and it may be inappropriate if the environment has changed. "Conservative" action may even be the riskiest course. Is it safe for managers to wait and see or to act timidly when a competitor starts to gobble their market share? Perhaps, but not often. On the other hand, the urge to act decisively should *not* mean flailing away in panic or with ill-considered knee-jerk reactions. The ability to test a variety of options in a simulated environment, where the cost of making mistakes is very low, is obviously quite an advantage.

How to Simulate?

Some simulations operate entirely through human interactions. Others run unattended on computers. And some combine humans and computers. Human simulations take relatively little time to set up and run (although they can still require extensive research). They may also capture the chemistry of the interactions among managers. However, purely human simulations cannot work well with quantitative data.

Simple computer simulations running on autopilot may oversimplify a competitive situation, while complex computer models are often time-consuming and expensive to create (especially if they're developed from scratch). However, the computer has an important advantage over human simulations: rapid what-if testing. Once information is in place, it becomes relatively easy to change one or more parameters. With this capability, managers can examine hundreds (or hundreds of thousands) of different possible scenarios played through years of competitive interactions. They can also back up to a given point and reevaluate a single decision. Because the computer can keep track of more data points and individual assumptions than a human could master, managers can ensure that assumptions are made explicit and are tested thoroughly.

Some simulations combine human and computer capabilities to reflect judgment and creativity as well as computational power. The Shell and Sterling cases described both worked in this fashion. They had teams of managers develop candidate competitive strategies that then served as input to a computer simulator, which handled the number crunching. Data for "calibrating" the simulator came from company data, surveys, and managers' judgment. This method—combining people and computers—works well for competitive strategy because strategy issues inherently involve both numbers and human behavior.

Benefits of Competitive Simulation

In deciding whether to use simulation, managers should consider the following benefits:

- *It provides time to prepare and act.* Simulations accelerate time, compressing years into minutes or days. With simulation, managers can see what the future might look like before it happens, and with that foresight, they can prepare for it.
- *It doesn't hurt.* Managers can get the gain without the pain. Because it is all simulated, the large losses of profits and market share are not real. (Of course, managers can't take the large gains to the bank either.)
- *It promotes creativity.* With risks removed, managers can experiment with how they might behave in unsafe, unpleasant, unexpected, or unconventional situations. As with flight simulators, they can make the daring move that would be too risky in real life, but that just might work out.
- *It's experimental.* Simulating competitive strategies makes it possible to test options in light of the strategies that competitors might adopt. Thus, although simulation doesn't tell managers what *will* happen, it helps them explore what *may* happen. In addition, by learning what has to happen to make a strategy work, they can develop contingency plans so that they can switch gears quickly, decisively, and only if really necessary. Simulation helps managers discover whether a strategy dominates (that is, whether it is always the best option) across a range of possible competitive scenarios.
- *It's experiential.* The process of creating and implementing simulations gives managers hands-on insights. Beyond the results, the process of creating and implementing a simulation is an education for the managers.
- *It helps managers to think like their competitors.* War games, war colleges, and other simulations don't just ask managers to anticipate their competitors' moves; they ask managers to *be* their competitors. These simulations give the managers and the company fresh insights into how their rivals think.

- *It's rigorous.* The simulation process captures and codifies the accumulated wisdom of the organization (which is usually more than managers think at first). It also forces managers to make their assumptions explicit. The simulation creates and applies a repository of competitive and market information.
- *It's unifying.* Managers develop a common view of their competitive situation and a shared language for strategy.
- *It's private.* Unlike test marketing, simulation occurs in the privacy of the company, allowing managers to test new ideas without tipping their hand.
- *It's useful.* Simulation facilitates generating and selecting a competitive strategy.

Changing Perspectives of Managers

One of the most powerful benefits of simulation is that it changes in a variety of ways the perspectives of the managers who participate. Going through a simulation changes how managers view their companies and their rivals. Simulation has the power to shock and enlighten managers in ways that detailed discussions or drawn-out analyses cannot match. Simulation gives managers a visceral feel for the impact of their strategies as well as the impact of their competitors' strategies. Here are some examples drawn from our experience:

Visiting the Ghost of Profits Future. Managers often become fixated on an approach to strategy. They usually don't change their approach until the company is in trouble. Like Scrooge in *A Christmas Carol,* managers can experience the future via simulation and still wake up in time to change their actions the next day. For example, the vice president of a company convened a war college to find a way to resurrect dismal profits. The firm's product had become a commodity business, managers insisted, and declining prices meant that the company would lose a projected $500 million over the next five years. Could the company differentiate itself to break this cycle? Impossible, said the managers, but they had a better solution. They would cut costs. The new strategy was put into the simulator immediately. The projected result: They would lose *only* $450 million. The model demonstrated that managers' habit of competing on price would lead them to pass the cost savings along to customers. This outcome was a shock, and convinced the managers that they had to do something more creative. By the end of the war college, they had filled a wall with ideas for differentiating their products. They implemented their ideas in real life—and begin making money.

Clearing the rose-colored glasses. Managers tend to paint too optimistic a view of the future; simulation can provide a much-needed reality check. For example, during simulations, teams of managers usually develop strategies for their company and its competitors. We often ask each team independently what share of the market it expects to capture. Summing the independent estimates usually produces a total well over 100 percent, which means that some or all of these rivals will be disappointed. Independent estimates may imply 123 percent share, but simulation forces internal consistency. By capturing all the known information in one coherent system, the simulation helps impose discipline on the strategy-development process.

Thinking long term. In another war college, a group of managers representing a rival company had developed a specific strategy. For six consecutive quarters, the managers watched their profits fall. For six quarters, this team resisted pressure to shift its strategy, but finally it gave up and changed course. The next quarter, profits went up, and they continued to rise for the rest of the five-year horizon. The managers were understandably pleased; they had turned the situation around. But what would have happened if they had held the course with their original strategy? In a few minutes, they found that profits would have turned around at the same time, and by the end of the simulation they would have made *twice as much* as they would have under their revised strategy. Simulation can help indicate when it might be judicious to hold the course, despite short-term profit pressures, and it can test whether a "fix" will really make matters better. Otherwise, how do managers know when they are sliding down a long-term decline or just about to turn around?

Obstacles to Simulations

With all these benefits, why don't more companies use simulation? We think there are several reasons:

- They are hard to build, as we know from our own and others' experience. For example, they should take into account processes such as customer purchase decisions and competitive dynamics, but those processes are hard to model.
- Because they are hard to build, they can be expensive to build. Computing power—that is, computer hardware and MIPS—is now almost free, but developing a realistic simulation can cost a great deal of time and money.
- They require new paradigms and analyses. For example, financial extrapolations and accounting rules don't work well in strategy simulation (or in real life), but they're hard to dislodge from conventional wisdom.
- Relatively few strategists know that they're possible (and that they work), so there's little explicit demand.
- Software developers usually aren't experts at competitive strategy, and competitive strategists usually aren't experts at software development. Or perhaps both developers and strategists see better job opportunities elsewhere.
- Some managers distrust the answers that they think computers will give them (which is not how most simulations work).
- Managers don't have enough hard data, and they worry about GIGO (garbage in, garbage out).

Cost issues are probably not to blame. As the Shell case demonstrates, simulations can produce enormous returns on investment because they affect competitive strategy, the highest-leverage decisions the firm has to make.

Maybe the fear of GIGO scares managers away from simulation. They apparently worry that using judgment and estimates instead of hard data will compromise the simulation's analysis. Unfortunately, there is no such thing as *data* about the future; the future hasn't happened yet. By the time data are available, it's too late. Meanwhile, managers must make decisions. They need to get comfortable with using the best information available—which may be judgments and estimates—to make the best decisions possible when the decisions need to be made.[3]

Whatever the cause(s) of the slow spread of simulations, the effect is that many more managers have experienced flight simulators than strategy simulations, even though they are far more likely to be engaged in shaping strategy than in flying planes. We expect that situation to change.

HOW TO DEVELOP AND APPLY A SIMULATION

What are the stages companies need to go through to develop an effective simulation? There are many ways to develop simulations, but the following is a typical approach that highlights some of the key stages of building and running a simulation. It is drawn from a simulation developed by ACS for a major airline.

Specify the Domain

The first step is to determine the specific market to model. Managers should simulate strategy on a market-by-market basis, since the set of competitors and customer demand and sensitivities differ significantly by market. In the airline simulation, the model was constructed on a route-by-route basis. A highly contested market was selected: the Detroit-Chicago route. The competitors were American Airlines, Midway Airlines, Northwest Airlines, Southwest Airlines, and United Airlines. The airline simulation modeled business and leisure travel separately because business and leisure travelers differ greatly on needs, prices paid, price sensitivity, and more.

Identify the Relevant Data

The next step is to determine what factors the simulation would have to use to model the positions and capabilities for each of the competitors. These data may include competitors' market shares, variable and fixed costs, capacities, the costs of and trigger levels for adding more capacity, time requirements for adding capacity, current price levels, market-perceived quality levels, awareness levels, and other factors. Table 17.2, showing some of the factors in ValueWar simulations, illustrates the wide range of possible factors that simulations can use.

Managers may want to use certain factors for which they lack data. They must decide whether to use only those factors for which they can obtain "objective" data, or whether to use the best information they *can* get so as to use the factors they consider relevant.

In the airline case, much of the data were readily available from public information. For example, airlines publish their flight schedules along with the type of aircraft, thereby providing the data for the capacity levels. Other data were reported to the FAA, and thus were easily retrievable. (Obviously, many other industries would not have the public-domain data that exist in the airline industry.) For other inputs, it was necessary to turn to data that had been gathered by one of the competitors based on customer surveys, such as market-perceived quality levels and awareness.

When they cannot obtain objective data, managers should use the best assumptions available to them. Relying on assumptions is often a sticky issue since almost everyone feels uncomfortable using "soft" data (see the previous discussion of GIGO). The alternative, however, is to ignore the factors for which assumptions would be required. Doing so doesn't take advantage of what knowledge of the market managers do have, however imperfect. More important, it implicitly, indiscriminately, and almost certainly incorrectly attributes capabilities to all competitors.

For example, suppose the firm does not know what level of awareness each of its competitors enjoys, and so it deletes the awareness factor from its simulation model. That deletion is equivalent to assuming that each competitor has 100 percent awareness and that none is limited by awareness in its access to the market. That assumption would do no harm if 100 percent awareness were as good as any other assumption, but omitting this factor from the model simply because the answer is not precisely known hides an important underlying assumption. Hidden assumptions make it hard for others to question (and learn from) the data and to modify the input as better information becomes available.

Table 17.2
Representative Factors Used in Simulations

Category	Representative Factors
Competitive Position (for each competitor)	• Perceived attribute levels (market-perceived quality (MPQ) ratings) • Price and perceived price • Market share, sales
Customer Preferences (by segment)	• Attribute (MPQ purchase criteria) importances/utilities/partworths • Evolution in customer preferences • Sensitivity to price and MPQ
Market Characteristics (by segment)	• Growth rate, cycles, and seasonality • Demand elasticities • Time to perceive competitors' moves
Competitors' Access to Customers (for each competitor, by segment)	• Awareness and consideration • Distribution • Suitability of product or service
Loyalty and Switching Costs (by segment)	• Customer loyalty • Disloyalty • Trends over time
Cost Structures (for each competitor)	• Fixed, variable, and capacity costs • Cost changes over time (e.g., productivity) • Costs of changing perceived attribute levels (levels of MPQ)
Competitors' Capabilities (for each competitor)	• Rates of and limits to change in perceived attribute levels (levels of MPQ) and price • Frequency of changes • Time to perceive competitors' moves and to act

Factors included in ValueWar simulations. Adapted from "Competitive-Strategy Simulation: Using Virtual Competition to Get the Jump on Real Competitors," *Advanced Competitive Strategies White Paper,* 1995.

Making uncertain factors explicit highlights candidates for sensitivity analysis. Perhaps managers "guesstimated" an airline's awareness at 80 percent. Would their strategy decision change if awareness levels were 50 percent or 95 percent? The numerical results will almost certainly change as the assumption about awareness changes, but managers need to know whether different levels of awareness should cause them to *act* differently.

Specify the Market-Response Model

Perhaps the most difficult task in developing a competitive-strategy simulation is specifying the market-response model. The model should capture the underlying drivers of the market; it should describe how the market demand (and the corresponding market shares) will be allocated to the different participants in the market.

One common way to determine the market-response model is to estimate it based on historical information. With a long enough time series, it would be possible to estimate the necessary response parameters. Note, though, that this approach makes a critical assumption: that the drivers of the past will also drive the future. Model builders can, of course, override this assumption with their judgment of what they believe will be the trends in the future.

The historical-data approach makes another, more subtle assumption, perhaps best described by example. Imagine that competitors in a market have always moved their prices in lockstep. What, then, would be the effect on demand of charging a price higher or lower than competitors in the future? If that event has not occurred in the past, then the future effect cannot be revealed by statistical analysis of historical data. Managers *must* make an assumption.

Finally, historical data may confound effects of multiple factors that, at least in the past, happened to move together. For example, if businesses in a market tended to cut prices in times of slow growth, then the historical effect of price changes would be entangled with the effect of slow growth. What would happen if a business cut its price during fast growth? It may be hard to tell.

A better approach may be to use the market-response model as a starting point for sensitivity analysis. That is, managers could estimate the historical market-response model, modified perhaps for the reasons just described and then simulate what would happen if, for example, the market were (or were to become) more or less price-sensitive. If a simulation leads managers to the same conclusions regardless of the level of price sensitivity, then they have learned something: They don't have to worry about price sensitivity. (In decision-analysis terms, they have found that the value of information regarding price sensitivity is zero.) On the other hand, if they find out that their best future actions change depending on price sensitivity, then they have learned something else: They had better do more rigorous analysis of price sensitivity, or at least monitor it so they can change course if it shifts.

Unfortunately, often, the historical information required to estimate the market-response model is not available. Under those circumstances, managers must gather the underlying data in other ways. Managers can use survey data (perhaps from conjoint analysis) or develop thoughtful judgments. In either case, it is prudent to contrast information with historical patterns and to run sensitivity analyses like those described.

In the airline simulation of the Chicago–Detroit market, managers felt there were two major segments and it would be best to specify two separate market-response functions. These two segments were the business and pleasure travelers, with the former caring more about quality[4] than price and the latter the reverse. It was also necessary to specify the costs associated with increasing or decreasing the market's perceived quality (for each component of quality; i.e., in-flight service, scheduling, on-time service, and so on) of each airline.

Input the Data

Once they've identified the relevant factors, defined the model, and gathered data on the factors (including estimates and assumptions), managers must get the data into the model. The first step includes the physical process of typing, scanning, or electronically transferring the numbers into the simulator. In addition, the user might have to adapt numbers to specific scales, translate financial data from different countries into a single currency, or adjust data to remove the effects of inflation.

But entering the numbers is not enough. Managers should perform validity and "sanity" checks on the data before running large-scale, high-visibility, big-impact simulations.

Validity checks ensure that the data are "legal." For example, sales and market-share data should never be negative; market-growth rates should not lead to absurdly large or small markets; financial data should add up (e.g., sales minus costs should equal profits).

Sanity checks require some judgment. They might involve running several simple simulations to see if the results make sense. Although this step might seem to incur a cost, it actually confers a benefit: It shows how the data work as a system, which often surfaces inconsistencies in data and assumptions that managers need to resolve. What if pursuing the current strategic course seems certain to lead to ruin? Such results should lead managers to question their inputs; then, if the inputs prove solid, managers have received their first insights from the simulation.

In the airline case, managers easily ensured the validity of the data, then proceeded to sanity checks. Given how customers perceived the airlines, did the market-share projections make sense? The people working on the simulation made sure that if the airlines made no changes in their prices or their market-perceived quality, then market share should shift over time toward the airlines offering high value and away from the airlines offering poor value.

Decide How to Handle Uncertainty

Managers will rarely feel completely confident that their input data are correct. (It's probably safe to say that if they are sure they are right, they are probably wrong. Nothing personal; it's just that most people tend to overestimate the accuracy of their data or estimates.) Simulation models can deal with uncertainty in two ways.

A *deterministic* model handles uncertainty as changes in the input data. Managers can run the model with different values for the input data, but each time they run a particular combination of inputs they will always get the same output. To observe the effects of uncertainty, they can change the input data, run the model, observe the results, and then repeat with different values for the input data. They may have to run each iteration by hand, or may be able to set up batch runs with appropriate ranges of input data.

A *stochastic* model directly associates uncertainty with the input data, selecting different values (within specific ranges) each time managers run a simulation. Thus, the simulation's output will be different in each run, and managers run the model repeatedly—perhaps many thousands of times—to see not only the most likely outcome but also the variation in outcomes.

Whatever the structure of the model they build or buy, managers can and generally should run multiple simulations to analyze the effects of uncertainty on their decisions. For example, in building the market response model, they could specify different relationships between competitors' marketing actions and the sales they generate. Then managers would run the simulation repeatedly, randomly sampling from the distribution of the parameter estimates (i.e., the distribution of relationships between actions and sales). The output of this process, called Monte Carlo simulation, would show the likelihood of the alternative results that could occur.

Given that the quality of the input data varies significantly, this approach offers one way to account for the differing levels of certainty in the data. For example, it can reveal whether an attractive strategy has a significant possibility of turning into a disaster under some circumstances.

The downside of developing a Monte Carlo simulation is that it increases the data and analytic demands. Managers must determine not only a best guess for each factor in the model but also specify a level of uncertainty around those best-guess numbers.[5]

Develop Strategy Options to Test

Once the model and data are in place, the next challenge is to develop the specific strategies to test in the simulation. The most common way to develop those strategies is to set up teams of managers who role-play the home company and its rivals. These managers develop initial strategies and then revise them based on feedback from the market during the simulation. They can derive strategies from competitors' actual planned strategies (as in the Sterling case) or from the planned strategies of the home company. The starting strategies can be an input to the process or they can be developed during a war game or war college program.

The objective of developing these strategy options is not to find "bad" strategies for competitors. It's easy to beat paper-tiger competitors by forcing them to follow a stupid or complacent strategy, but that's neither realistic nor helpful. True competitors often compete vigorously and tenaciously. It's important to explore the strategies that competitors actually may adopt in real life.

Similarly, the objective is not to find "good" strategies if those strategies cannot be implemented. What good is it to discover that unprecedented improvements in perceived quality, coupled with simultaneous and similarly unprecedented reductions in costs, produce better profits? Managers should try to develop realistic strategies, including "stretch" goals, but be wary of overly optimistic strategies that won't come true and that will discredit the strategy-development process.

It helps to populate the firm's home team *and* the competitors' teams with comparably skilled managers. (In other words, don't stack the deck by putting the best people on the home team.) Give all the teams incentives to try to win, and make sure the teams define *winning* as the real-life competitors do. The best results come from competing against worthy adversaries, not against pushovers.

Analyze Simulated Outcomes and Track Real Outcomes

Quantitative simulations can display outcomes not only at the end of the time horizon but also at points along the way. Managers can use this capability to further analyze their strategies and to develop implementation road maps. Further analysis can address concerns such as short-term sacrifices for long-term gains, the robustness of strategy options, and contingency planning. Implementation road maps can help with internal management, performance monitoring, and decisions to switch strategies.

Analysis: Short- versus Long-Term.   All else being equal, managers will obviously prefer a strategy with a higher expected outcome than one with a lower expected outcome. But all else is not always equal. For example, what if the strategy with the highest market share after five years involves seriously negative profits for the next two years? Such a pill might be too bitter to swallow, especially if the future benefit looks too distant or uncertain. Check intermediate-term results and examine multiple measures of success before adopting a strategy.

Analysis: Robustness.   The sensitivity-analysis techniques described can also provide valuable insights before selecting a strategy. Perhaps the most likely outcome of a strategy looks attractive, but it carries volatility or downside risk that the firm cannot tolerate. Managers might prefer a strategy whose most likely outcome is slightly worse if it is less vulnerable to external events or to internal hiccups. A strategy that's relatively insensitive to other forces—that is, a strategy whose outcome is primarily under the firm's control—is called a *robust* strategy.[6]

Analysis: Contingency Planning.   Managers may discover during a war college or sensitivity analysis that their strategy works beautifully if (for example) a key competitor focuses its product line on new features, but that the strategy flops if the competitor emphasizes image and service. If managers reach such a conclusion, they should explore different strategy options in case the competitor takes the latter tack. They can then develop a contingency plan: Do strategy A if the competitor works on new features, and do strategy B if it promotes image and service. Contingency plans need to link tightly to decisions to switch strategies, as described next.

Implementation: Internal Management.   The simulation should show not just outcomes (market share, profits, and so on), but also what has to happen to make those outcomes come true. Many of those have-to-happen events refer to actions that the business takes. For example, perhaps the simulated strategy involves improving market-perceived quality on reliability from a rating (by the market) of 55 to 80 within two years. That part of the strategy then should translate into action for those parts of the organization that affect reliability and market perceptions of reliability. The results also have implications for performance monitoring, as described next.

Implementation: Performance Monitoring. In the preceding example, the strategy calls for a significant improvement in the firm's market ratings on reliability. For the quickest feedback on whether the strategy is on course, the firm can periodically measure market perceptions of its reliability. If managers find that market ratings lag behind their expectations, then they know they must take remedial action or adjust their strategy and expectations. Monitoring leading indicators in this way provides two big advantages over just monitoring outcomes (market share, profits, and so on): First, managers see whether they are on track early, rather than late; second, they see *what* is going right or wrong, which helps to direct corrective measures.

Implementation: Decisions to Switch Strategies. Suppose managers have developed contingency plans to identify under which circumstances they need to shift strategies. They need to know if those circumstances come to pass. They should set up market- and competitive-intelligence operations to monitor those key events.[7] After all, it doesn't do any good to have contingency plans if no one tracks the triggers that would demand a change in course.

Ongoing Strategy and the War Room

As discussed, companies are starting to couple competitive-strategy war rooms with strategy simulators. Managers use the war room as a place to collect up-to-date market and competitive intelligence that they then analyze through simulation. This approach helps them react quickly and appropriately to changes in their competitive environment. Equally important, it helps them know when *not* to react.

Managers naturally want to *do* something when confronted with a change or event—they feel that they're not "managing" if they don't act—and so the ability to quickly analyze the incoming intelligence can prevent wasting effort or even making a situation worse.

Managers should consider the possibility of creating such a war room as they design or select a strategy simulator. Using or building a simulation that's narrowly focused on a specific strategy decision may be efficient, but it may be unable to handle an unexpected event. For example, imagine that a company has built a custom simulation to test the impact of pricing moves against its current competitors and their existing product lines. That simulation won't help much if a competitor exits the market, if a new competitor enters the market, or if a competitor changes its product line, or even if the firm itself scores a new-product breakthrough.

A simulation better suited to the war room would have the flexibility to adapt rapidly to internal and external events. Look for (or build in) a broad, structured framework designed to accept new data easily and to analyze what-if questions quickly.

Teaching Strategy, and the Selected Strategy, to the Organization

The impact of the simulation doesn't end with the close of the formal simulation. Managers can apply the simulation in two more ways after they have completed their strategy development.

First, they can make it part of the firm's management-development programs. Simulation works well at enlivening the educational process and at engaging people from a variety of functional backgrounds. Further, it helps them better understand how their market behaves.

Second, managers can use the simulation to communicate their selected strategy and to convince people that it's the right way to go. Letting colleagues go through a similar (or abbreviated) war college can be more persuasive than simply announcing that everyone must immediately and fondly embrace the new strategy. For example, one company embedded simulation results into an interactive presentation that individual managers could run to test their strategy skills against the selected strategy.

CONCLUSION: DECISIONS, NOT PRECISION

Simulation can play a powerful role in developing and analyzing competitive-strategy options. Using simulation, managers have developed successful strategies, anticipated events that later occurred in real life, and learned about strategy, and their own businesses, at each step of the simulation process.

On the other hand, sometimes managers spin their wheels in a well-intentioned quest for precision. Such efforts are inevitably doomed to fail for two reasons. One: Too many things can go off in wildly different directions (which is why exploring different scenarios is vital). Two: There is no such thing as *data* about the future that managers can use as input to their simulations.

The key to using simulation effectively is to focus on exploring options to find the best strategy for the possible multiple futures and the various competitive dynamics that affect them. The result is *better competitive-strategy decisions*. And, as a side benefit, the simulation process creates better strategists.

After participating in a war college, Barbara McCloskey, manager of Leisure Strategy at British Airways, summarized the major benefits of simulation: "There's huge value in being able to test your assumptions and your customers' perceptions of you before you put your strategy into place. You see things you normally don't even recognize because they are so pervasive. Plus, the work you go through in building the model is like a master's-level course in your own business."

Simulations can take some of the "luck" out of formulating a successful strategy. They give managers something that athletes have always had: the opportunity to practice before facing actual competitors. As Arnold Palmer is reputed to have said: "The more I practice, the luckier I get."

NOTES

Introduction

1. Paul R. LaMonica, "Battling Batteries: Why Duracell and Eveready Are Neck and Neck in Market Share, But Not in Brand Value," *Financial World,* (January 30, 1996), p. 58.

2. Richard Gibson, "Battle over New Battery May Keep Going and Going," *Wall Street Journal,* (January 2, 1996), p. 11.

3. Carolee Aker, "Testing, Testing . . . New On-Battery Testers," *The Christian Science Monitor,* (June 13, 1996), p. 8.

4. Richard A. D'Aveni, *Hypercompetition: Managing The Dynamics of Strategic Maneuvering,* (New York: Free Press, 1994).

5. Michael S. Malone, "Can Silicon Graphics Hold Off Hewlett-Packard?" *Fortune,* (October 30, 1995), pp. 119–126.

6. Judy Ward, "I Won't Dance. Don't Ask Me. Don't Talk Mass Market to Silicon Graphics. Don't Even Think about It," *Financial World,* (March 11, 1996), p. 42.

7. "Life on the Visual Edge," *Computer Business Review,* (April 1, 1996).

8. Barbara Robertson, "Battling for Dominance: Silicon Graphics Finds Competition in 3D Graphics Workstation Market," *Computer Graphics World,* (March 1996), p. 52.

9. "Life on the Visual Edge," *Computer Business Review,* (April 1, 1996).

10. *Ibid.*

11. Ward, "I Won't Dance."

12. Randy Myers, "The Art of Partnering," *CFO,* (December 1995), pp. 26–34.

13. Thomas Nagel, "Managing Price Competition," *Marketing Management,* 2(1), pp. 37–38.

14. C. K. Prahalad and Gary Hamel, "The Core Competence of the Corporation," *Harvard Business Review,* (May–June 1990), pp. 79–91.

Chapter 1

1. For a representative application, see Rajendra K. Srivastava, Robert P. Leone, and Allan Shocker, "Market Structure Analysis: Hierarchical Clustering of Products Based on Substitution-in-Use," *Journal of Marketing,* (Summer 1981), pp. 38–48.

2. Some switching also reflects complementarity due to variety-seeking behavior. A model to distinguish substitute versus complementary brands is found in James M. Lattin and Leigh McAlister, "Using a Variety Seeking Model to Identify Substitute and Complementary Relationships among Competing Products," *Journal of Marketing Research,* 22 (August 1985), pp. 330–339.

3. Adapted from Douglas Tigert and Stephen Arnold, "Nordstrom: How Good Are They?" Babson College Retailing Research Reports, (September 1990); as shown in Michael Levy and Barton A. Weitz, *Retailing Management,* (Burr Ridge, IL: Irwin, 1992), p. 205.

4. John McGee and Howard Thomas, "Strategic Groups: Theory, Research, and Taxonomy," *Strategic Management Journal,* 7 (1986), pp. 141–160.

5. Richard P. Rumelt ("Towards a Strategic Theory of the Firm," in Robert B. Lamb, ed., *Competitive Strategic Management,* New York: Prentice-Hall, 1984) expands the notion of mobility barriers to any mechanism that isolates firms and limits equalization of profit rates or differential expansion.

6. J. A. Bleeke, "Strategic Choices for Newly Opened Markets," *Harvard Business Review,* (September–October 1990).

7. Michael E. Porter, *Competitive Strategy,* (New York: Free Press, 1980).

8. George S. Yip, *Barriers to Entry: A Corporate Strategy Perspective,* (Lexington, MA: Lexington Books, 1982).

9. Other aspects of the shakeout phenomena are discussed in David A. Aaker and George S. Day, "The Perils of High-Growth Markets," *Strategic Management Journal,* 7 (September–October 1986), pp. 409–422.

10. John Hagel III, "Spider versus Spider," *The McKinsey Quarterly*, 1 (1996), pp. 4–18.

11. Richard P. Rumelt, "How Much Does Industry Matter?" *Strategic Management Journal*, 12 (March 1991), pp. 167–185.

Chapter 2

1. David S. Landes, "Time Runs Out on the Swiss," *Across the Board*, (January 1984), pp. 46–55.

2. Michael E. Porter, *Competitive Strategy*, (New York: Free Press, 1980).

3. Richard P. Rumelt, Dan Schendel, and David Teece, "Strategic Management and Economics," *Strategic Management Journal*, 12 (Winter 1991), pp. 5–30; and Berger Wernerfelt, "A Resource-Based Theory of the Firm," *Strategic Management Journal*, 5 (March 1984), pp. 171–180.

4. Michael E. Porter, *Competitive Advantage*, (New York: Free Press, 1985).

5. Lynn Philips, Dae Chang, and Robert Buzzell, "Product Quality, Cost Position, and Business Performance: A Test of Some Key Hypotheses, *Journal of Marketing*, 42 (1983), pp. 26–43.

6. Michael Treacy and Fred Wiersema, *The Discipline of Market Leaders*, (Reading, MA: Addison-Wesley, 1995).

7. Dorothy Leonard-Barton, "Core Capabilities and Core Rigidities: A Paradox in Managing New Product Development," *Strategic Management Journal*, 13 (Summer 1992), pp. 111–125.

8. George Stalk, Philip Evans, and Lawrence Shulman, "Competing on Capabilities: The New Rules of Corporate Strategy," *Harvard Business Review*, (March–April 1992), pp. 57–69.

9. C. K. Prahalad and Gary Hamel, "The Core Competence of the Corporation," *Harvard Business Review*, (May–June 1990), pp. 79–91.

10. Robert D. Buzzell and Bradley T. Gale, *The PIMS Principles*, (New York: The Free Press, 1987).

11. Frederick Reicheld and W. Earl Sasser, "Zero Defections: Quality Comes to Services," *Harvard Business Review*, (September–October 1990), pp. 301–307.

12. George S. Day and Prakash Nedungadi, "Managerial Representations of Competitive Positions," *Journal of Marketing*, (April 1994).

13. George S. Day and Robin Wensley, "Assessing Advantage: A Framework for Diagnosing Competitive Superiority," *Journal of Marketing*, (April 1988), pp. 1–20.

14. Pankaj Ghemawat, "Sustainable Advantage," *Harvard Business Review*, 64 (September–October 1986), pp. 55–58.

15. Richard P. Rumelt, "Towards a Strategic Theory of the Firm," in Robert Lamb, ed., *Competitive Strategic Management,* (Englewood Cliffs, NJ: Prentice-Hall, 1984), pp. 556–570.

16. Jeffrey Williams, "How Sustainable Is Your Competitive Advantage?" *California Management Review,* (1992), pp. 1–23.

17. *Ibid.*

18. Robert M. Grant, "The Resource-Based Theory of Competitive Advantage: Implications for Strategy Formulation," *California Management Review,* (Spring 1991), pp. 114–135.

19. Jay B. Barney, "Organization Culture: Can It Be a Source of Sustained Competitive Advantage?" *Academy of Management Review,* 11 (1986), pp. 656–665.

20. By definition, these resources are also rare, since anything possessed by many present or prospective competitors has already been neutralized and cannot yield superior rents. We don't consider rarity a separate condition, as does Jay B. Barney in "Firm Resources and Sustained Competitive Advantage," *Journal of Management,* 17 (March 1991), pp. 99–120.

21. This is called absorptive capacity. See Wesley M. Cohen and Daniel A. Leventhal, "Absorptive Capacity: A New Perspective on Learning and Innovation," *Administrative Science Quarterly,* 35 (1990), pp. 128–152.

22. I. Dierkx and K. Cool, "Asset Stock Accumulation and Sustainability of Competitive Advantage," *Management Science,* 35 (November 1989), pp. 1504–1511.

23. Pankaj Ghemawat, *Commitment,* (New York: Free Press, 1991).

24. Gwen Ortmeyer, John A. Quelch, and Walter Salmon, "Restoring Credibility to Retail Pricing," *Sloan Management Review,* 33 (Fall 1991), pp. 55–66.

25. Gary Hamel and C. K. Prahalad, "Strategic Intent," *Harvard Business Review,* 67 (May–June 1989), pp. 63–76.

Chapter 3

1. Michael E. Porter, *Competitive Strategy,* (New York: Free Press, 1980).

2. See Margaret A. Peteraf, "The Cornerstones of Competitive Advantage: A Resource-Based View," *Strategic Management Journal,* 14 (1993), pp. 179–191.

3. See Dennis Yao, "Beyond the Reach of the Invisible Hand: Impediments to Economic Activity, Market Failures, and Profitability," *Strategic Management Journal,* 9 (1988), pp. 39–70.

4. Richard H. K. Vietor, *Strategic Management in the Regulatory Environment,* (Englewood Cliffs, NJ: Prentice-Hall, 1989), p. 25.

5. See Elizabeth E. Bailey and William J. Baumol, "Deregulation and the Theory of Contestable Markets," *Yale Journal on Regulation,* 1 (1984), pp. 111–137.

6. David Vogel, "The Study of Business and Politics," *California Management Review,* 38 (Spring 1996), pp. 146–165.

7. Robert W. Hahn and Thomas D. Hopkins, "Regulation/Deregulation: Looking Backward, Looking Forward," *The American Enterprise,* 3 (July–August 1992), pp. 70–79.

8. David P. Baron, *Business and Its Environment,* (Englewood Cliffs, NJ: Prentice-Hall, 1996).

9. For another view of these relationships, see Sharon M. Oster, *Modern Competitive Analysis,* (Oxford: Oxford University Press, 1990).

10. As described in J. Kingdon, "The Policy Window and Joining the Streams," in *Agendas, Alternatives and Public Policies,* (1984), pp. 173–179.

11. See James Q. Wilson, *The Politics of Regulation,* (New York: Basic Books, 1980).

12. See Elizabeth E. Bailey and Jeffrey R. Williams, "Sources of Economic Rent in the Deregulated Airline Industry," *Journal of Law and Economics,* 31 (1988), pp. 173–202.

13. See David P. Baron, *Business and Its Environment,* (Englewood Cliffs, NJ: Prentice-Hall, 1996).

14. See Yiorgos Mylonadis, "Peripheries Matter: Negotiated Ordering and Core Change in an Industrial Firm, 1983–1987," Wharton working paper, (March 1995).

Chapter 4

1. Eric K. Clemons, "Creating the Forgetting Organization: Using the Scenario Process to Facilitate Learning During Rapid Technology-Driven Environmental Change," working paper, The Wharton School, (November 1996).

2. Signet has spun off its credit card business, which is now operated by Capital One, a separate company.

3. We have previously termed such markets *newly contestable* (cf., E. K. Clemons, D. C. Croson, and B. W. Weber, "Market Dominance as a Precursor of Firms' Underperformance: Emerging Technologies and the Advantages of New Entrants," in press, *Journal of Management Information Systems,* Fall 1996). We have changed our terminology to avoid confusion with the well-defined regulatory concept of contestable markets (cf., W. Baumol, J. C. Panzar, and R. D. Willig, *Contestable Markets and the Theory of Industry Structure,* New York: Harcourt Brace Jovanovich, 1982).

4. See, for example, W. Baumol, J. C. Panzar, and R. D. Willig, *Contestable Markets and the Theory of Industry Structure,* (New York: Harcourt Brace Jovanovich, 1982), or the more recent W. J. Baumol and J. G. Sidak, *Toward Competition in Local Telephony,* (Cambridge, MA: MIT Press, 1994).

5. Surprisingly, those Bell Holding companies that might be considered most vulnerable—Pacific Telesis and Nynex—have recently been purchased by other Bell companies. It remains to be seen whether these were effective moves toward surviving shakeouts, or inappropriate actions in which the purchasers acquired both "love 'ems" and "kill yous," and the regulatory restrictions that accompany incumbency.

6. The London Stock Exchange has recently (October 1995) made changes to its rule 4.18, and now allows its member firms to quote better prices to off-exchange customers than it does to those trading on the Exchange. However, its off-exchange competitors have a rational economic basis for deciding how to price their dealing services; if exchange member firms cut their dealing prices without using data or predictive models to determine how to price their services for different customers, they are likely to sustain serious losses.

7. Eric K. Clemons, "Using Scenario Analysis to Manage the Strategic Risks of Business Reengineering," *Sloan Management Review,* (Summer 1995), pp. 61–71.

Chapter 5

1. For a formal exposition of game theory, see the following works: Roger Myerson, *Game Theory: Analysis of Conflict,* (Cambridge, MA: Harvard University Press, 1991); Jean Tirole, *The Theory of Industrial Organization,* (Cambridge, MA: The MIT Press, 1990); Ken Binmore, *Fun and Games: A Text on Game Theory,* (Lexington, MA: D.C. Heath and Company, 1992).

2. In normal form games, the convention is to list the payoffs to the row player (Firm B) first, followed by the payoffs to the column player (Firm A).

3. Named for the mathematician John Nash who developed the concept in 1951, and was awarded the 1994 Nobel prize for this idea.

4. The seven military classics are: *Ssu-ma Fa, The Art of War, Wu-tzu, Wei Liao-tzu, Six Secret Teachings, Three Strategies,* and *Questions and Answers.*

5. "Manzi Quits at IBM and His Many Critics Are Not at All Surprised," *Wall Street Journal,* (October 12, 1995), p. A1.

6. "Why AT&T Takeover of NCR Hasn't Been a Real Bell Ringer," *Wall Street Journal,* (September 19, 1995), p. A1.

7. "Caesar's Chairman Gluck Quits, Citing Diminished Role after ITT Breakup," *Wall Street Journal,* (June 29, 1995), p. B13.

8. This example is loosely based on Harvard Business School case 9-190-102.

9. Experimental evidence suggests that correctly structured incentive schemes can induce individuals to consider the long-term consequences of their decisions. See Andrew Schotter and Keith Weigelt, "Behavioral Consequences of Corporate Incentives and Long-Term Bonuses: An Experimental Study," *Management Science,* 38 (September 1992), pp. 1280–1298.

10. In fact, given the current climate where firms pay consultants large sums of money to build game theoretic models for them, Meyer may be wrong to state that corporations have not noticed the competitive disadvantages of failing to provide more game theoretic training to their managers.

11. Of course, the absolute level would affect payoffs.

12. While space does not permit a detailed explanation of incomplete information game models, interested readers should consult Keith Weigelt and Ian MacMillan, "An Interactive Strategic Analysis Framework," *Strategic Management Journal,* 9 (1988), pp. 27–40.

13. Teck Hua Ho, "Finite Automata Play Repeated Prisoner's Dilemma with Information Processing Costs," *Journal of Economic Dynamics and Control,* 20 (1996), pp. 173–207.

14. In fact, these are Nash strategies.

15. Because if entry occurs, the incumbent must start a price war and realize a payoff of 0 versus 2.

16. "Frito-Lay Devours Snack-Food Business," *Wall Street Journal,* (October 27, 1995), p. B1.

17. For a review, see Keith Weigelt and Colin Camerer, "Reputation and Corporate Strategy: A Review of Recent Theory and Applications," *Strategic Management Journal,* 9 (1988), pp. 443–454.

18. J. B. Van Huyck, R. B. Battalio, and R. Beil, "Strategic Uncertainty, Equilibrium Selection Principles, and Coordination Failure in Average Opinion Games," *Quarterly Journal of Economics,* 106 (1990), pp. 885–910; J. B. Van Huyck, R. B. Battalio, and R. Beil, "Tacit Coordination Games, Strategic Uncertainty, and Coordination Failure," *American Economic Review,* 80 (1991), pp. 234–248; Mark Knez and Colin Camerer, "Expectational Assets in the Laboratory," *Strategic Management Journal,* 15 (Winter 1994), pp. 101–119.

19. See *The Economist,* (December 16, 1995), p. 61.

Chapter 6

1. See Richard D. McKelvey and Thomas R. Palfrey, "An Experimental Study of the Centipede Game," *Econometrica,* 4 (July 1992), pp. 803–836.

Notes

2. *Ibid.*

3. Steven L. Lippman and John Mamer, "Preemptive Innovation," *Journal of Economic Theory,* 61 (1993), pp. 104–119.

4. For a detailed exposition, see Lippman and Mamer.

5. See Richard Thaler, *Quasi-Rational Economics,* (New York: The Russell-Sage Foundation, 1991).

6. Itzhak Gilboa and David Schmeidler, "Case-Based Decision Theory," *Quarterly Journal of Economics,* (November 1995), pp. 605–630; Caroline Zsambok, "Implications of a Recognition Decision Model for Consumer Behavior," in L. McAlister and M. Rothschild (ed.), *Advances in Consumer Research,* 20 (1993), pp. 239–244.

7. *Los Angeles Times,* (March 14, 1986).

8. Robert J. Meyer, Rajeev Tyagi, and John Walsh, "Heuristic Reasoning in Intuitive Pricing Under Uncertainty," working paper, Department of Marketing, Wharton School, University of Pennsylvania (1996).

9. Russell Winer, "A Reference-Price Model of Brand Choice for Frequently Purchased Branded Products," *Journal of Consumer Research,* 13 (September 1986), pp. 250–256.

10. Daniel Kahneman, "Reference Points, Anchors, Norms, and Mixed Feelings," *Organizational Behavior and Human Decision Processes,* 51 (1992), pp. 296–312; Amos Tversky and Itamar Simonson, "Context-Dependent Preferences," *Management Science,* 39, 10 (1993), pp. 1179–1189.

11. Robert J. Meyer and Joao Assuncao, "The Optimality of Consumer Stockpiling Strategies," *Marketing Science,* 9 (Winter 1990), pp. 18–41.

12. Amos Tversky and Daniel Kahneman, "Loss Aversion in Riskless Choice: A Reference Dependent Model," *Quarterly Journal of Economics,* 106 (November 1991), pp. 1039–1062.

13. Meyer, Tyagi, and Walsh, 1996.

14. John C. Cripps and Robert J. Meyer, "Heuristics and Biases in Timing the Replacement of Durable Products," *Journal of Consumer Research,* 21 (September 1994).

15. Daniel Kahneman and Amos Tversky, "On the Psychology of Prediction," *Psychological Review,* 80 (1973), pp. 237–251.

16. Kahneman and Tversky, 1973.

17. B. Hayes-Roth and F. Hayes-Roth, "A Cognitive Model of Planning," *Cognitive Science,* 3 (1979), pp. 275–310.

18. Colin F. Camerer, Eric J. Johnson, Talia Rymon, and Sankar Sen, "Cognition and Framing in Sequential Bargaining for Gains and Losses," in K. Binmore, A. Karman, and P. Tani (eds.), *Proceedings of the International Conference on Game Theory,* (Cambridge, MA: The MIT Press, 1993).

19. James C. Cox and Ronald L. Oaxaca, "Laboratory Experiments with a Finite-Horizon Job Search Model," *Journal of Risk and Uncertainty,* 2 (September 1989), pp. 301–329; Andrew Schotter and Yale M. Braunstein, "Economic Search: An Experimental Study," *Economic Inquiry,* 19 (January 1981), pp. 1–25.

20. Meyer and Assuncao, (1990); Cripps and Meyer, (1994).

21. From Robert Meyer, Steven Lippman, and Daryl Banks, "Imperfect Evolution in Game of Preemptive Innovation," working paper, Department of Marketing, The Wharton School, University of Pennsylvania, (1996).

22. See, for example, Douglas D. Davis and Charles A. Holt, *Experimental Economics,* (Princeton, NJ: Princeton University Press, 1993); Vernon L. Smith, "Economics in the Laboratory," *Journal of Economic Perspectives,* 8 (Winter 1994), pp. 113–131.

23. Jorgen W. Weibull, *Evolutionary Game Theory,* (Cambridge, MA: The MIT Press, 1995); Drew Frudenberg and David Levine, *Theory of Learning in Games,* manuscript, Department of Economics, University of California, Los Angeles, 1996.

24. We might add, however, that the mechanism does not appear to converge to *full* co-operation. An extension of this simulation to 5,000 periods suggested a price asymptote of about .8—suggesting that while firms may display a cooperative evolution, occasional price variation will persist.

Chapter 7

1. Paul J. H. Schoemaker and J. Edward Russo, "Frames of Mind," working paper, Johnson Graduate School of Management, Cornell University, May 1993.

2. M. E. Porter, *Competitive Strategy,* (New York, Free Press, 1980).

3. Al Ries and Jack Trout, *Marketing Warfare,* (New York: McGraw-Hill, 1986), and David J. Rogers, *Waging Business Warfare,* (New York: Scribner, 1987).

4. Robert Keidel, *Game Plans: Sport Strategies for Business,* (New York: E. P. Dutton, 1985).

5. M. E. Porter and A. M. Spence, "The Capacity Expansion Process in a Growing Oligopoly: The Case of Corn Wet Milling," in J. J. McCall (ed.), *The Economics of Information and Uncertainty,* (Chicago: University of Chicago Press, 1982), pp. 259–309.

6. K. Weigelt and C. Camerer, "Reputation and Corporate Strategy: A Review of 30 Recent Theory and Applications," *Strategic Management Journal,* 9 (1988), pp. 453–454.

7. A. Jacquemin, *The New Industrial Organizations: Market Forces and Strategic Behavior,* (Cambridge, MA: MIT Press, 1987). See also Edward J. Zajac and Max H. Bazerman, *Academy of Management Review,* 16, 1 (1991), pp. 37–56.

8. Lee Ross, David Green, and Pamela House, "The 'False Consensus Effect': An Egocentric Bias in Social Perception and Attribution Processes," *Journal of Experimental Social Psychology,* 13 (1977), pp. 279–301.

9. Stephen J. Hoch, "Perceived Consensus and Predictive Accuracy: The Pros and Cons of Projection." *Journal of Personality and Social Psychology,* 53, 2 (1987), pp. 221–234.

10. Zajac and Bazerman, 1991.

11. Brian Mullen, John F. Dovidio, Craig Johnson, and Carolyn Copper, "In-group Out-group Differences in Social Projection," *Journal of Experimental Social Psychology,* 28, 5 (1992), pp. 422–440.

12. Stephen J. Hoch, "Perceived Consensus and Predictive Accuracy: The Pros and Cons of Projection," *Journal of Personality and Social Psychology,* 53, 2 (1987), pp. 221–234.

13. Deborah J. Mitchell, Marjorie E. Adams, and Eric J. Johnson, "Your Preferences May Be Hazardous to Your Health: How False Consensus and Overconfidence Influence Judgments of Product Success," Wharton School Marketing Department, 1995.

14. B. Fischhoff, P. Slovic, and S. Lichtenstein, "Knowing with Certainty: The Appropriateness of Extreme Confidence," *Journal of Experimental Psychology: Human Perception and Performance,* 3 (1977), pp. 552–564.

15. J. Edward Russo and Paul J. H. Schoemaker, "Managing Overconfidence," *Sloan Management Review,* 33, 2 (Winter 1992).

16. Colin Camerer and Martin Weber, "Recent Developments in Modeling Preferences: Uncertainty and Ambiguity," *Journal of Risk and Uncertainty,* (in press).

17. Hillel J. Einhorn and Robin M. Hogarth, "Ambiguity and Uncertainty in Probablistic Inference," *Annual Review of Psychology,* 92 (1985), pp. 433–461.

18. Risto Karajalainen and Colin Camerer, "Ambiguity in Non-Cooperative Games," *Theory and Decision,* (in press).

19. Timothy W. McGuire, Sara Kiesler, and Jane Siegel, "Group and Computer-Mediated Discussion Effects in Risk Decision Making," *Journal of Personality & Social Psychology,* 52, 5 (1987), pp. 917–930.

20. Glen Whyte, "Escalating Commitment in Individual and Group Decision Making: A Prospect Theory Approach?" *Organizational Behavior and Human Decision Processes,* 54 (1993), pp. 430–455.

21. Michael T. Hannan and John Freeman, *Organizational Ecology,* (Cambridge, MA: Harvard University Press, 1989).

22. J. R. Anderson, *The Adaptive Character of Thought,* (Hillsdale: Lawrence Erlbaum Associates, 1990).

23. For an example of where adaptive learning does and does not produce predicted equilibria, see A. E. Roth and Ido Erev, "Learning in Extensive-Form Games:

Experimental Data and Simple Dynamic Models in the Intermediate Term," working paper, Department of Economics, University of Pittsburgh, 1993.

24. Jessica Goodfellow and Charles R. Plott, "An Experimental Examination of the Simultaneous Determination of Input Prices and Output Prices," *Southern Economics Journal,* 56 (1990), pp. 969–983.

25. DeLong, Shleifer, Summer, and Waldmann, 1990.

26. Paul J. H. Schoemaker and J. Edward Russo, "Frames of Mind," working paper, Johnson Graduate School of Management, Cornell University, May 1993.

27. John W. Payne, James R. Bettman, and Eric J. Johnson, *The Adaptive Decision Maker,* (Cambridge: Cambridge University Press, 1993).

28. Herbert A. Simon, "Rationality in Psychology and Economics," *Journal of Business,* 59 (1986), p. 209.

29. As Richard Thaler argues in "The Psychology and Economics Conference Handbook," *Journal of Business,* 59 (1986), S279, it is as if each frame believes in at least one of the following two false statements:

1. All behavior is rational.
2. Rational models are useless.

Moreover, as DeLong, Shleifer, Summers, and Waldmann argue, a limited time horizon combined with risk aversion, present real limits on the ability of a rational agent to eliminate noise through arbitrage. J. DeLong, A. Shleifer, L. Summers, and R. J. Waldman, "Noise Trader Risk in Financial Markets," *Journal of Political Economy,* 98 (1990), pp. 703–738.

30. Richard Zeckhauser, "Comments: Behavioral versus Rational Economics: What You See Is What You Conquer," *Journal of Business,* 59 (1986), p. 439.

31. Cited in M. R. Hogan and M. Redev, "Introduction: Perspectives from Economics & Psychology," *Journal of Business,* 59 (1986), p. 185.

32. The modern origins of these ideas are due to Ehrlich and Raven (1964).

33. William H. Durham, *Coevolution: Genes Culture and Human Diversity,* (Stanford, CA: Stanford University Press, 1991).

34. Brent Schlender, "Software Hardball," *Fortune,* (September 30, 1996), pp. 114–116.

35. J. Huber, J. Payne, and C. Puto, "Adding Asymmetrically Dominated Alternatives: Violations of Regularity and the Similarity Hypothesis," *Journal of Consumer Research,* 9 (1982), pp. 90–98.

36. Charles D. Darwin, *On the Origin of Species,* (Cambridge, MA: Harvard University Press, 1959/1964), p. 102.

Chapter 8

1. Some classics in this theory are James G. March and Herbert A. Simon, *Organizations,* (New York: Wiley, 1958); Richard M. Cyert and James G. March, *A Behavioral Theory of the Firm,* (Englewood Cliffs, NJ: Prentice-Hall, 1963); Graham T. Allison, *Essence of Decision: Explaining the Cuban Missile Crisis,* (Boston, MA: Little, Brown & Co., 1971); Richard R. Nelson and Sidney Winter, *An Evolutionary Theory of Economic Change,* (Cambridge, MA: Harvard University Press, 1982); and James G. March, *Decision and Organizations,* (New York: Basil Blackwell, 1988).

2. One of the crucial steps in using game theory is specifying the game. Game theory can become an academic exercise if the game is not specified in some descriptively accurate manner. In this regard, behavioral theory of the firm can facilitate by pointing out the crucial variables that must be considered in an environment of poor information.

3. The emphasis of *Aviation Daily* on information release is illustrated by the fact that 45 percent of the sample competitive moves from two years' data, as part of the pilot test, was formally announced by corporate executives at the level of senior VPs or above. One executive from United Airlines noted that, *Aviation Daily* is "the bible of the airline industry. Nothing of significance escapes them." Another officer from Pan Am noted that "*Aviation Daily* is most accurate and very comprehensive." Similar comments were made by many airline executives and experts interviewed.

4. To assure the strategic significance of price actions, this study included only those with change magnitude greater than 10 percent.

5. Certainly a set of similar competitive moves may be motivated by a common industry change rather than by one another. To a great extent, a keyword search method excluded this possibility, but to ensure that no such competitive moves remained in the sample, the keyword search method was supplemented by a thorough reexamination of the entire database. This additional analysis identified two cases that might have met the conditions described. These two cases were removed from the sample. Thus the sample includes only action/response pairs identified by the major daily publication devoted exclusively to the industry.

6. These types of competitive moves include almost all the most important competitive methods identified by Michael E. Levine in his comprehensive review of airline competition since deregulation. (Michael E. Levine, "Airline Competition in Deregulated Markets: Theory, Firm Strategy, and Public Policy," *Yale Journal on Regulation,* 4 (1987), pp. 393–494.) Competition in computerized reservation systems seems to be the only noticeable omission in the current study.

7. The survey had a response rate of 42 percent. Respondents were asked to rate each of the 13 competitive moves in terms of their external visibility and logistical complexity. Multiple dimensions were used to obtain the score on each dimension. Cronbach alpha scores indicate interitem reliability to be high.

8. For classic examples of such studies, see Barry M. Staw and J. Ross, "Behavior in Escalation Situations: Antecedents, Prototypes, and Solutions," *Research in Organizational Behavior,* 9 (1987), pp. 39–78; and Pankaj Ghemawat, *Commitment: The Dynamic of Strategy,* (New York: Wiley, 1991). Escalation theory actually predicts that under the new threat of competitor response, an initiator of a highly committed move will in all likelihood be heavily influenced by a "breakdown or pathology in the pattern of decision making," and will escalate its commitment to the course of action. Indeed, if the responder is not careful, it could also be caught up in this loop of action and response, and both attacker and defender could end up in an "escalation war" to the detriment of both. For example, Martin Shubik ("The Dollar Action Game: A Paradox in Noncooperative Behavior and Escalation," *Journal of Conflict Resolution,* 15 (1971), pp. 109–111) performed an experimental auction where the highest bidder won a dollar prize, but the loser had to pay the amount bid. The participants continued to bid in order to avoid net loss and come out ahead. In real life, such compulsive counteraction could spiral into a never-ending war.

9. The weight for each of these items to create the index was calculated in the following manner: Performance data on each of the items for the sample 32 airlines were obtained for the eight years from 1979 to 1986. This yielded 256 observations (32 airlines multiplied by eight years of observations) on each of the four variables. We then performed a factor analysis on the four performance variables. A one-factor solution was selected based on the SCREE test and the traditional eigen value cutoff criterion of 1.0. This factor accounted for 57.2 percent of the variance in the performance data and had an eigen value of 2.29. The relative factor loadings for each of the four performance measures were then used as the weightage for each measure in the final performance index. The factor loadings were as follows: 0.67 for revenues per revenue-passenger-mile, 0.94 for operating profit per revenue-passenger-mile, 0.76 for profit margin, and 0.61 for S&P stock rating.

10. An airline was deemed to have been affected by an action if it had flights into and from the airports that were targets of a given competitive action.

Chapter 9

1. T. F. Bresnahan, "Competition and Collusion in the American Automobile Industry: The 1955 Price War," *Journal of Industrial Economics,* 35 (June 1987), pp. 457–482.

2. A. Roy, D. M. Hanssens, and J. S. Raju, "Competitive Pricing by a Price Leader," *Management Science,* 40, 7 (1994), pp. 809–823.

3. F. Gasmi, J. J. Laffont, and Q. H. Vuong, "Econometric Analysis of Collusive Behavior in a Soft Drink Market," working paper, University of Southern California, Los Angeles, 1988.

4. F. Gasmi, J. J. Laffont, and Q. H. Vuong, "A Structural Approach to Empirical Analysis of Collusive Behavior," *European Economic Review,* 34 (1990), pp. 513–523.

Notes

5. D. M. Hanssens, "Market Response, Competitive Behavior, and Time Series Analysis," *Journal of Marketing Research,* 17 (November 1980), pp. 470–485.

6. V. Kadiyali, "Pricing, Advertising, and Product Mix: Entry and Accommodation Strategy in the U.S. Photographic Film Industry," working paper, Department of Economics, Northwestern University, 1992.

7. V. Kadiyali, N. J. Vilcassim, and P. K. Chintagunta, "Empirical Analysis of Competitive Product Line Pricing Decisions: Lead, Follow, or Move Together?" working paper, S. C. Johnson Graduate School of Management, Cornell University, 1994.

8. G. Iwata, "Measurement of Conjectural Variations in Oligopoly," *Econometrica,* 42 (March 1974), pp. 947–966.

9. F. M. Scherer, *Industrial Market Structure and Economic Performance,* (Chicago: Rand McNally Publishing Co., 1980).

10. *Ibid.*

11. *Ibid.*

12. P. E. Green, *Analyzing Multivariate Data,* (Hinsdale, IL: The Dryden Press, 1978); G. S. Day, A. D. Shocker, and R. K. Srivastava, "Customer-Oriented Approaches to Identifying Product Markets," *Journal of Marketing,* 43 (Fall 1979), pp. 8–19.

13. C. W. J. Granger, "Investigating Causal Relations by Econometric Models and Cross-Spectral Methods," *Econometrica,* 37 (1969), pp. 424–438.

14. In more technical terms, leadership is assumed to exist if an apparently unexplainable part of the strategic action of the follower is correlated with the corresponding action of the leaders from an earlier period. In the context of time series analysis, it suggests that there exists a correlation between the random shocks in each firm's series of strategic actions.

15. A. Roy and J. S. Raju, "Statistical Tests for Price Leadership," working paper, University of California, Riverside, 1994.

16. These include D. R. Cox, "Further Results on Tests of Separate Families of Hypotheses," *Journal of the Royal Statistical Society,* Series B 24 (1962), pp. 406–424; J. A. Hausman, "Specification Tests in Econometrics," *Econometrica,* 46 (1978), pp. 1251–1272; H. White, "Maximum Likelihood Estimation of Misspecified Models," *Econometrica,* 50 (1982), pp. 1–25. Recent studies have used Vuong's nonnested model tests. Vuong derives likelihood ratio tests for comparing nested, overlapping, and nonnested models. Vuong's method, unlike the other methods described, does not assume either of the models being compared to be the true model. This makes the Vuong test flexible and especially suitable when demand and cost equations are kept simple so as to enable estimation. (Q. H. Vuong, "Likelihood Ratio Tests for Model Selection and Non-Nested Hypotheses," *Econometrica,* 57 (1989), pp. 307–333.)

17. If sales in the current period are affected by marketing decisions made in previous time periods, the traditional static definition of conjectural variations will not yield

good results (Roy and Raju, 1994). Some attempts have been made to extend the CV concept to a multiperiod context and to account for intertemporal conjectures that can change from period to period. (M. E. Slade, "Interfirm Rivalry in a Repeated Game: An Empircal Test of Tacit Collusion," *Journal of Industrial Economics,* 35 (June 1987), pp. 499–516.) Such *modified CV coefficients* should be able to capture dynamic demand structures with carryover effects.

Chapter 10

1. Hubert Gatignon and Pradeep Bansal, "Market Entry and Defensive Strategies," in George Day, Barton Weitz, and Robin Wensley (eds.), *The Interface of Marketing and Strategy,* (JAI Press Inc., 1990); Thomas S. Robertson and Hubert Gatignon, "How Innovators Thwart New Entrants into Their Markets," *Planning Review,* 19, 5 (1991), pp. 4–11; Oliver Heil and Thomas S. Robertson, "Toward a Theory of Competitive Market Signaling: A Research Agenda," *Strategic Management Journal,* 12 (1991), pp. 403–418; Douglas Bowman and Hubert Gatignon "Determinants of Competitor Response Time to a New Product Introduction," *Journal of Marketing Research,* 32 (February 1995), pp. 42–53.

2. Frederic M. Scherer outlines three possibilities regarding the direction of reaction of the incumbent firms to the entry. Frederic M. Scherer, *Industrial Market Structure and Economic Performance,* (Boston, MA: Houghton Mifflin Company, 1980), p. 244.

3. Venkatram Ramaswamy, Hubert Gatignon, and David Reibstein, "Competitive Marketing Behavior in Industrial Markets," *Journal of Marketing,* 58 (April 1994), pp. 45–55.

4. Bowman and Gatignon, 1995.

5. Hubert Gatignon, Erin Anderson, and Kristiaan Helsen, "Competitive Reactions to Market Entry: Explaining Interfirm Differences," *Journal of Marketing Research,* 26 (February 1989), pp. 44–55.

6. Hubert Gatignon, Thomas S. Robertson, and Adam Fein, " Incumbent Defense Strategies against Innovative Entry," proceedings of the European Marketing Academy Conference, May 1995, Paris, pp. 329–350.

7. John R. Hauser and Steven M. Shugan, "Defensive Market Strategies," *Marketing Science,* 2, 4 (Fall 1983), pp. 319–360.

8. Ian MacMillan, Mary Lynn McCaffery, and Gilles Van Wijk, "Competitors' Responses to Easily Imitated New Products—Exploring Commercial Banking Product Introductions," *Strategic Management Journal,* 6 (1985), pp. 75–86; Ian MacMillan and Mary Lynn McCaffery, "Strategy for Low-Entry Barriers," *Journal of Business Strategy,* 2, 3 (Spring 1982), pp. 115–119.

9. John B. Frey, "Commentary on 'Marketing Mix Reactions to Entry,' " *Marketing Science,* 7 (Fall 1988), pp. 386–387.

10. George S. Day, *Analysis for Strategic Market Decisions,* (St. Paul, MN: West Publishing Co., 1986).

11. Day, 1986.

12. Robinson, 1988; and Bowman and Gatignon, 1995.

13. Ramaswamy, Gatignon, and Reibstein, 1994.

14. Bowman and Gatignon, 1995.

15. *Ibid.*

16. "Kodak's Rivalry with Fuji Heats Up," *Manufacturing Week,* (April 18, 1988), p. 28.

17. L. W. Phillips, D. R. Chang, and R. D. Buzzell, "Product Quality, Cost Position, and Business Performance: A Test of Some Key Hypotheses," *Journal of Marketing,* 47, 2 (Spring 1983), pp. 26–43.

18. Venkatram Ramaswamy, Hubert Gatignon, and David Reibstein, "Competitive Marketing Behavior in Industrial Markets," *Journal of Marketing,* 58 (April 1994), pp. 45–55.

19. Ken G. Smith, Curtis M. Grimm, Ming-Jer Chen, and Martin J. Gannon, "Predictors of Response Time to Competitive Strategic Actions: Preliminary Theory and Evidence," *Journal of Business Research,* 18 (1989), pp. 245–258.

20. MacMillan, McCaffery, and Van Wijk, 1985.

21. *Ibid.,* p. 77.

22. Bowman and Gatignon, 1995.

23. MacMillan, McCaffery, and Van Wijk, 1985; and Smith *et al.,* 1989.

24. Ming-Jer Chen and Ian C. MacMillan, "Non-Response and Delayed Response to Competitive Moves: The Roles of Competitor Dependence and Action Irreversibility," *Academy of Management Journal,* 35, 3 (1992), pp. 539–570.

Chapter 11

1. Williamson, 1995.

2. R. Kohli, D. Lehmann, and J. Pae, "New Product Forecasting: The Extent and Impact of Incubation Time," paper presented at the JMR conference on Innovation in New Product Development: "Best Practice" in Research, Modeling and Applications, May 1995.

3. Other approaches for generating creative new ideas or new products are described by Y. Wind, *Product Policy: Concepts, Methods, and Strategy,* (Reading, MA: Addison Wesley, 1982); J. L. Adams, *Conceptual Blockbusting: A Guide to Better Ideas,* (San Francisco: West Freeman and Company, 1974); and T. Proctor, *The Essence of Management Creativity,* (London: Prentice-Hall International, 1995).

4. T. L. Saaty, *The Analytic Hierarchy Process,* (New York: McGraw-Hill, 1980); T. L. Saaty, *Multicriteria Decision Making: The Analytic Hierarchy Process,* (Pittsburgh, PA: RWS Publications, 1990); Y. Wind and T. L. Saaty, "Marketing Applications of the Analytic Hierarchy Process," *Management Science,* 26 (1980).

5. Expert Choice, (Pittsburgh, PA: Expert Choice, Inc., 1996).

Chapter 12

1. Bruce H. Clark and David B. Montgomery, "Deterrence, Reputations, and Competitive Cognition," Research Paper No. 1261R, Stanford University, 1994.

2. Oliver P. Heil and Kris Helson, "A Conceptual Framework about the Emergence of Price Wars," working paper, University of Chicago, 1994.

3. Oliver P. Heil and Thomas S. Robertson, "Toward a Theory of Competitive Market Signaling: A Research Agenda," *Strategic Management Journal,* (September/October 1991), pp. 403–418.

4. Jehoshua Eliashberg, Thomas S. Robertson, and Talia Rymon, "Market Signaling and Competitive Bluffing," working paper, The Wharton School, 1992.

5. Stephen Kreider Yoder, "Computer Makers Defend 'Vaporware,'" *Wall Street Journal,* (February 16, 1995); Oliver P. Heil and Arlen Langvardt, "The Interface between Competitive Market Signaling and Antitrust Legislation," *Journal of Marketing,* 58 (July 1994), pp. 81–96.

6. Jehoshua Eliashberg, Thomas S. Robertson, and Talia Rymon, "Market Signaling and Competitive Bluffing," working paper, The Wharton School, 1993.

7. Oliver P. Heil and Barton A. Weitz, "Marketing Signals and Competitive Activity: An Exploratory Study," working paper, The Wharton School, 1985.

8. This study is reported in Jehoshua L. Eliashberg and Thomas S. Robertson, "New Product Preannouncing Behavior: A Market Signaling Study," *Journal of Marketing Research,* 25 (1988), pp. 282–292. The implications for whether to preannounce are adapted from Thomas S. Robertson, "How to Reduce Penetration Cycling Time," *Sloan Management Review,* 35 (Fall 1993), pp. 87–96.

9. Representative papers are by Marian Moore, "Signals and Choices in Competitive Interactions," *Management Science,* 38 (March 1992), pp. 483–500, and Marian Moore and Michael Moore, "Cooperation, Hierarchy and Structure," in *Research on Negotiations in Organizations,* vol. 2, (JAI Press), 1990, pp. 207–217.

10. Oliver P. Heil and Rockney G. Walters, "Explaining Competitive Reactions to New Product Signals: An Empirical Study," *The Journal of New Product Innovation Management,* 10 (1993), pp. 53–65.

11. Robert Axelrod, *The Evolution of Competition,* (New York: Basic Books, 1984).

12. Oliver P. Heil, Donald G. Morrison, and Rockney G. Walters, "A Market Signaling Framework to Explain Competitive Reactions to Price Reduction Signals," working paper, UCLA, 1993.

Chapter 13

1. P. Ghemawat, *Commitment: The Dynamic of Strategy,* (New York: Free Press, 1992).

2. L. Thomas, "Brand Capital and Incumbent Firms' Positions in Evolving Markets," *Review of Economics and Statistics,* 77 (1995), pp. 522–534.

3. *Ibid.,* and L. Thomas, "Brand Capital and Entry Order," *Journal of Economics and Management Strategy,* (1996).

4. J. Sutton, *Sunk Costs and Market Structure,* (Boston: MIT Press, 1980).

5. D. Fudenberg and J. Tirde, "The Fat Cat Effect, the Puppy Dog Ploy, and the Lean and Hungry Look." *American Economic Review, Papers and Proceedings,* 74 (1984), pp. 361–368.

6. M. E. Porter, *Competitive Strategy,* (New York: Free Press, 1980).

Chapter 14

1. FTC Press Release, "FTC Requires Restructuring of Time-Warner/Turner Deal: Settlement Resolves Charges That Deal Would Reduce Cable Industry Competition," (September 12, 1996).

2. Catherine Yang, "Time Warner-Turner Ready for Prime Time," *Business Week,* (July 29, 1996), p. 38.

3. The offense of monopoly . . . has two elements: the possession of monopoly power in the relevant market, and the willful acquisition or maintenance of that power as distinguished from growth or development as a consequence of a superior product, business acumen, or historic accident." *United States v Grinnell Corp.,* 384 US 563, 570-71 (1966).

4. The Federal Trade Commission has recently changed its policy from the frequent and broad use of prior approval restrictions in orders regarding mergers.

5. See Michael E. Porter, *Competitive Advantage: Creating and Sustaining Superior Performance,* (New York: Free Press, 1985), p. 494; and *Competitive Strategy: Techniques for Analyzing Industries and Competitors,* (New York: Free Press, 1980), p. 50.

6. This section is excerpted from D. Yao, "United States Competition Policy: Laws, Institutions, and Experience," unpublished speech given at INDECOPI/World Bank seminar, Lima, Peru, 1994.

7. *United States v Topco Assocs.,* 405 US 596 (1972).

8. The goals of enforcement agencies around the world differ to some extent. For example, the European Union and many other countries have a broader set of goals for competition policy that include some consideration of "industrial policy."

9. The statutes enacted by the U.S. Congress that prohibit these practices are the Sherman Act, the Clayton Act (the U.S. merger regulation statute), and the Federal Trade Commission Act, which was passed in 1914 and established the Federal Trade Commission.

10. The antitrust laws also apply to the relationship between a manufacturer and its distributors or customers. In this kind of "vertical" relationship, the antitrust laws leave room for considerably more latitude, since a manufacturer must have contracts and agreements with its own distributors and customers.

11. Where private suits seem likely to address the alleged anticompetitive action, the agencies will sometimes delay their own investigation pending the outcome of private litigation.

12. 15 USC Sec 15 (1988). The requirement to show antitrust injury makes it difficult for private parties to challenge acquisitions and mergers.

13. *United States v Topco Assocs.,* 405 US 596, 609, 612 (1972), as noted in Frank E. Easterbrook, "The Limits of Antitrust," *Texas Law Review,* 63 (1984), pp. 1–39.

14. R. Nelson, "Why Do Firms Differ, and How Does It Matter?" *Strategic Management Journal,* 12 (Winter 1991), pp. 61–74.

15. Gary Hamel, Yves L. Doz, and C. K. Prahalad, "Collaborate with Your Competitors—and Win," *Harvard Business Review,* (Jan.–Feb. 1989), p. 133.

16. For example, Kenichi Ohmae argues that "Globalization mandates alliances, makes them absolutely essential to strategy." K. Ohmae, *The Borderless World: Power and Strategy in the Interlinked Economy,* (New York: Harper Business, 1990), p. 114.

17. B. Kogut "Joint Ventures: Theoretical and Empirical Perspectives," *Strategic Management Journal,* 9 (1988), pp. 319–332. Kogut includes strategic behavior (including deterring entry and eroding competitors' positions) as one of three justifications for joint ventures.

18. While FTC and DOJ receive roughly 1,500–3,000 filings per year, the number of FTC second requests is more than a magnitude less, and formal enforcement actions many fewer still.

19. *United States v Foley,* 1979-1 Trade Cas. (CCH) 62,577 (4th Cir. 1979).

20. Quality Trailer Products, 57 Fed. Reg. 37004, Aug. 17, 1992.

21. Phillip Areeda, *Antitrust Law: An Analysis of Antitrust Principles and Their Application,* 7 (Boston: Little, Brown and Company, 1986), p. 29.

22. *United States v Airline Tariff Publishing Co.,* Civ. No. 92–2584 (D.D.C. Dec. 21, 1992).

23. See Heil and Langvardt (1994) for a general discussion of signaling and antitrust and its managerial implications. Oliver P. Heil and Arlen W. Langvardt, "The Interface between Competitive Market Signaling and Antitrust Law," *Journal of Marketing,* (July 1994).

24. General Motors Corp., 103 F.T.C. 374 (1984). Order Granting Petition to Reopen and Set Aside Order in General Motors Corp., Dkt. No. 3132 (Oct. 29, 1993). See John E. Kwoka, Jr. "International Joint Venture: General Motors and Toyota," in J. Kwoka, Jr. and L. J. White (eds.), *The Antitrust Revolution,* (Glenview, IL: Scott, Foresman and Co., 1989), pp. 46–79. See also Martin Marietta (File No. 941 0038 Consent Order accepted for public comment on March 25, 1994).

25. Toby G. Singer, "The Scope of Permissible Coordination between Merging Entities Prior to Consummation," outline for presentation before ABA Section of Antitrust Law, 42nd annual spring meeting.

26. No cases have been brought in this area, though some information exchanges in the premerger context have been investigated. Mary Lou Steptoe, acting director, Bureau of Competition, Federal Trade Commission, prepared remarks before ABA Section of Antitrust Law, spring meeting, April 7, 1994, pp. 7, 10.

27. "60 Minutes with the Honorable James F. Rill, Assistant Attorney General, Antitrust Division, U.S. Department of Justice," 59 *Antitrust Law Journal,* 45 (1990), pp. 57–58.

28. See e.g., Kevin J. Arquit, director, Bureau of Competition, Federal Trade Commission, Dec. 14, 1989 speech.

29. See, generally, U.S. Department of Justice and Federal Trade Commission, "Antitrust Guidelines for the Licensing of Intellectual Property," ("IP guidelines") April 6, 1995.

30. The first cause of action listed in *United States v Pilkington plc,* DC Ariz, No. 94–345, May 26, 1994.

31. 1992, "DOJ/FTC Horizontal Merger Guidelines."

32. *United States v Penn-Olin Chemical Co.,* 246 F. Supp. 917 (D. Del 1965), aff'd per curiam.

33. General Motors Corporation 103 F.T.C. 374 (1984), Order Granting Petition to Reopen and Set Aside Order in General Motors Corporation, Dkt. No. 3132 (Oct. 29, 1993).

34. Proposed settlement, published for public comment, August 1994.

35. *Broadcast Music, Inc., v Columbia Broadcasting System, Inc.,* 441 U.S. 1, 99 (1979) S. Ct. 1551, 60 L Ed2d 1.

36. Brunswick Corp., 94 FTC 1174 (1979), *modified,* 96 FTC 151 (1980).

37. *Affirmed, Yamaha Motor Co. v Federal Trade Commission,* 657 F2d 971 (8th Cir. 1981).

38. Portions of this section are excerpted from remarks of FTC Commissioner D. Yao "Anticompetitive Concerns Relating to Information Sharing in Health Care Markets" before Charles River Associates conference, Boston, MA, April 28, 1994.

39. Benchmarking is a process through which competing firms can seek information from each other in order to discover how to improve their various functional practices and institute initiatives to emulate the best practice—learning from the successes and mistakes of others. Benchmarking is seen as a way of changing one's thinking.

40. "The agency will delineate the product market to be a product or group of products such that a hypothetical profit-maximizing firm that was the only present and future seller of those products (monopolist) likely would impose at least a 'small but significant and nontransitory' increase in price." U.S. Department of Justice and Federal Trade Commission, "Horizontal Merger Guidelines," (April 2, 1992), p. 6. An antitrust product market can be thought of as a grouping of products for which products excluded from the group are not relatively close substitutes for products in the group. The "hypothetical monopolist" product market test—often referred to as the 5- percent test"—described is an analytical way of defining such a market. In practice, evidence used to determine the antitrust product market includes evidence of actual (or considered) shifts in demand caused by changes in past price (or other competitive variables), how seller's view likely buyer substitution, switching costs, etc. (See 1992 "Horizontal Merger Guidelines," pp. 6–7.)

41. *United States v United States Gypsum Co.,* 438 US 422, 446 (1978).

42. In re Coordinated Proceedings in Petroleum Products Antitrust Litig., 906 F2d 432 (9th Cir. 1990) *cert. denied* 111 S.Ct. 2274 (1991). Court denied summary judgment to defendant oil companies, finding sufficient evidence to support an inference of conspiracy where current and prospective price information was allegedly shared through press releases, price postings, and direct contacts among competitors.

43. See J. J. Anton and D. A. Yao, "Standard-Setting Consortia, Antitrust, and High-Technology Industries," *Antitrust Law Journal,* 64, 1 (Fall 1995), pp. 247–265.

44. U.S. Department of Justice and the Federal Trade Commission, "Statements of Enforcement Policy and Analytical Principles Relating to Health Care and Antitrust," September 27, 1994, p. 55. (Revised 1996)

45. *Ibid.,* p. 56.

46. See Steven C. Salop and Lawrence J. White, "Economic Analysis of Private Antitrust Litigation," *Georgetown Law Journal,* 74 (April 1986), p. 1, and a summary of the Georgetown Private Antitrust Litigation Project in Milton Handler, et al. *Cases and Materials on Trade Regulation* (3rd ed.), (Westbury, NY: The Foundation Press, 1990), p. 376.

47. Thomas E. Kauper and Edward A. Snyder, "An Inquiry into the Efficiency of Private Antitrust Enforcement: Follow-on and Independently Initiated Cases Compared," *Georgetown Law Journal,* 74 (April 1986), p. 1163.

48. See e.g., Michael Slater, "AMD Loses 287 Microcode Case," *Microprocessor Report,* (July 8, 1992). Reprinted in microprocessor report, *Understanding X86 Microprocessors,* (Emeryville, CA: Ziff-Davis Press, 1993).

49. Private firms often have an influence over whether a case is investigated by the government. A primary source of government cases is through complaints lodged by private parties—often competitors. Private companies can also be helpful in providing information (and sometimes even analyses!) to the government agencies.

Chapter 15

1. S. Addelman, "Orthogonal Main-Effect Plans for Asymmetrical Factorial Experiments," *Technometrics,* 4 (1962), pp. 21–46; P. E. Green, "On the Design of Choice Experiments Involving Multifactor Alternatives," *Journal of Consumer Research,* 1 (1974), pp. 61–68.

2. P. E. Green, "Hybrid Models for Conjoint Analysis: An Expository Review," *Journal of Marketing Research,* 21 (1984), pp. 155–159.

3. V. Srinivasan and G. A. Wyner, "CASEMAP: Computer-Assisted Self-Explication of Multiattribute Preference," in W. Henry, M. Menasco, and H. Takada (eds.), *New Product Development and Testing,* (Lexington, MA: Lexington Books, 1989), pp. 81–112.

4. Green, 1984.

5. R. M. Johnson, "Adaptive Conjoint Analysis," *Sawtooth Software Conference on Perceptual Mapping, Conjoint Analysis, and Computer Interviewing,* (Ketchum, ID: Sawtooth Software, 1987), pp. 253–266.

6. P. E. Green and V. R. Rao, "Nonmetric Approaches to Multivariate Analysis in Marketing," working paper, Wharton School, University of Pennsylvania, Philadelphia, PA, 1969; P. E. Green and V. R. Rao, "Conjoint Measurement for Quantifying Judgmental Data," *Journal of Marketing Research,* 8 (1971), pp. 355–363.

7. P. E. Green and V. Srinivasan, "Conjoint Analysis in Marketing: New Developments with Implications for Research and Practice," *Journal of Marketing,* 54 (1990), pp. 3–19; P. Cattin and D. R. Wittink, "Commercial Use of Conjoint Analysis: A Survey," *Journal Marketing,* 46 (1982), pp. 44–53; D. R. Wittink and P. Cattin, "Commercial Use of Conjoint Analysis: An Update," *Journal of Marketing,* 53 (1989), pp. 91–96.

8. P. E. Green and A. M. Krieger, "Choice Rules and Sensitivity Analysis in Conjoint Simulators." *Journal of the Academy of Marketing Science,* 16 (1988), pp. 114–127.

9. Green and Krieger (1989) provide a review of product optimization models based on both multidimensional scaling and conjoint analysis.

10. N. Allison, "Conjoint Analysis across the Business System," *Sawtooth Software Conference Proceedings,* (Ketchum, ID: Sawtooth Software, 1989), pp. 183–196.

11. P. E. Green and A. M. Krieger, "An Application of a Product Positioning Model to Pharmaceutical Products," *Marketing Science,* 11 (Spring 1992), pp. 117–132.

12. Green, 1984.

13. S. C. Choi, W. S. DeSarbo, and P. T. Harker, "Product Positioning under Price Competition," *Management Science,* 36 (1990), pp. 175–199.

14. R. M. Johnson, "Trade-Off Analysis of Consumer Values," *Journal of Marketing Research,* 11 (1974), pp. 121–127; S. Herman, "Software for Full-Profile Conjoint Analysis," *Proceedings of the Sawtooth Software Conference on Perceptual Mapping, Conjoint Analysis, and Computer Interviewing,* (Ketchum, ID: Sawtooth Software, 1988), pp. 117–130.; SPSS, Inc., *SPSS Categories,* (Chicago: SPSS, Inc., 1990).

Chapter 16

1. The situation is further complicated by the FTC's filing of charges against the manufacturers regarding a collusive arrangement not to advertise directly to consumers. Earlier, there also had been price-fixing charges and penalties, in Florida and other states, against the leading companies.

2. J. A. deVasconcellos and D. C. Hambrick, "Key Success Factors: Test of a General Theory in the Mature Industrial-Product Sector," *Strategic Management Journal,* 10 (1989), pp. 367–382.

3. P. Ghemawat, *Commitment,* (New York: Free Press, 1991).

4. See Richard Schmalansee, "Do Markets Differ Much?" *American Economic Review,* 75 (June 1985), pp. 341–351; D. Mueller, "Persistent Performance among Large Corporations," in L. Thomas (ed.), *The Economics of Strategic Planning,* (Lexington, MA: Lexington Books, 1986); R. Jacobson, "The Persistence of Abnormal Returns," *Strategic Management Journal,* 9 (1988), pp. 415–430; and R. P. Rumelt, "How Much Does Industry Matter?" *Strategic Management Journal,* 12, 3 (1991), pp. 167–185.

5. In their pathbreaking article, Prahalad and Hamel offer four tests to identify core competencies. First, a core competence must provide potential access to a wide variety of market segments. Second, it should enhance the benefits of the product or service in the eye of the customer. Third, a core competence should be hard for competitors to imitate. Last, the list of core competencies must not be too long (fewer than ten). See C. K. Prahalad and Gary Hamel, "The Core Competence of the Corporation," *Harvard Business Review,* (May/June 1990), pp. 79–91.

6. P. J. H. Schoemaker and R. Amit, "Investment in Strategic Assets," *Advances in Strategic Management,* 10A (1994), pp. 3–33; and R. Amit and P. J. H. Schoemaker, "Strategic Assets and Organizational Rent," *Strategic Management Journal,* 1, 4 (1993), pp. 33–46.

7. This figure elaborates and synthesizes notions developed in Barney (1989, 1991); Conner (1991); Dierickx & Cool (1989a, 1989b, & 1990); Ghemawat (1991b); Nelson & Winter (1982); Penrose (1959); Peteraf (1993); Porter (1980); Rumelt (1984); Teece (1982, 1997); Wernerfelt (1984). It augments Amit & Schoemaker (1993).

8. See, for example, P. Wack, "Scenarios: Uncharted Waters Ahead," *Harvard Business Review,* (September/October, 1985), pp. 72–89; or P. J. H. Schoemaker, "Scenario Planning: A Tool for Strategic Thinking," *Sloan Management Review,* (Winter 1995), pp. 25–40.

9. The combining of the basic scenario building blocks (trends, outcomes, and stakeholders) can be done in at least three different ways: 1. *Intuitively.* Once all the pieces are laid out, you have to find some major themes and story lines around which to organize all the elements; 2. *Heuristically.* Select the two most important uncertainties (e.g., by asking members of the management team to vote for them individually) and cross them into a 2 × 2 matrix, as in the example; 3. *Statistically.* Systematically combine the outcomes of all the key uncertainties into internally consistent strings to provide outer boundaries. For details, see P. J. H. Schoemaker, "How to Link Strategic Vision to Core Capabilities," *Sloan Management Review,* 34, 1 (Fall 1992), pp. 67–81; and P. J. H. Schoemaker, "Scenario Planning: A Tool for Strategic Thinking."

10. R. P. Rumelt, 1991.

11. P. E. Green and D. S. Tull, *Research for Marketing Decisions,* (New York: Prentice-Hall, 1978).

12. At this point in the analysis, these are actually hypotheses about the SIFs in the industry. To truly assess future SIFs, the second phase of our analysis also needs to be completed. This is a complex, iterative process, but it is represented more simply here.

13. Once all firms have been analyzed in terms of their most attractive SA bundles, it should be verified that the asymmetries in these various bundles are consistent with the SIFs postulated at the start of the process. The more asymmetry we observe across firms, the greater the profit variance will be and the more pronounced the SIFs will be when examined ex post.

14. P. J. H. Schoemaker and C. A. J. M. van der Heijden, "Strategic Planning at Royal Dutch/Shell," *Journal of Strategic Change,* 12 (1993), pp. 157–171.

15. J. Rosenhead, *Strategies for Change: Logical Incrementalism,* (Homewood, IL: Richard D. Irwin, 1980).

16. E. F. Fama, *Foundations of Finance,* (New York: Basic Books, 1976).

17. See R. L. Keeney and H. Raiffa, *Decisions with Multiple Objectives: Preferences and Value Trade-offs,* (2nd ed.), (New York: John Wiley & Sons, Inc., 1993). In either analysis, it is important to properly assess the options value inherent in each

possible investment (stemming from decisions that can be made later to enlarge or reduce the investment). See, for example, A. K. Dixit and R. S. Pindyck, "The Options Approach to Capital Investment," *Harvard Business Review,* (May/June 1995), pp. 105–115.

Chapter 17

1. Simulated test markets offer a twist on the traditional test market. In a simulated test market, the researcher constructs a simulated (artificial) store, places products on a shelf, brings in respondents, and asks those respondents to select products. This simulation of the shopping experience offers major advantages over traditional test markets, such as testing a wider variety or number of alternative products, revealing less information to competitors, costing less, providing results more quickly, and being much easier to implement.

2. Our evidence, not as good as data but better than just haphazard anecdotes, has convinced us that people are often more certain of the correctness of their favorite alternatives than they should be. For example, managers usually assume that businesses with heavy fixed costs should cut their prices to maximize volume, which they believe in turn will boost profits. In fact, many such businesses would benefit more from higher prices (obviously depending on the price elasticity), even if volume suffers, if they want profits. Experiment with a simple spreadsheet and you'll see. J. Edward Russo and Paul J. H. Schoemaker discuss overconfidence in their book *Decision Traps: The Ten Barriers to Brilliant Decision-Making and How to Overcome Them,* (Simon & Schuster, 1989), especially pp. 70–80.

3. Some forms of simulation support sensitivity analysis, which can relieve some of the anxiety over GIGO. When one or more numbers seem prohibitively soft, sensitivity analysis can test whether the *decision* depends on getting better accuracy. For example, perhaps managers don't know whether a market will grow at 5 percent or 10 percent over the next few years. They can run the simulation at 5 percent growth and at 10 percent growth, and see if they should change their strategy. If so, they've learned that they should develop contingency plans, or that they should invest in better research or forecasts of market growth. (The simulation results can even help calculate how much they should be willing to pay for that information.) If not, they've learned that they don't need better data on market growth; they can proceed with their strategy.

4. Remember that quality means perceived attribute levels, combined into a measure of market-perceived quality (MPQ). One of the airlines in the market gathered survey data on what attributes travelers use to decide on an airline (by segment) and how important they considered each of those attributes (also by segment). In this case, MPQ included attributes, such as on-time service, convenience of schedule, safety, and in-flight service, that travelers use to select an airline. The simulation also included passengers' perceptual ratings on those attributes of the airlines competing on the Detroit-Chicago route.

448

5. When simulation inputs are estimated from historical data, the statistical analysis leading to parameter estimates automatically includes uncertainty. However, this uncertainty refers to the confidence (or lack thereof) that the parameter estimate is correct *given* the historical data. Unrepresentative or constrained historical data has a kind of hidden uncertainty. For example, if one gathers market data from a brief period of stable and steady growth, then one will not observe the uncertainty in market growth rates that could come from future changes in the economic climate.

6. We tried to find a good adjective to describe the opposite, that is, a strategy whose outcome depends a great deal on forces outside its control. The thesaurus gave us words such as frail, shaky, weak, infirm, and even wishy-washy. The best we found was fragile. We leave finding a better adjective as an exercise for the reader.

7. Note that those events might be internal to the business. For example, managers may wish to switch to a more aggressive strategy if an R&D project achieves a breakthrough.

INDEX

INDEX